Dance In The Vampire Bund 12

VAMPIRE BUND
12

NOZOMU TAMAKI

松明の如く汝の身より炎の爆ぜるとき
汝は知らず
その身を焦がしつつ自由の身とならんことを
汝の持てる全ては消滅する運命とならんことを

ただ灰と、地の底へと汝を導く
混迷だけが残されんことを

永遠の勝利の暁に
燃え残るの灰の奥底深く
燦然と輝ける
ダイヤモンドの残らんことを！

From you, as from burning chips of resin,
Fiery fragments circle far and near:
Ablaze, you don't know if you are to be free,
Or if all that is yours will disappear.

Will only ashes and confusion remain,
Leading into the abyss?—or will there be
In the depths of the ash a star-like diamond,
The dawning of eternal victory!

Cyprian kamil Norwid, Prolog-Tragedia fantastyczna

Dance In The Vampire Bund 12

Contents

Tamaki Nozomu Presents Dance In The Vampire Bund 12

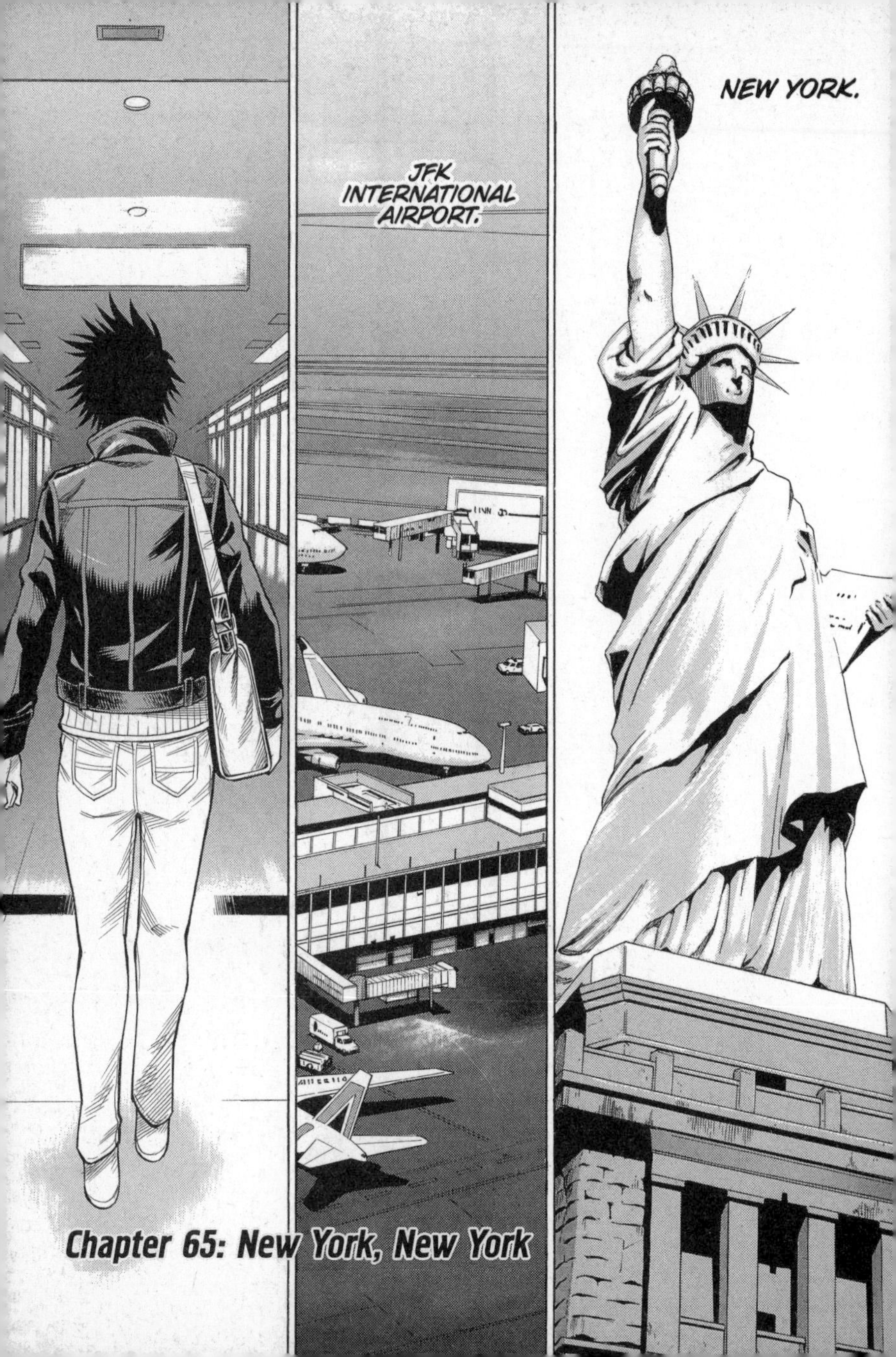
NEW YORK.
JFK INTERNATIONAL AIRPORT.
Chapter 65: New York, New York

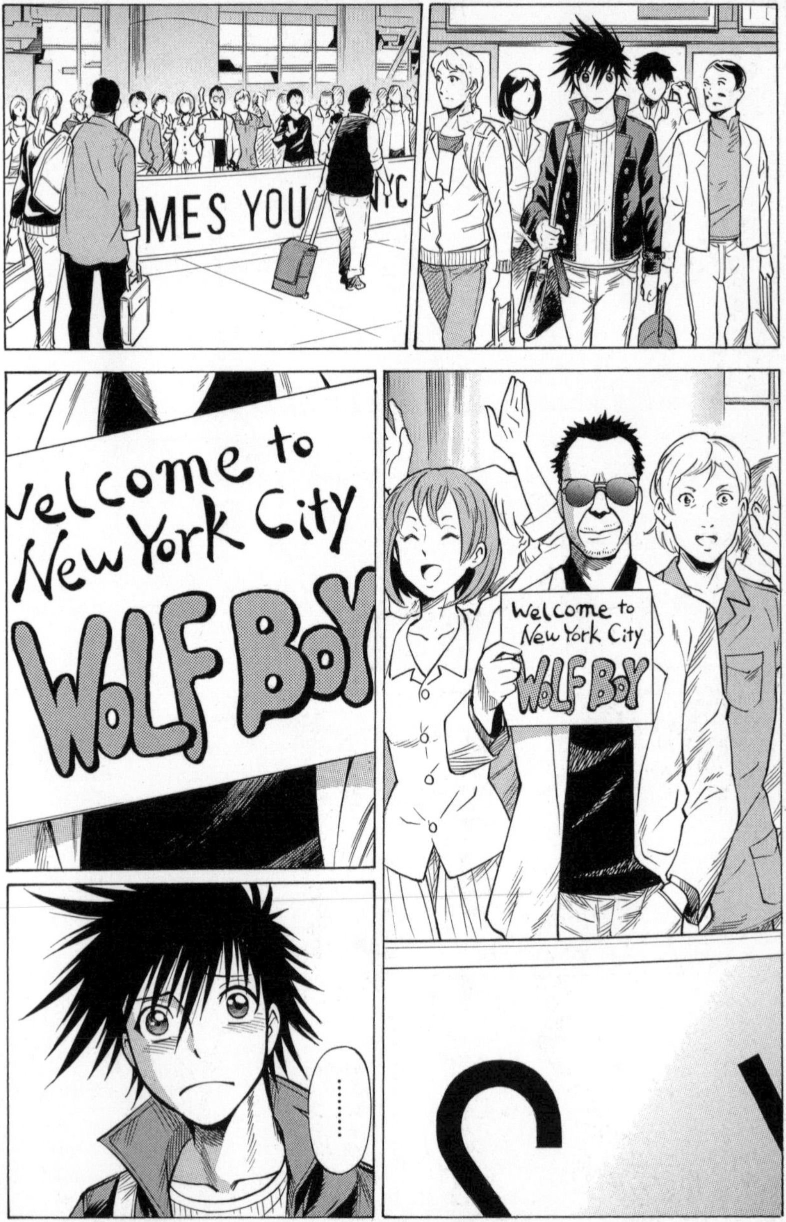
MES YOU
Welcome to New York City WOLF BOY
Welcome to New York City WOLF BOY
………

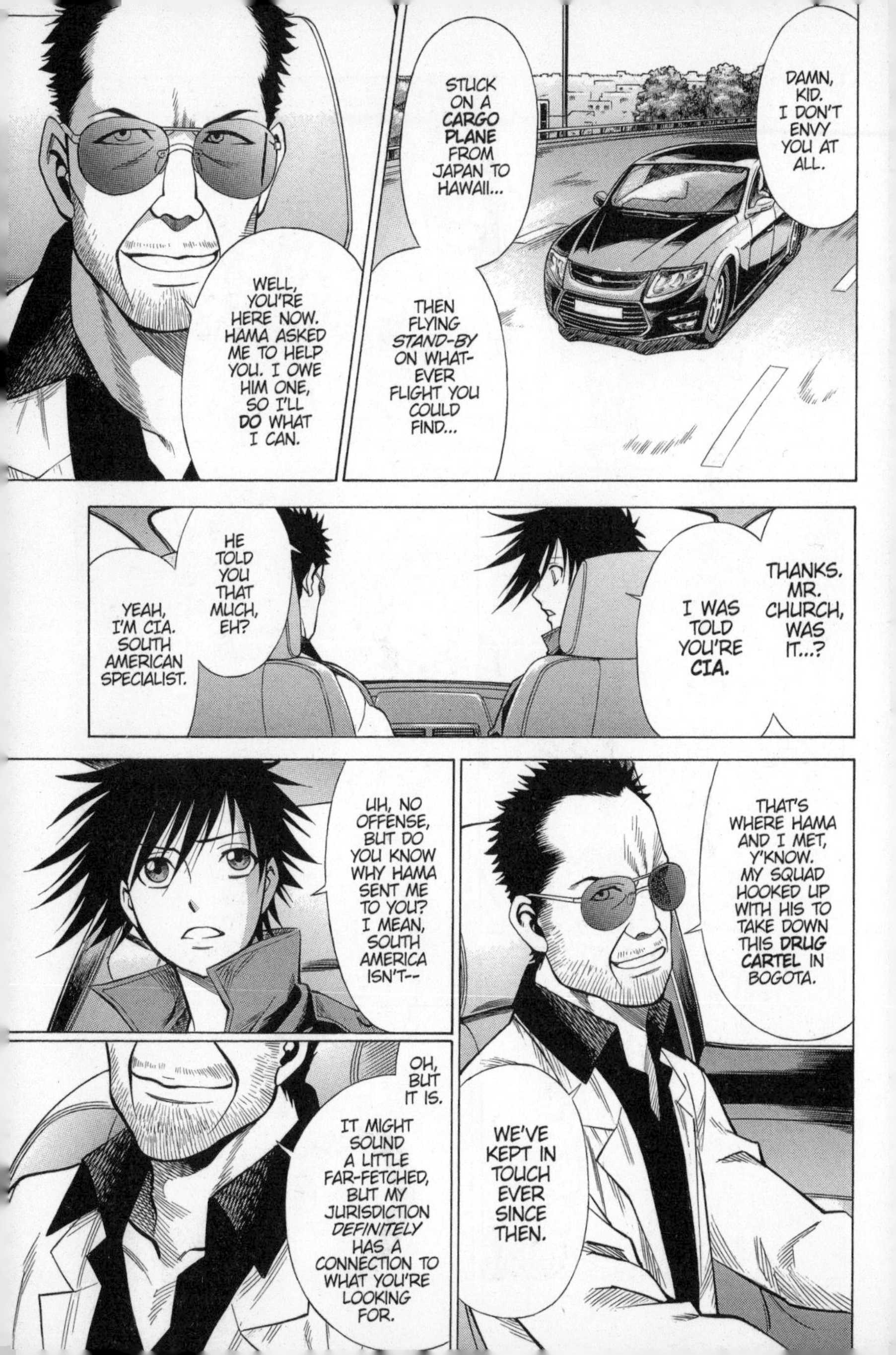
DAMN, KID. I DON'T ENVY YOU AT ALL.
STUCK ON A CARGO PLANE FROM JAPAN TO HAWAII...
THEN FLYING STAND-BY ON WHAT-EVER FLIGHT YOU COULD FIND...
WELL, YOU'RE HERE NOW. HAMA ASKED ME TO HELP YOU. I OWE HIM ONE, SO I'LL DO WHAT I CAN.
THANKS. MR. CHURCH, WAS IT...?
I WAS TOLD YOU'RE CIA.
HE TOLD YOU THAT MUCH, EH?
YEAH, I'M CIA. SOUTH AMERICAN SPECIALIST.
UH, NO OFFENSE, BUT DO YOU KNOW WHY HAMA SENT ME TO YOU? I MEAN, SOUTH AMERICA ISN'T--
OH, BUT IT IS.
IT MIGHT SOUND A LITTLE FAR-FETCHED, BUT MY JURISDICTION DEFINITELY HAS A CONNECTION TO WHAT YOU'RE LOOKING FOR.
THAT'S WHERE HAMA AND I MET, Y'KNOW. MY SQUAD HOOKED UP WITH HIS TO TAKE DOWN THIS DRUG CARTEL IN BOGOTA.
WE'VE KEPT IN TOUCH EVER SINCE THEN.

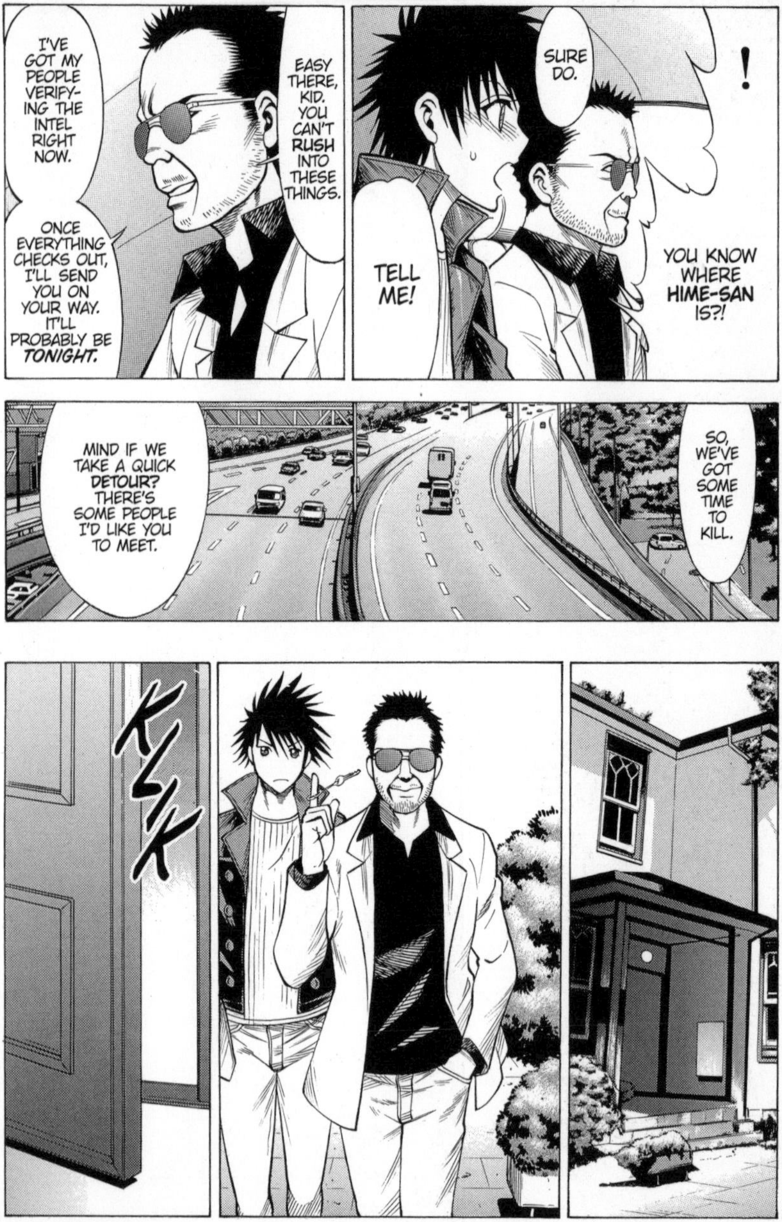
!
YOU KNOW WHERE HIME-SAN IS?!
SURE DO.
TELL ME!
EASY THERE, KID. YOU CAN'T RUSH INTO THESE THINGS.
I'VE GOT MY PEOPLE VERIFYING THE INTEL RIGHT NOW.
ONCE EVERYTHING CHECKS OUT, I'LL SEND YOU ON YOUR WAY. IT'LL PROBABLY BE TONIGHT.
SO, WE'VE GOT SOME TIME TO KILL.
MIND IF WE TAKE A QUICK DETOUR? THERE'S SOME PEOPLE I'D LIKE YOU TO MEET.
KLIK

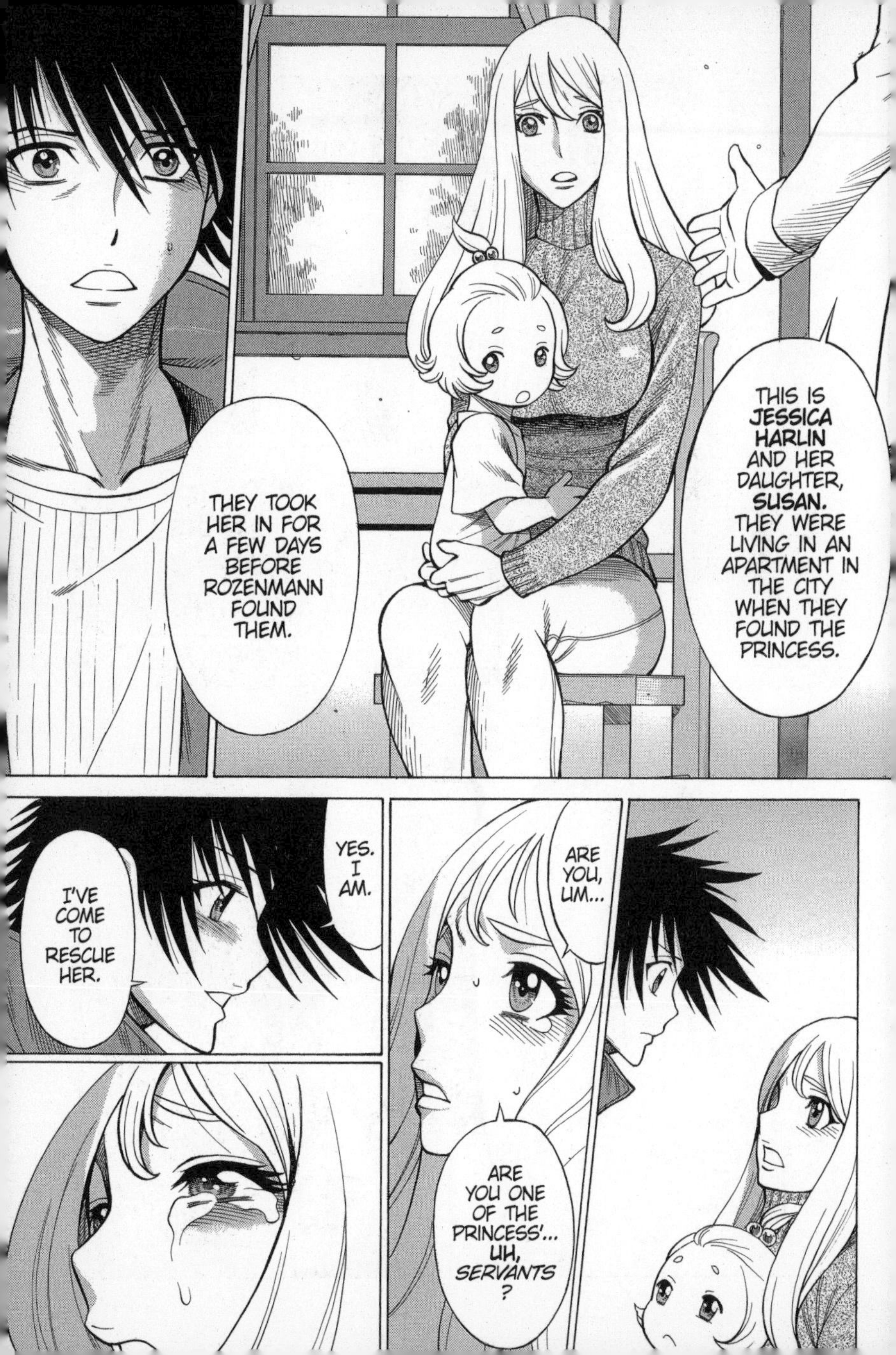
THIS IS **JESSICA HARLIN** AND HER DAUGHTER, **SUSAN.** THEY WERE LIVING IN AN APARTMENT IN THE CITY WHEN THEY FOUND THE PRINCESS.
THEY TOOK HER IN FOR A FEW DAYS BEFORE ROZENMANN FOUND THEM.
ARE YOU, UM...
ARE YOU ONE OF THE PRINCESS'... **UH,** *SERVANTS* ?
YES. I AM.
I'VE COME TO RESCUE HER.

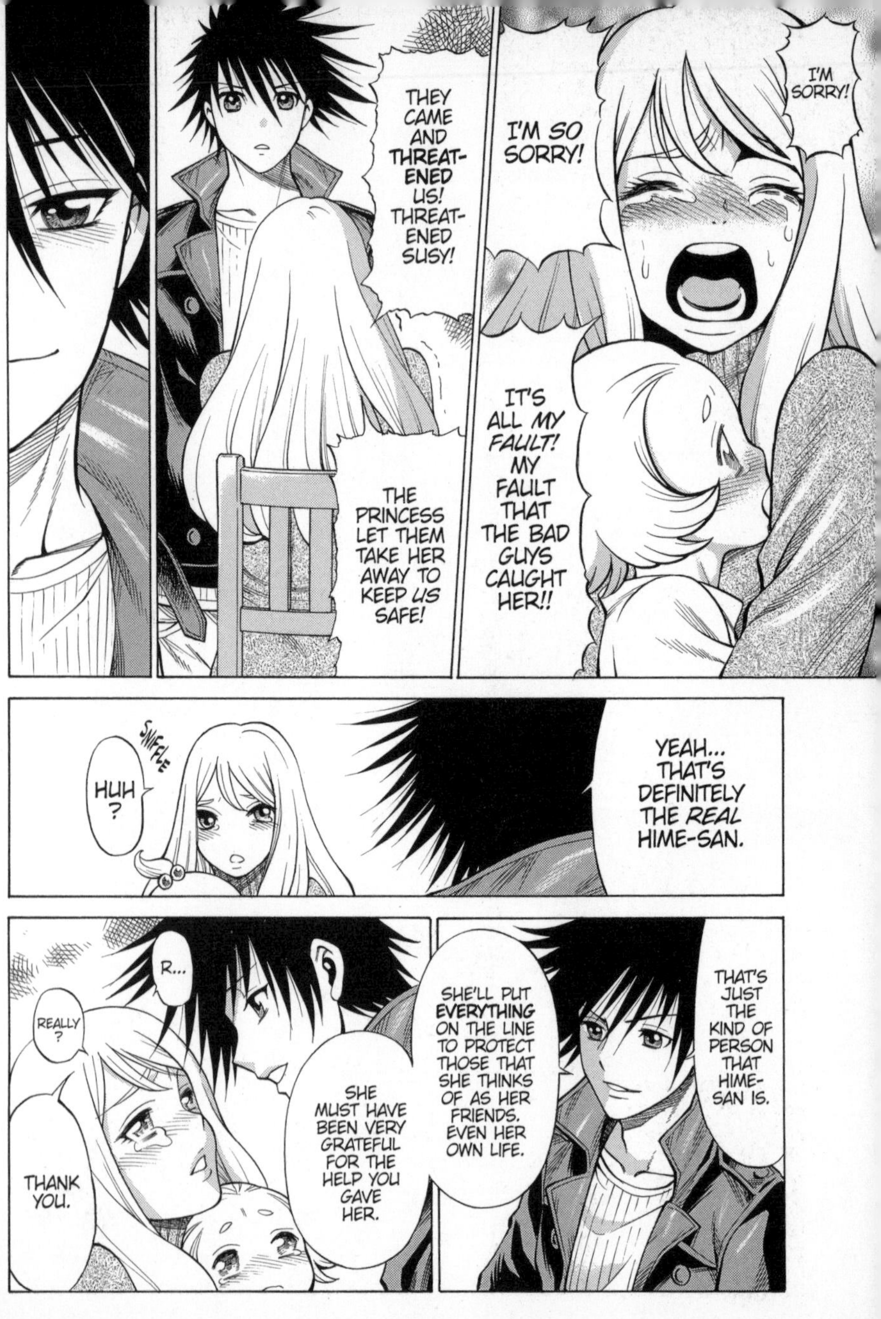
I'M SORRY!
I'M SO SORRY!
IT'S ALL MY FAULT! MY FAULT THAT THE BAD GUYS CAUGHT HER!!
THEY CAME AND THREATENED US! THREATENED SUSY!
THE PRINCESS LET THEM TAKE HER AWAY TO KEEP US SAFE!
YEAH... THAT'S DEFINITELY THE REAL HIME-SAN.
SNIFFLE
HUH?
THAT'S JUST THE KIND OF PERSON THAT HIME-SAN IS.
SHE'LL PUT EVERYTHING ON THE LINE TO PROTECT THOSE THAT SHE THINKS OF AS HER FRIENDS. EVEN HER OWN LIFE.
SHE MUST HAVE BEEN VERY GRATEFUL FOR THE HELP YOU GAVE HER.
R...
REALLY?
THANK YOU.

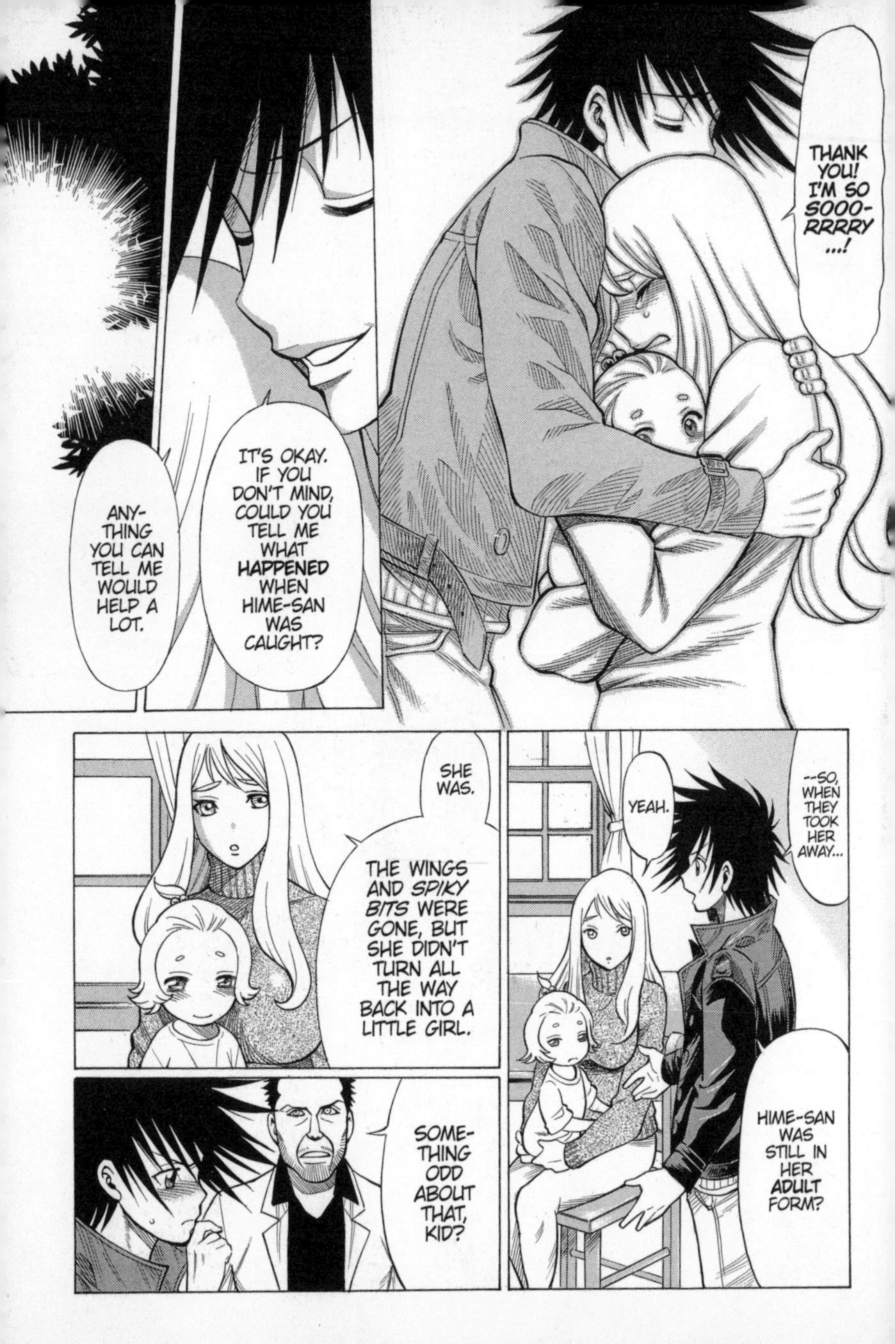
THANK YOU! I'M SO SOOOO-RRRRY ...!
IT'S OKAY. IF YOU DON'T MIND, COULD YOU TELL ME WHAT **HAPPENED** WHEN HIME-SAN WAS CAUGHT?
ANY-THING YOU CAN TELL ME WOULD HELP A LOT.
--SO, WHEN THEY TOOK HER AWAY...
YEAH.
HIME-SAN WAS STILL IN HER **ADULT** FORM?
SHE WAS.
THE WINGS AND *SPIKY BITS* WERE GONE, BUT SHE DIDN'T TURN ALL THE WAY BACK INTO A LITTLE GIRL.
SOME-THING ODD ABOUT THAT, KID?

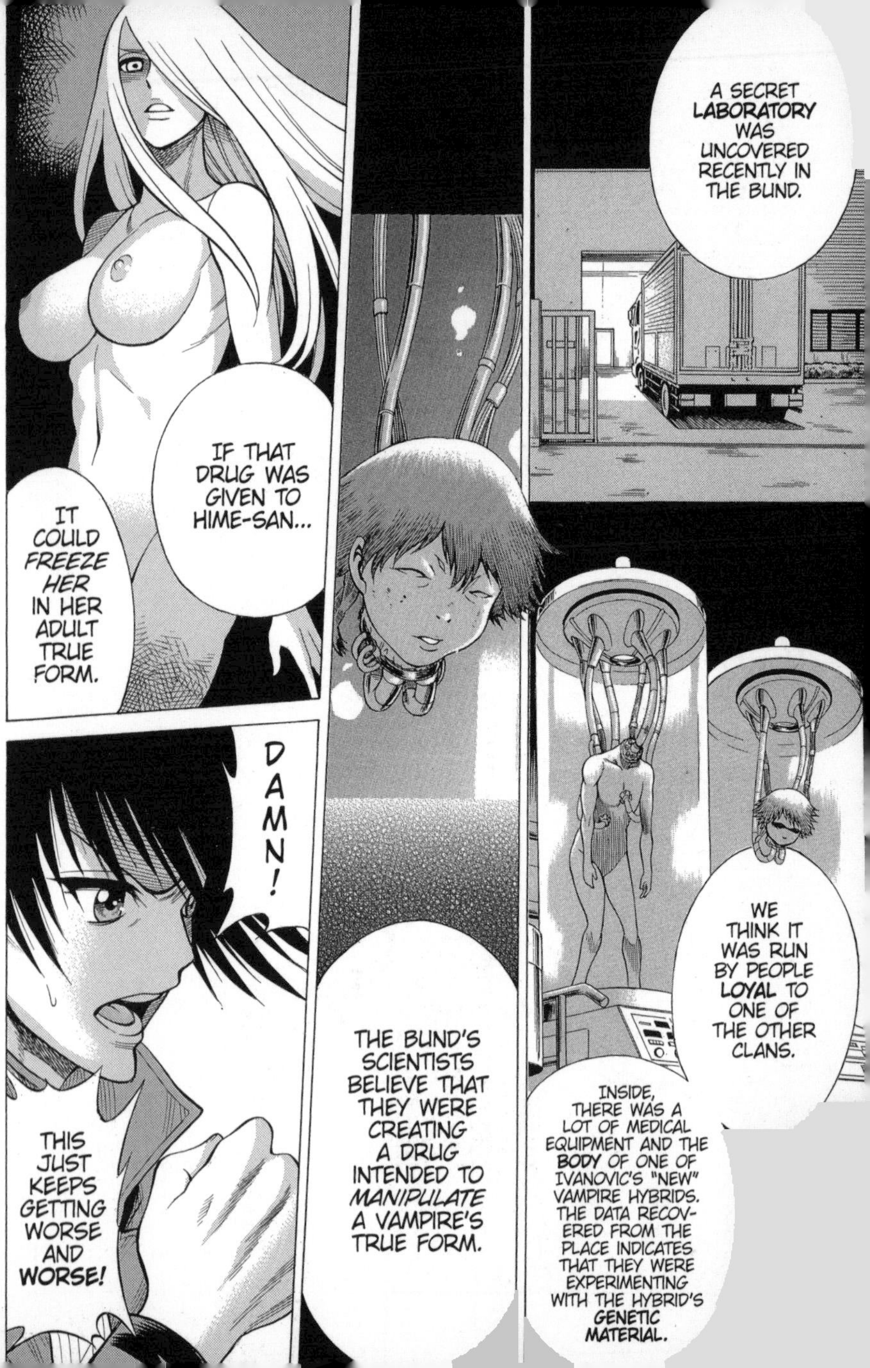
A SECRET LABORATORY WAS UNCOVERED RECENTLY IN THE BUND.
WE THINK IT WAS RUN BY PEOPLE LOYAL TO ONE OF THE OTHER CLANS.
INSIDE, THERE WAS A LOT OF MEDICAL EQUIPMENT AND THE BODY OF ONE OF IVANOVIC'S "NEW" VAMPIRE HYBRIDS. THE DATA RECOVERED FROM THE PLACE INDICATES THAT THEY WERE EXPERIMENTING WITH THE HYBRID'S GENETIC MATERIAL.
THE BUND'S SCIENTISTS BELIEVE THAT THEY WERE CREATING A DRUG INTENDED TO MANIPULATE A VAMPIRE'S TRUE FORM.
IF THAT DRUG WAS GIVEN TO HIME-SAN...
IT COULD FREEZE HER IN HER ADULT TRUE FORM.
DAMN!
THIS JUST KEEPS GETTING WORSE AND WORSE!

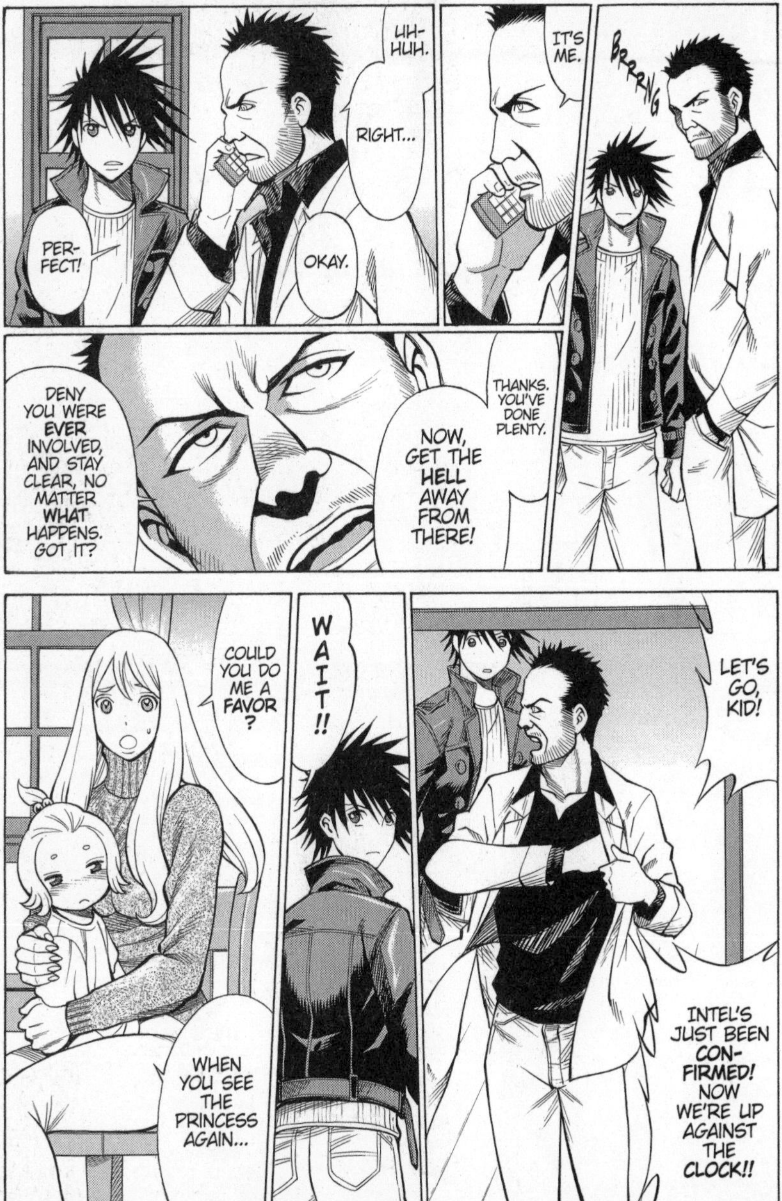
BRRRRNG
IT'S ME.
UH-HUH.
RIGHT...
OKAY.
PERFECT!
THANKS. YOU'VE DONE PLENTY.
NOW, GET THE HELL AWAY FROM THERE!
DENY YOU WERE EVER INVOLVED, AND STAY CLEAR, NO MATTER WHAT HAPPENS. GOT IT?
LET'S GO, KID!
INTEL'S JUST BEEN CONFIRMED! NOW WE'RE UP AGAINST THE CLOCK!!
WAIT!!
COULD YOU DO ME A FAVOR?
WHEN YOU SEE THE PRINCESS AGAIN...

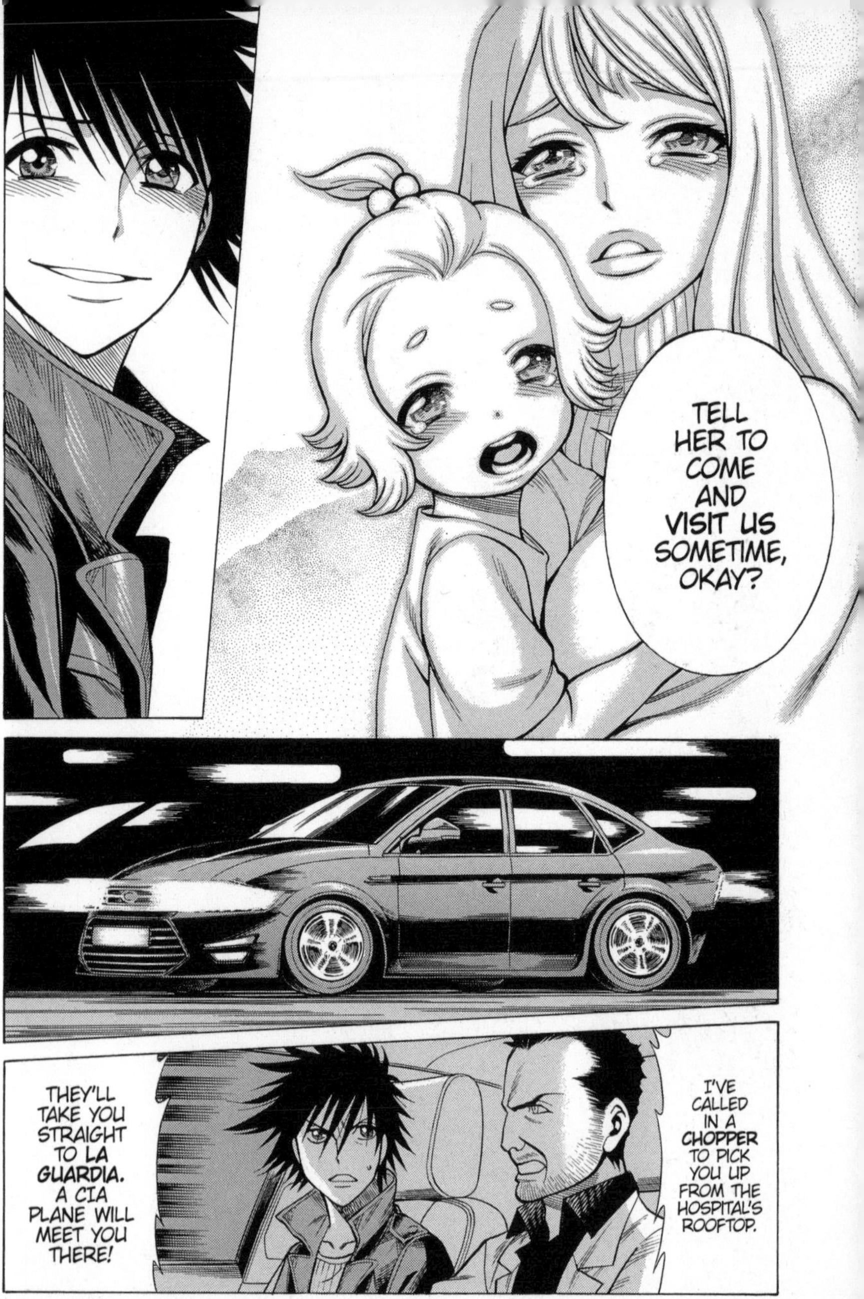
TELL HER TO COME AND VISIT US SOMETIME, OKAY?
I'VE CALLED IN A CHOPPER TO PICK YOU UP FROM THE HOSPITAL'S ROOFTOP.
THEY'LL TAKE YOU STRAIGHT TO LA GUARDIA. A CIA PLANE WILL MEET YOU THERE!

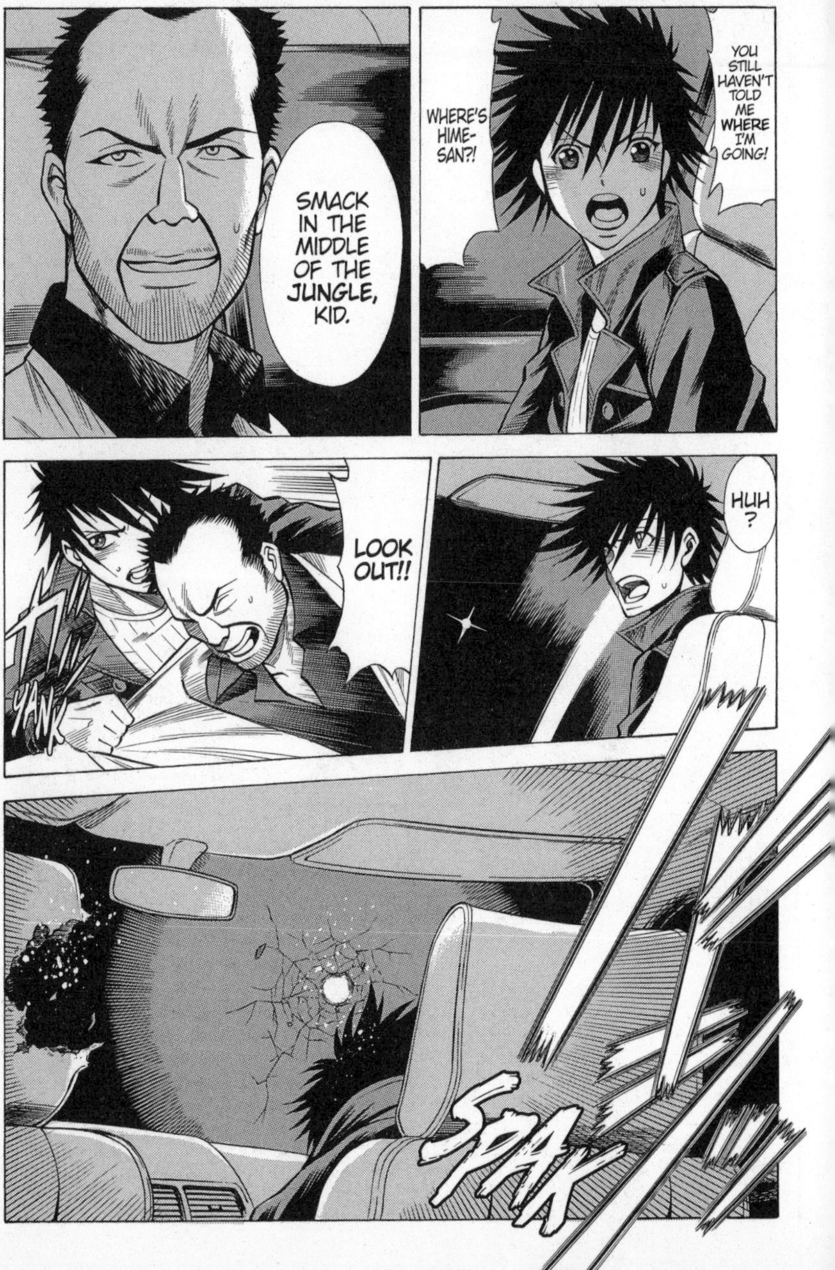
YOU STILL HAVEN'T TOLD ME WHERE I'M GOING!
WHERE'S HIME-SAN?!
SMACK IN THE MIDDLE OF THE JUNGLE, KID.
HUH?
LOOK OUT!!
YANK
SPAK

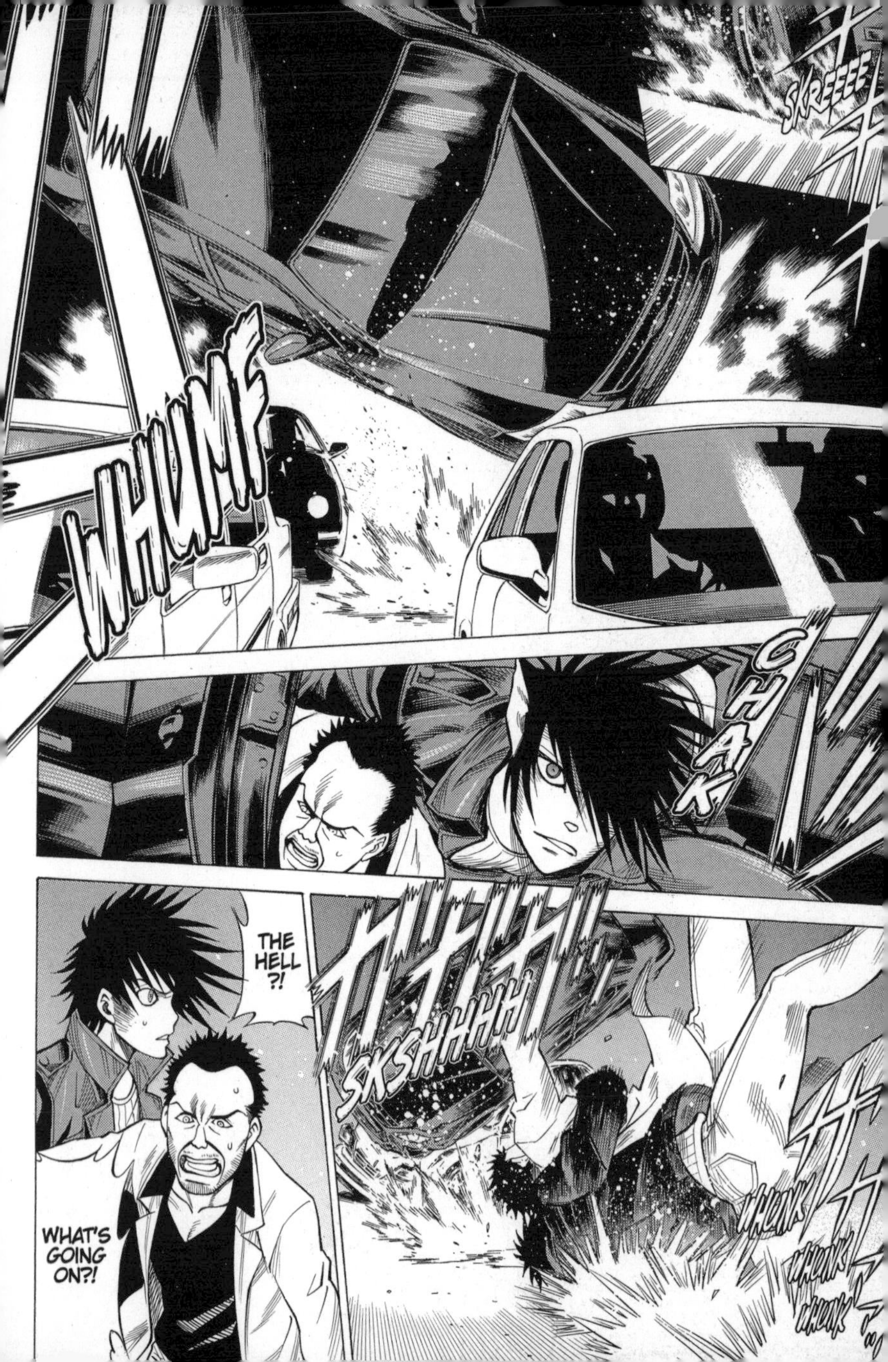
SKREEEE
WHUMF
CHAK
SKSHHHH
WHUNK
WHUNK
WHUNK
THE HELL?!
WHAT'S GOING ON?!

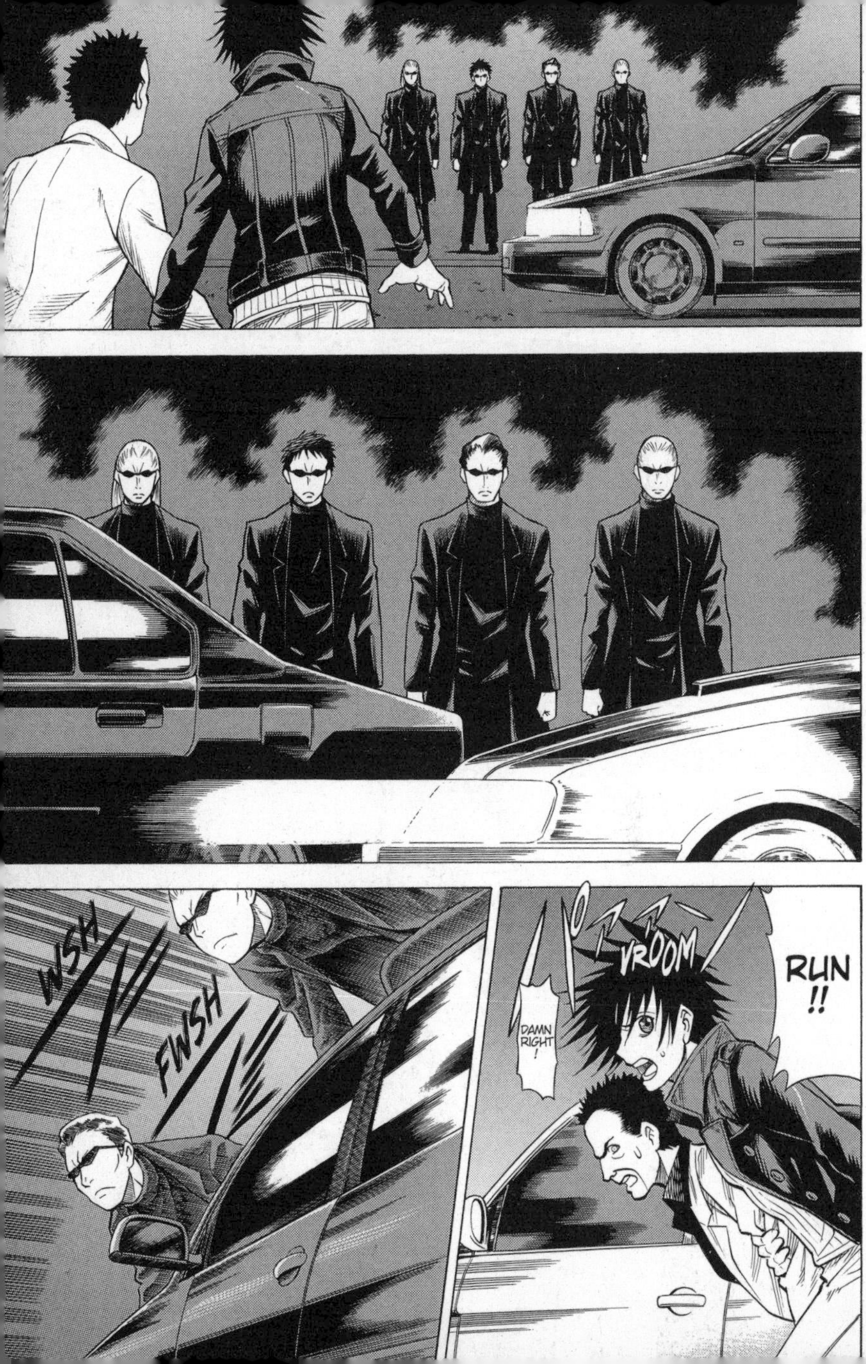
RUN !!
VROOM
DAMN RIGHT !
WSH
FWSH

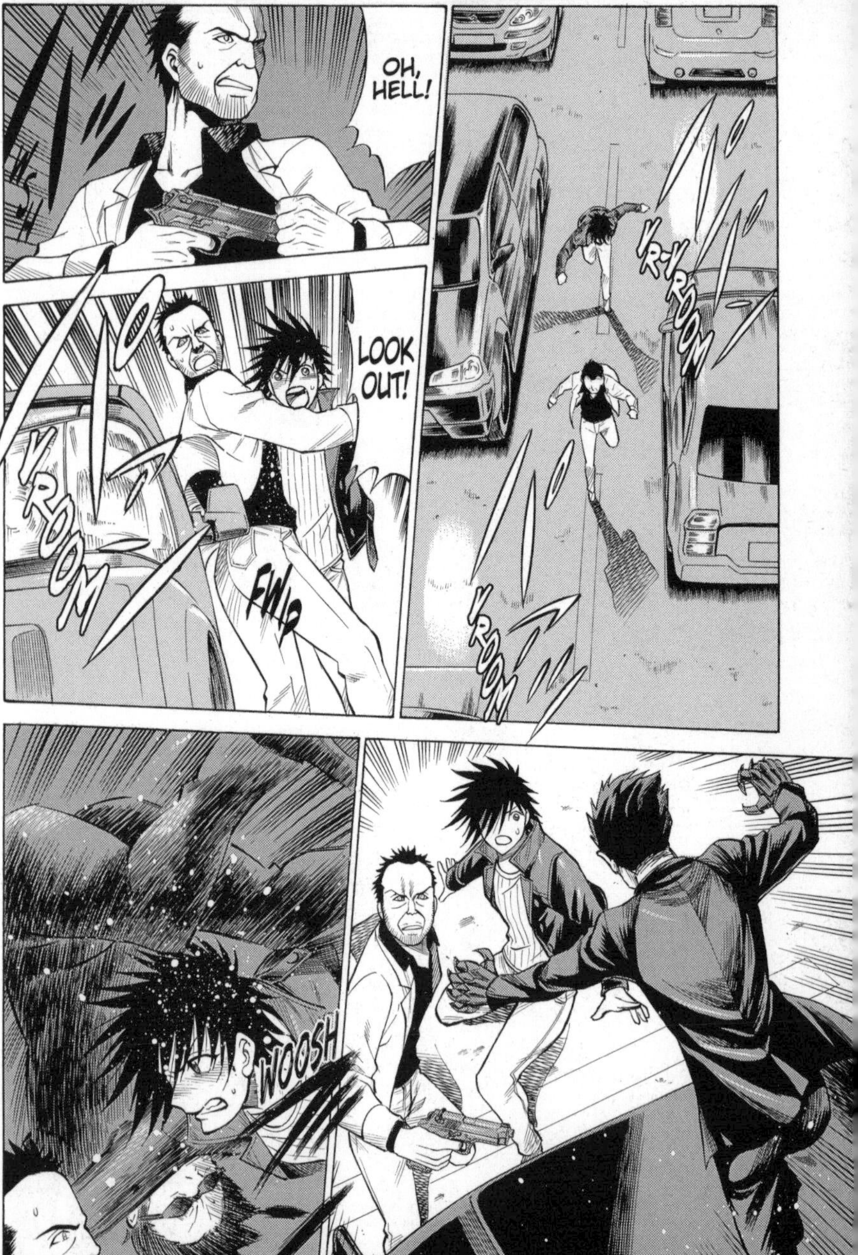
VR-VROOM
VROOM
OH, HELL!
LOOK OUT!
VROOM
FWIP
WOOSH

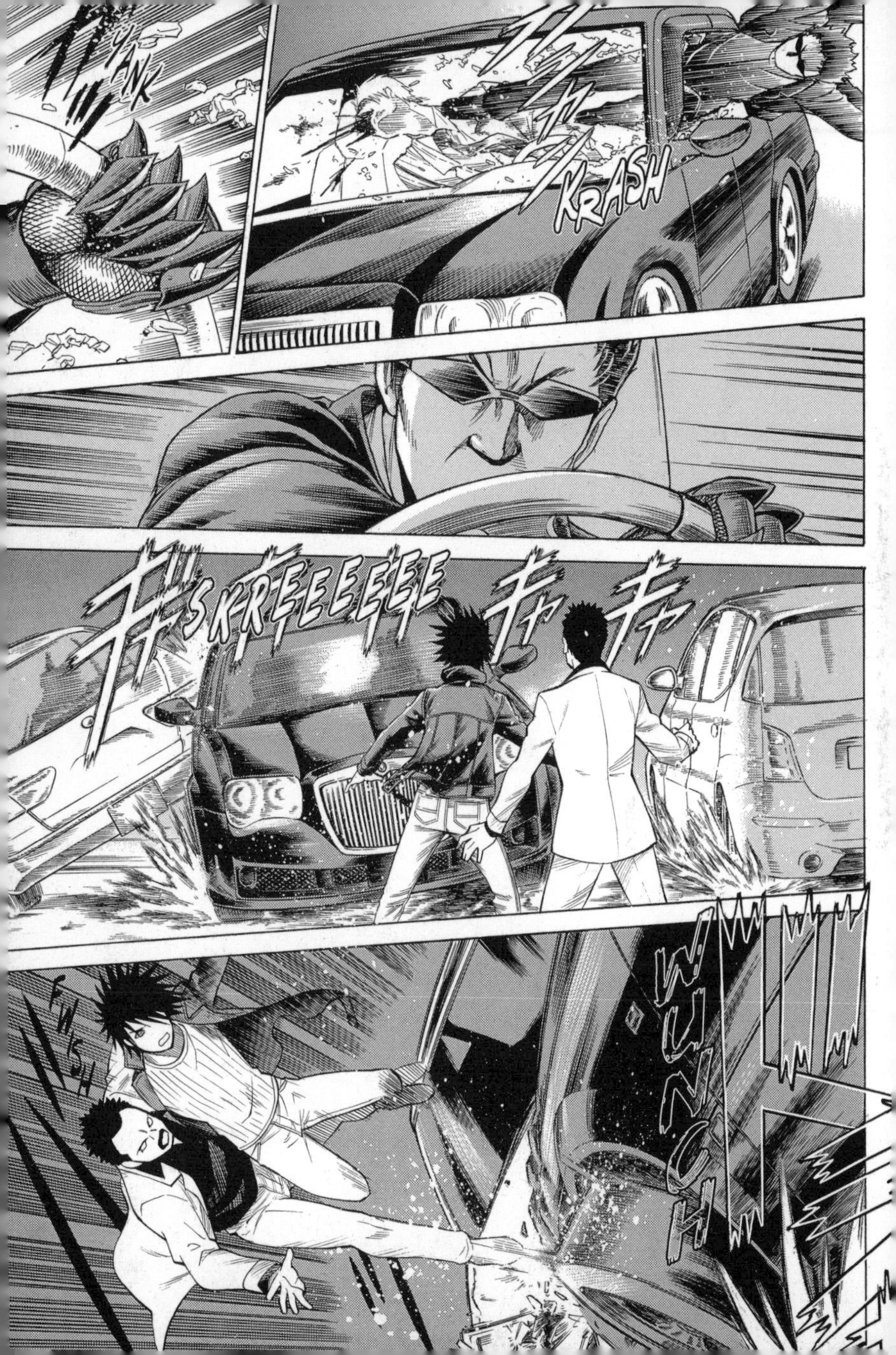
KRASH
YANK
SKREEEEEEE
キャキャ
WUNCH
FWISH

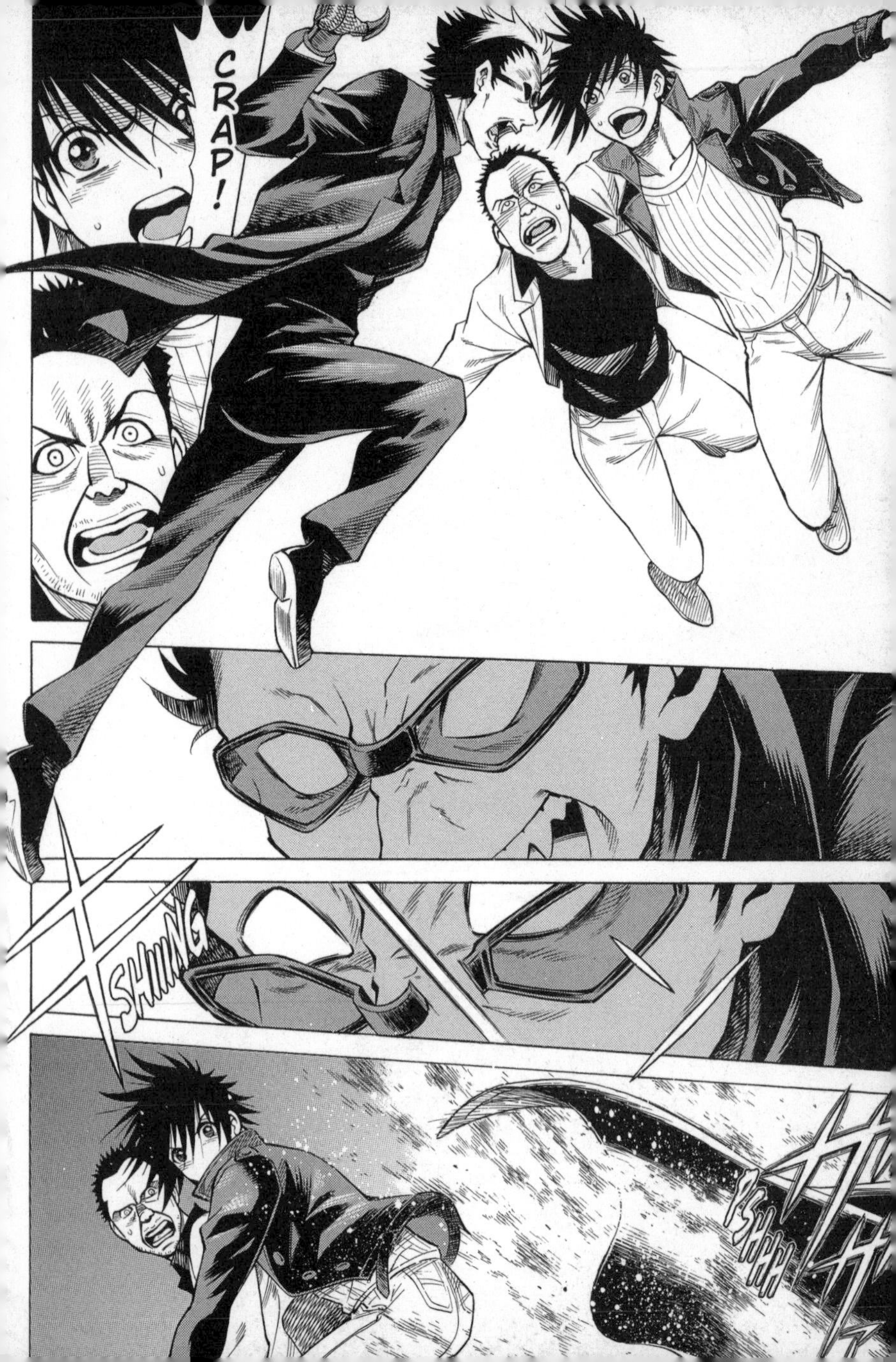
CRAP!
SHIIING
PSHHH

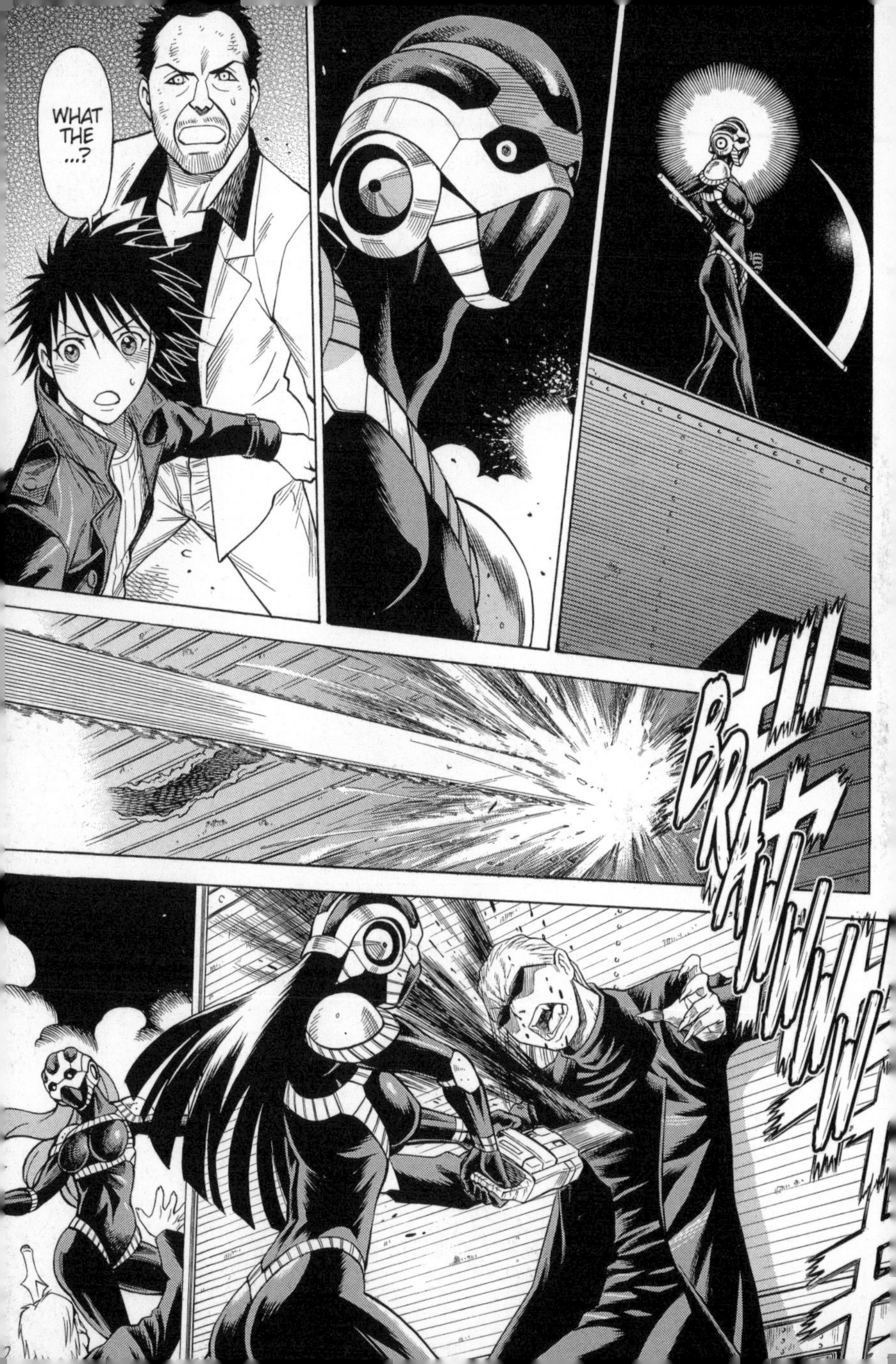
WHAT THE ...?
BRA

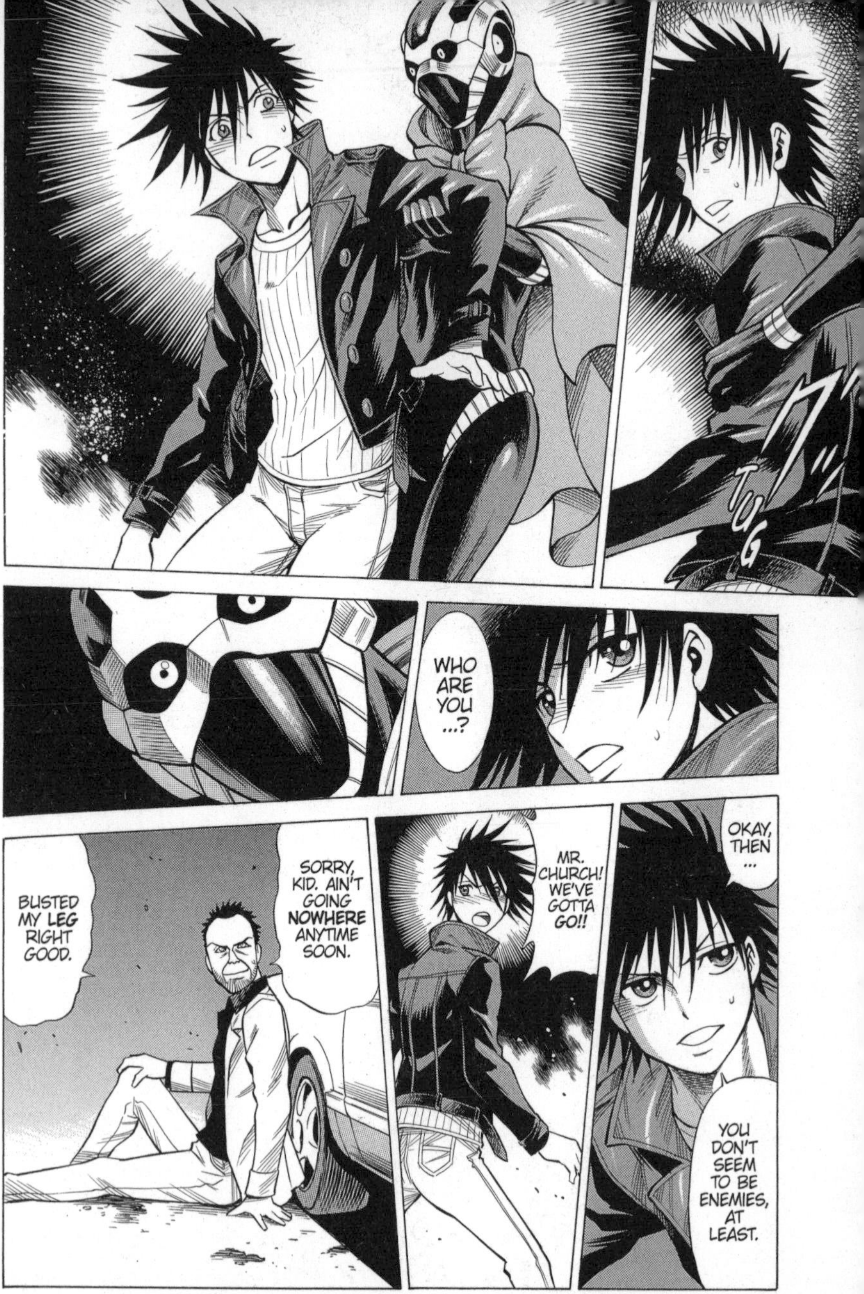
TUG
WHO ARE YOU ...?
OKAY, THEN ...
YOU DON'T SEEM TO BE ENEMIES, AT LEAST.
MR. CHURCH! WE'VE GOTTA GO!!
SORRY, KID. AIN'T GOING NOWHERE ANYTIME SOON.
BUSTED MY LEG RIGHT GOOD.

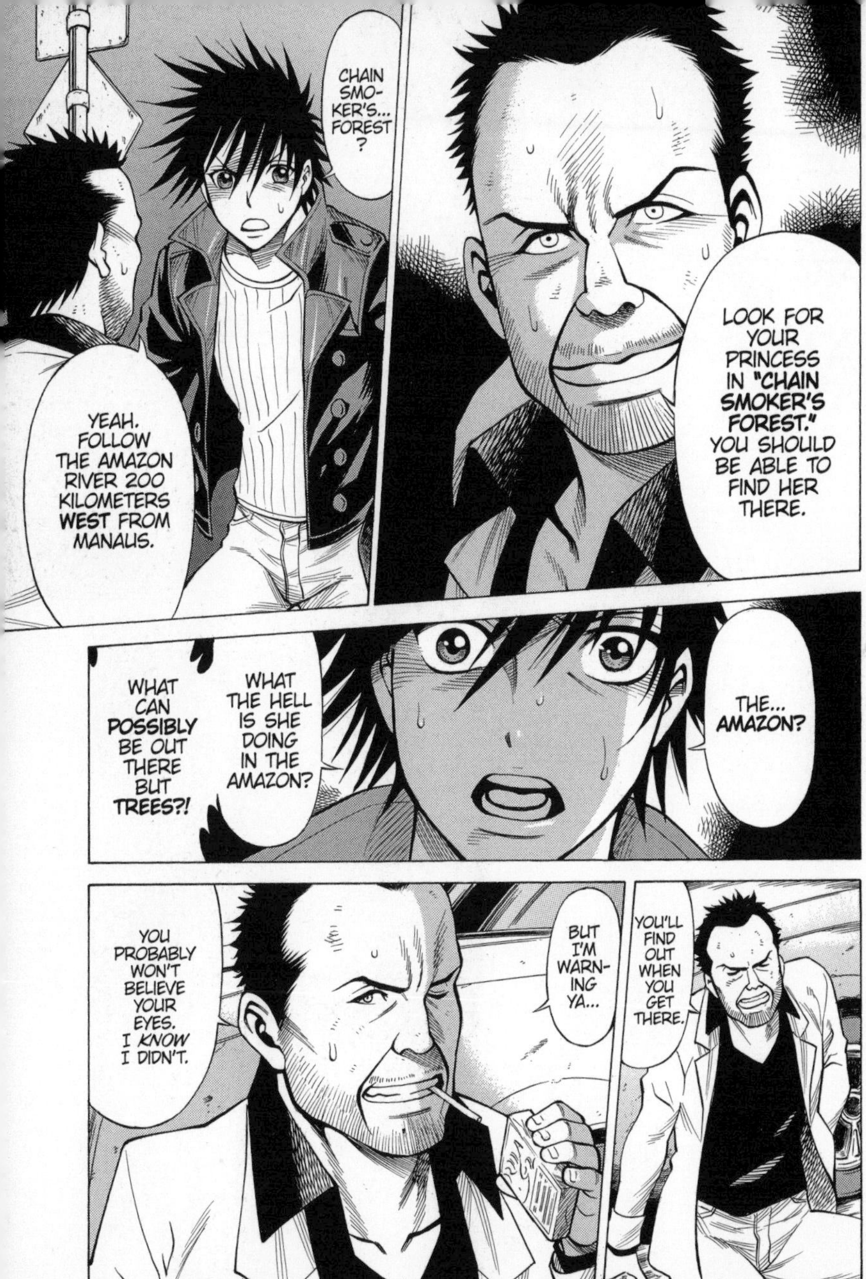
LOOK FOR YOUR PRINCESS IN "CHAIN SMOKER'S FOREST." YOU SHOULD BE ABLE TO FIND HER THERE.
CHAIN SMOKER'S... FOREST?
YEAH. FOLLOW THE AMAZON RIVER 200 KILOMETERS WEST FROM MANAUS.
THE... AMAZON?
WHAT THE HELL IS SHE DOING IN THE AMAZON?
WHAT CAN POSSIBLY BE OUT THERE BUT TREES?!
YOU'LL FIND OUT WHEN YOU GET THERE.
BUT I'M WARNING YA...
YOU PROBABLY WON'T BELIEVE YOUR EYES. I KNOW I DIDN'T.

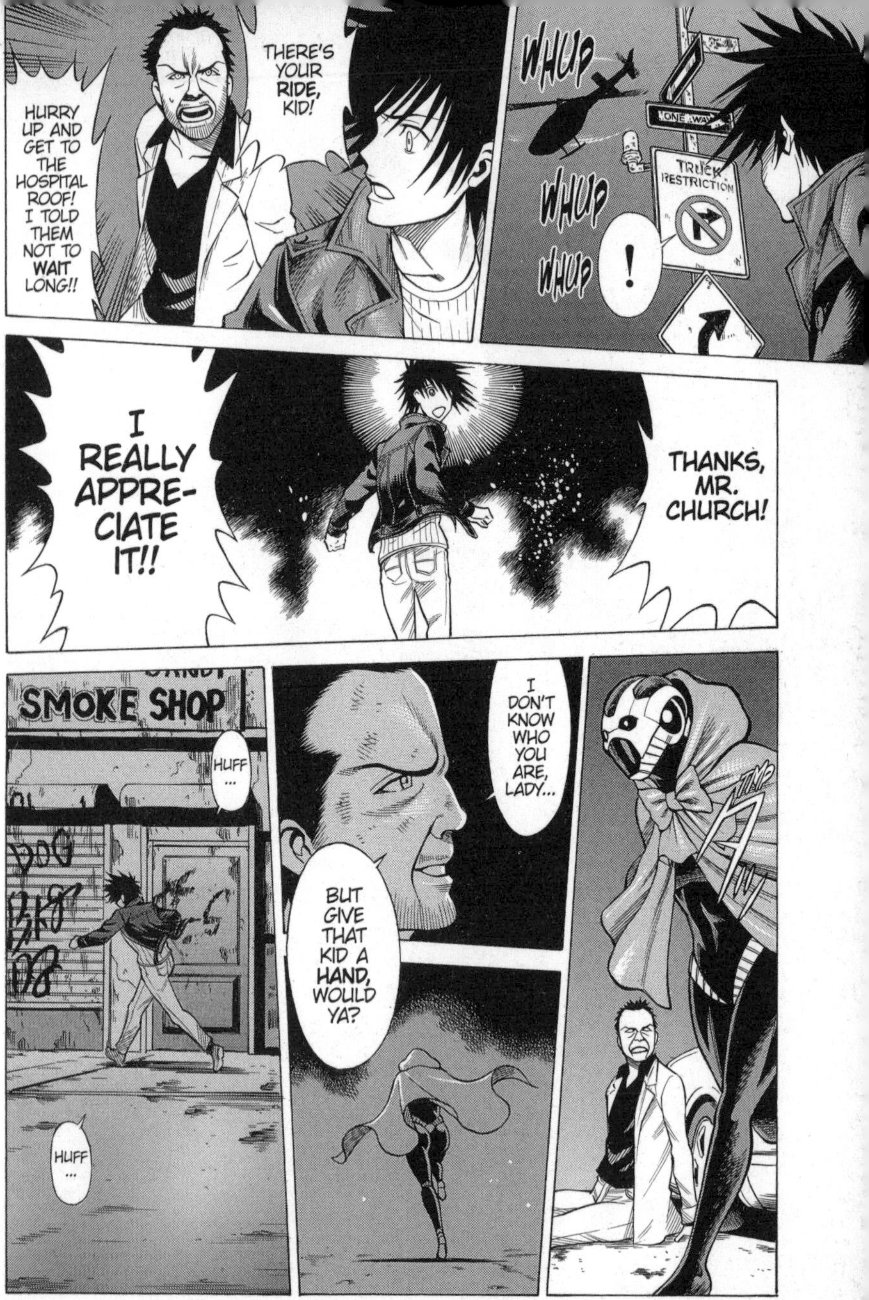
WHUP
WHUP
WHUP
ONE WAY
TRUCK RESTRICTION
!
THERE'S YOUR RIDE, KID!
HURRY UP AND GET TO THE HOSPITAL ROOF! I TOLD THEM NOT TO WAIT LONG!!
THANKS, MR. CHURCH!
I REALLY APPRE-CIATE IT!!
I DON'T KNOW WHO YOU ARE, LADY...
BUT GIVE THAT KID A HAND, WOULD YA?
SMOKE SHOP
HUFF...
HUFF...

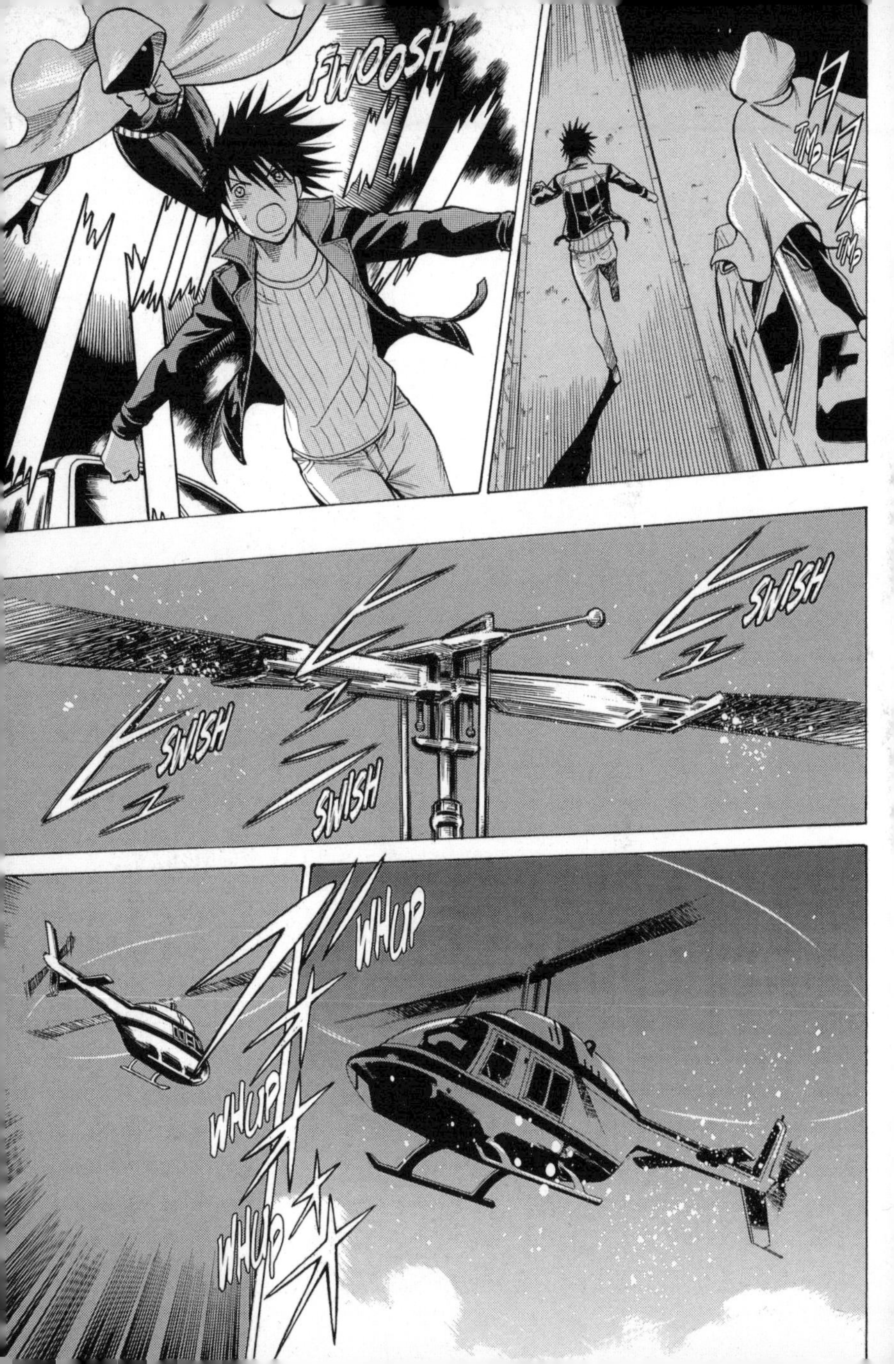
TMP
TMP
FWOOSH
SWISH
SWISH
SWISH
WHUP
WHUP
WHUP

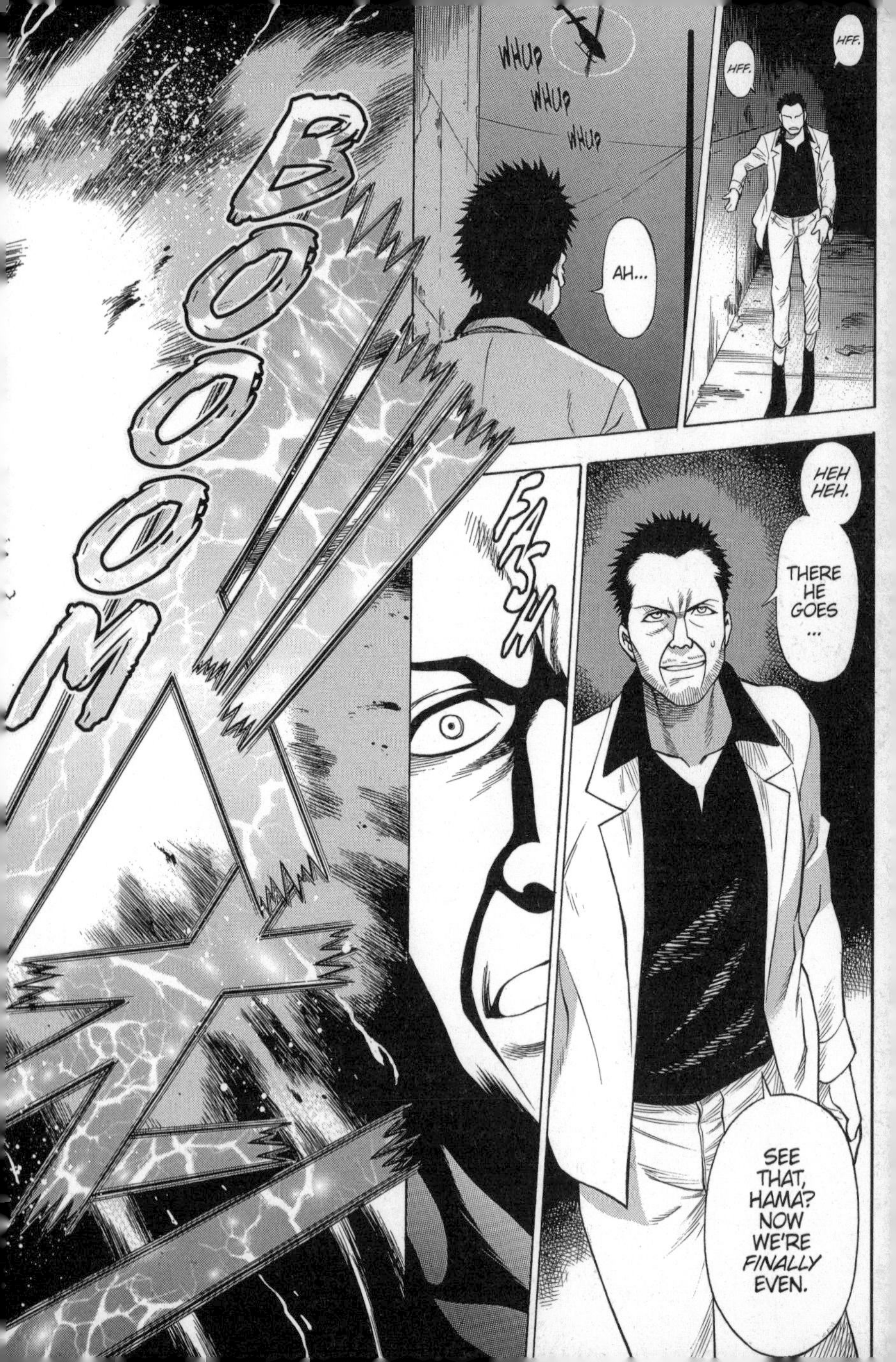
HFF.
HFF.
WHUP
WHUP
WHUP
AH...
HEH HEH.
THERE HE GOES ...
SEE THAT, HAMA? NOW WE'RE *FINALLY* EVEN.
FASH
BOOOOM

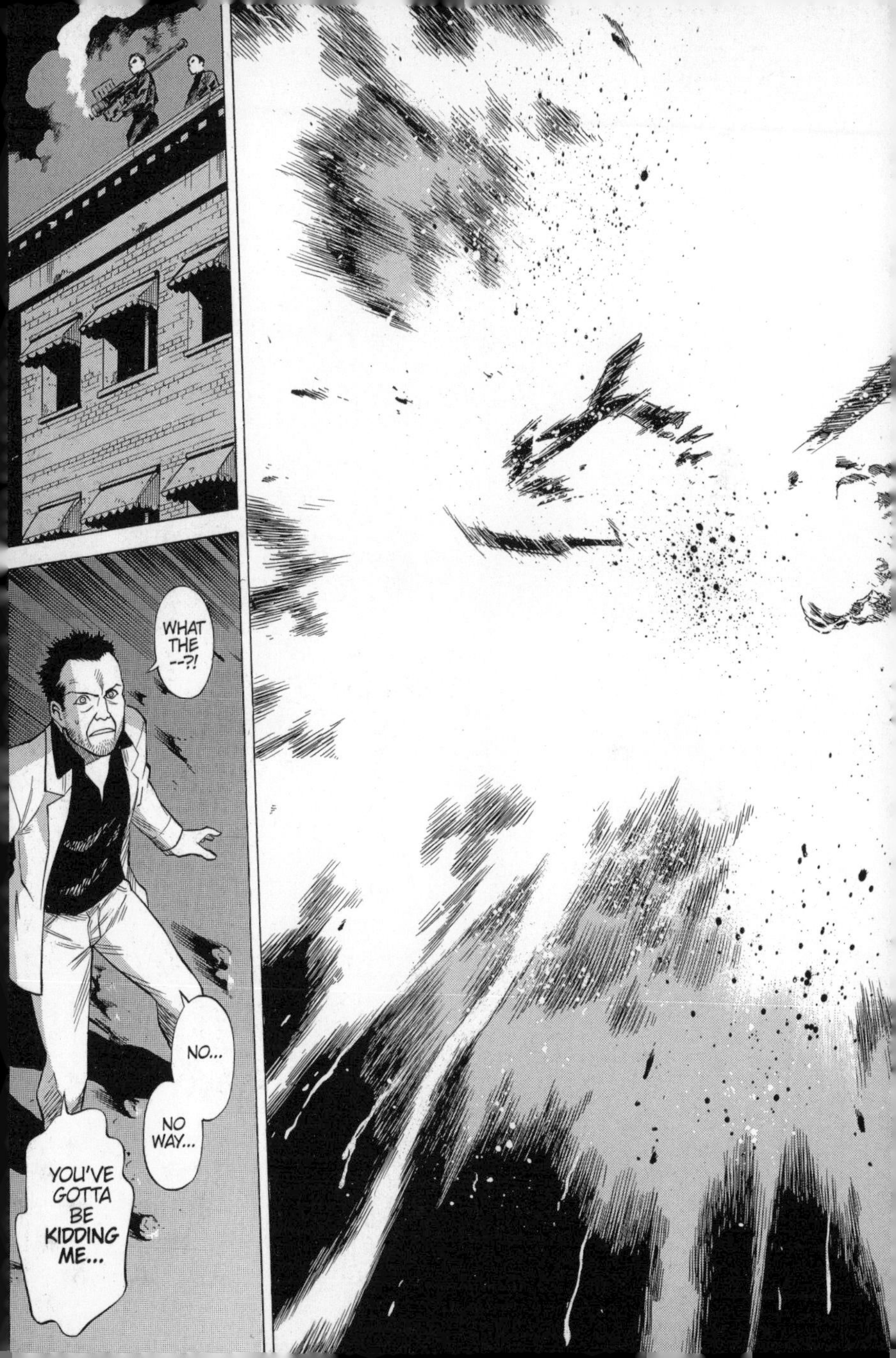
WHAT THE --?!
NO...
NO WAY...
YOU'VE GOTTA BE KIDDING ME...

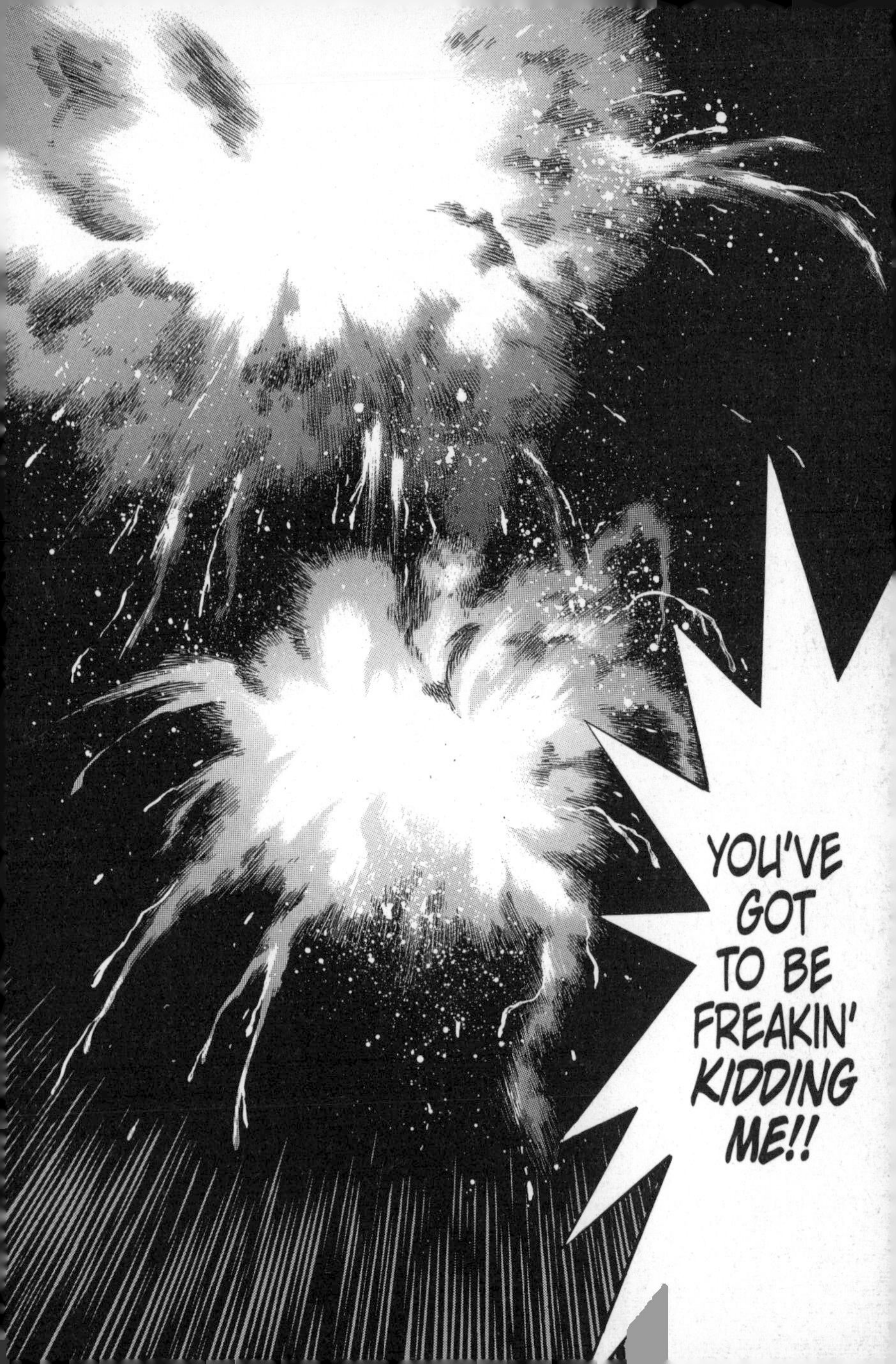
YOU'VE GOT TO BE FREAKIN' KIDDING ME!!

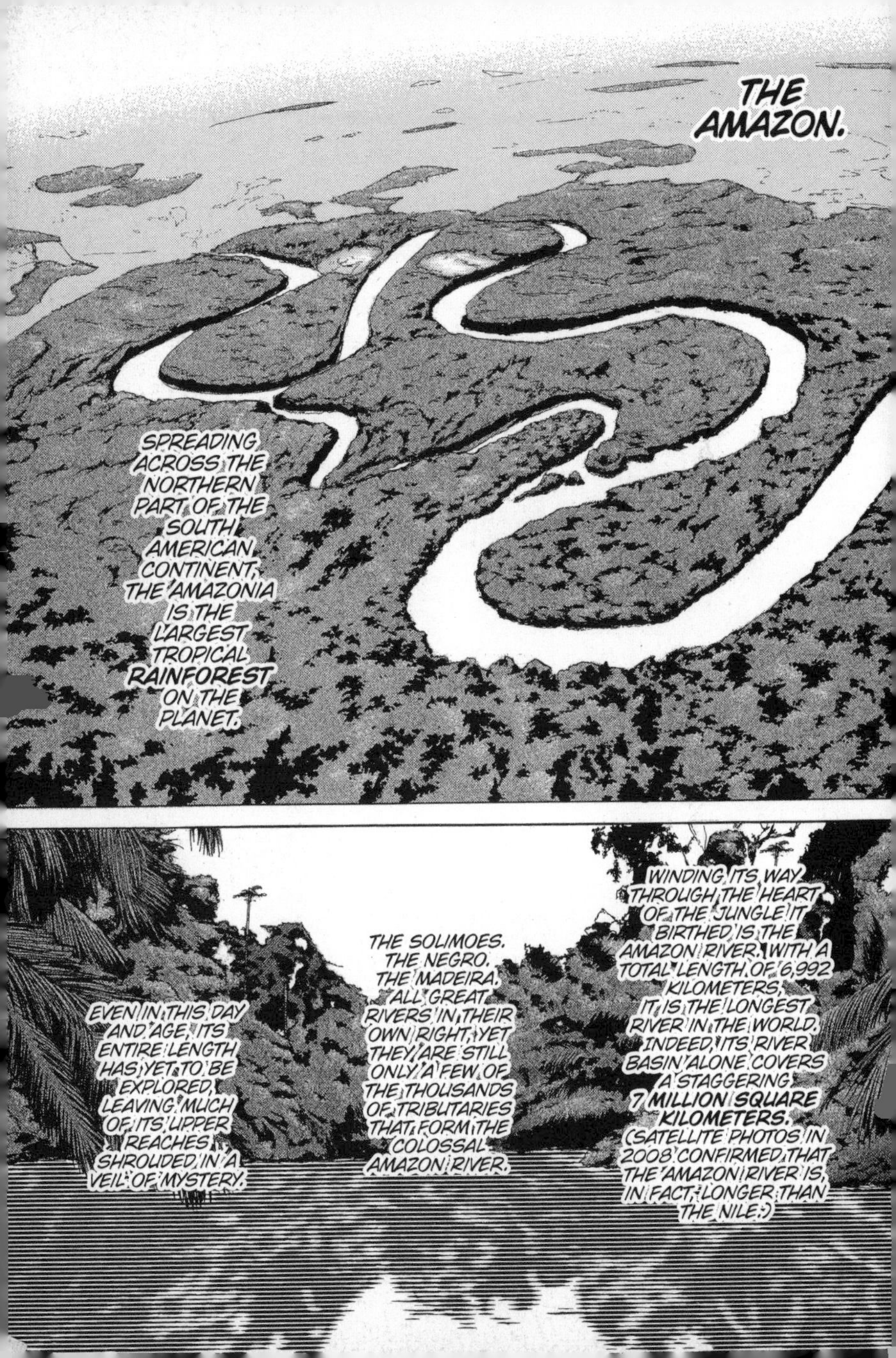
THE AMAZON.
SPREADING ACROSS THE NORTHERN PART OF THE SOUTH AMERICAN CONTINENT, THE AMAZONIA IS THE LARGEST TROPICAL **RAINFOREST** ON THE PLANET.
WINDING ITS WAY THROUGH THE HEART OF THE JUNGLE IT BIRTHED IS THE AMAZON RIVER. WITH A TOTAL LENGTH OF 6,992 KILOMETERS, IT IS THE LONGEST RIVER IN THE WORLD. INDEED, ITS RIVER BASIN ALONE COVERS A STAGGERING **7 MILLION SQUARE KILOMETERS.**
(SATELLITE PHOTOS IN 2008 CONFIRMED THAT THE AMAZON RIVER IS, IN FACT, LONGER THAN THE NILE.)
THE SOLIMOES. THE NEGRO. THE MADEIRA. ALL GREAT RIVERS IN THEIR OWN RIGHT, YET THEY ARE STILL ONLY A FEW OF THE THOUSANDS OF TRIBUTARIES THAT FORM THE COLOSSAL AMAZON RIVER.
EVEN IN THIS DAY AND AGE, ITS ENTIRE LENGTH HAS YET TO BE EXPLORED, LEAVING MUCH OF ITS UPPER REACHES SHROUDED IN A VEIL OF MYSTERY.

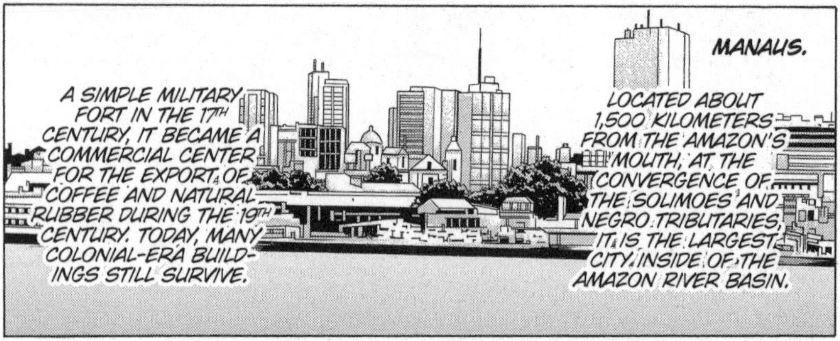
MANAUS.
LOCATED ABOUT 1,500 KILOMETERS FROM THE AMAZON'S MOUTH, AT THE CONVERGENCE OF THE SOLIMOES AND NEGRO TRIBUTARIES, IT IS THE LARGEST CITY INSIDE OF THE AMAZON RIVER BASIN.
A SIMPLE MILITARY FORT IN THE 17TH CENTURY, IT BECAME A COMMERCIAL CENTER FOR THE EXPORT OF COFFEE AND NATURAL RUBBER DURING THE 19TH CENTURY. TODAY, MANY COLONIAL-ERA BUILDINGS STILL SURVIVE.

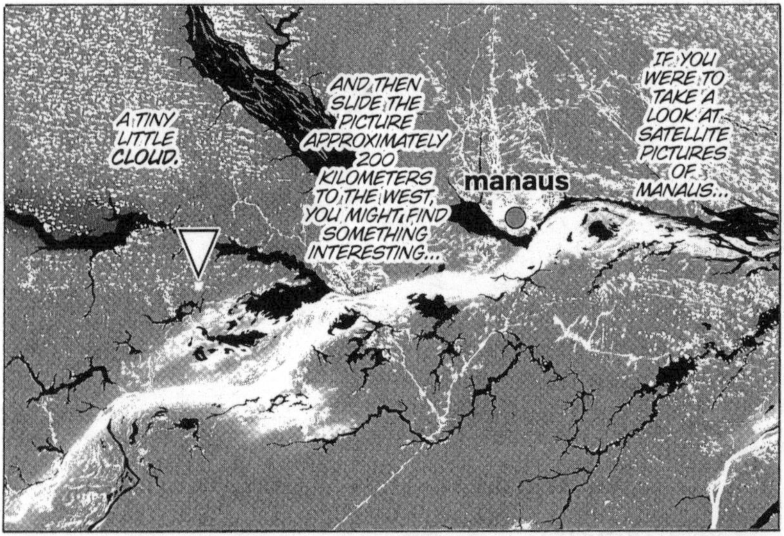
IF YOU WERE TO TAKE A LOOK AT SATELLITE PICTURES OF MANAUS...
manaus
AND THEN SLIDE THE PICTURE APPROXIMATELY 200 KILOMETERS TO THE WEST, YOU MIGHT FIND SOMETHING INTERESTING...
A TINY LITTLE CLOUD.

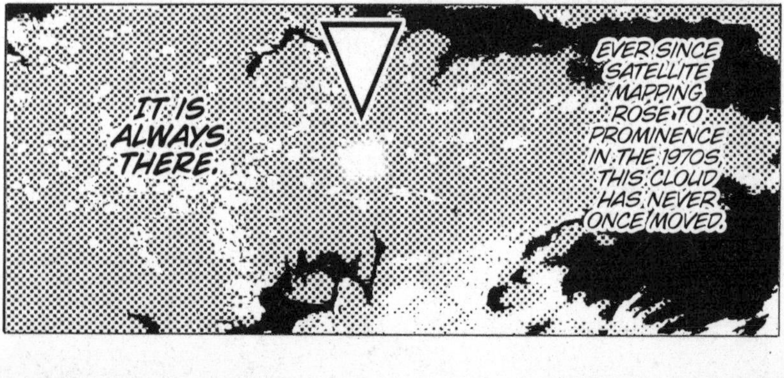
EVER SINCE SATELLITE MAPPING ROSE TO PROMINENCE IN THE 1970S, THIS CLOUD HAS NEVER ONCE MOVED.
IT IS ALWAYS THERE.

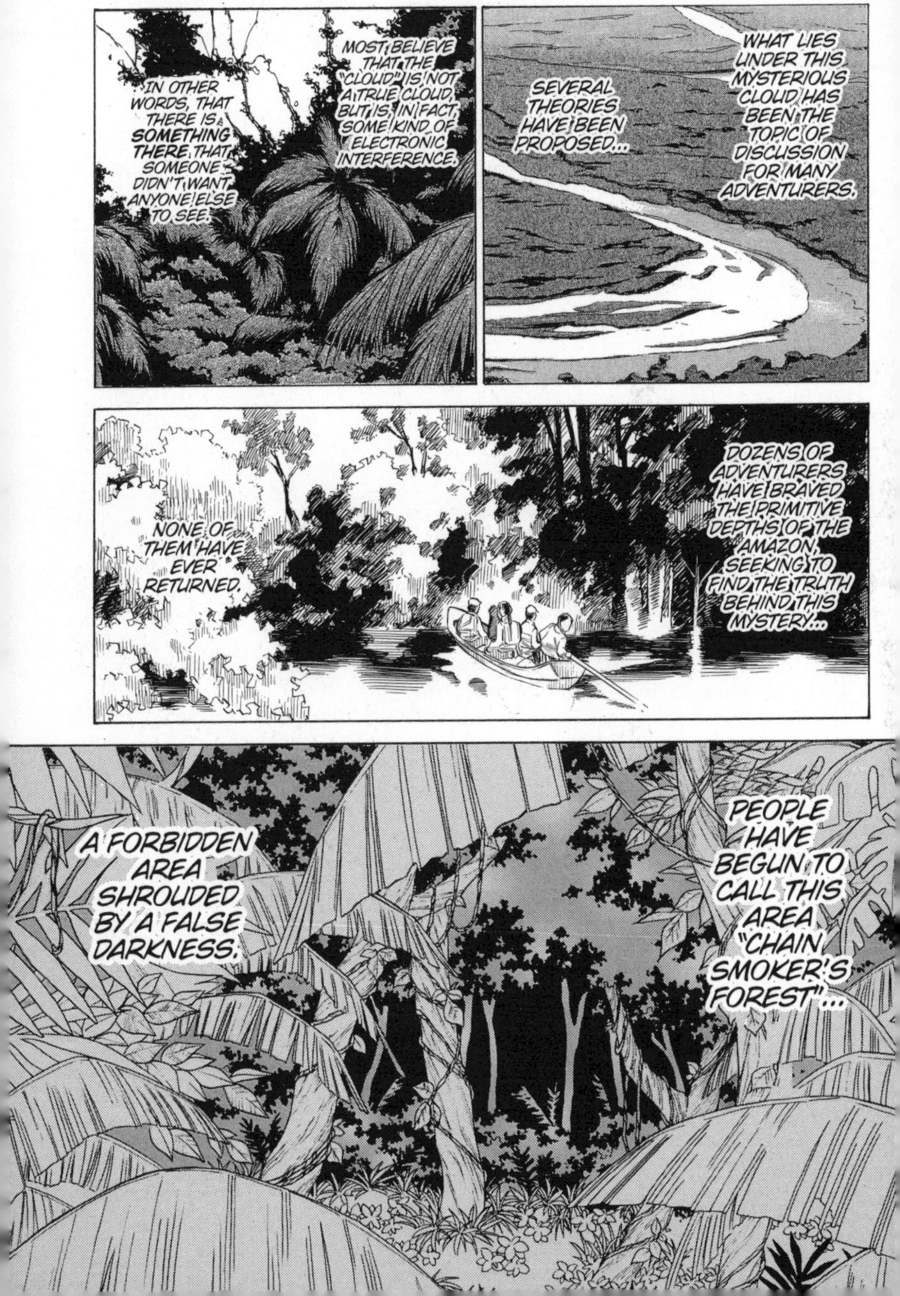
WHAT LIES UNDER THIS MYSTERIOUS CLOUD HAS BEEN THE TOPIC OF DISCUSSION FOR MANY ADVENTURERS.
SEVERAL THEORIES HAVE BEEN PROPOSED...
MOST BELIEVE THAT THE "CLOUD" IS NOT A TRUE CLOUD, BUT IS, IN FACT, SOME KIND OF ELECTRONIC INTERFERENCE.
IN OTHER WORDS, THAT THERE IS **SOMETHING THERE** THAT SOMEONE DIDN'T WANT ANYONE ELSE TO SEE.
DOZENS OF ADVENTURERS HAVE BRAVED THE PRIMITIVE DEPTHS OF THE AMAZON, SEEKING TO FIND THE TRUTH BEHIND THIS MYSTERY...
NONE OF THEM HAVE EVER RETURNED.
PEOPLE HAVE BEGUN TO CALL THIS AREA "CHAIN SMOKER'S FOREST"...
A FORBIDDEN AREA SHROUDED BY A FALSE DARKNESS.

Chapter 66: A Verdant Hell

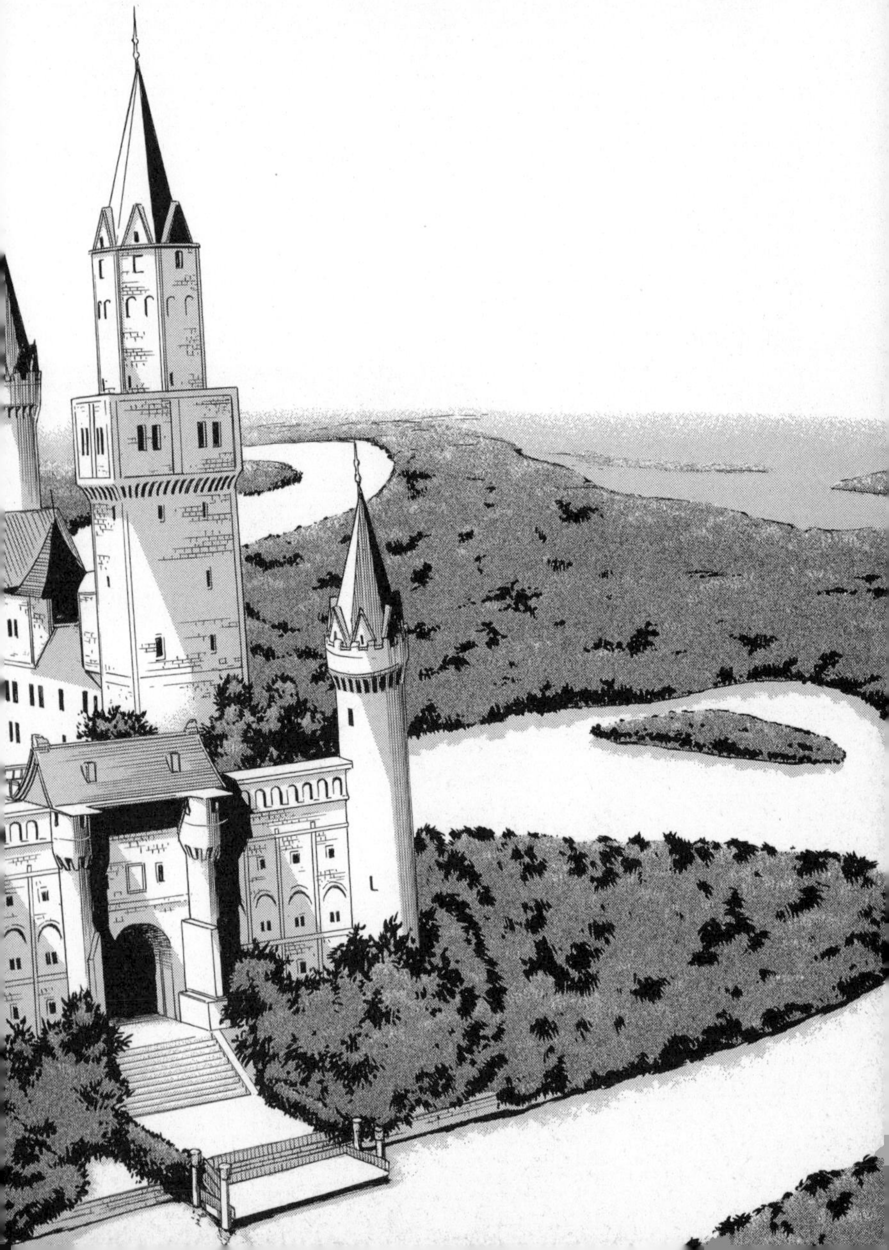

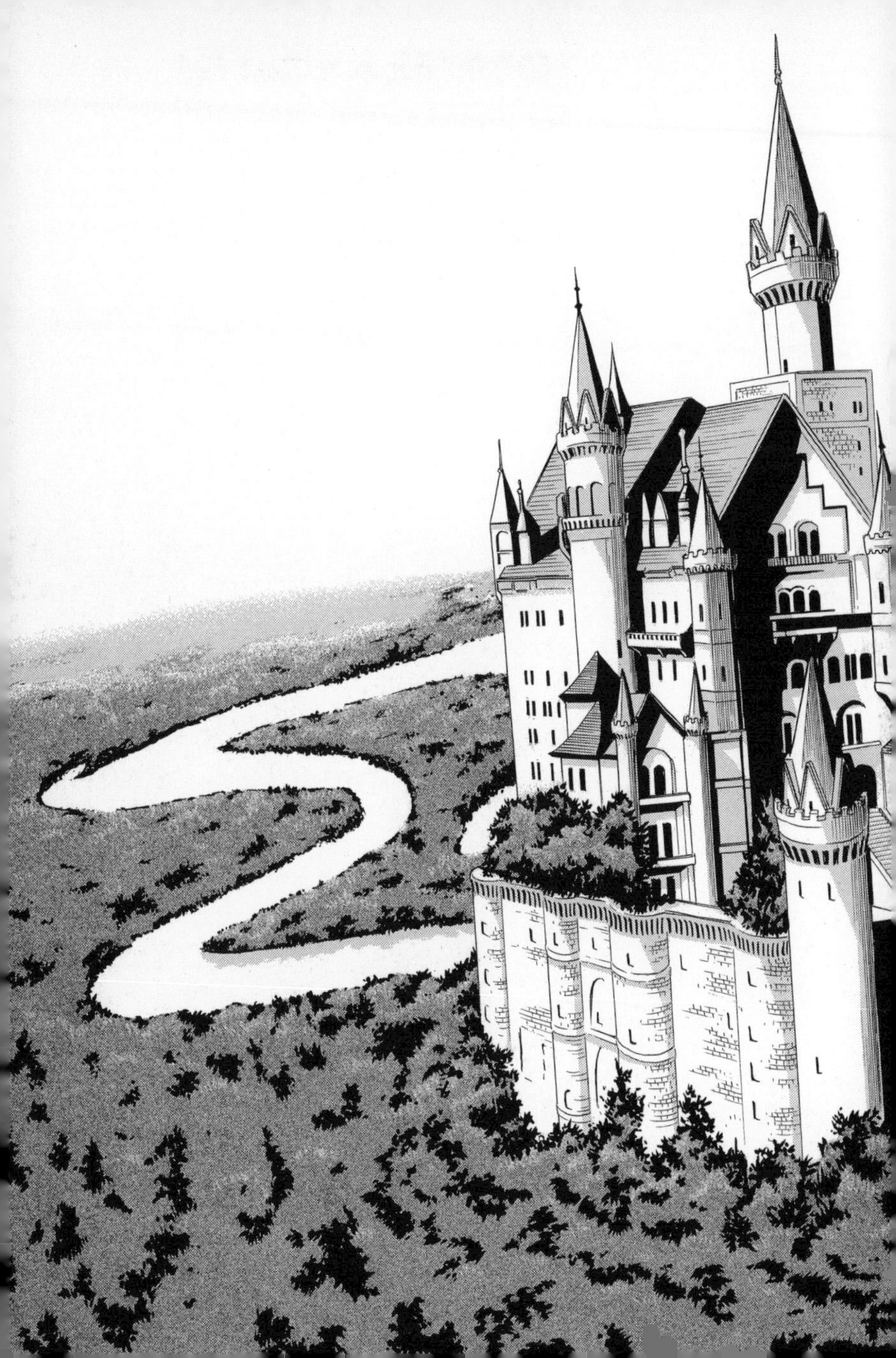

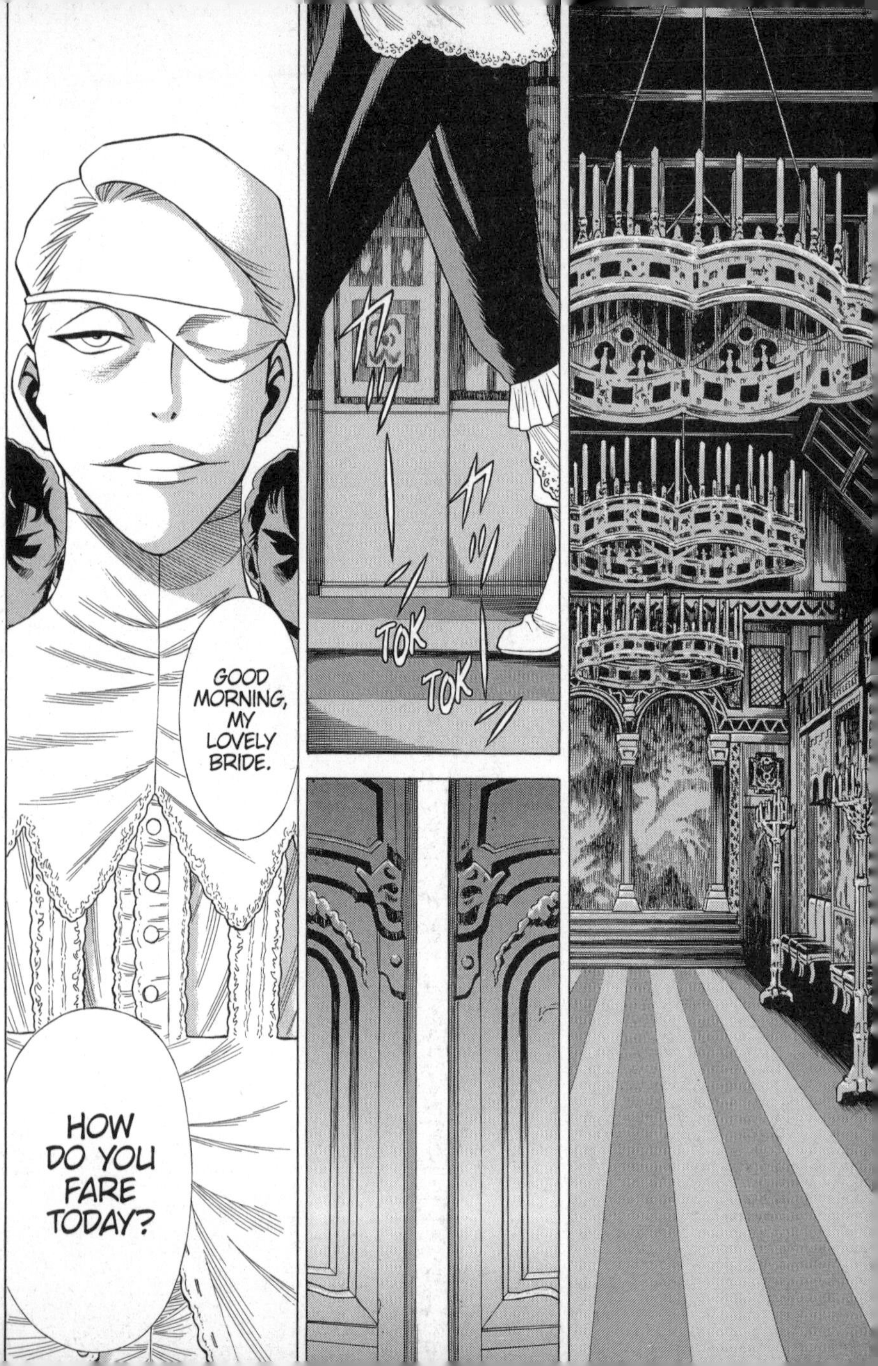
TOK
TOK
GOOD MORNING, MY LOVELY BRIDE.
HOW DO YOU FARE TODAY?

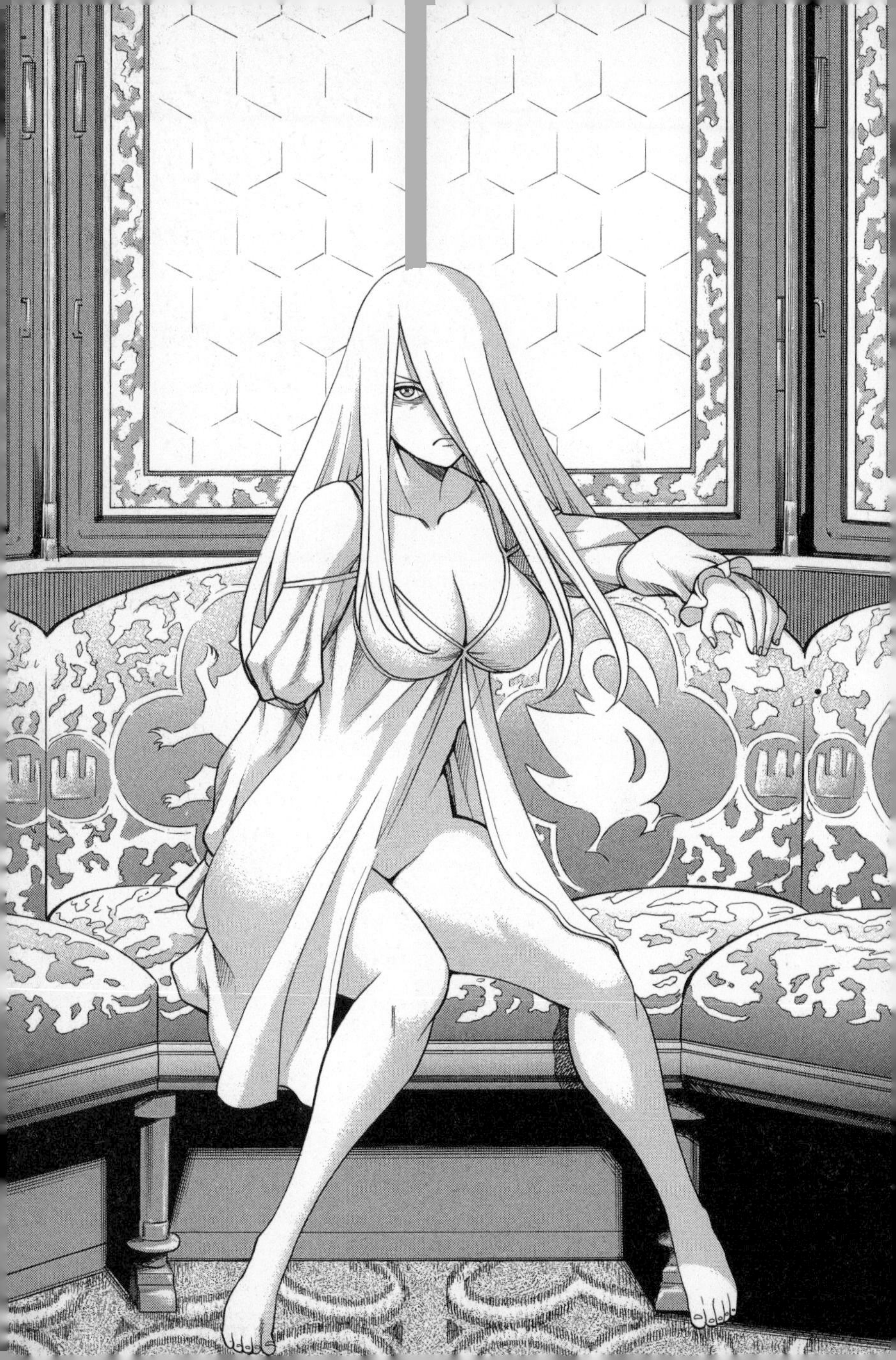

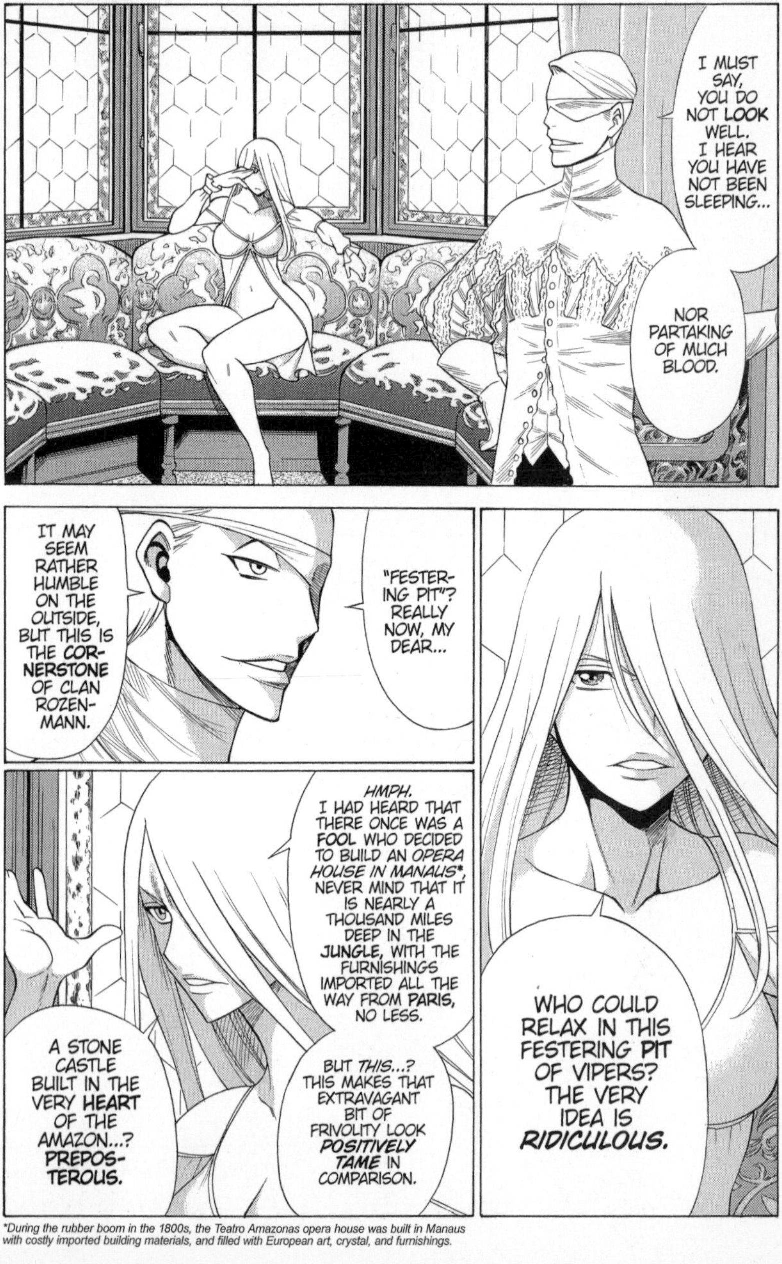
I MUST SAY, YOU DO NOT LOOK WELL. I HEAR YOU HAVE NOT BEEN SLEEPING...
NOR PARTAKING OF MUCH BLOOD.
WHO COULD RELAX IN THIS FESTERING PIT OF VIPERS? THE VERY IDEA IS RIDICULOUS.
"FESTER-ING PIT"? REALLY NOW, MY DEAR...
IT MAY SEEM RATHER HUMBLE ON THE OUTSIDE, BUT THIS IS THE COR-NERSTONE OF CLAN ROZEN-MANN.
HMPH. I HAD HEARD THAT THERE ONCE WAS A FOOL WHO DECIDED TO BUILD AN OPERA HOUSE IN MANAUS*, NEVER MIND THAT IT IS NEARLY A THOUSAND MILES DEEP IN THE JUNGLE, WITH THE FURNISHINGS IMPORTED ALL THE WAY FROM PARIS, NO LESS.
BUT THIS...? THIS MAKES THAT EXTRAVAGANT BIT OF FRIVOLITY LOOK POSITIVELY TAME IN COMPARISON.
A STONE CASTLE BUILT IN THE VERY HEART OF THE AMAZON...? PREPOS-TEROUS.

*During the rubber boom in the 1800s, the Teatro Amazonas opera house was built in Manaus with costly imported building materials, and filled with European art, crystal, and furnishings.

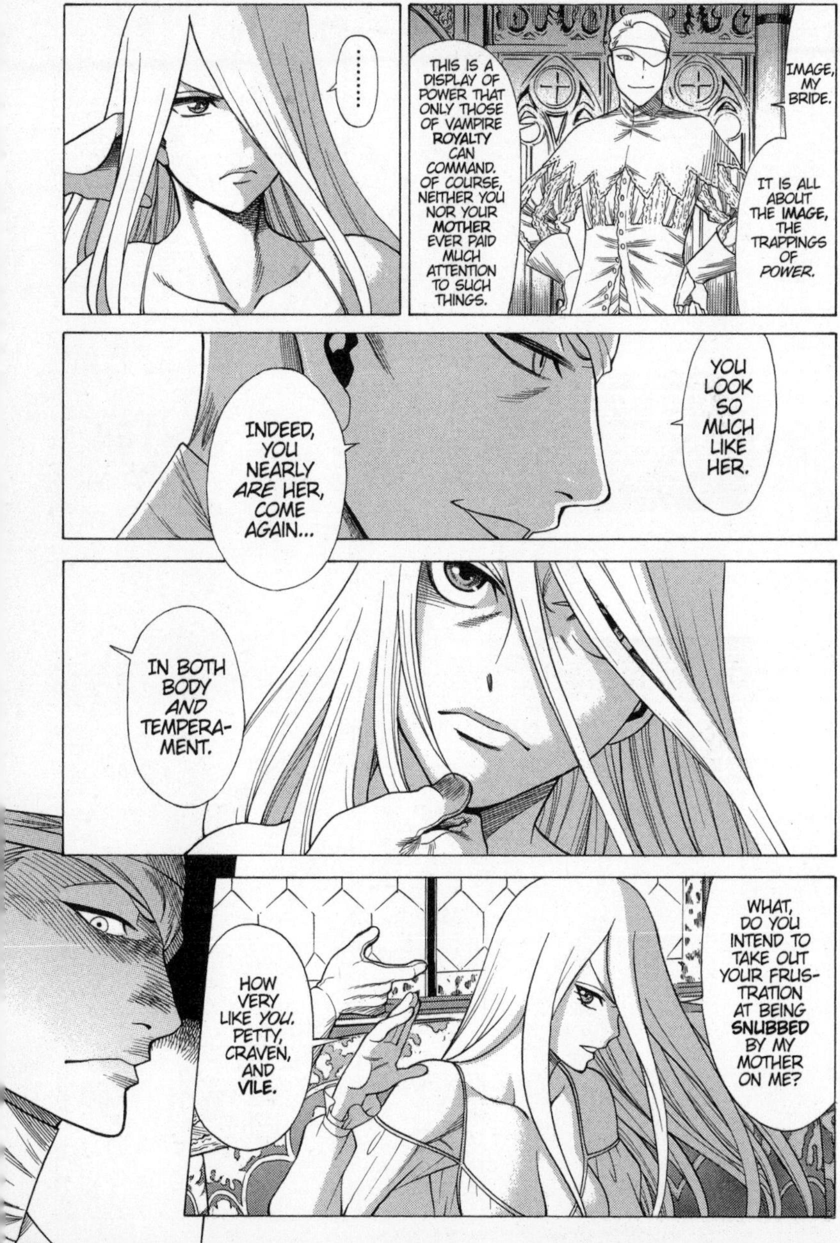
IMAGE, MY BRIDE.
IT IS ALL ABOUT THE IMAGE, THE TRAPPINGS OF POWER.
THIS IS A DISPLAY OF POWER THAT ONLY THOSE OF VAMPIRE ROYALTY CAN COMMAND. OF COURSE, NEITHER YOU NOR YOUR MOTHER EVER PAID MUCH ATTENTION TO SUCH THINGS.
....
YOU LOOK SO MUCH LIKE HER.
INDEED, YOU NEARLY ARE HER, COME AGAIN...
IN BOTH BODY AND TEMPERA-MENT.
WHAT, DO YOU INTEND TO TAKE OUT YOUR FRUS-TRATION AT BEING SNUBBED BY MY MOTHER ON ME?
HOW VERY LIKE YOU. PETTY, CRAVEN, AND VILE.

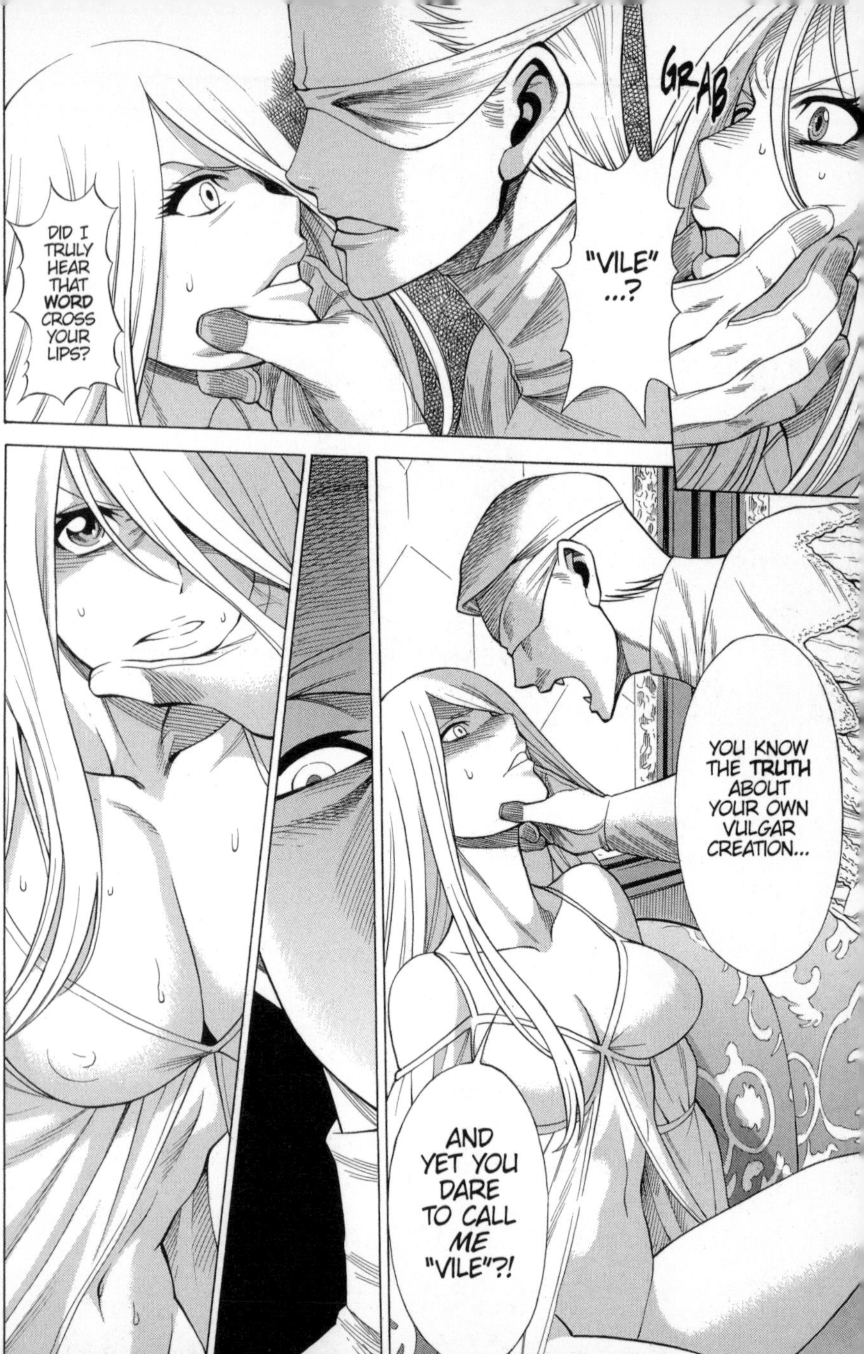
GRAB
"VILE" ...?
DID I TRULY HEAR THAT WORD CROSS YOUR LIPS?
YOU KNOW THE TRUTH ABOUT YOUR OWN VULGAR CREATION...
AND YET YOU DARE TO CALL ME "VILE"?!

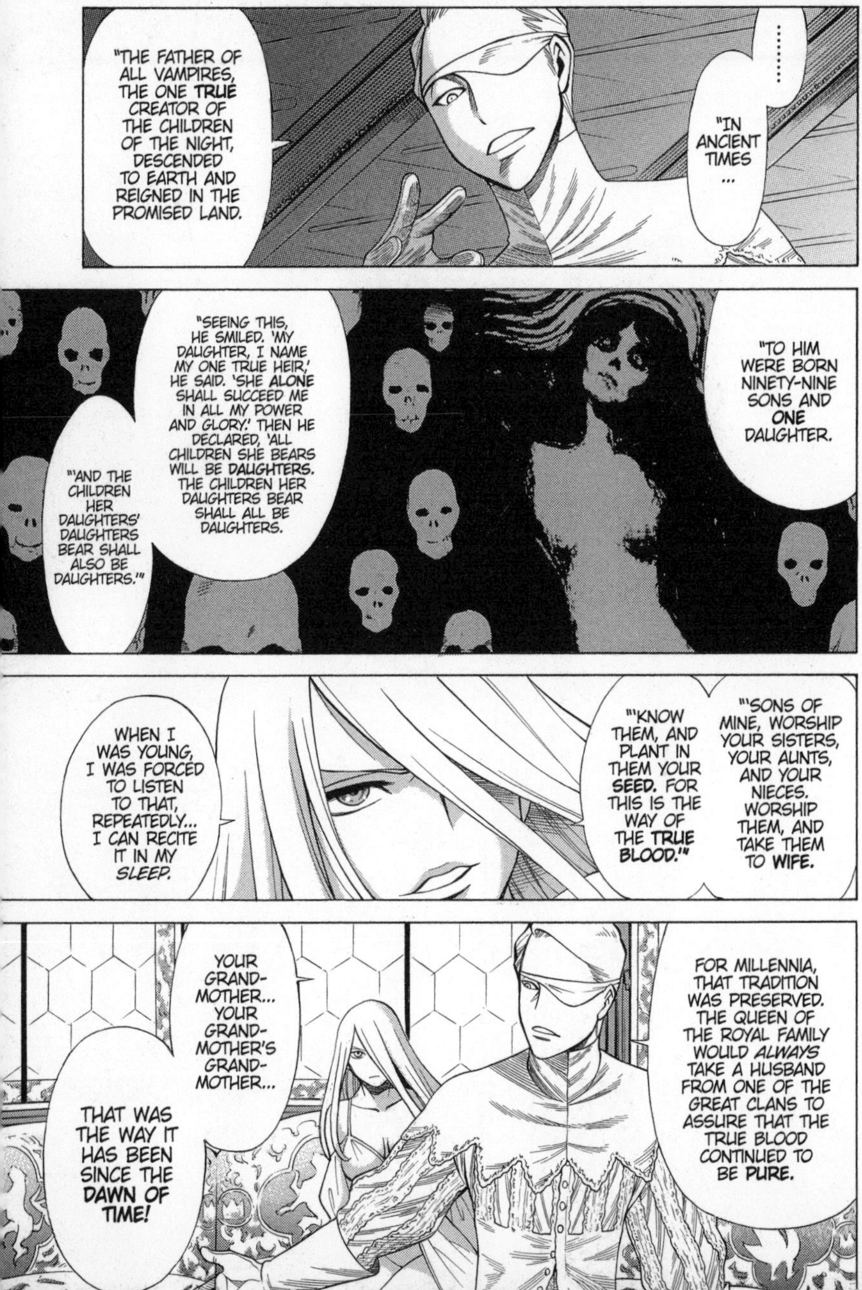
……
"IN ANCIENT TIMES ...
"THE FATHER OF ALL VAMPIRES, THE ONE TRUE CREATOR OF THE CHILDREN OF THE NIGHT, DESCENDED TO EARTH AND REIGNED IN THE PROMISED LAND.
"TO HIM WERE BORN NINETY-NINE SONS AND ONE DAUGHTER.
"SEEING THIS, HE SMILED. 'MY DAUGHTER, I NAME MY ONE TRUE HEIR,' HE SAID. 'SHE ALONE SHALL SUCCEED ME IN ALL MY POWER AND GLORY.' THEN HE DECLARED, 'ALL CHILDREN SHE BEARS WILL BE DAUGHTERS. THE CHILDREN HER DAUGHTERS BEAR SHALL ALL BE DAUGHTERS.
"'AND THE CHILDREN HER DAUGHTERS' DAUGHTERS BEAR SHALL ALSO BE DAUGHTERS.'"
"'SONS OF MINE, WORSHIP YOUR SISTERS, YOUR AUNTS, AND YOUR NIECES. WORSHIP THEM, AND TAKE THEM TO WIFE.
"'KNOW THEM, AND PLANT IN THEM YOUR SEED. FOR THIS IS THE WAY OF THE TRUE BLOOD.'"
WHEN I WAS YOUNG, I WAS FORCED TO LISTEN TO THAT, REPEATEDLY... I CAN RECITE IT IN MY SLEEP.
FOR MILLENNIA, THAT TRADITION WAS PRESERVED. THE QUEEN OF THE ROYAL FAMILY WOULD ALWAYS TAKE A HUSBAND FROM ONE OF THE GREAT CLANS TO ASSURE THAT THE TRUE BLOOD CONTINUED TO BE PURE.
YOUR GRAND-MOTHER... YOUR GRAND-MOTHER'S GRAND-MOTHER...
THAT WAS THE WAY IT HAS BEEN SINCE THE DAWN OF TIME!

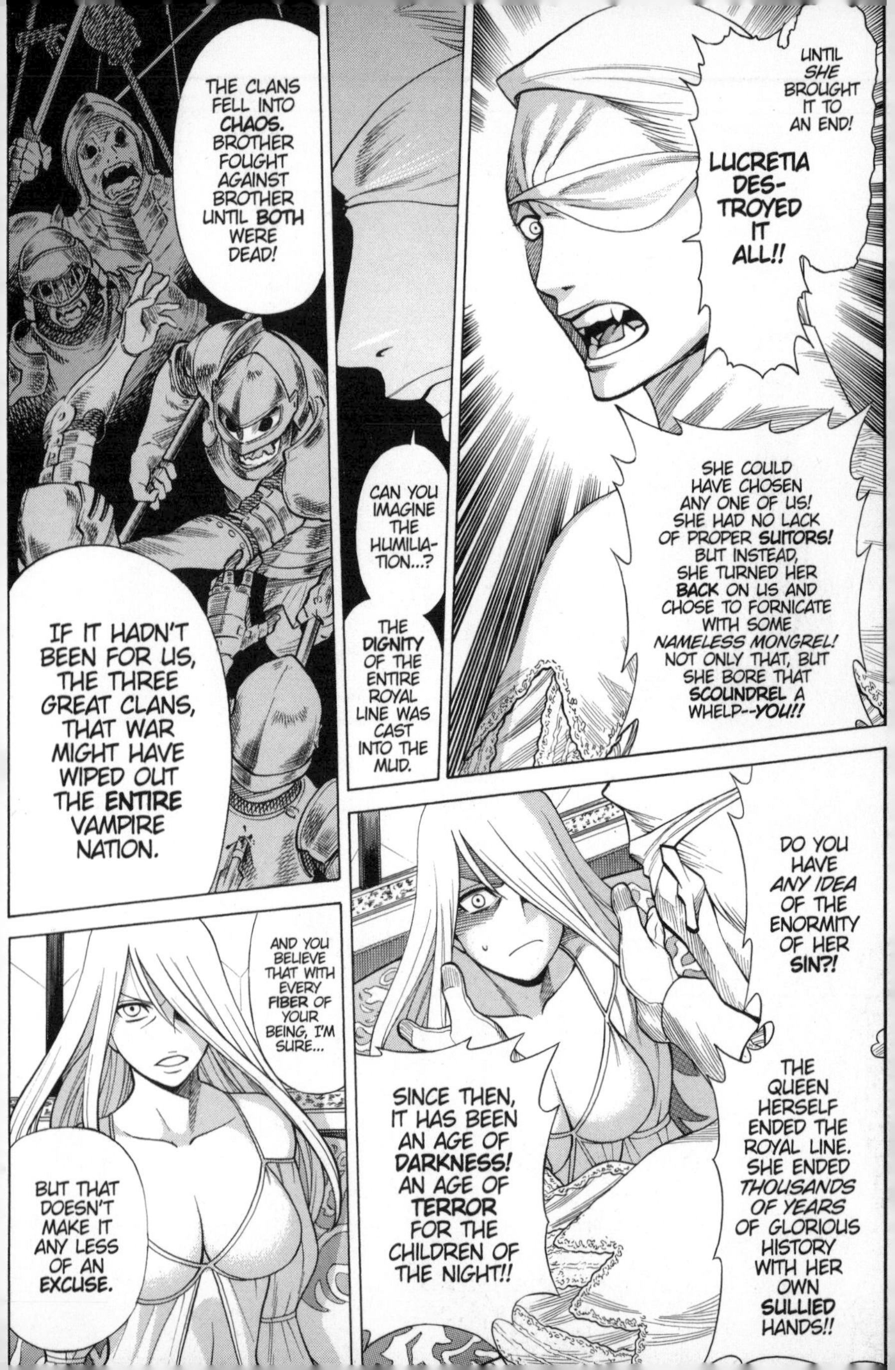

UNTIL SHE BROUGHT IT TO AN END!
LUCRETIA DES-TROYED IT ALL!!
SHE COULD HAVE CHOSEN ANY ONE OF US! SHE HAD NO LACK OF PROPER SUITORS! BUT INSTEAD, SHE TURNED HER BACK ON US AND CHOSE TO FORNICATE WITH SOME NAMELESS MONGREL! NOT ONLY THAT, BUT SHE BORE THAT SCOUNDREL A WHELP--YOU!!
CAN YOU IMAGINE THE HUMILIA-TION...?
THE DIGNITY OF THE ENTIRE ROYAL LINE WAS CAST INTO THE MUD.
THE CLANS FELL INTO CHAOS. BROTHER FOUGHT AGAINST BROTHER UNTIL BOTH WERE DEAD!
IF IT HADN'T BEEN FOR US, THE THREE GREAT CLANS, THAT WAR MIGHT HAVE WIPED OUT THE ENTIRE VAMPIRE NATION.
DO YOU HAVE ANY IDEA OF THE ENORMITY OF HER SIN?!
THE QUEEN HERSELF ENDED THE ROYAL LINE. SHE ENDED THOUSANDS OF YEARS OF GLORIOUS HISTORY WITH HER OWN SULLIED HANDS!!
SINCE THEN, IT HAS BEEN AN AGE OF DARKNESS! AN AGE OF TERROR FOR THE CHILDREN OF THE NIGHT!!
AND YOU BELIEVE THAT WITH EVERY FIBER OF YOUR BEING, I'M SURE...
BUT THAT DOESN'T MAKE IT ANY LESS OF AN EXCUSE.

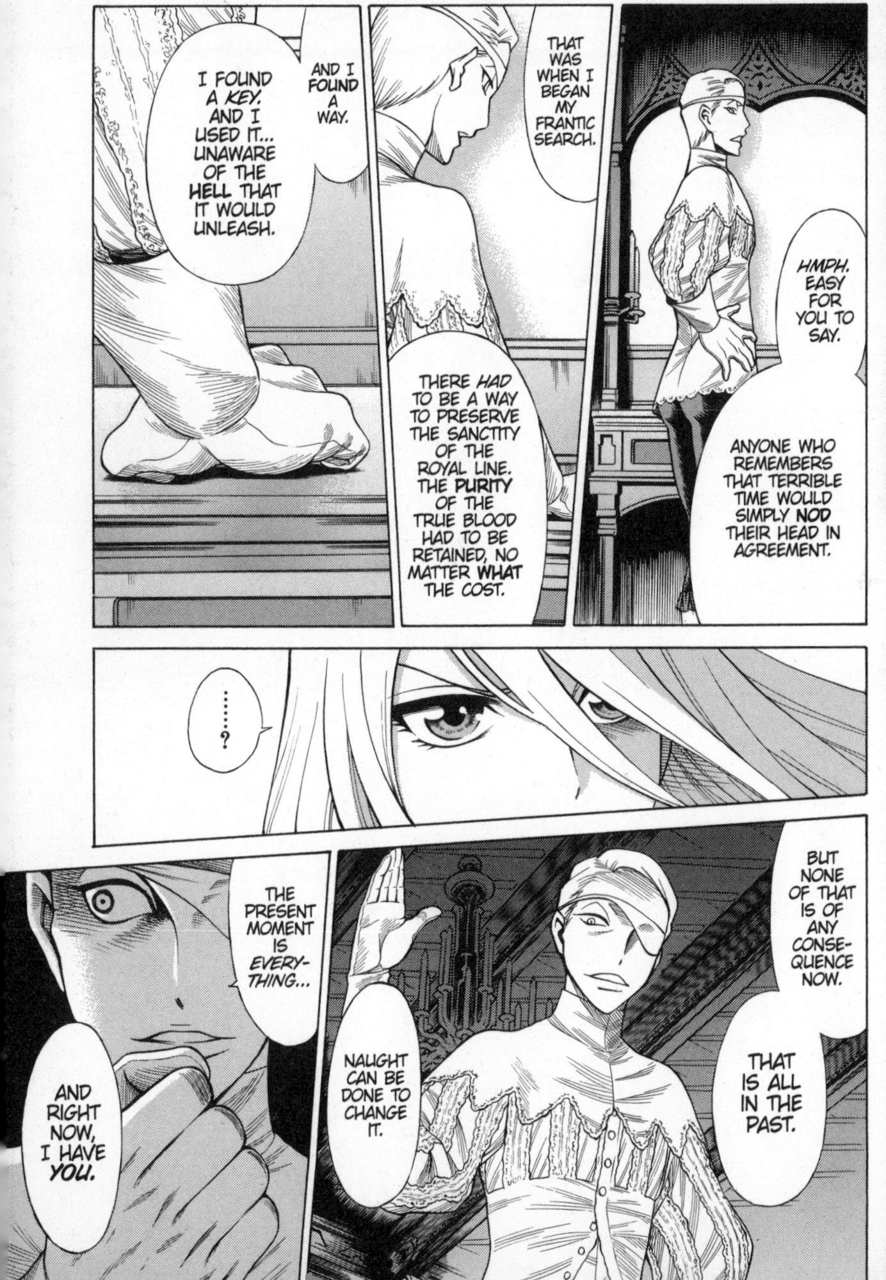
HMPH. EASY FOR YOU TO SAY.
ANYONE WHO REMEMBERS THAT TERRIBLE TIME WOULD SIMPLY **NOD** THEIR HEAD IN AGREEMENT.
THAT WAS WHEN I BEGAN MY FRANTIC SEARCH.
THERE *HAD* TO BE A WAY TO PRESERVE THE SANCTITY OF THE ROYAL LINE. THE **PURITY** OF THE TRUE BLOOD HAD TO BE RETAINED, NO MATTER **WHAT** THE COST.
AND I FOUND A WAY.
I FOUND A *KEY.* AND I USED IT... UNAWARE OF THE **HELL** THAT IT WOULD UNLEASH.
......?
BUT NONE OF THAT IS OF ANY CONSE-QUENCE NOW.
THAT IS ALL IN THE PAST.
NAUGHT CAN BE DONE TO CHANGE IT.
THE PRESENT MOMENT IS *EVERY-THING...*
AND RIGHT NOW, I HAVE ***YOU.***

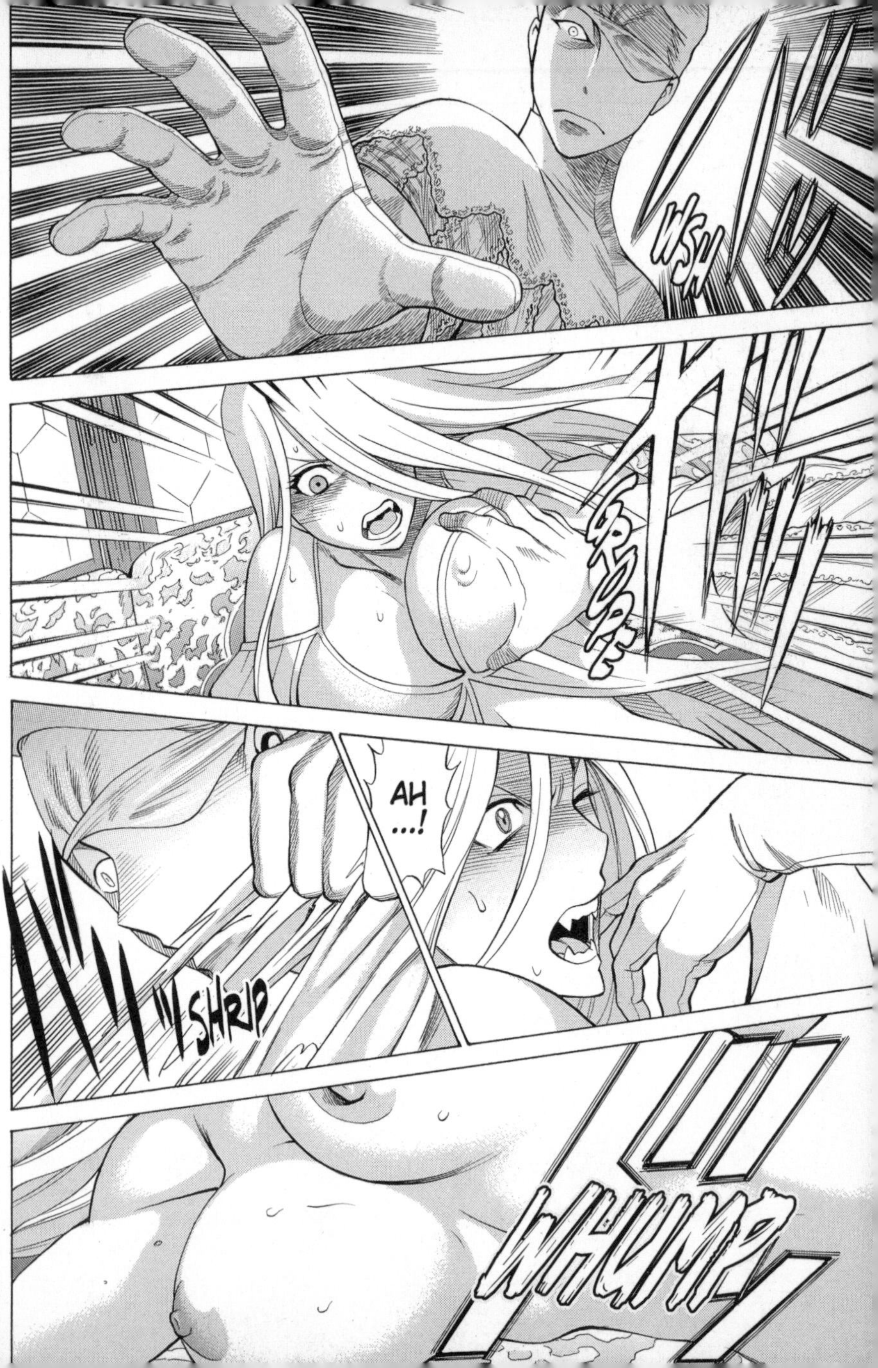
WSH
GROPE
AH ...!
SHRIP
WHUMP

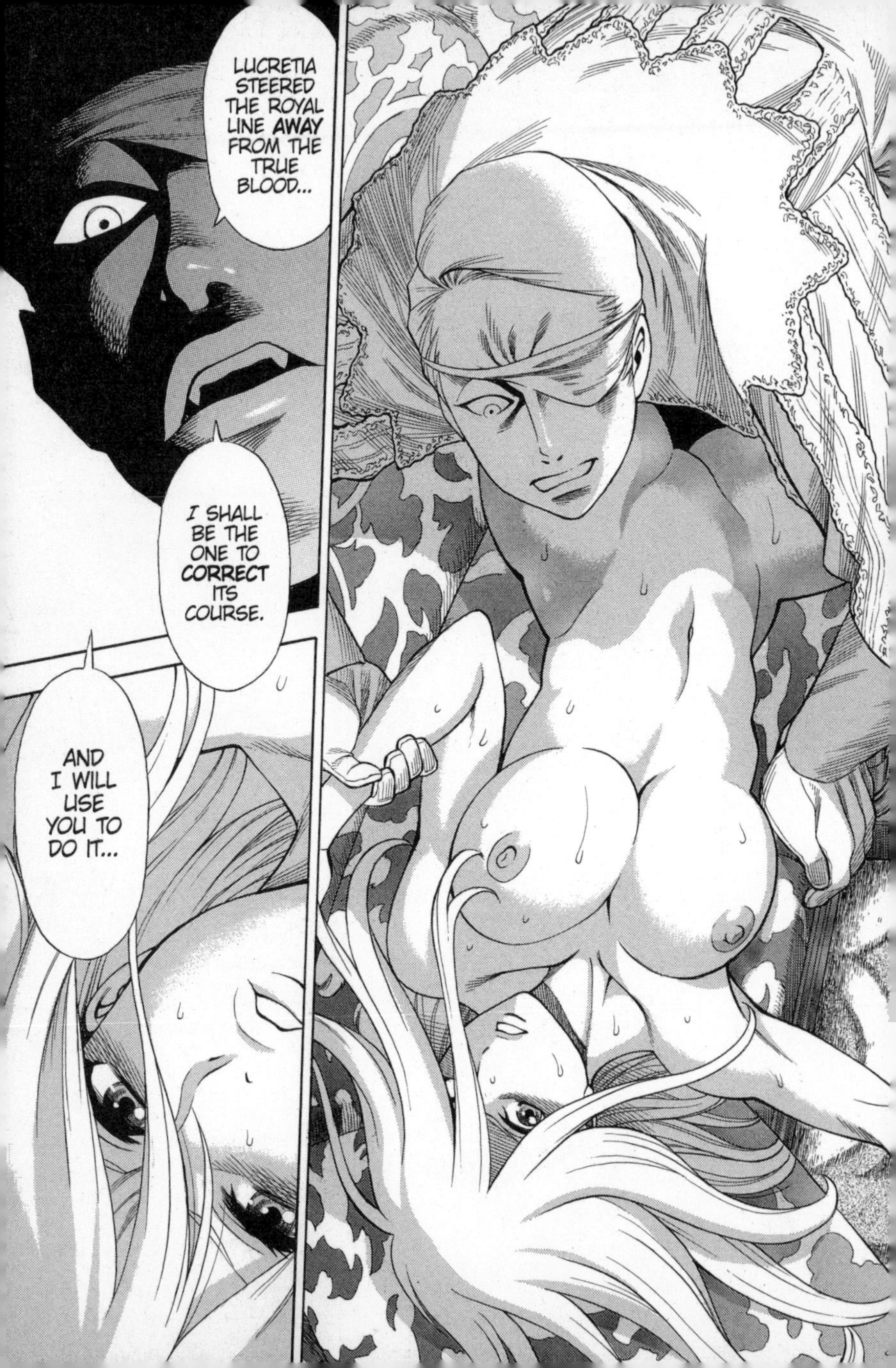
LUCRETIA STEERED THE ROYAL LINE AWAY FROM THE TRUE BLOOD...
I SHALL BE THE ONE TO CORRECT ITS COURSE.
AND I WILL USE YOU TO DO IT...

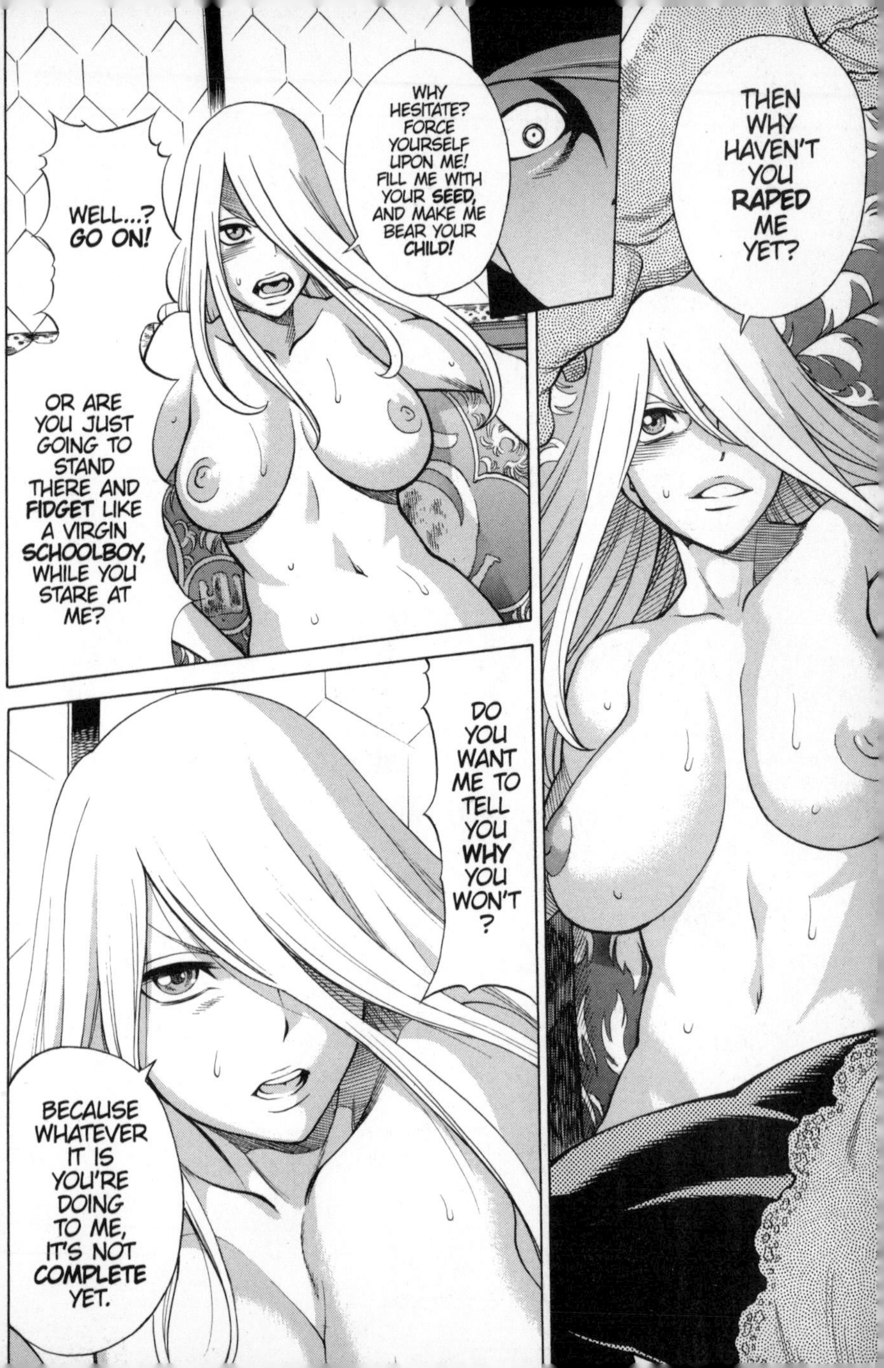
THEN WHY HAVEN'T YOU RAPED ME YET?
WHY HESITATE? FORCE YOURSELF UPON ME! FILL ME WITH YOUR SEED, AND MAKE ME BEAR YOUR CHILD!
WELL...? GO ON!
OR ARE YOU JUST GOING TO STAND THERE AND FIDGET LIKE A VIRGIN SCHOOLBOY, WHILE YOU STARE AT ME?
DO YOU WANT ME TO TELL YOU WHY YOU WON'T ?
BECAUSE WHATEVER IT IS YOU'RE DOING TO ME, IT'S NOT COMPLETE YET.

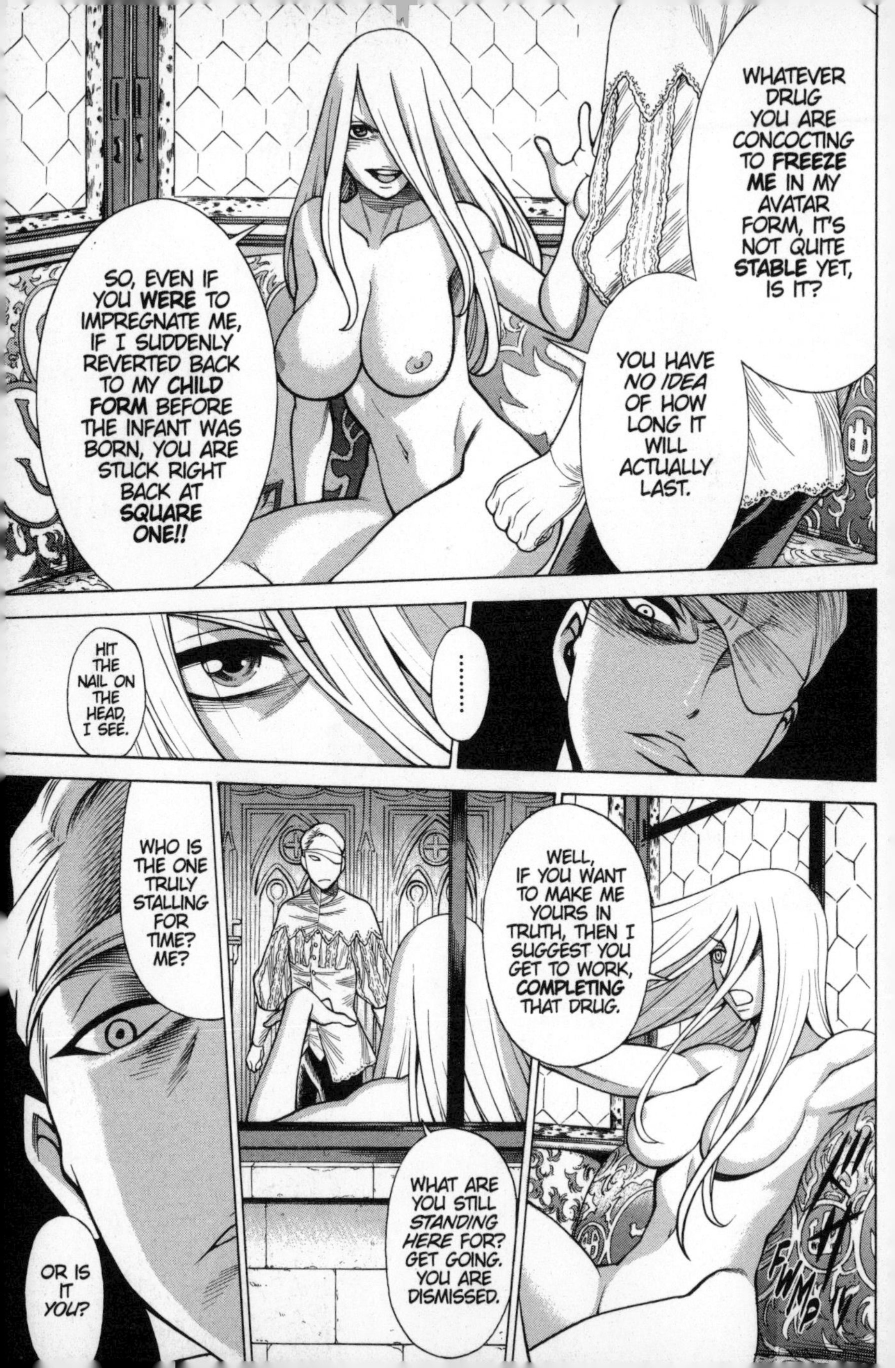
WHATEVER DRUG YOU ARE CONCOCTING TO FREEZE ME IN MY AVATAR FORM, IT'S NOT QUITE STABLE YET, IS IT?
YOU HAVE NO IDEA OF HOW LONG IT WILL ACTUALLY LAST.
SO, EVEN IF YOU WERE TO IMPREGNATE ME, IF I SUDDENLY REVERTED BACK TO MY CHILD FORM BEFORE THE INFANT WAS BORN, YOU ARE STUCK RIGHT BACK AT SQUARE ONE!!
......
HIT THE NAIL ON THE HEAD, I SEE.
WELL, IF YOU WANT TO MAKE ME YOURS IN TRUTH, THEN I SUGGEST YOU GET TO WORK, COMPLETING THAT DRUG.
WHAT ARE YOU STILL STANDING HERE FOR? GET GOING. YOU ARE DISMISSED.
FWMP
WHO IS THE ONE TRULY STALLING FOR TIME? ME?
OR IS IT YOU?

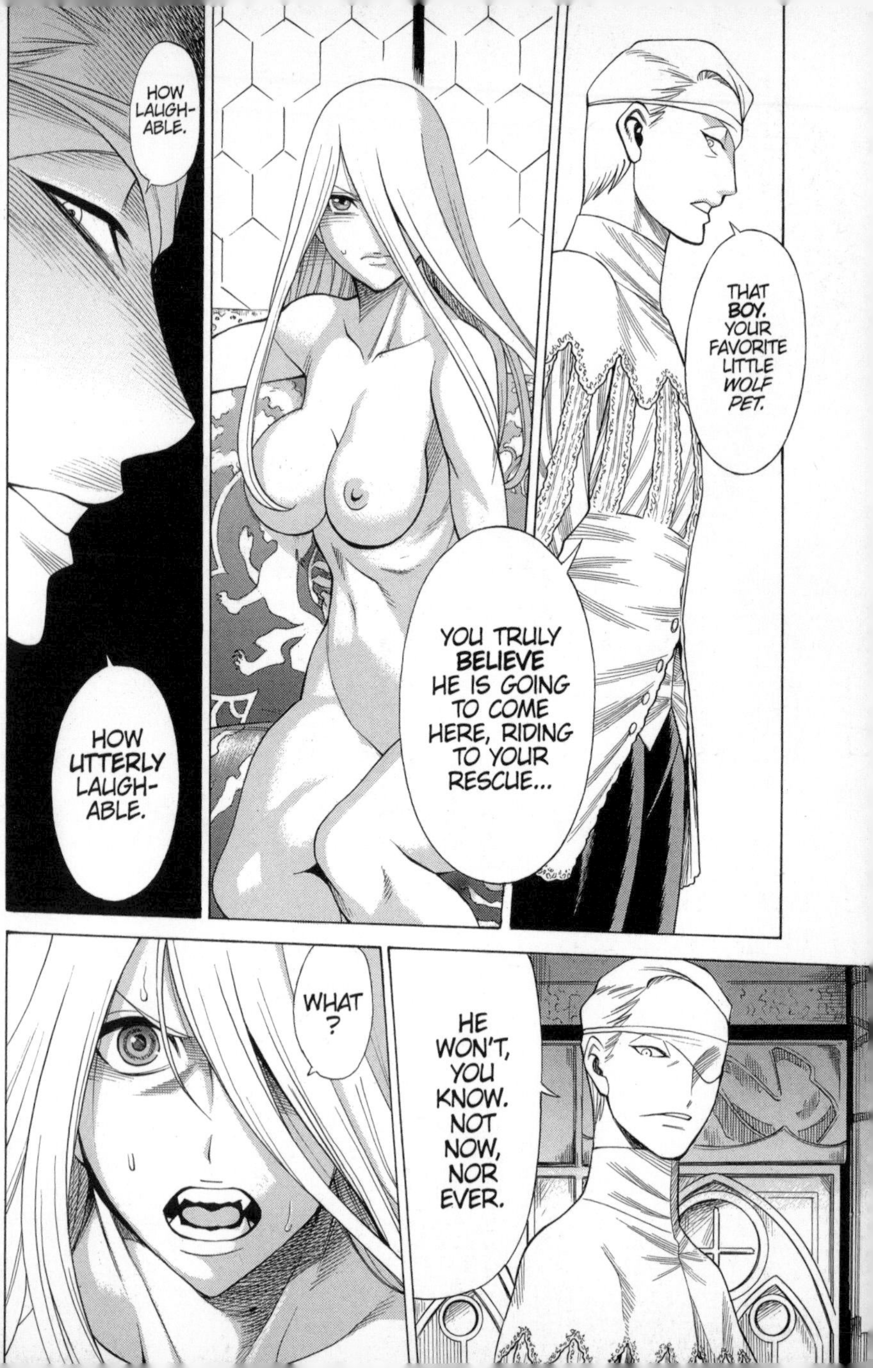
THAT BOY. YOUR FAVORITE LITTLE WOLF PET.
YOU TRULY BELIEVE HE IS GOING TO COME HERE, RIDING TO YOUR RESCUE...
HOW LAUGHABLE.
HOW UTTERLY LAUGHABLE.
HE WON'T, YOU KNOW. NOT NOW, NOR EVER.
WHAT?

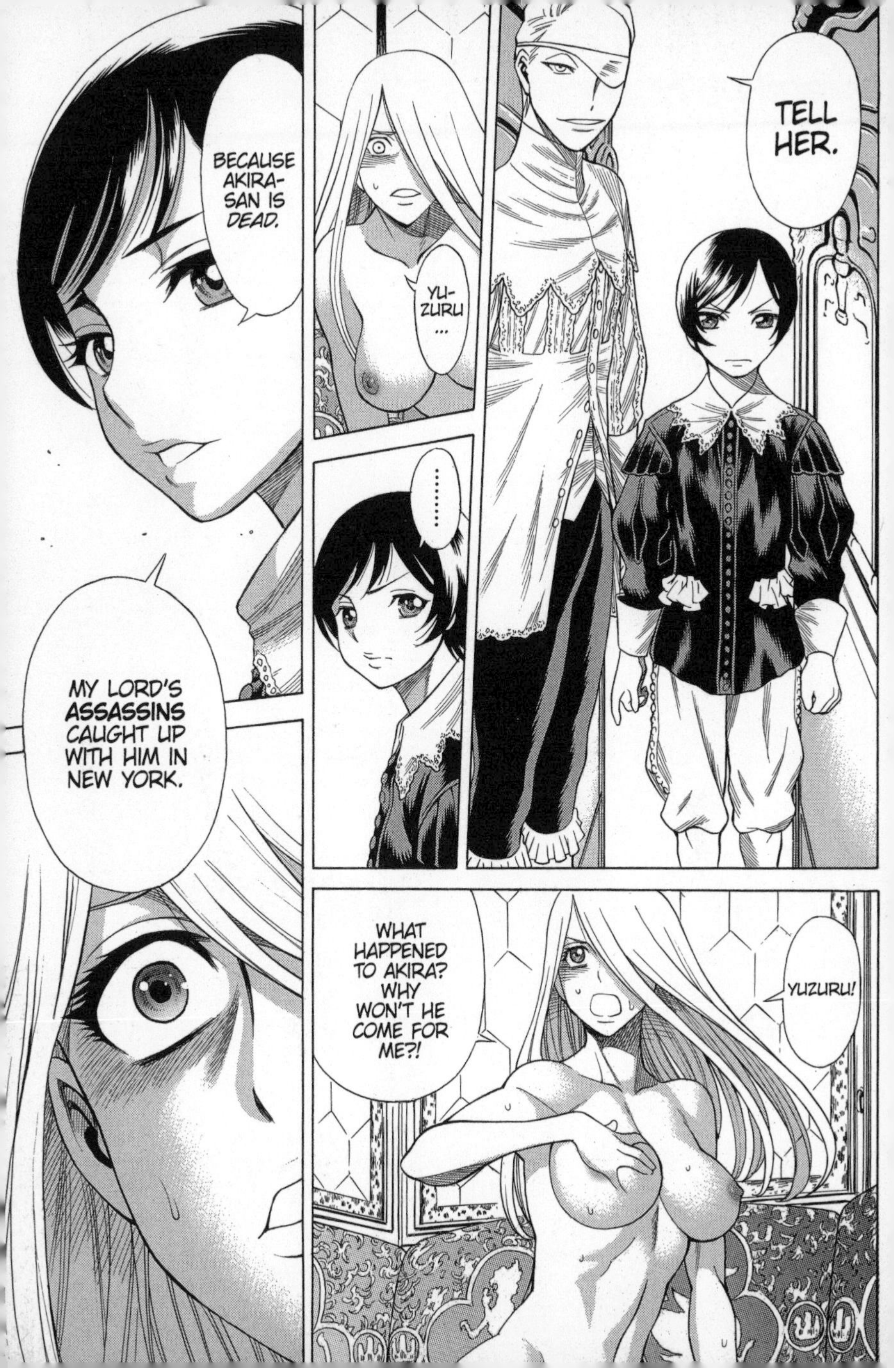
TELL HER.
YU-ZURU ...
....
YUZURU!
WHAT HAPPENED TO AKIRA? WHY WON'T HE COME FOR ME?!
BECAUSE AKIRA-SAN IS DEAD.
MY LORD'S ASSASSINS CAUGHT UP WITH HIM IN NEW YORK.

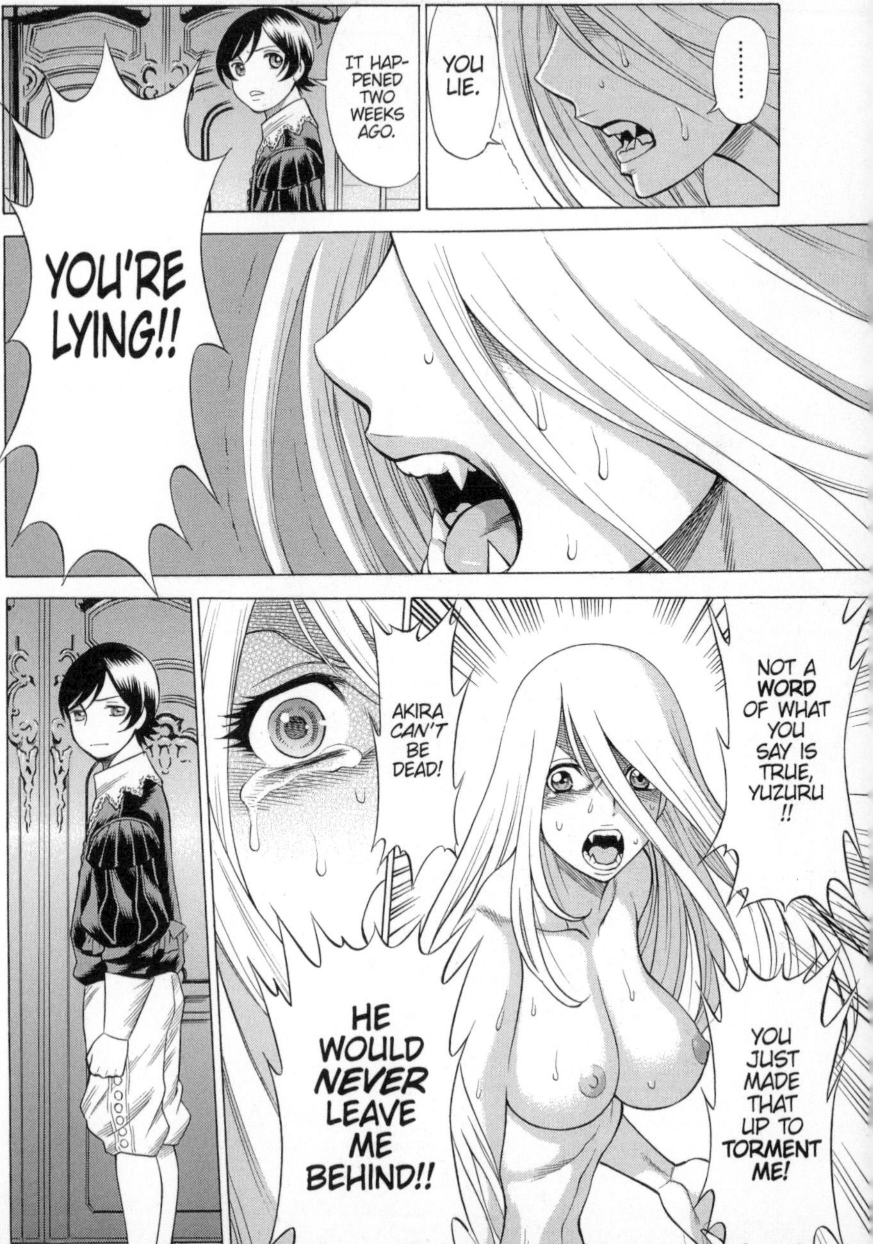
……
YOU LIE.
IT HAP-PENED TWO WEEKS AGO.
YOU'RE LYING!!
NOT A WORD OF WHAT YOU SAY IS TRUE, YUZURU!!
AKIRA CAN'T BE DEAD!
YOU JUST MADE THAT UP TO TORMENT ME!
HE WOULD NEVER LEAVE ME BEHIND!!

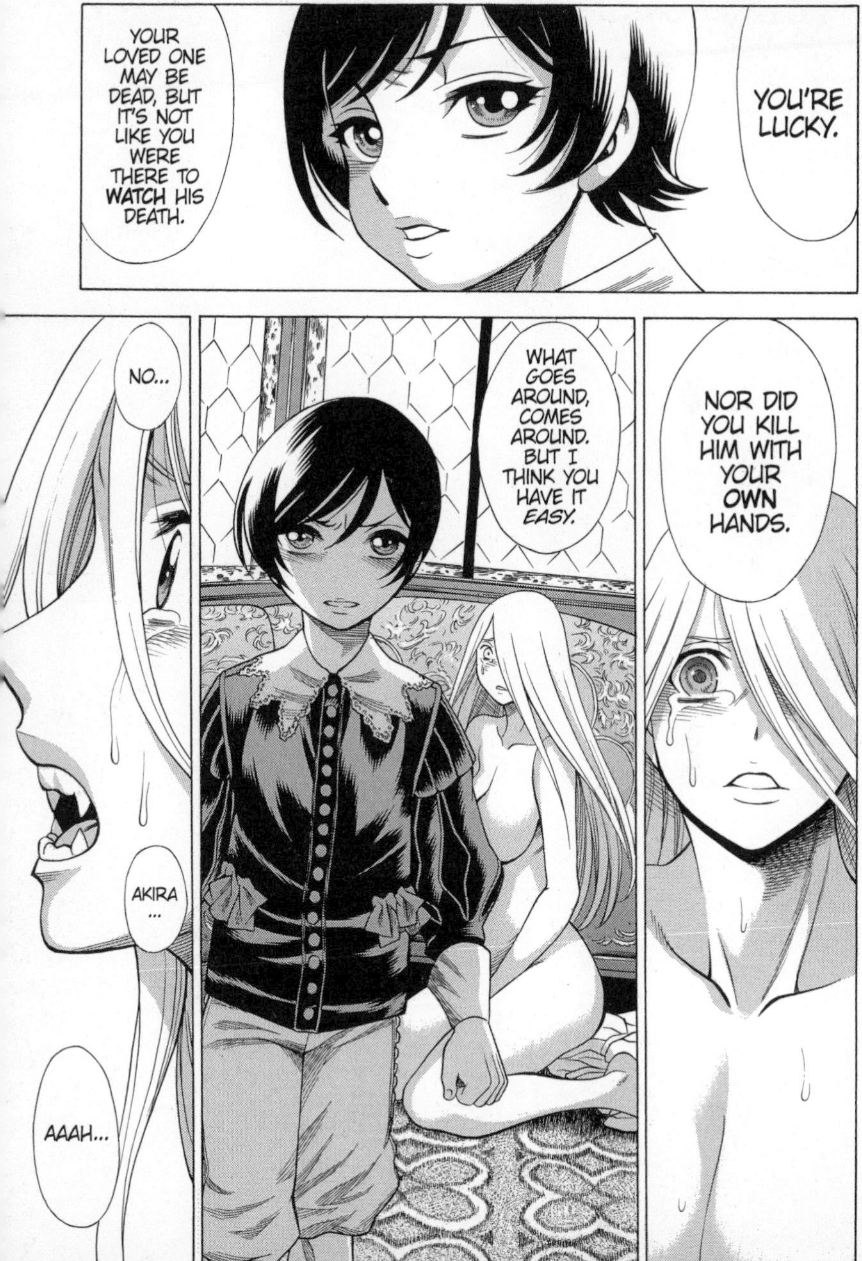
YOU'RE LUCKY.
YOUR LOVED ONE MAY BE DEAD, BUT IT'S NOT LIKE YOU WERE THERE TO **WATCH** HIS DEATH.
NOR DID YOU KILL HIM WITH YOUR OWN HANDS.
WHAT GOES AROUND, COMES AROUND. BUT I THINK YOU HAVE IT *EASY.*
NO...
AKIRA ...
AAAH...

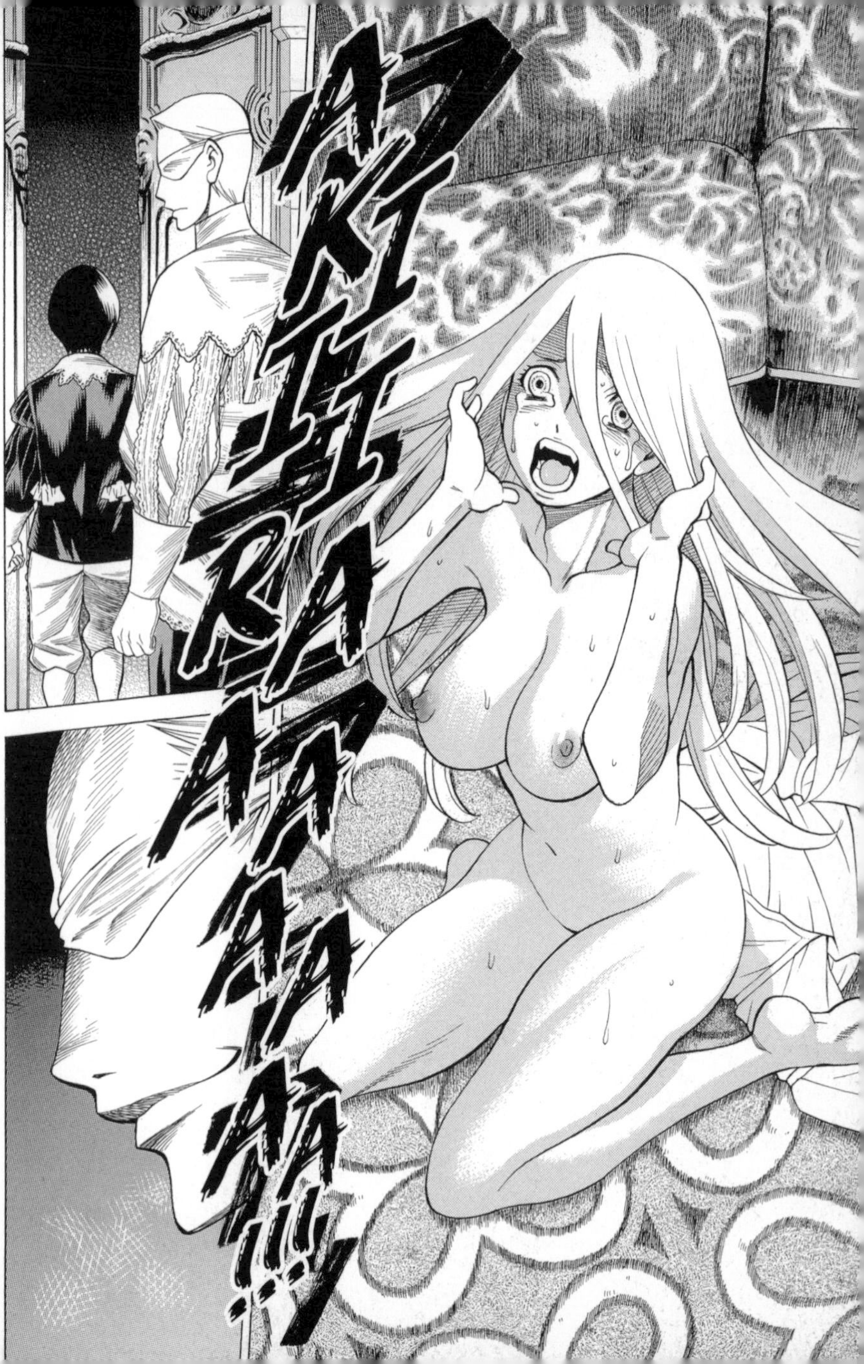

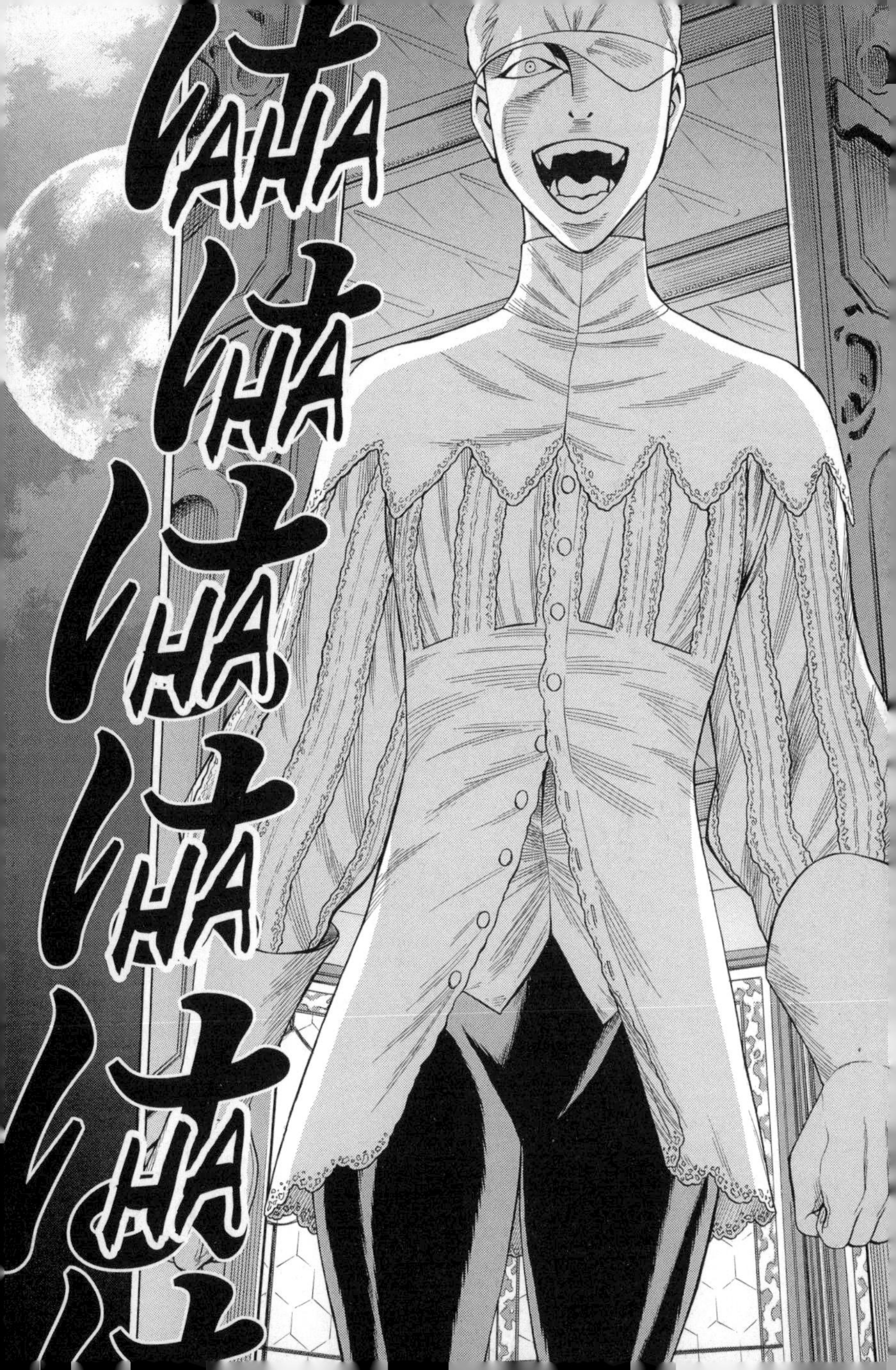
AHA
HA
HA
HA
HA

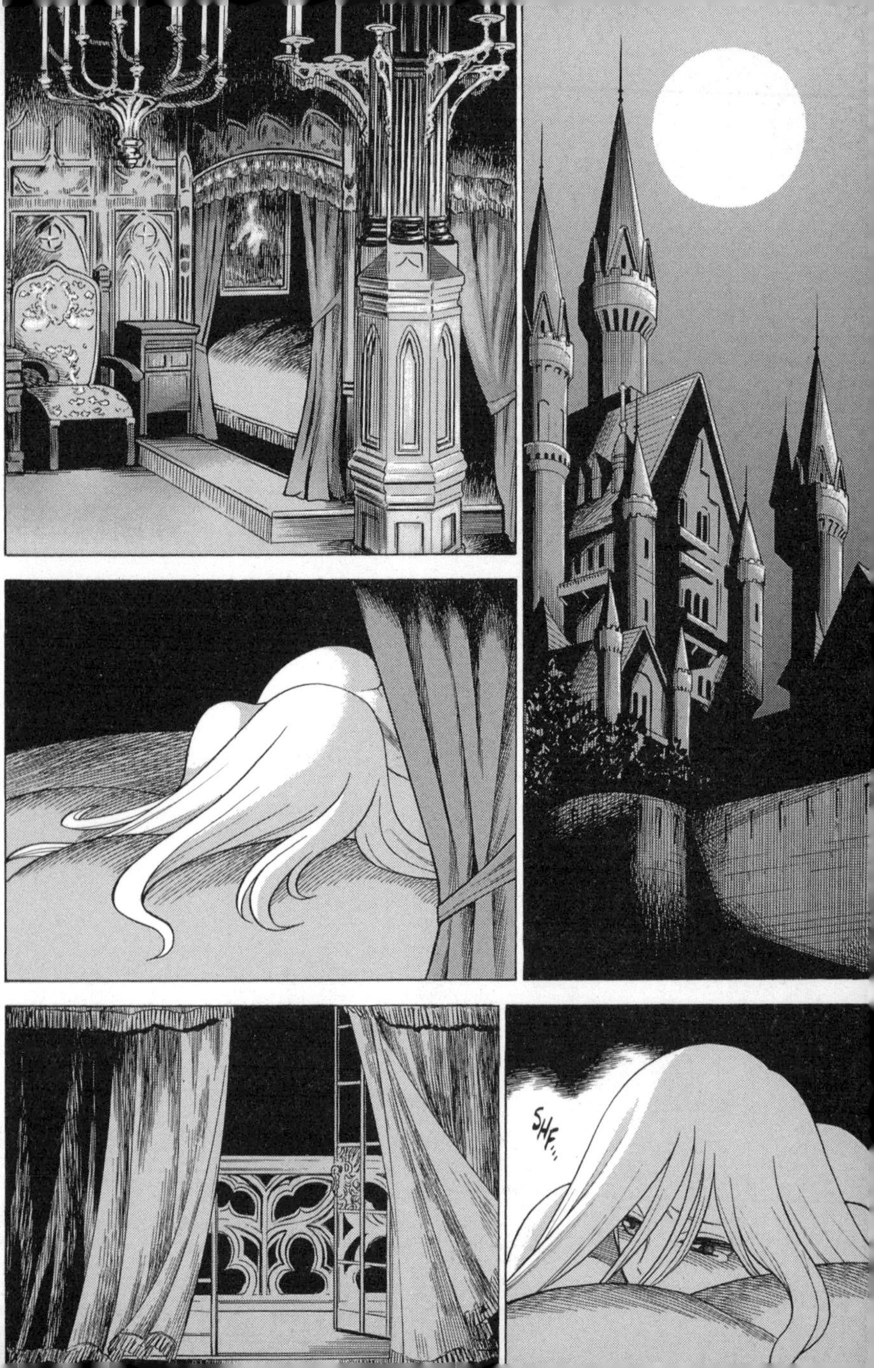
SHF...

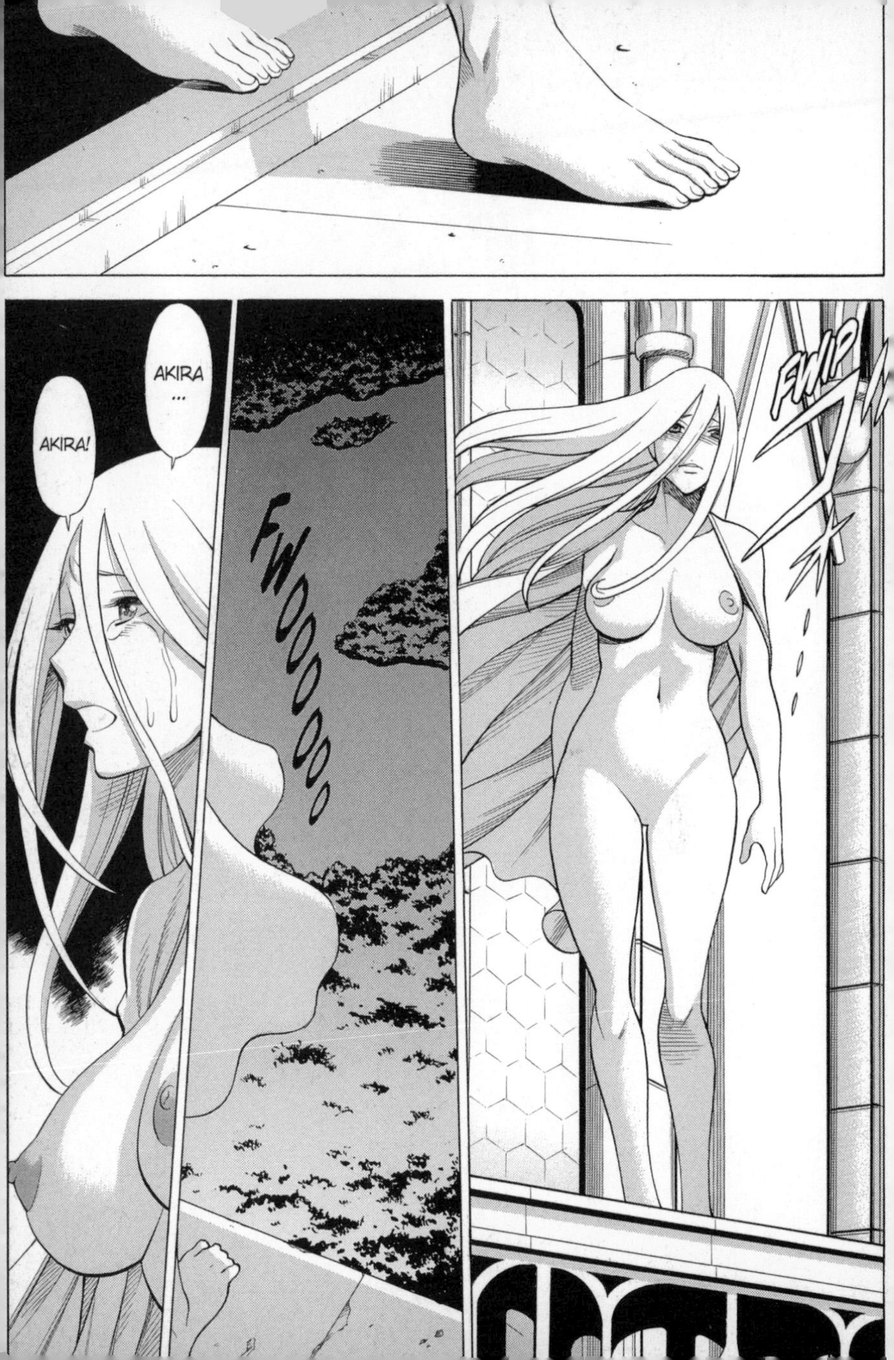
FWIP
FWOOOOOOO
AKIRA ...
AKIRA!

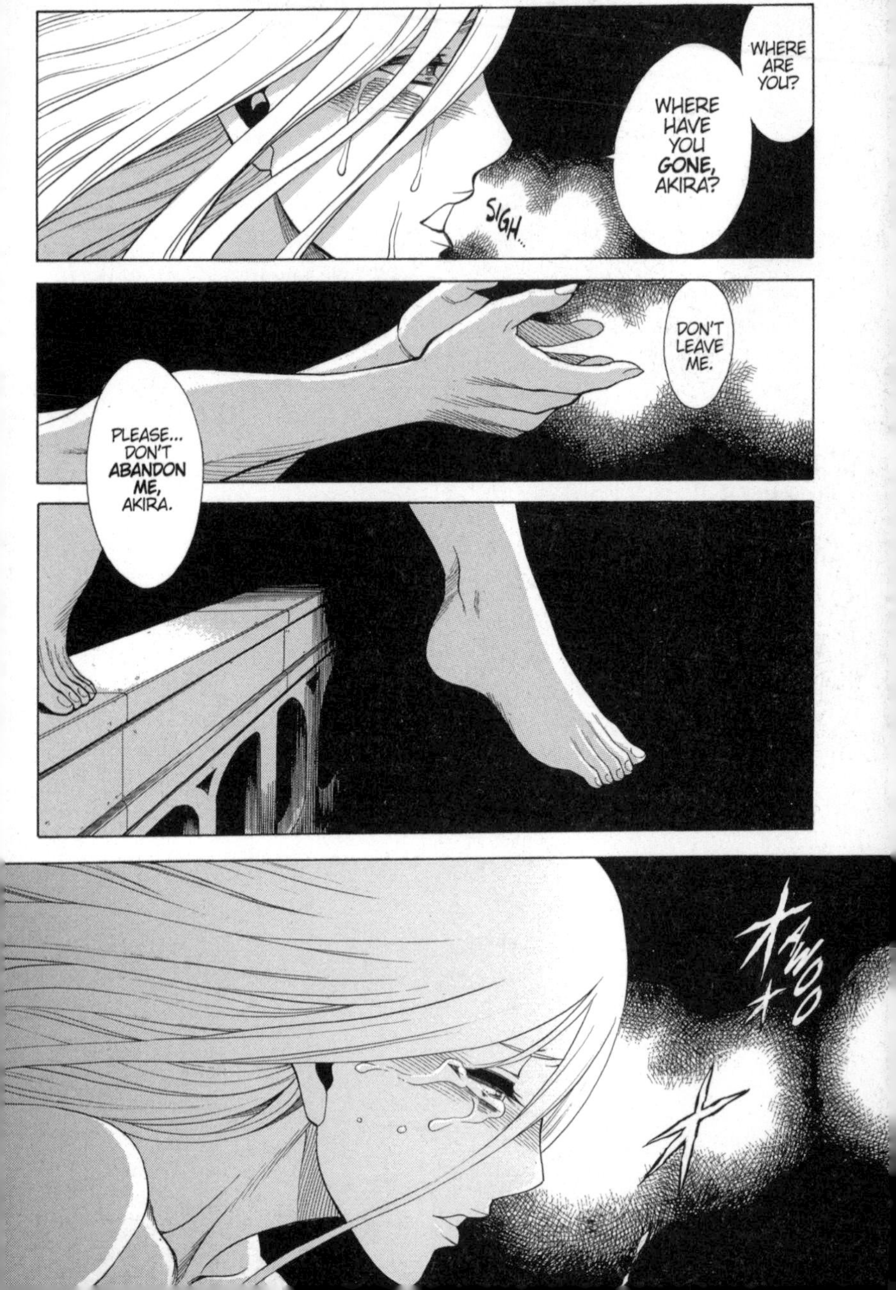
WHERE ARE YOU?
WHERE HAVE YOU GONE, AKIRA?
SIGH...
DON'T LEAVE ME.
PLEASE... DON'T ABANDON ME, AKIRA.
AWOO

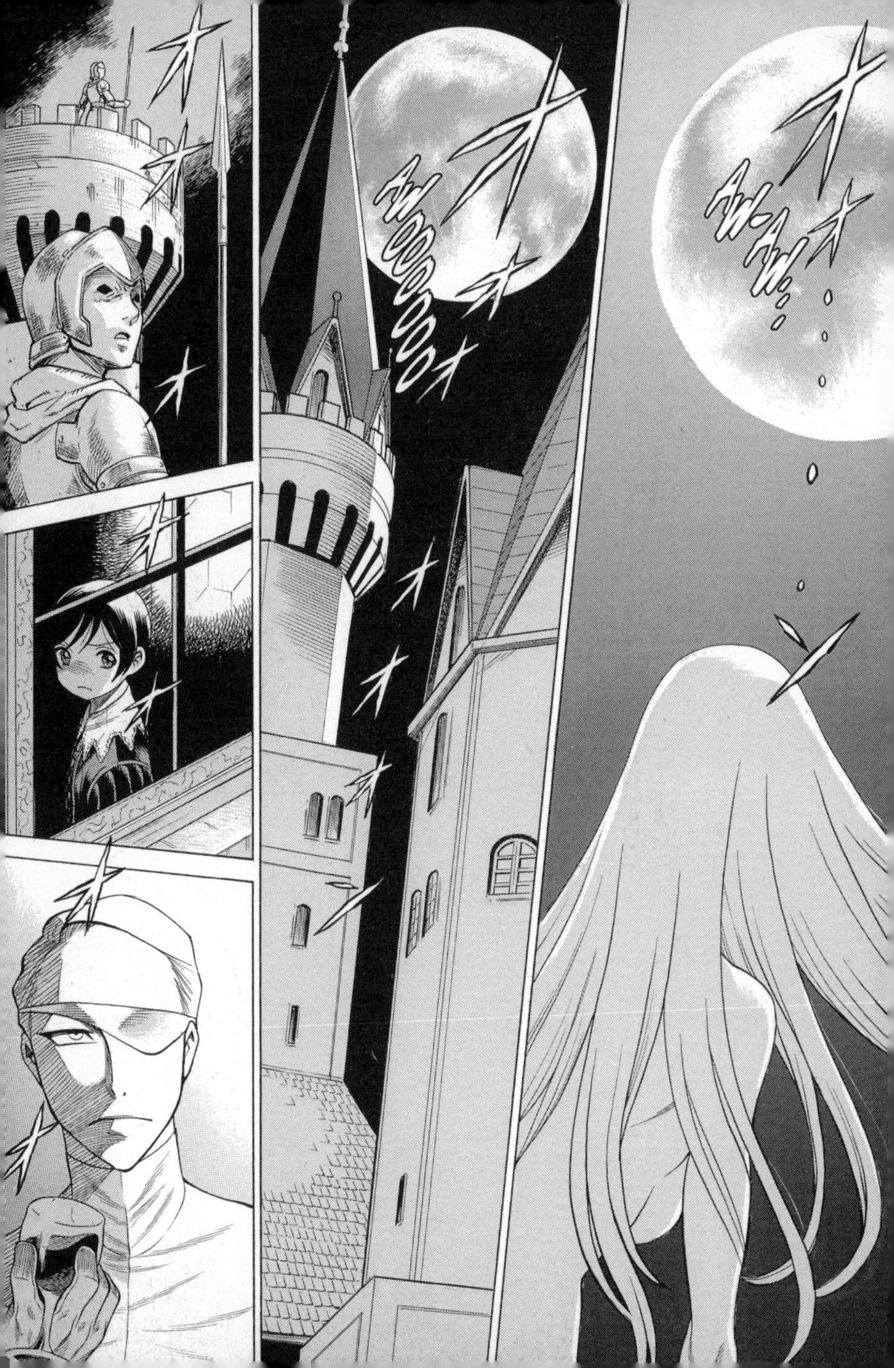
AW-AW-AW...
AWOOOOOOO

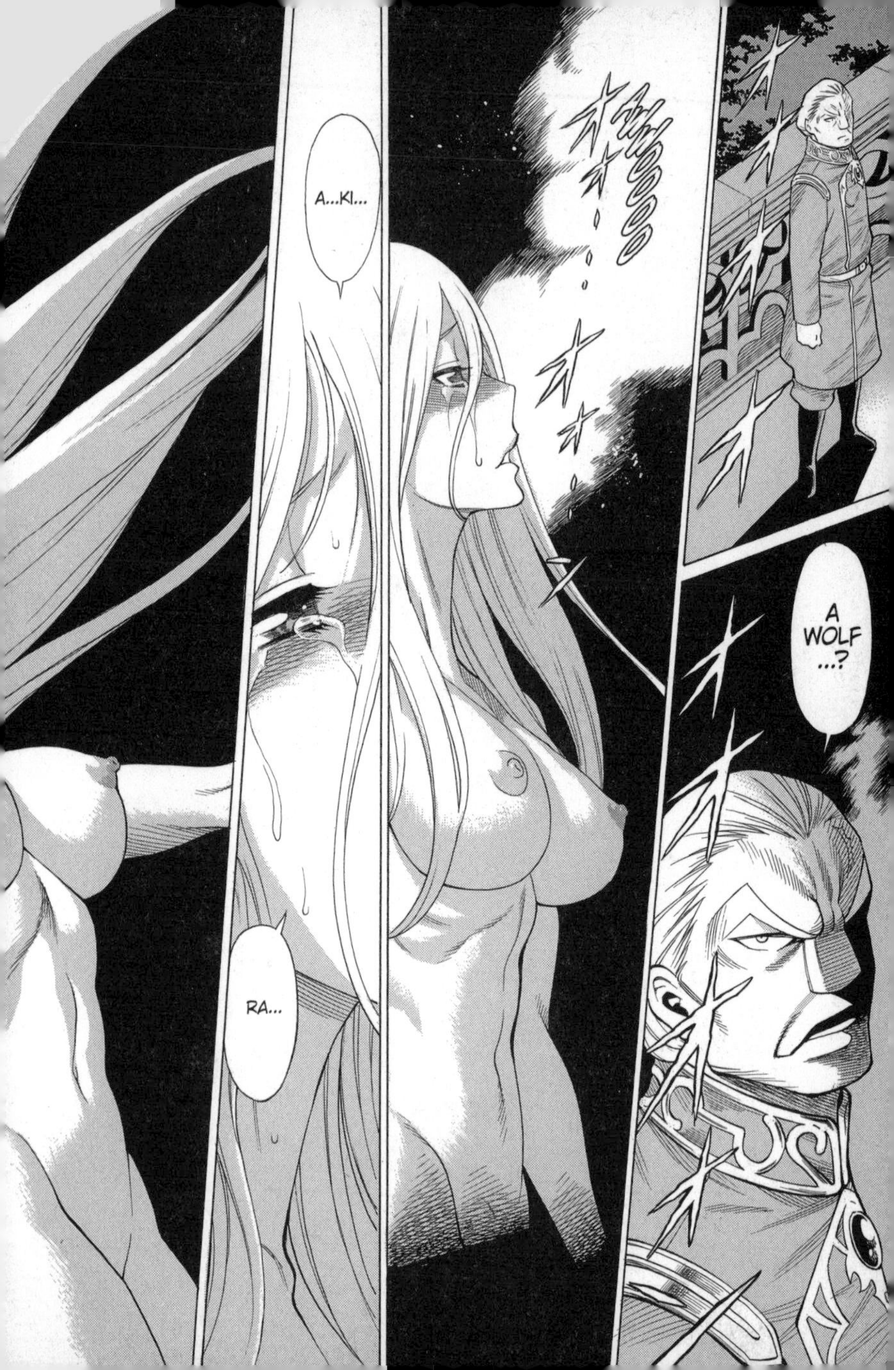
A WOLF ...?
A...KI...
RA...

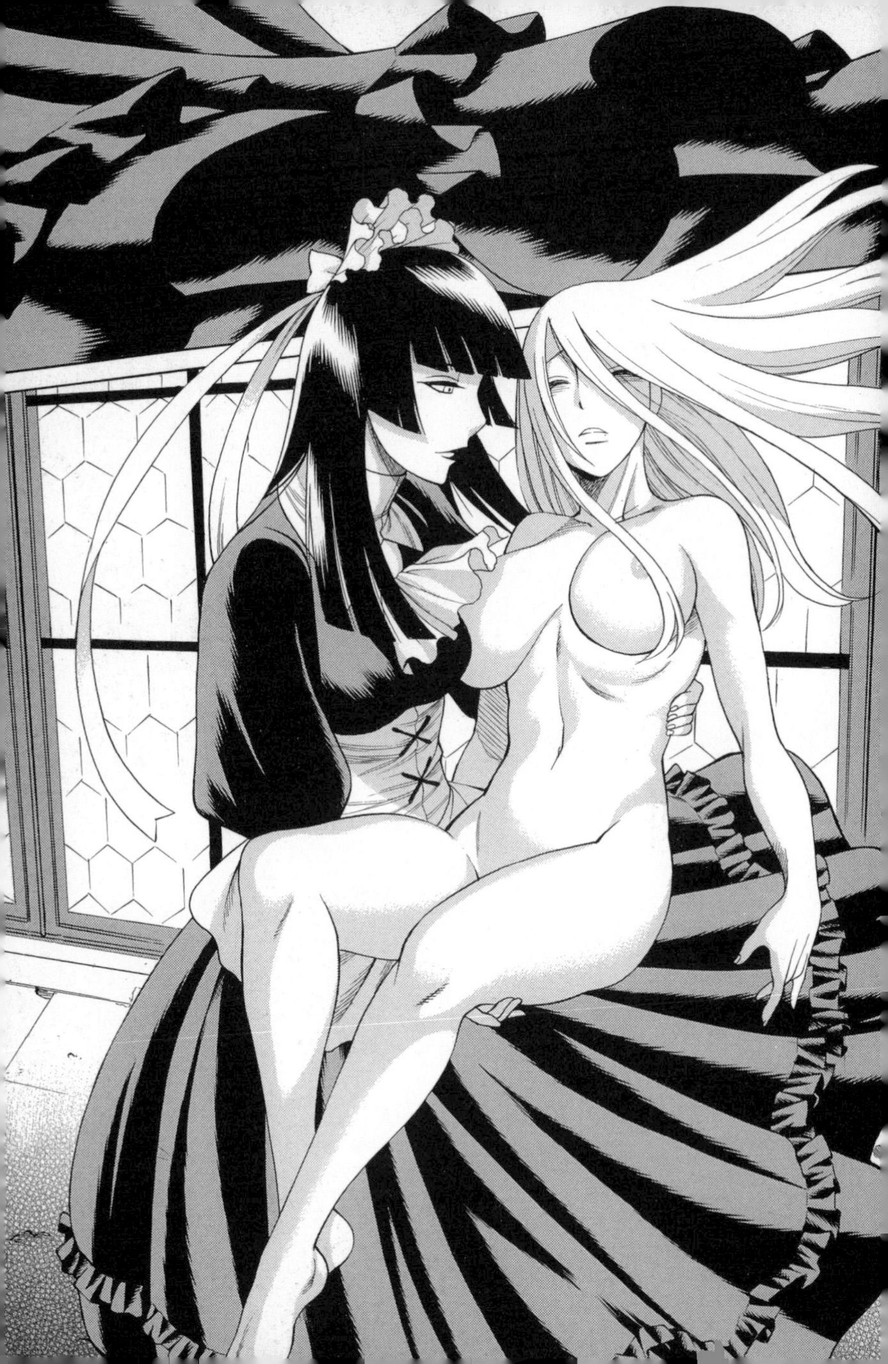

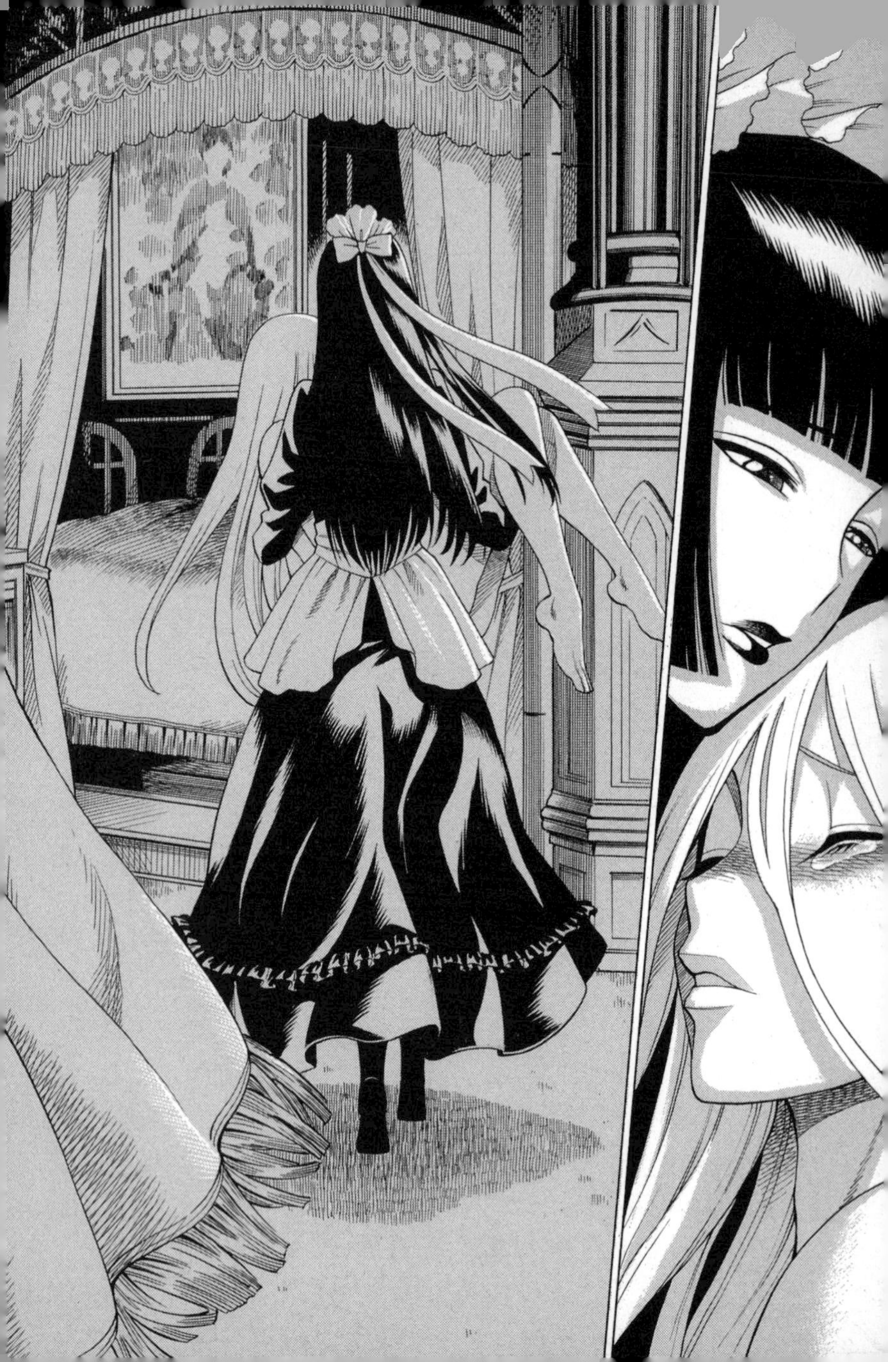

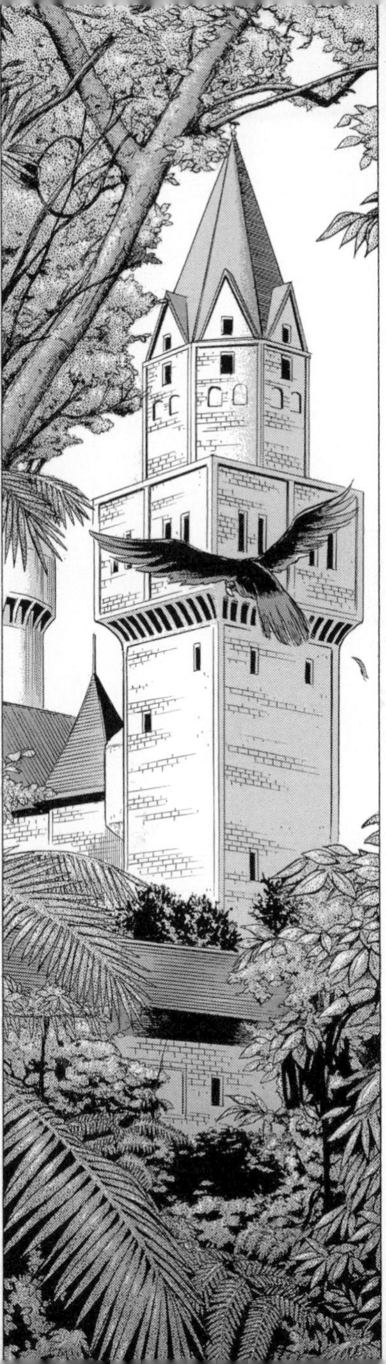

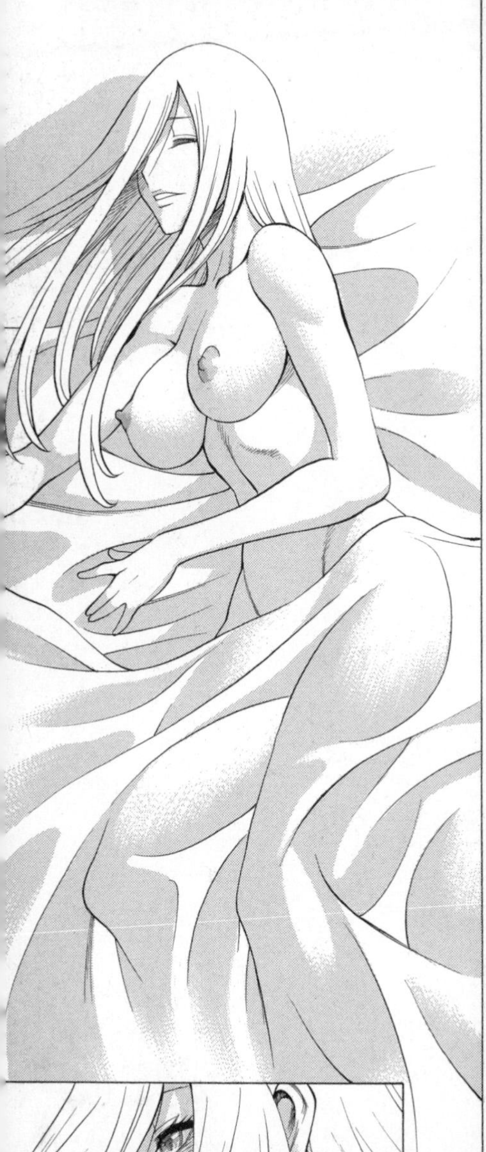

Chapter 67: Machinations

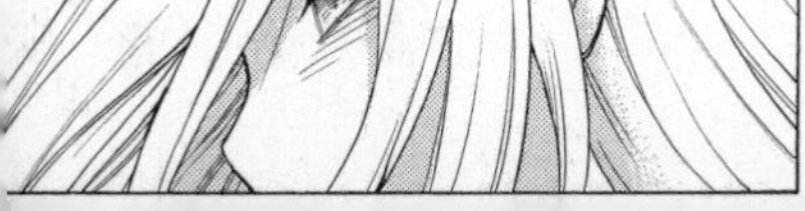

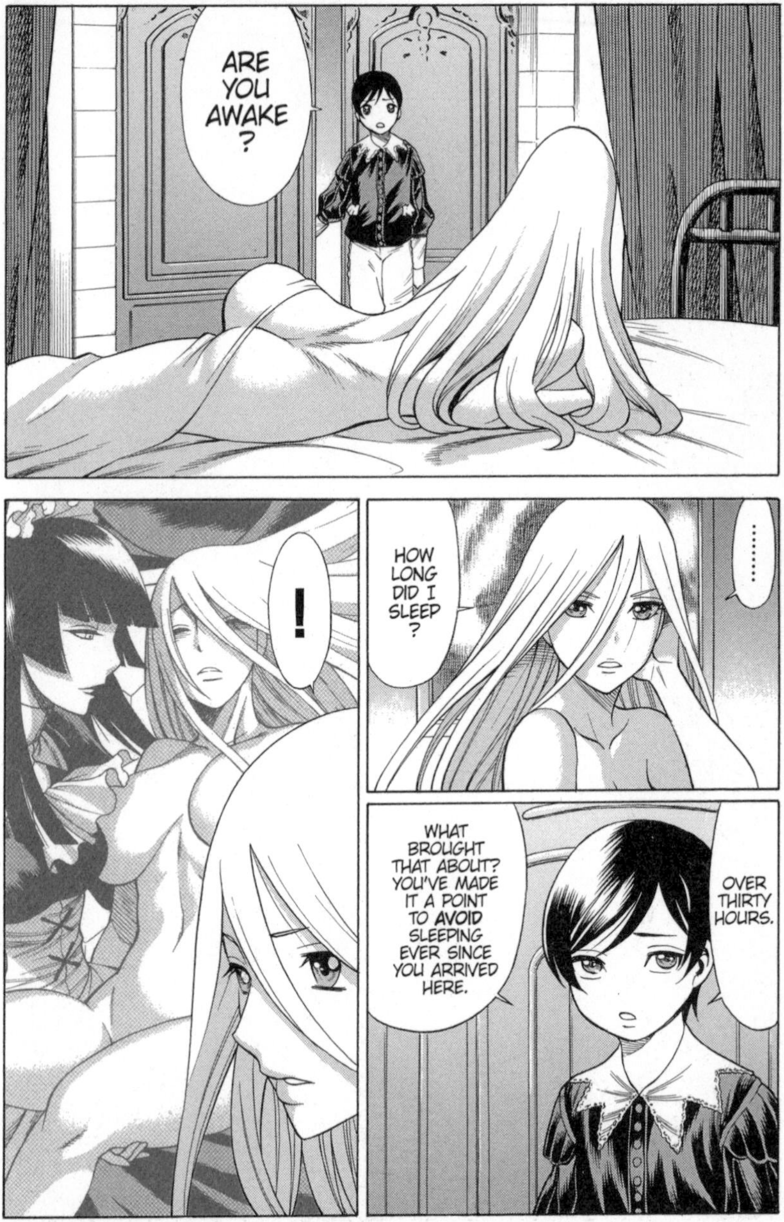
ARE YOU AWAKE?
....
HOW LONG DID I SLEEP?
OVER THIRTY HOURS.
WHAT BROUGHT THAT ABOUT? YOU'VE MADE IT A POINT TO **AVOID** SLEEPING EVER SINCE YOU ARRIVED HERE.
!

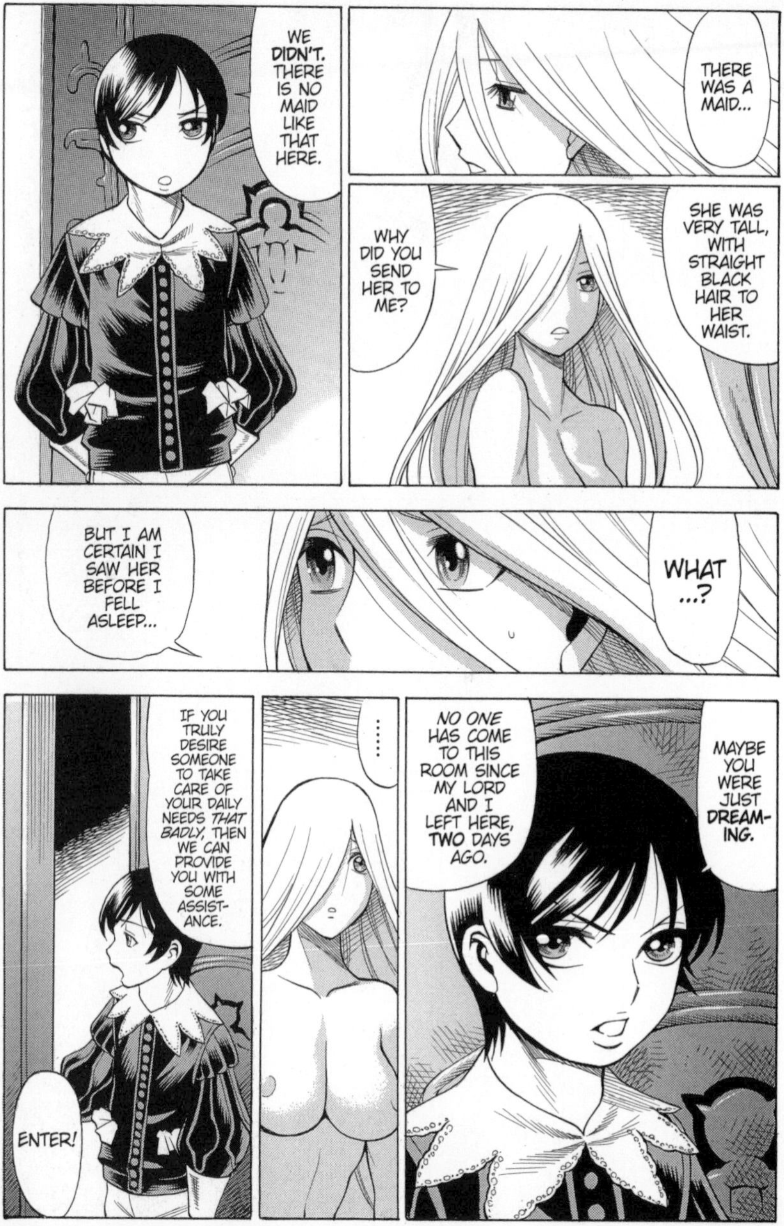
THERE WAS A MAID...
SHE WAS VERY TALL, WITH STRAIGHT BLACK HAIR TO HER WAIST.
WHY DID YOU SEND HER TO ME?
WE DIDN'T. THERE IS NO MAID LIKE THAT HERE.
WHAT ...?
BUT I AM CERTAIN I SAW HER BEFORE I FELL ASLEEP...
MAYBE YOU WERE JUST DREAMING.
NO ONE HAS COME TO THIS ROOM SINCE MY LORD AND I LEFT HERE, TWO DAYS AGO.
......
IF YOU TRULY DESIRE SOMEONE TO TAKE CARE OF YOUR DAILY NEEDS THAT BADLY, THEN WE CAN PROVIDE YOU WITH SOME ASSISTANCE.
ENTER!

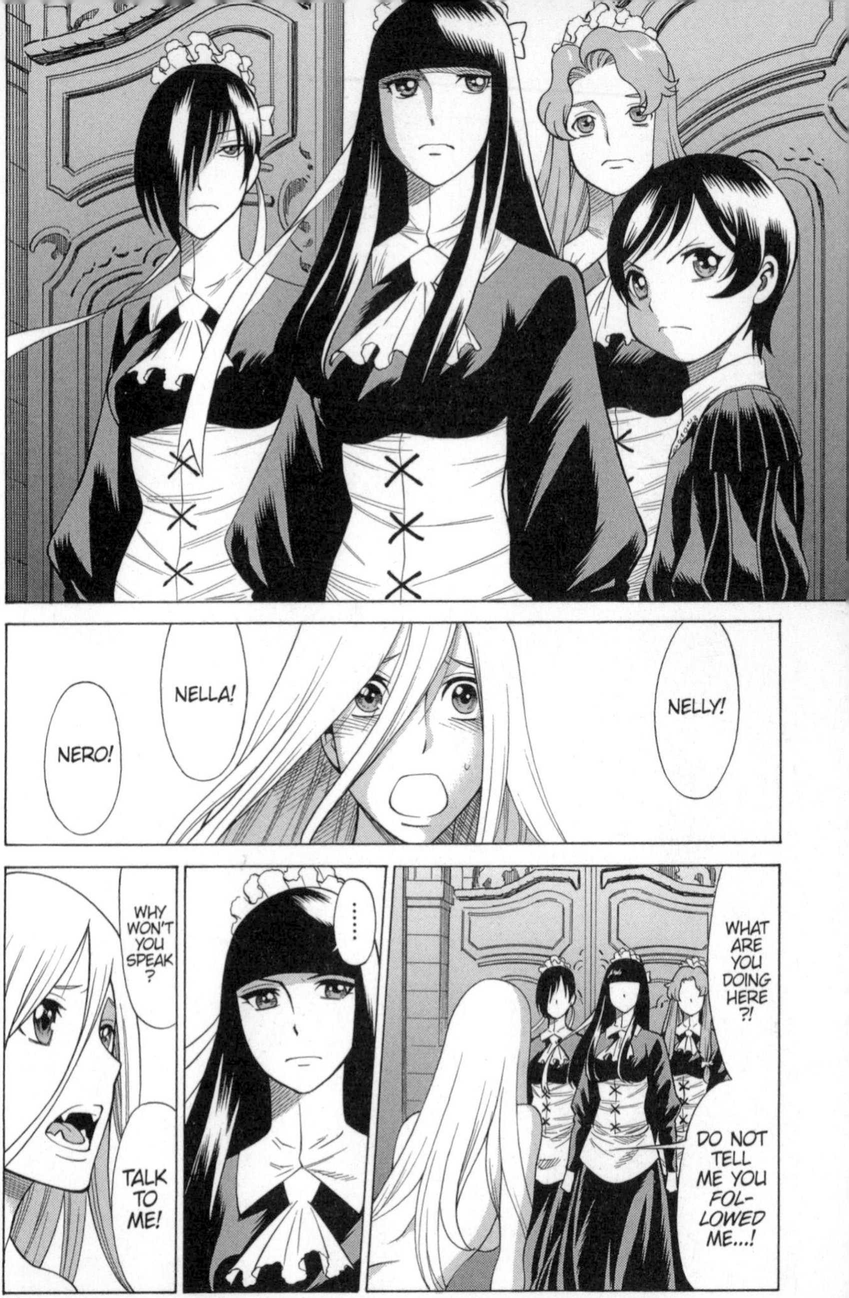
NELLY!
NELLA!
NERO!
WHAT ARE YOU DOING HERE?!
DO NOT TELL ME YOU FOL-LOWED ME...!
......
WHY WON'T YOU SPEAK?
TALK TO ME!

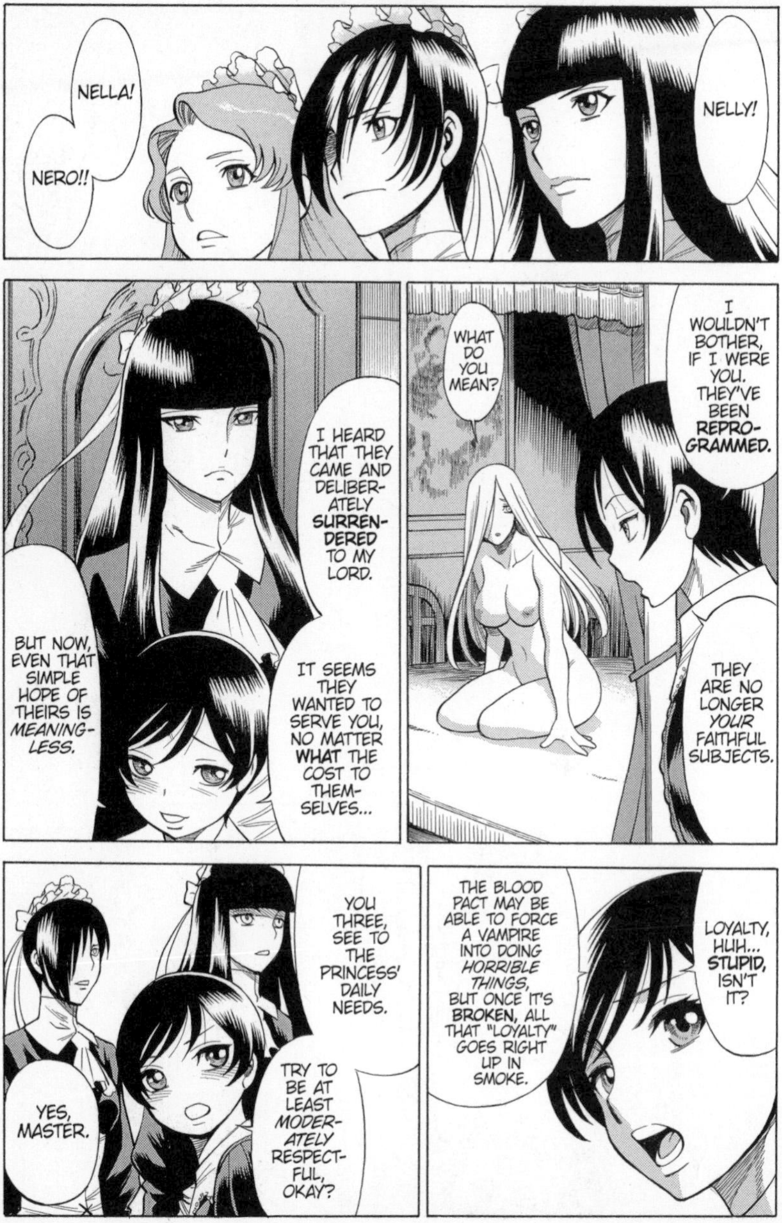
NELLY!
NELLA!
NERO!!
I WOULDN'T BOTHER, IF I WERE YOU. THEY'VE BEEN **REPROGRAMMED.**
WHAT DO YOU MEAN?
THEY ARE NO LONGER *YOUR* FAITHFUL SUBJECTS.
I HEARD THAT THEY CAME AND DELIBERATELY **SURRENDERED** TO MY LORD.
IT SEEMS THEY WANTED TO SERVE YOU, NO MATTER **WHAT** THE COST TO THEMSELVES...
BUT NOW, EVEN THAT SIMPLE HOPE OF THEIRS IS *MEANINGLESS.*
LOYALTY, HUH... **STUPID,** ISN'T IT?
THE BLOOD PACT MAY BE ABLE TO FORCE A VAMPIRE INTO DOING *HORRIBLE THINGS,* BUT ONCE IT'S **BROKEN,** ALL THAT "LOYALTY" GOES RIGHT UP IN SMOKE.
YOU THREE, SEE TO THE PRINCESS' DAILY NEEDS.
TRY TO BE AT LEAST *MODERATELY* RESPECTFUL, OKAY?
YES, MASTER.

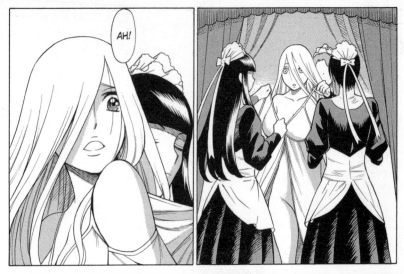

AH!

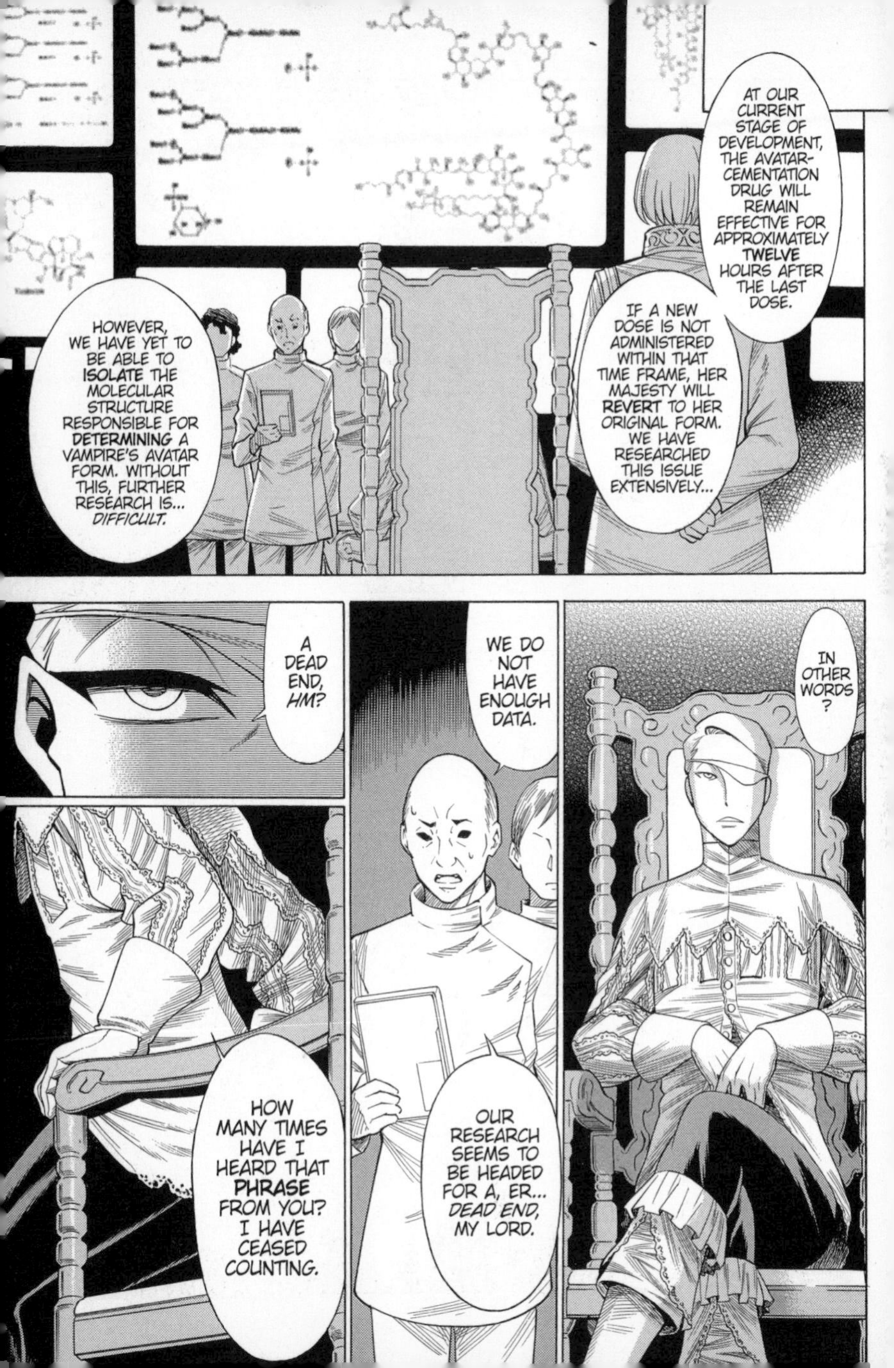
AT OUR CURRENT STAGE OF DEVELOPMENT, THE AVATAR-CEMENTATION DRUG WILL REMAIN EFFECTIVE FOR APPROXIMATELY TWELVE HOURS AFTER THE LAST DOSE.
IF A NEW DOSE IS NOT ADMINISTERED WITHIN THAT TIME FRAME, HER MAJESTY WILL REVERT TO HER ORIGINAL FORM. WE HAVE RESEARCHED THIS ISSUE EXTENSIVELY...
HOWEVER, WE HAVE YET TO BE ABLE TO ISOLATE THE MOLECULAR STRUCTURE RESPONSIBLE FOR DETERMINING A VAMPIRE'S AVATAR FORM. WITHOUT THIS, FURTHER RESEARCH IS... DIFFICULT.
IN OTHER WORDS?
WE DO NOT HAVE ENOUGH DATA.
OUR RESEARCH SEEMS TO BE HEADED FOR A, ER... DEAD END, MY LORD.
A DEAD END, HM?
HOW MANY TIMES HAVE I HEARD THAT PHRASE FROM YOU? I HAVE CEASED COUNTING.

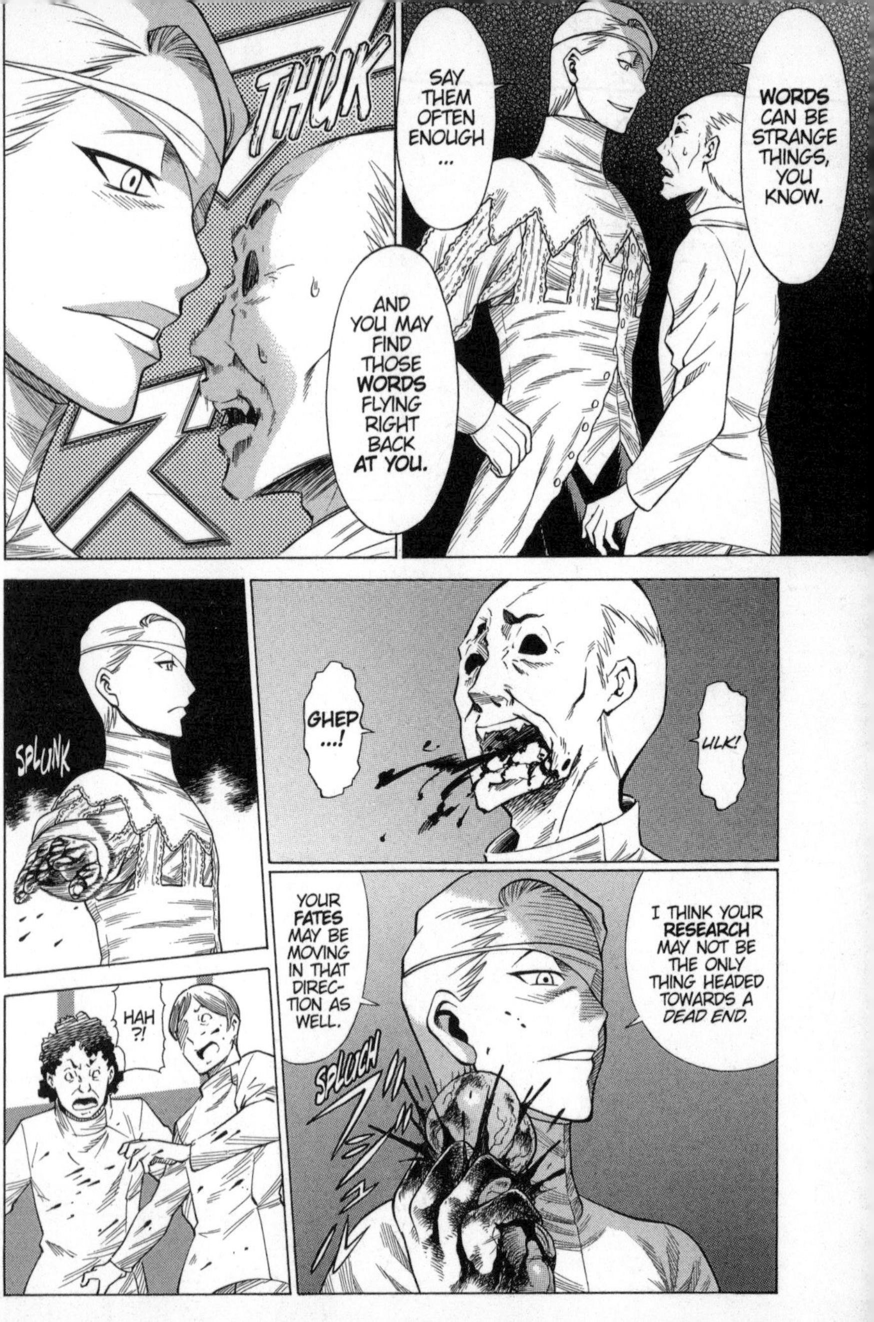
WORDS CAN BE STRANGE THINGS, YOU KNOW.
SAY THEM OFTEN ENOUGH ...
AND YOU MAY FIND THOSE WORDS FLYING RIGHT BACK AT YOU.
THUK
ULK!
GHEP ...!
SPLUNK
I THINK YOUR RESEARCH MAY NOT BE THE ONLY THING HEADED TOWARDS A DEAD END.
YOUR FATES MAY BE MOVING IN THAT DIRECTION AS WELL.
SPLUCH
HAH ?!

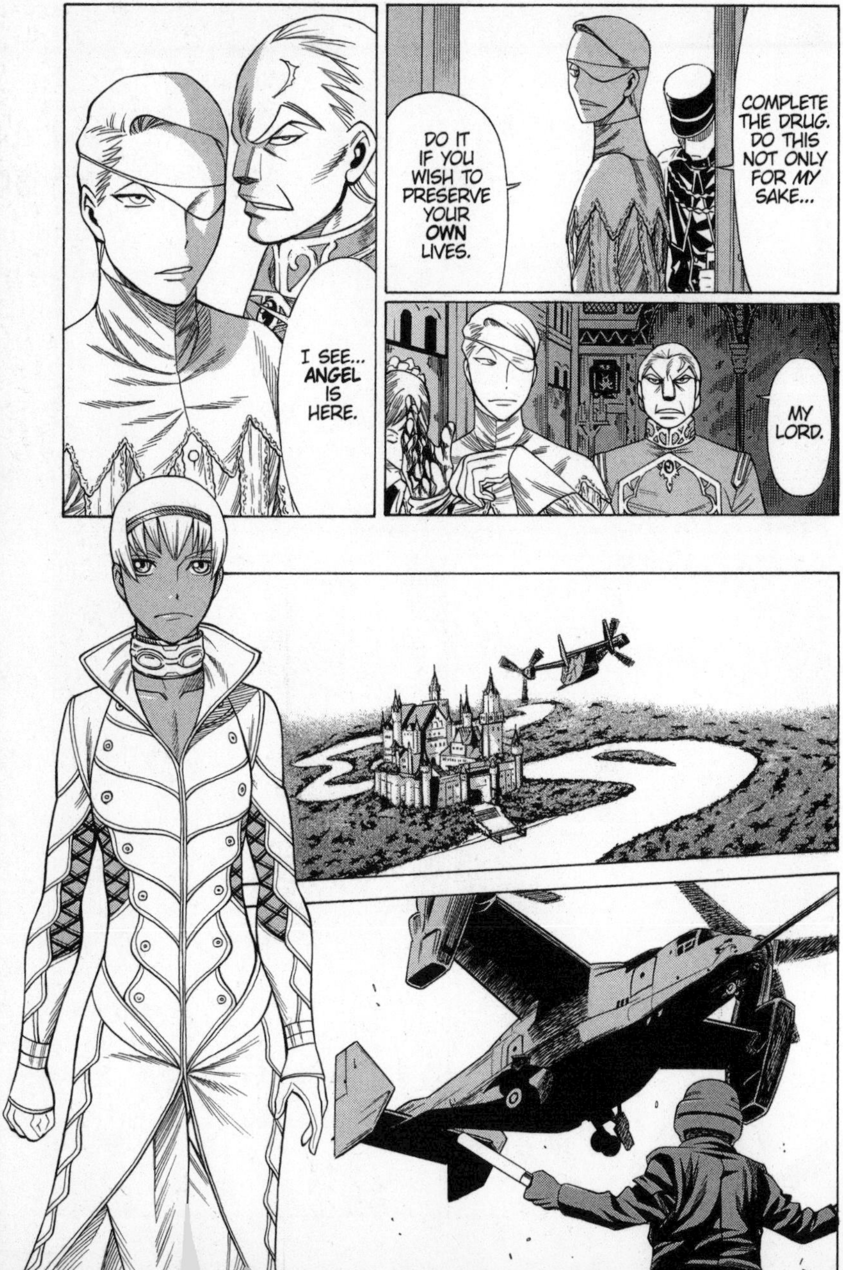
COMPLETE THE DRUG. DO THIS NOT ONLY FOR *MY* SAKE...
DO IT IF YOU WISH TO PRESERVE YOUR **OWN** LIVES.
MY LORD.
I SEE... **ANGEL** IS HERE.

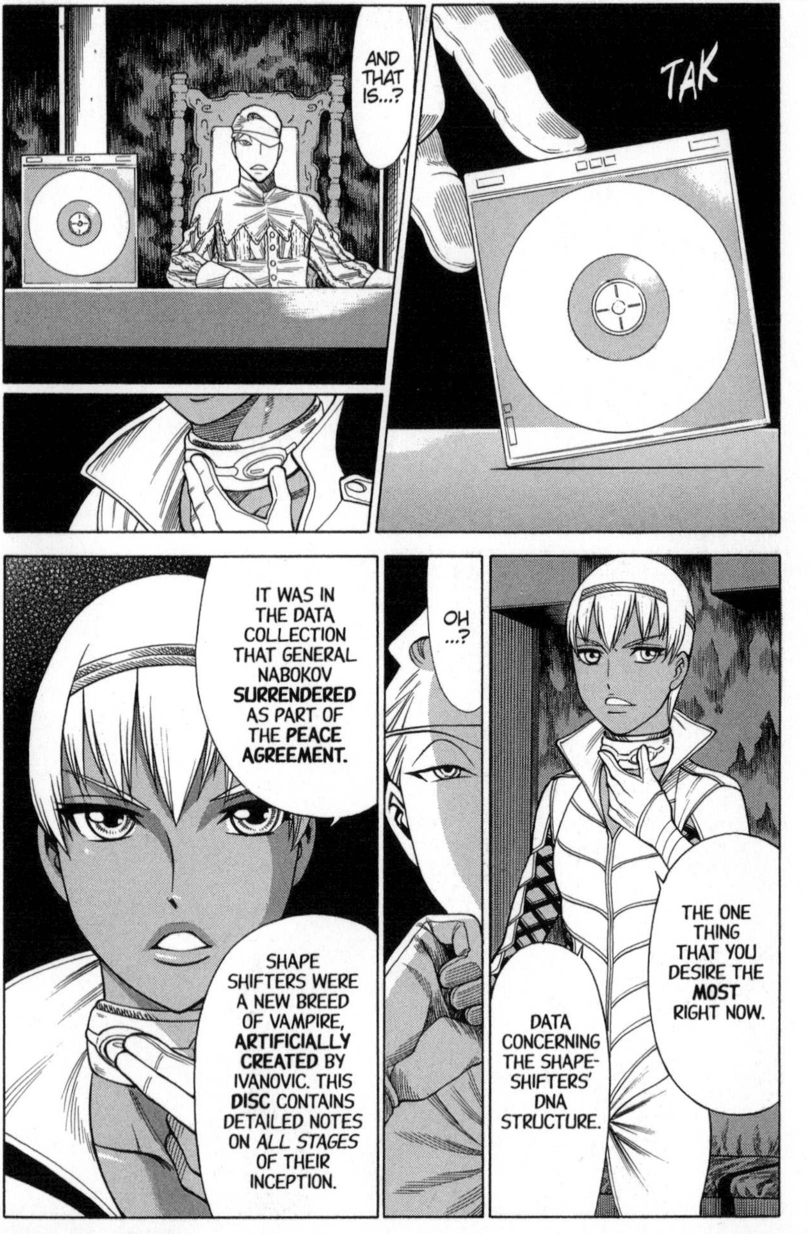
TAK
AND THAT IS...?
THE ONE THING THAT YOU DESIRE THE MOST RIGHT NOW.
DATA CONCERNING THE SHAPE-SHIFTERS' DNA STRUCTURE.
OH ...?
IT WAS IN THE DATA COLLECTION THAT GENERAL NABOKOV SURRENDERED AS PART OF THE PEACE AGREEMENT.
SHAPE SHIFTERS WERE A NEW BREED OF VAMPIRE, ARTIFICIALLY CREATED BY IVANOVIC. THIS DISC CONTAINS DETAILED NOTES ON ALL STAGES OF THEIR INCEPTION.

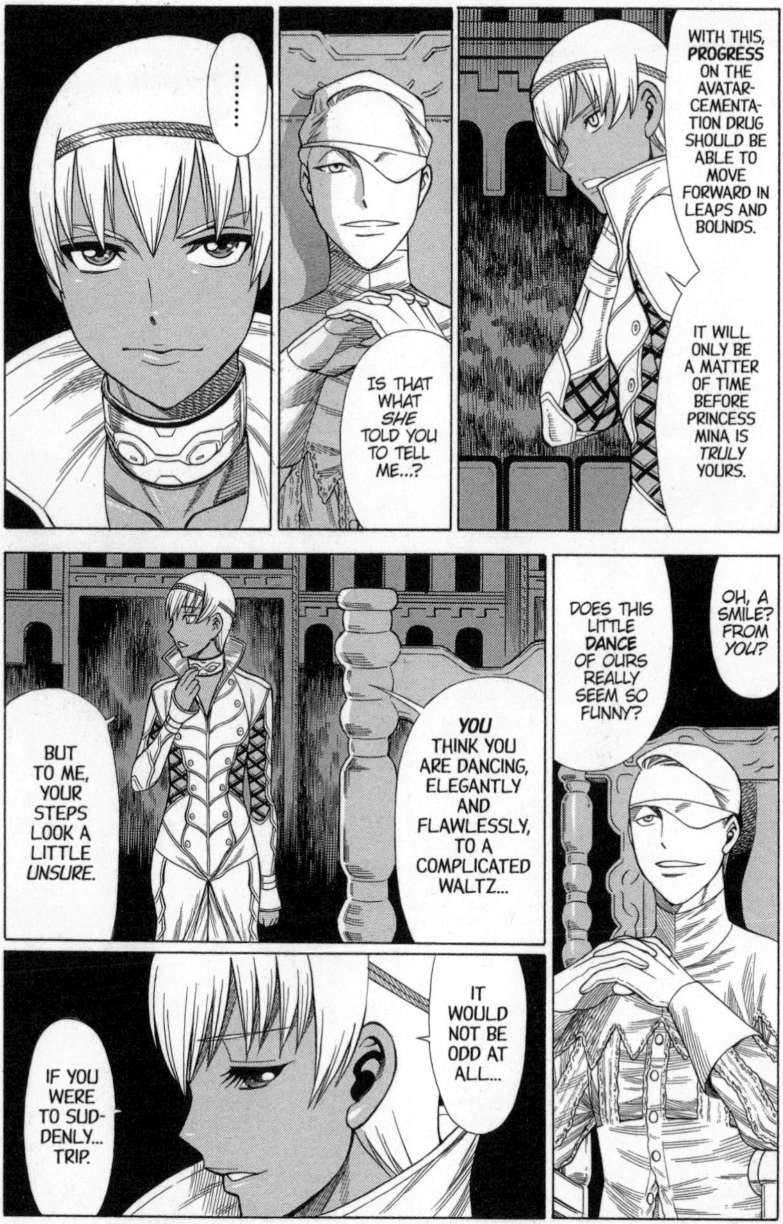
WITH THIS, PROGRESS ON THE AVATAR-CEMENTATION DRUG SHOULD BE ABLE TO MOVE FORWARD IN LEAPS AND BOUNDS.
IT WILL ONLY BE A MATTER OF TIME BEFORE PRINCESS MINA IS TRULY YOURS.
IS THAT WHAT SHE TOLD YOU TO TELL ME...?
......
OH, A SMILE? FROM YOU?
DOES THIS LITTLE DANCE OF OURS REALLY SEEM SO FUNNY?
YOU THINK YOU ARE DANCING, ELEGANTLY AND FLAWLESSLY, TO A COMPLICATED WALTZ...
BUT TO ME, YOUR STEPS LOOK A LITTLE UNSURE.
IT WOULD NOT BE ODD AT ALL...
IF YOU WERE TO SUDDENLY... TRIP.

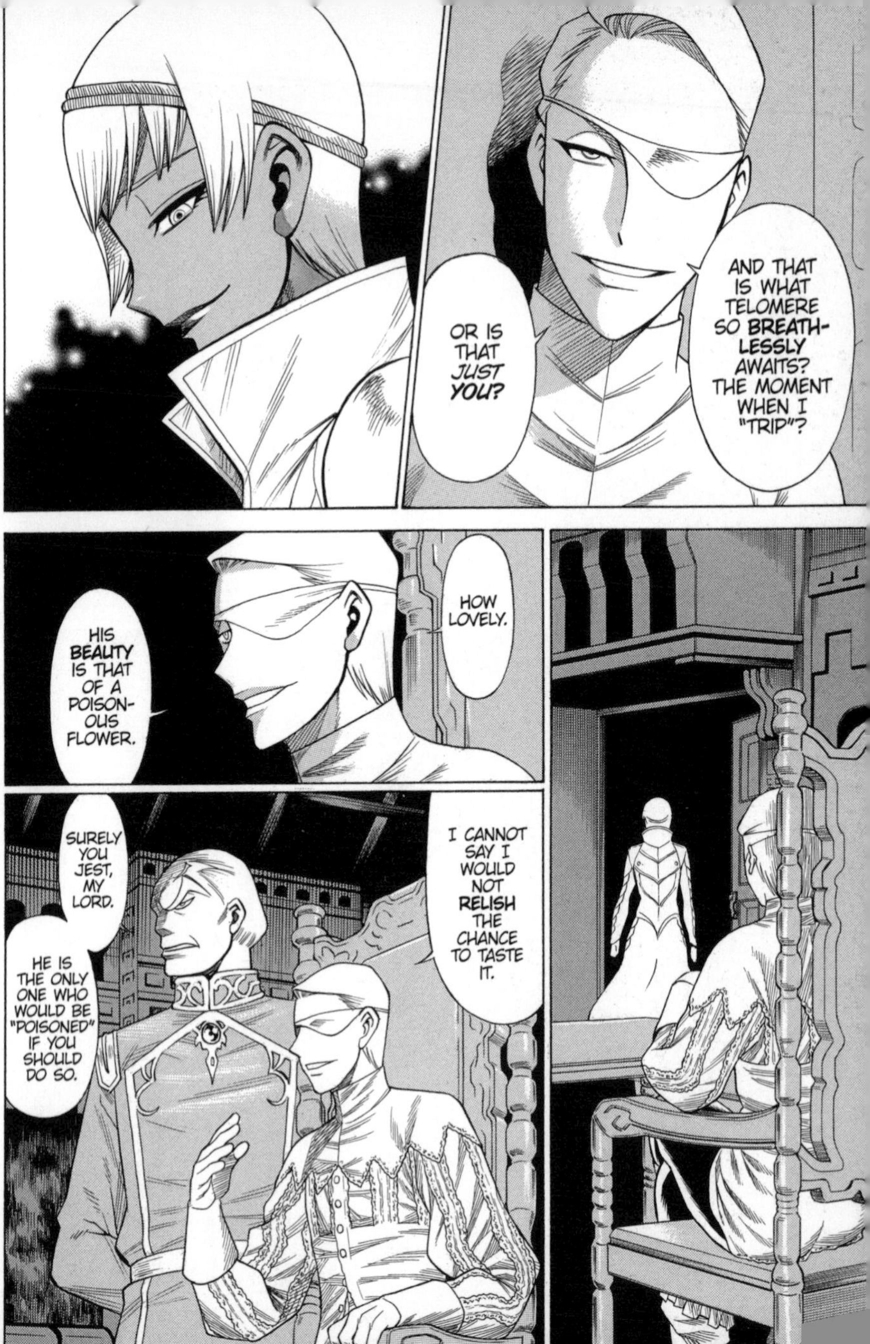
AND THAT IS WHAT TELOMERE SO BREATHLESSLY AWAITS? THE MOMENT WHEN I "TRIP"?
OR IS THAT JUST YOU?
HOW LOVELY.
HIS BEAUTY IS THAT OF A POISONOUS FLOWER.
I CANNOT SAY I WOULD NOT RELISH THE CHANCE TO TASTE IT.
SURELY YOU JEST, MY LORD.
HE IS THE ONLY ONE WHO WOULD BE "POISONED" IF YOU SHOULD DO SO.

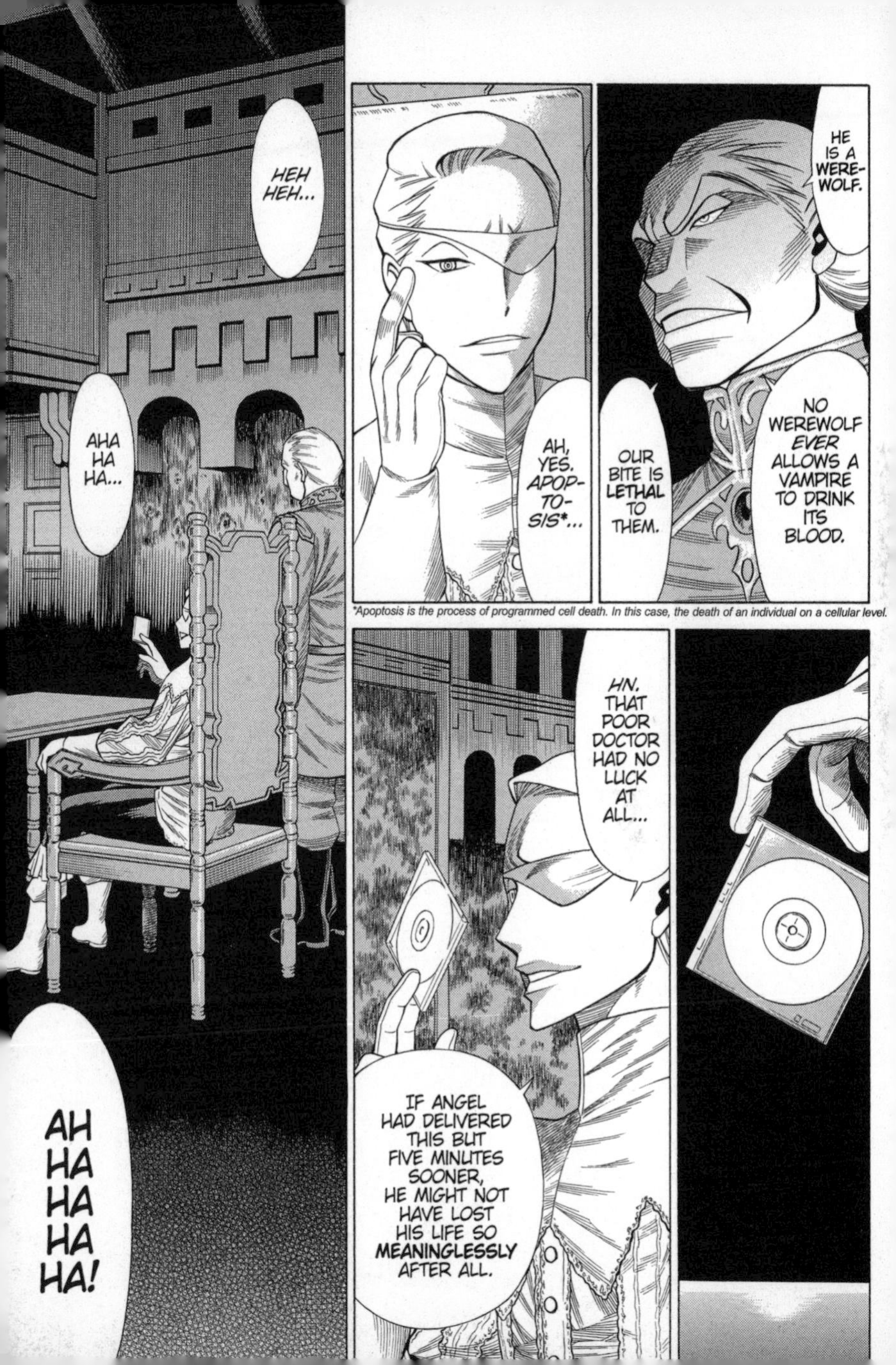
HE IS A WEREWOLF.
NO WEREWOLF *EVER* ALLOWS A VAMPIRE TO DRINK ITS BLOOD.
OUR BITE IS **LETHAL** TO THEM.
AH, YES. *APOPTOSIS**...
HN. THAT POOR DOCTOR HAD NO LUCK AT ALL...
IF ANGEL HAD DELIVERED THIS BUT FIVE MINUTES SOONER, HE MIGHT NOT HAVE LOST HIS LIFE SO **MEANINGLESSLY** AFTER ALL.
HEH HEH...
AHA HA HA...
AH HA HA HA HA!

*Apoptosis is the process of programmed cell death. In this case, the death of an individual on a cellular level.

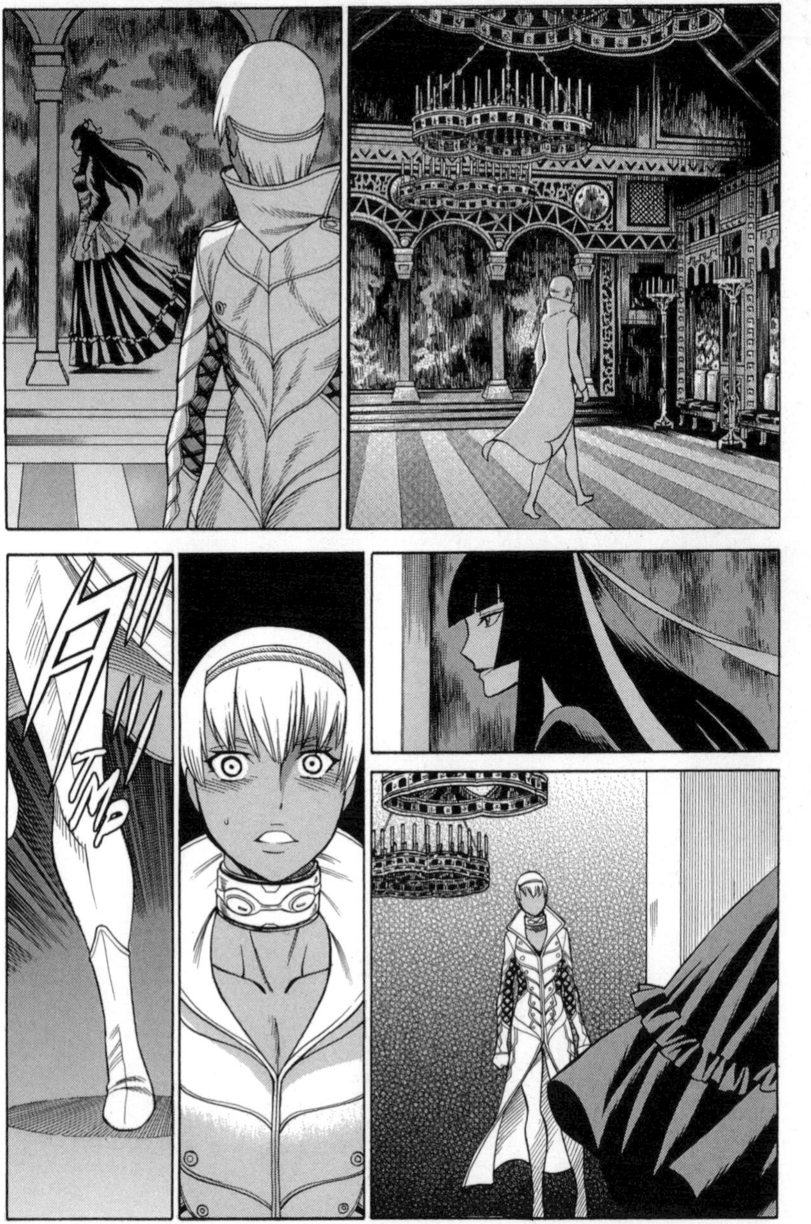
STMP

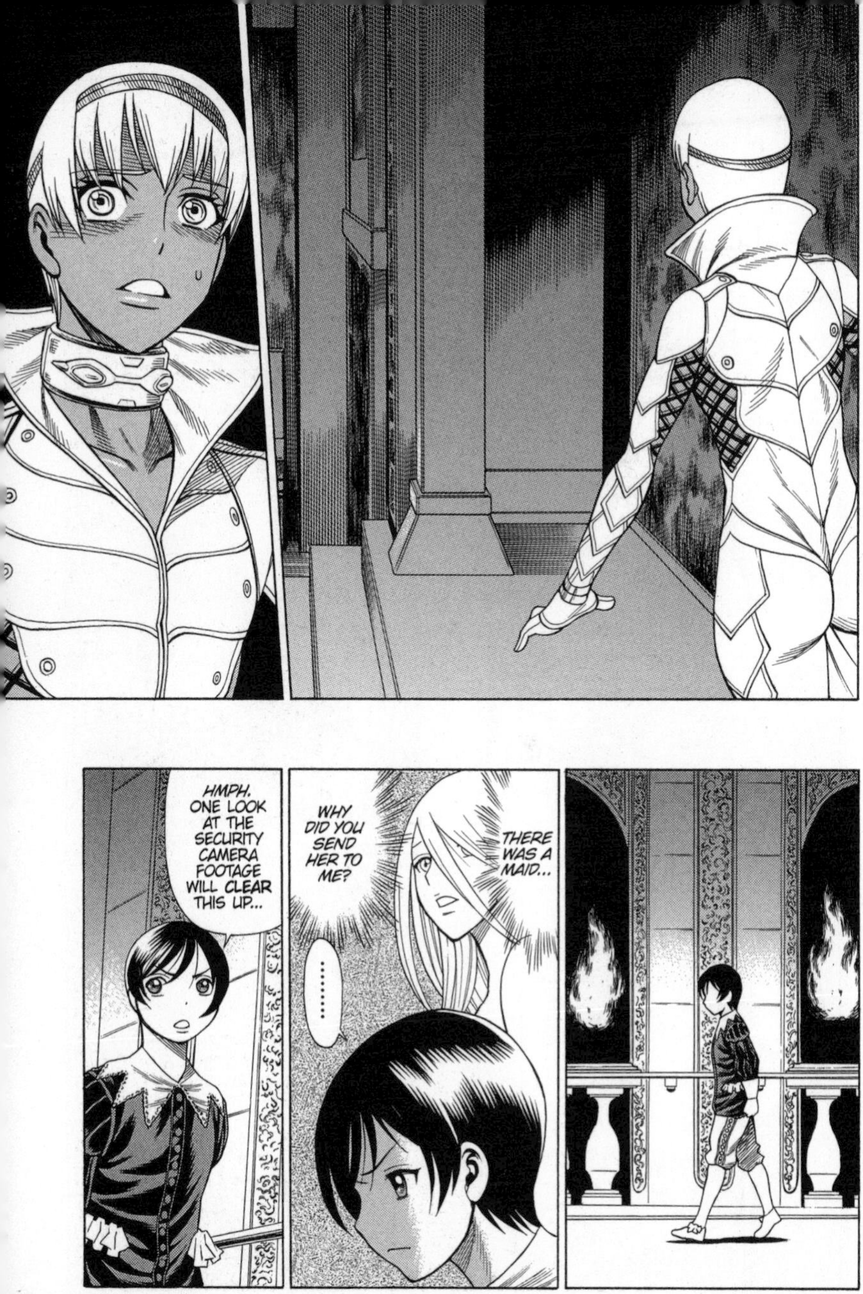
THERE WAS A MAID...
WHY DID YOU SEND HER TO ME?
....
HMPH. ONE LOOK AT THE SECURITY CAMERA FOOTAGE WILL CLEAR THIS UP...

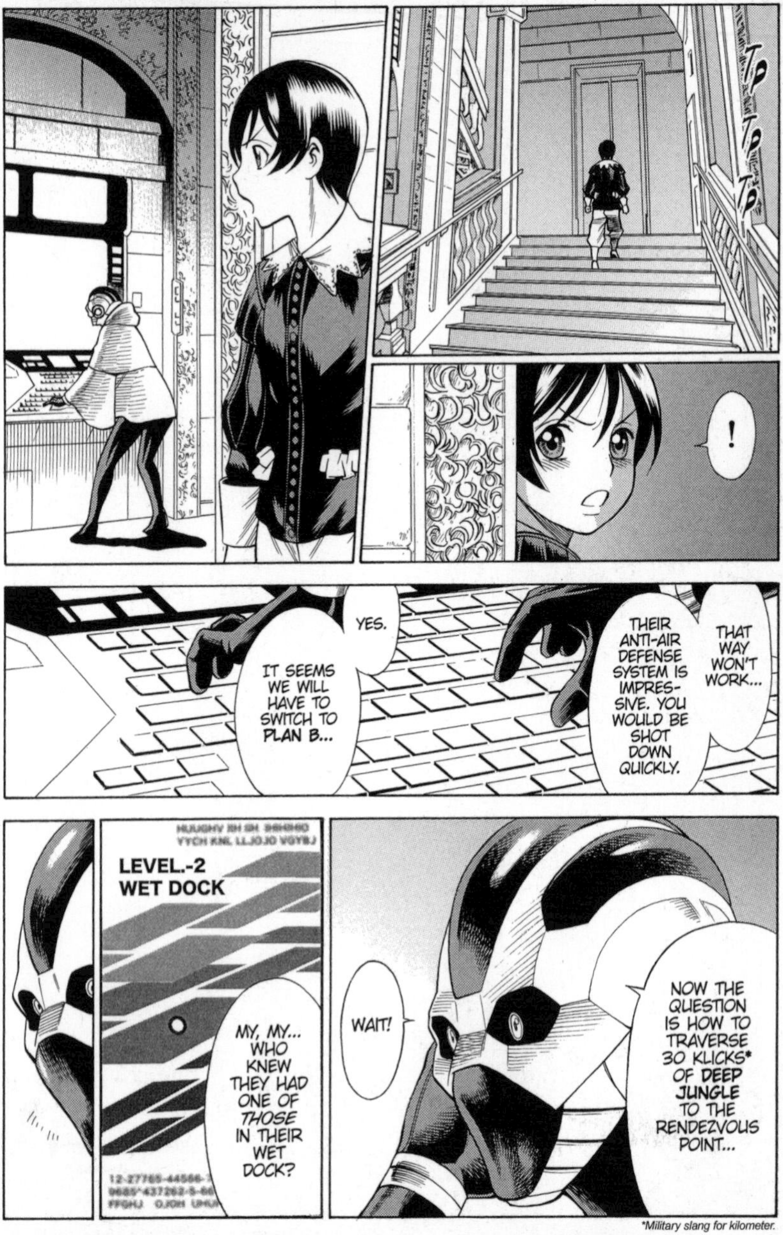
TP TP TP TP TP
!
THAT WAY WON'T WORK...
THEIR ANTI-AIR DEFENSE SYSTEM IS IMPRESSIVE. YOU WOULD BE SHOT DOWN QUICKLY.
YES.
IT SEEMS WE WILL HAVE TO SWITCH TO **PLAN B**...
NOW THE QUESTION IS HOW TO TRAVERSE 30 KLICKS* OF **DEEP JUNGLE** TO THE RENDEZVOUS POINT...
WAIT!
LEVEL.-2 WET DOCK
MY, MY... WHO KNEW THEY HAD ONE OF *THOSE* IN THEIR WET DOCK?

*Military slang for kilometer.

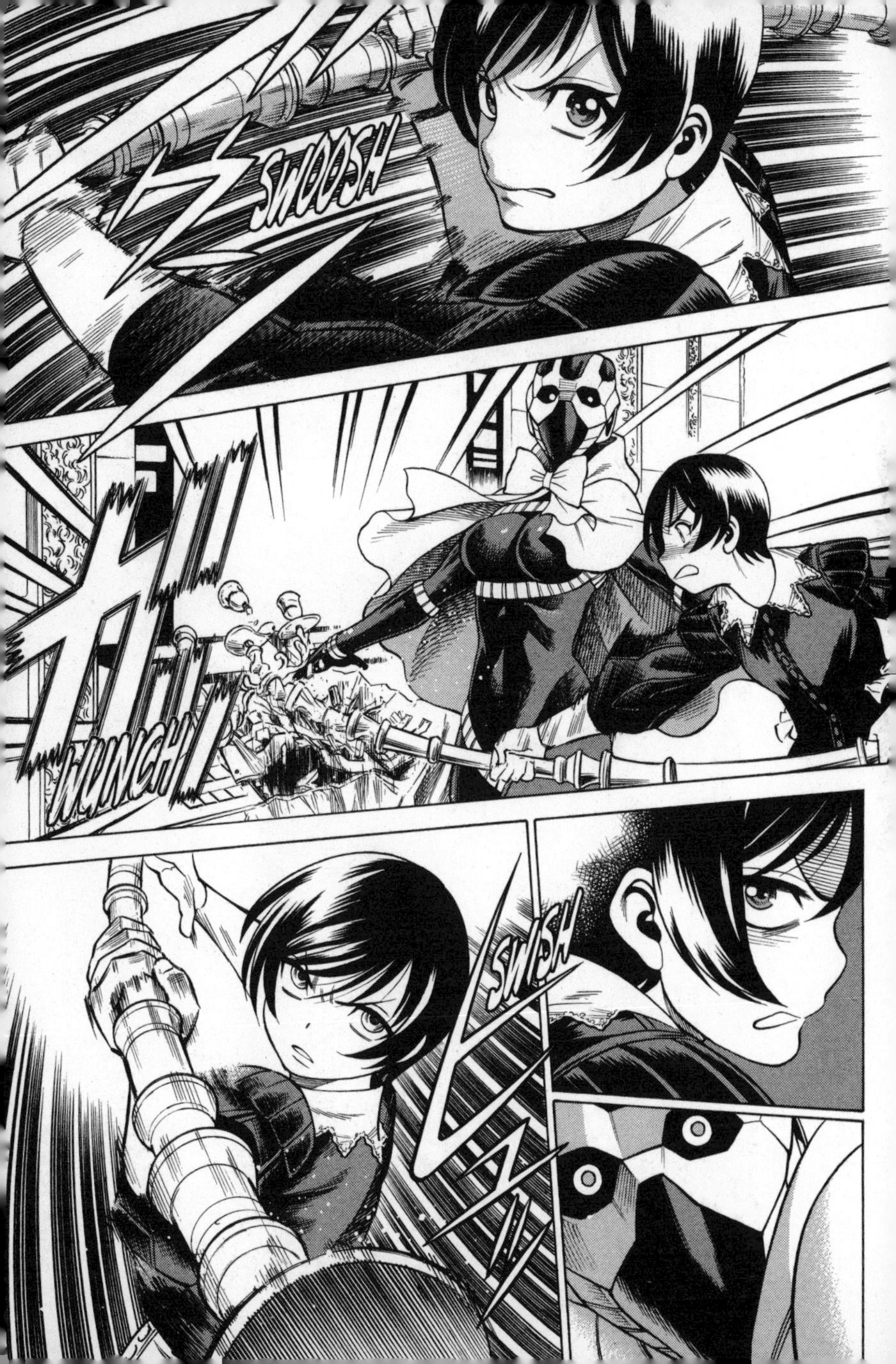
SWOOSH
WUNCH!
SWISH

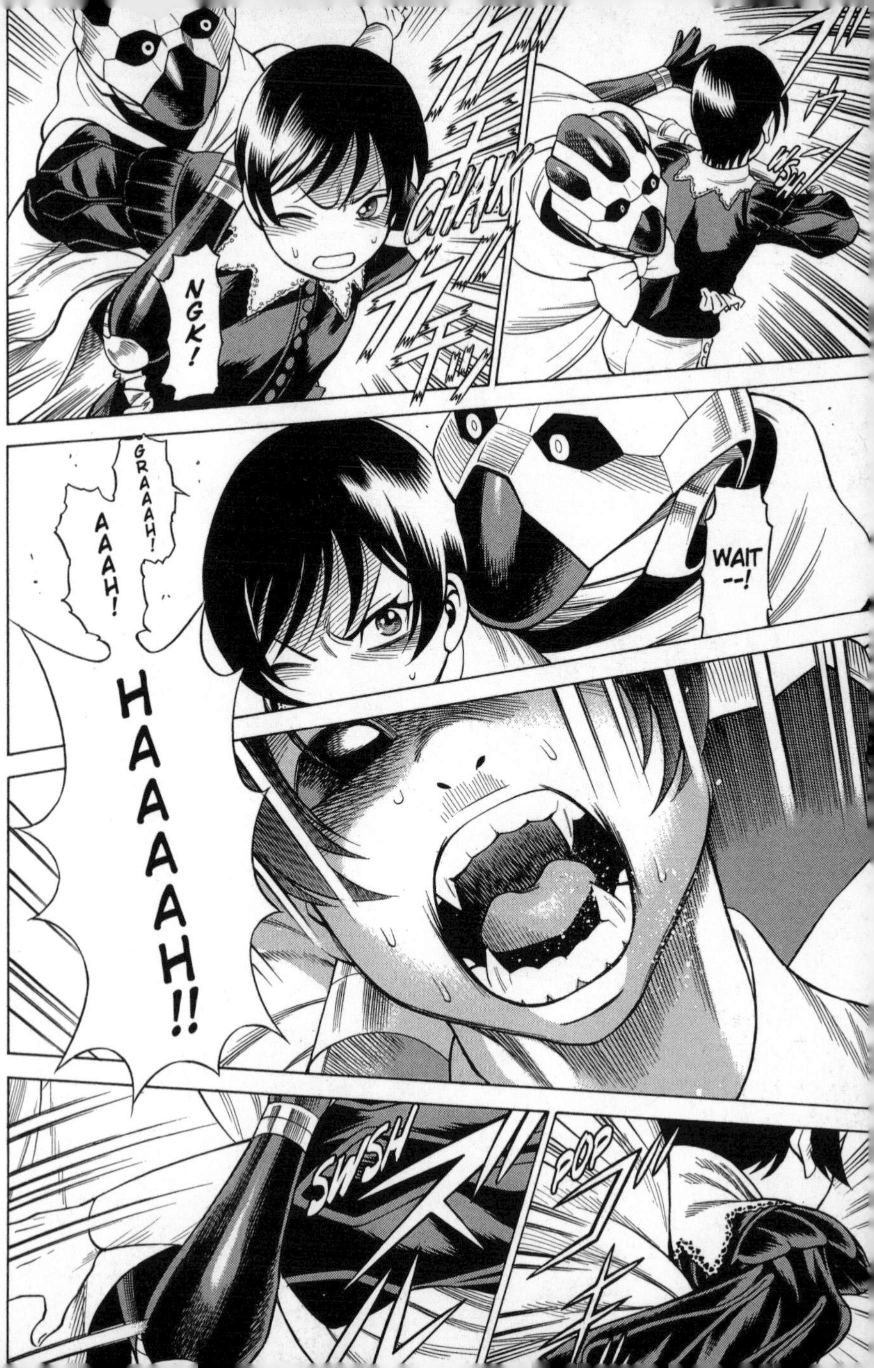
WSH
CHAK
NGK!
WAIT --!
GRAAAAH! AAAAH!
HAAAAAH!!
POP
SWISH

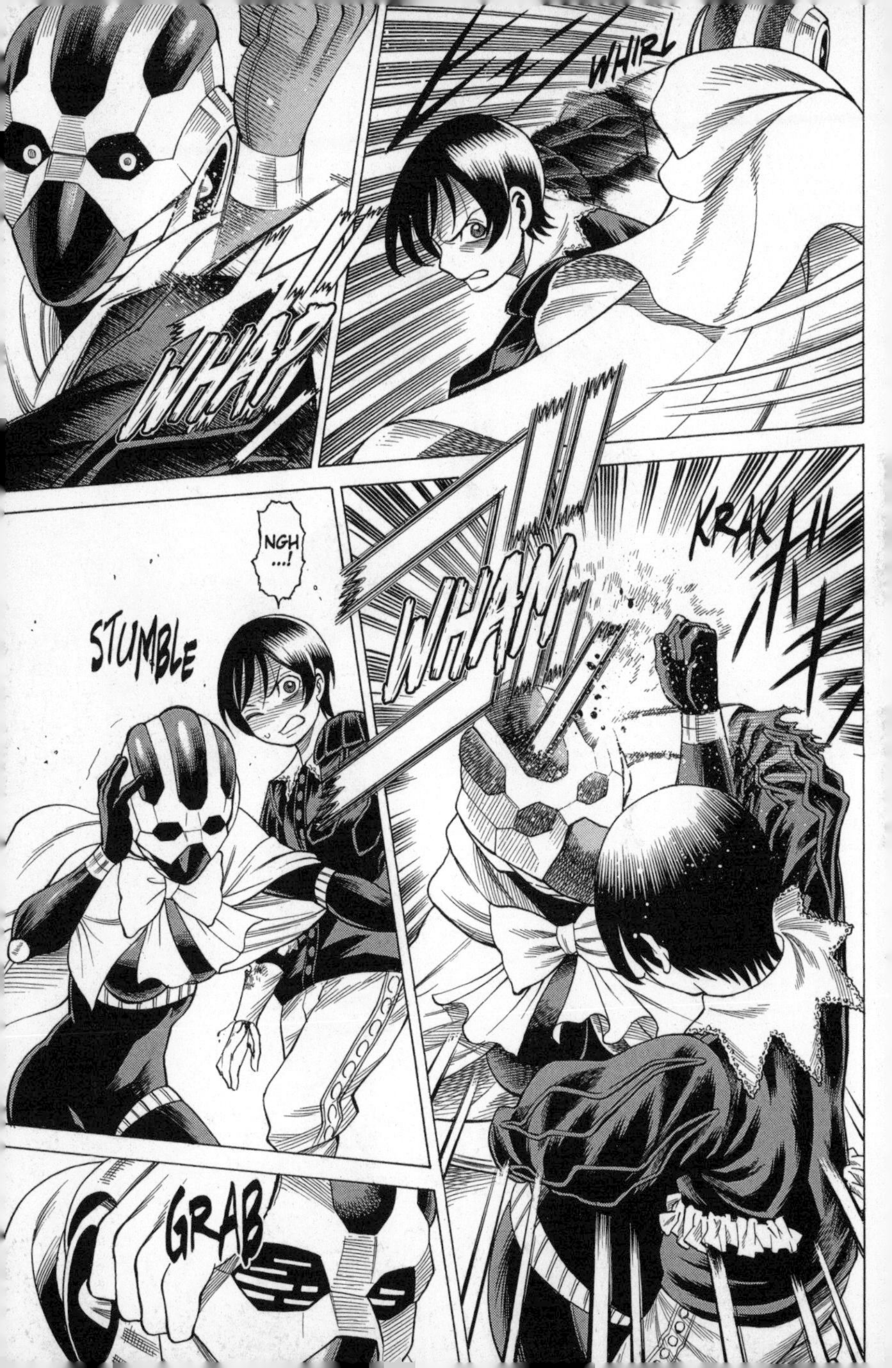
WHIRL
WHAP
KRAK
WHAM
NGH ...!
STUMBLE
GRAB

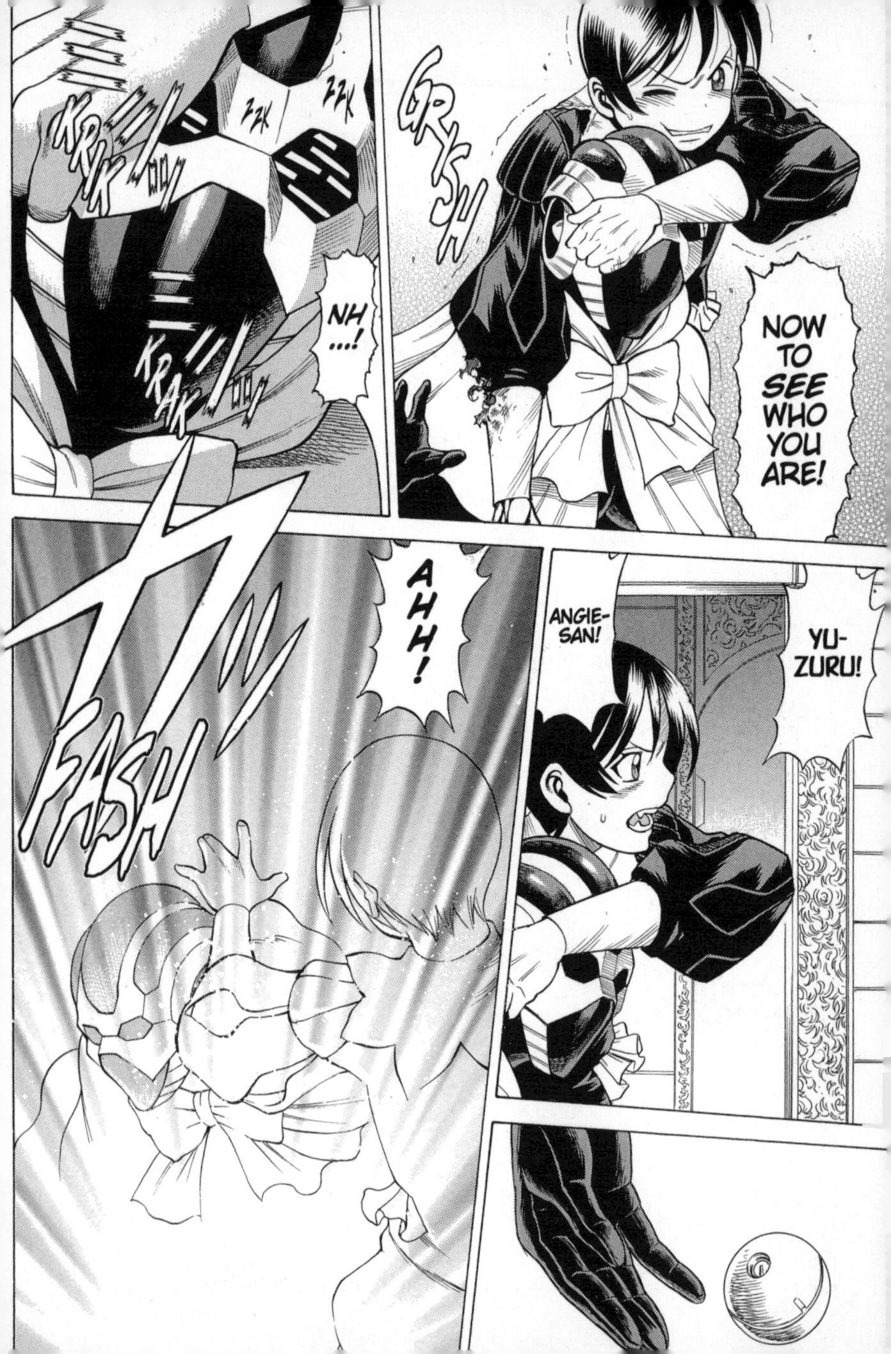
GRKSH
NOW TO SEE WHO YOU ARE!
ZZK
ZZK
KRIK
KRAK
NH ...!
YU-ZURU!
ANGIE-SAN!
AHH!
FASH

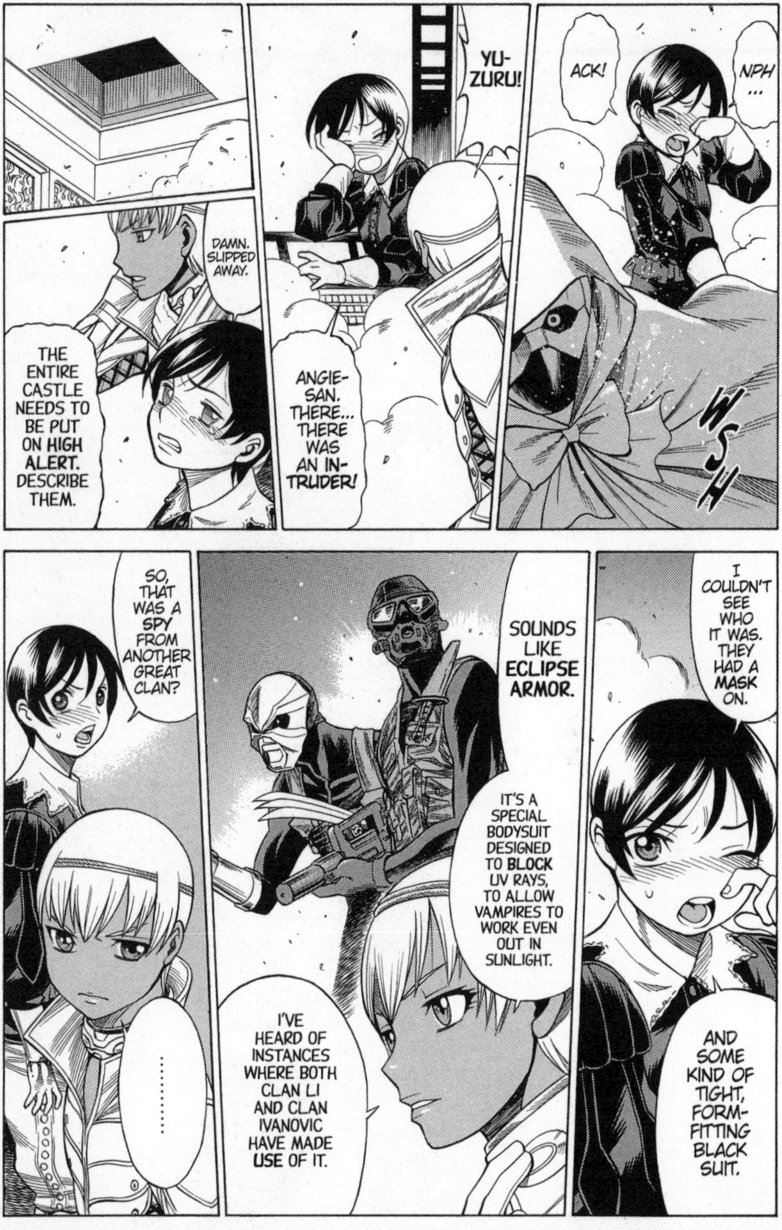

NPH ...
ACK!
WSH
YU-ZURU!
ANGIE-SAN. THERE... THERE WAS AN IN-TRUDER!
DAMN. SLIPPED AWAY.
THE ENTIRE CASTLE NEEDS TO BE PUT ON HIGH ALERT. DESCRIBE THEM.
I COULDN'T SEE WHO IT WAS. THEY HAD A MASK ON.
AND SOME KIND OF TIGHT, FORM-FITTING BLACK SUIT.
SOUNDS LIKE ECLIPSE ARMOR.
IT'S A SPECIAL BODYSUIT DESIGNED TO BLOCK UV RAYS, TO ALLOW VAMPIRES TO WORK EVEN OUT IN SUNLIGHT.
I'VE HEARD OF INSTANCES WHERE BOTH CLAN LI AND CLAN IVANOVIC HAVE MADE USE OF IT.
SO, THAT WAS A SPY FROM ANOTHER GREAT CLAN?
....

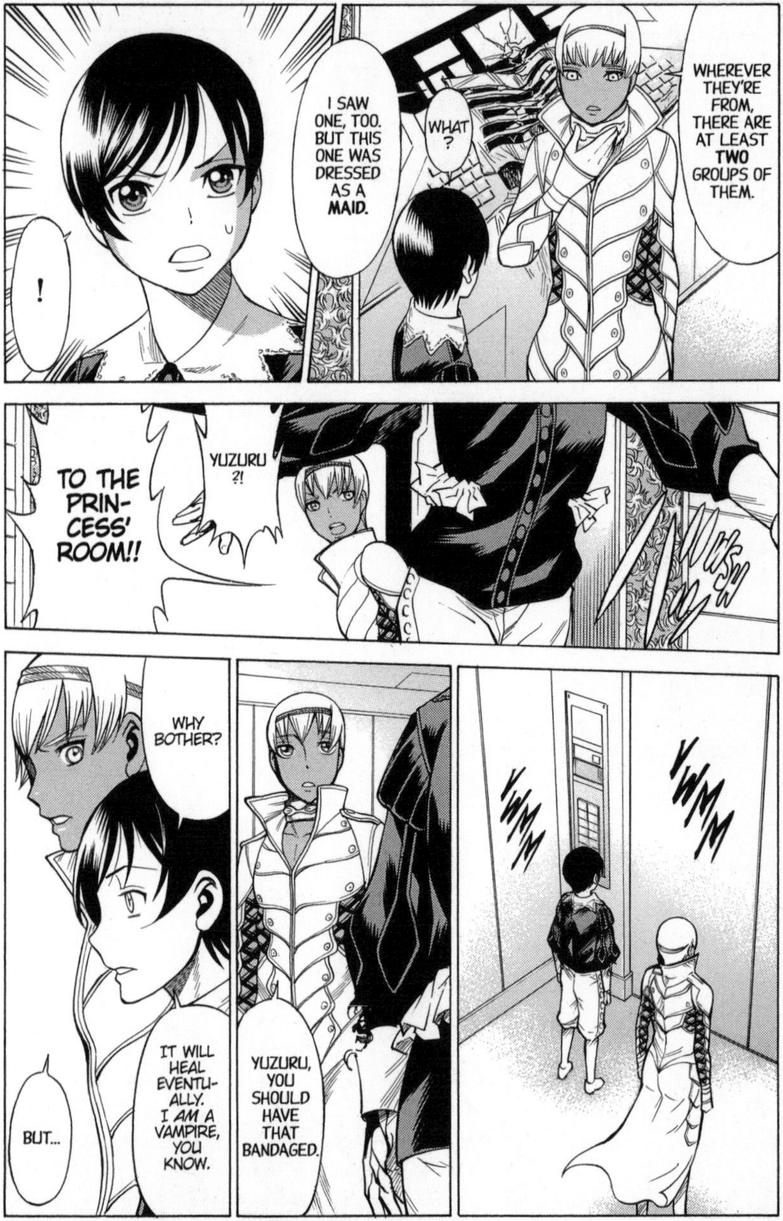
WHEREVER THEY'RE FROM, THERE ARE AT LEAST **TWO** GROUPS OF THEM.
WHAT?
I SAW ONE, TOO. BUT THIS ONE WAS DRESSED AS A **MAID**.
!
YUZURU?!
TO THE PRINCESS' ROOM!!
VWMM
VWMM
YUZURU, YOU SHOULD HAVE THAT BANDAGED.
WHY BOTHER?
IT WILL HEAL EVENTUALLY. I *AM* A VAMPIRE, YOU KNOW.
BUT...

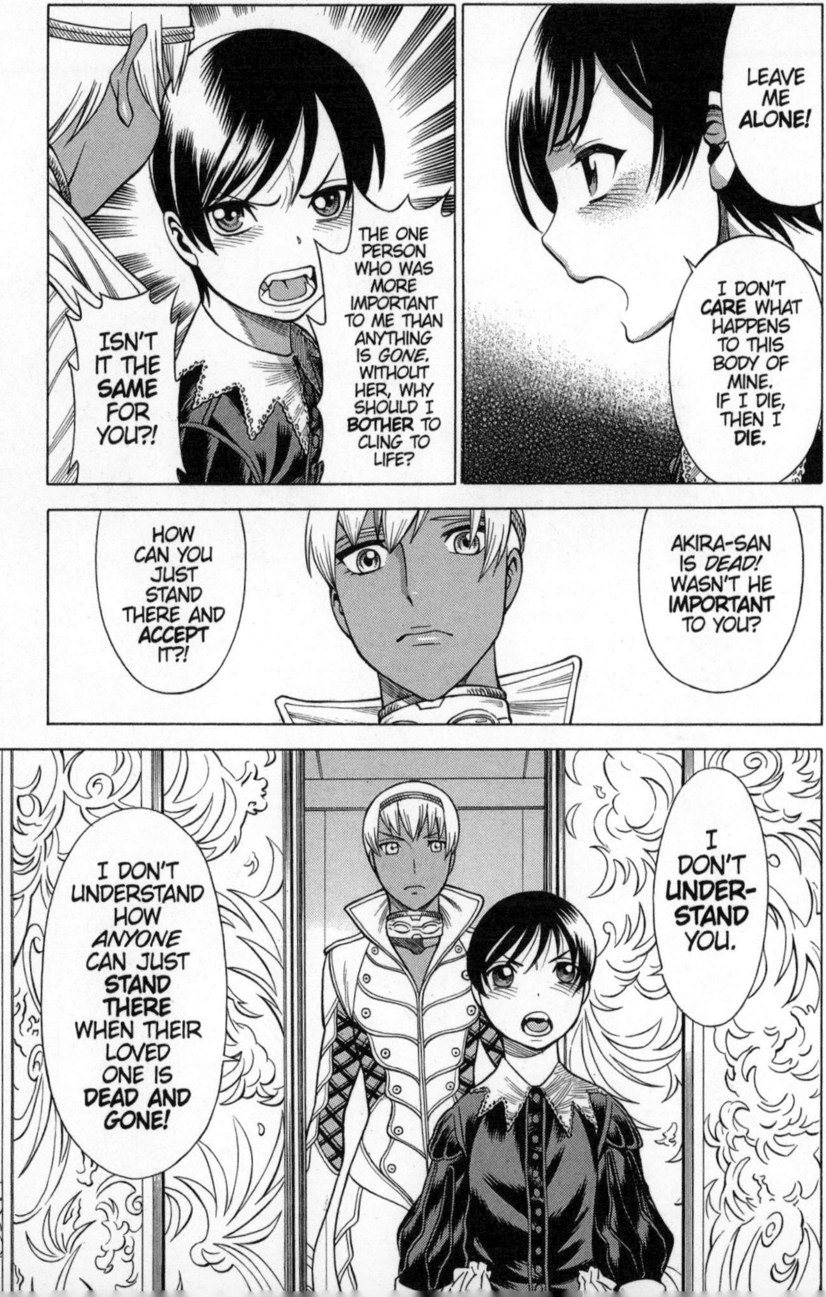
LEAVE ME ALONE!
I DON'T CARE WHAT HAPPENS TO THIS BODY OF MINE. IF I DIE, THEN I DIE.
THE ONE PERSON WHO WAS MORE IMPORTANT TO ME THAN ANYTHING IS GONE. WITHOUT HER, WHY SHOULD I BOTHER TO CLING TO LIFE?
ISN'T IT THE SAME FOR YOU?!
AKIRA-SAN IS DEAD! WASN'T HE IMPORTANT TO YOU?
HOW CAN YOU JUST STAND THERE AND ACCEPT IT?!
I DON'T UNDER-STAND YOU.
I DON'T UNDERSTAND HOW ANYONE CAN JUST STAND THERE WHEN THEIR LOVED ONE IS DEAD AND GONE!

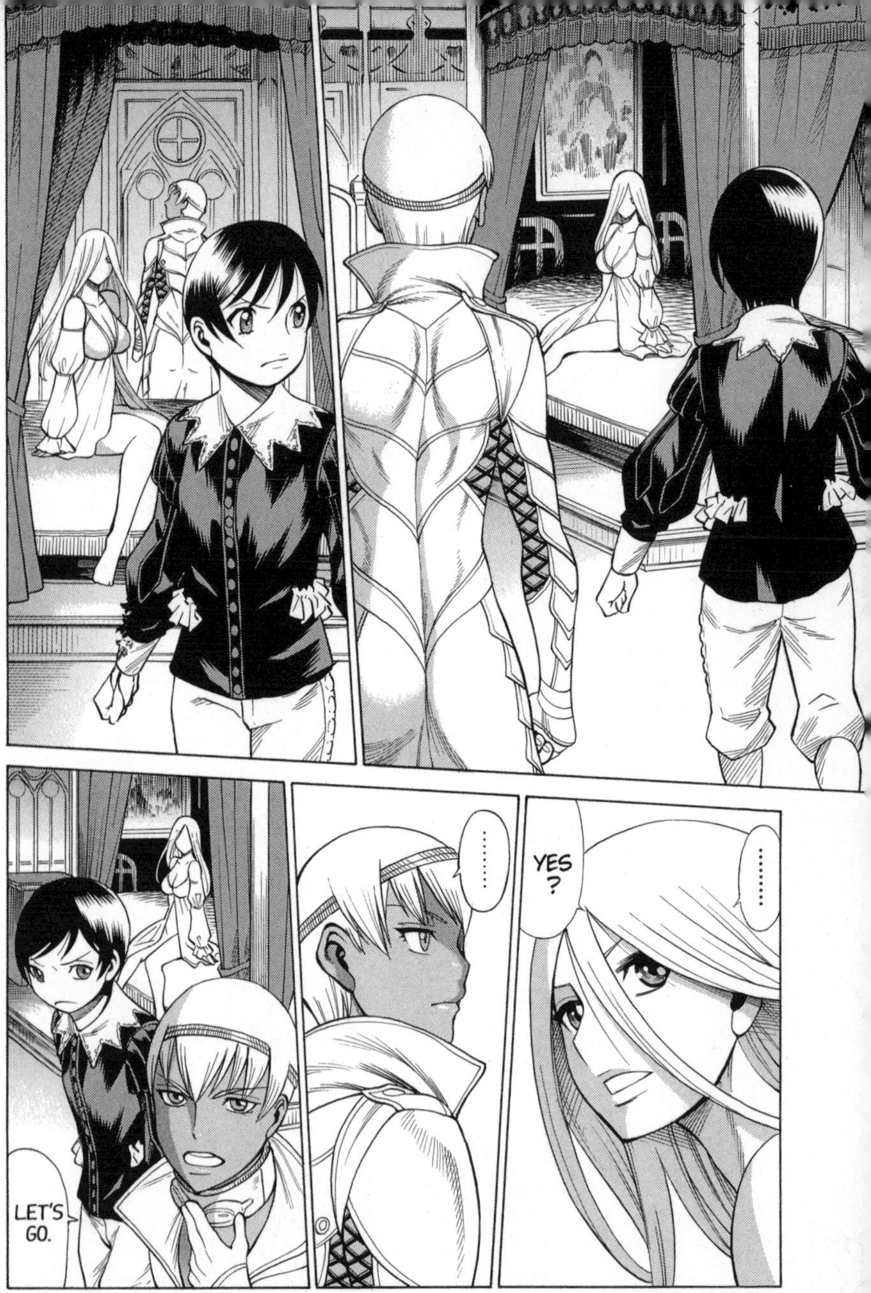
....
YES?
....
LET'S GO.

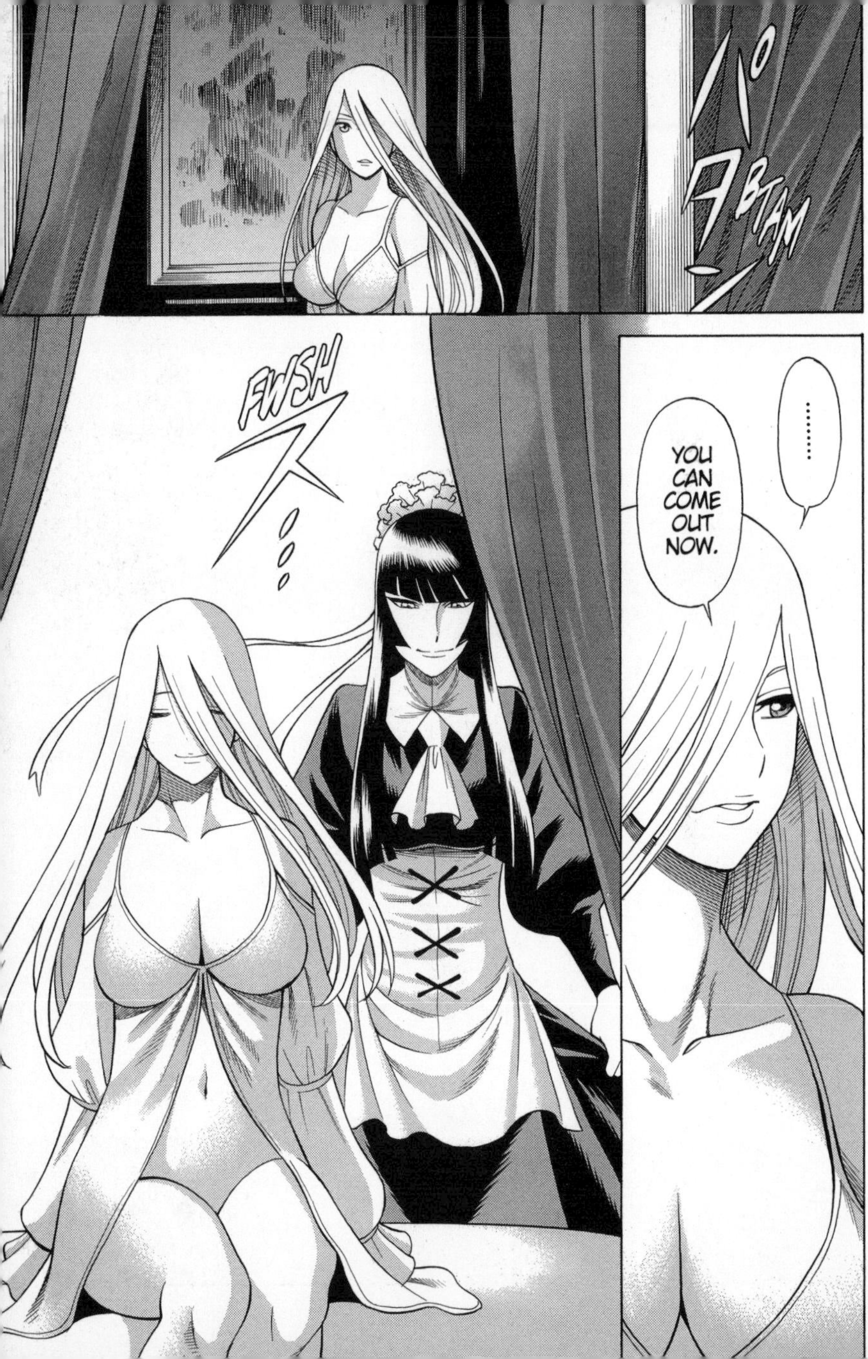
BTAM
....
YOU CAN COME OUT NOW.
FWSH

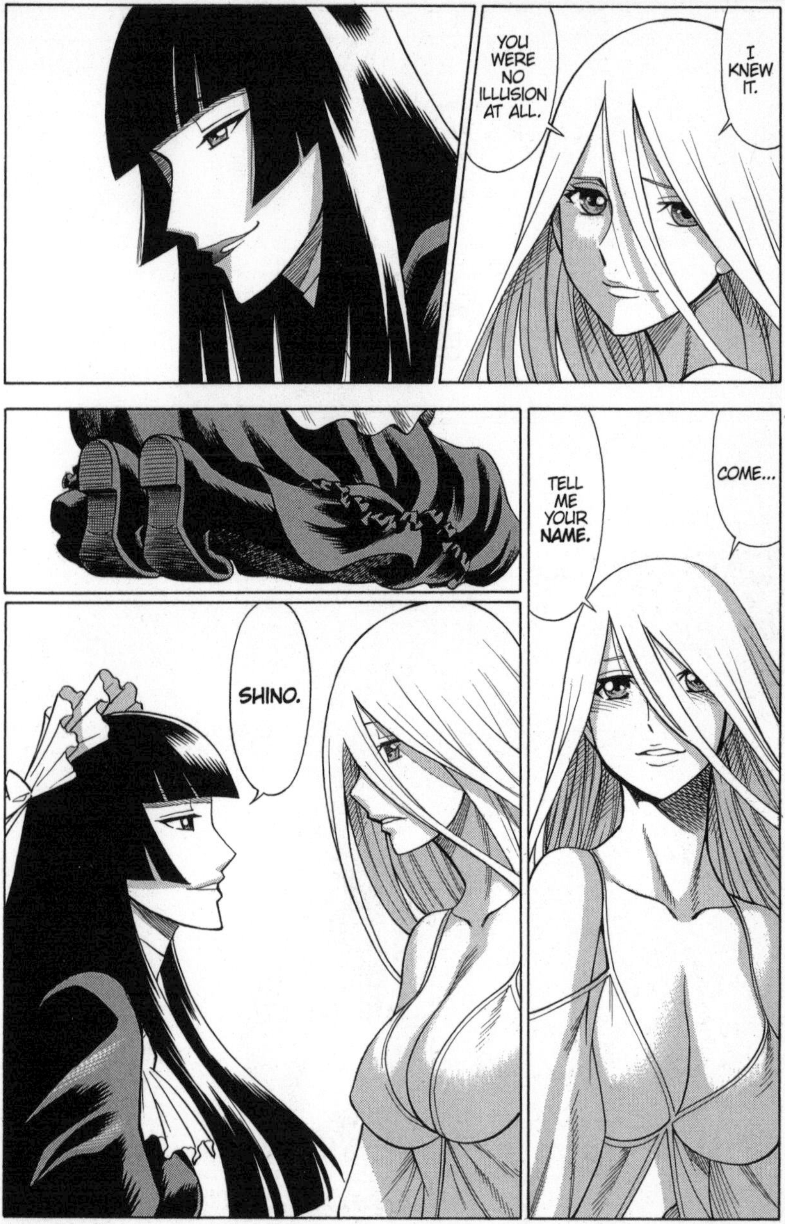
I KNEW IT.
YOU WERE NO ILLUSION AT ALL.
COME...
TELL ME YOUR NAME.
SHINO.

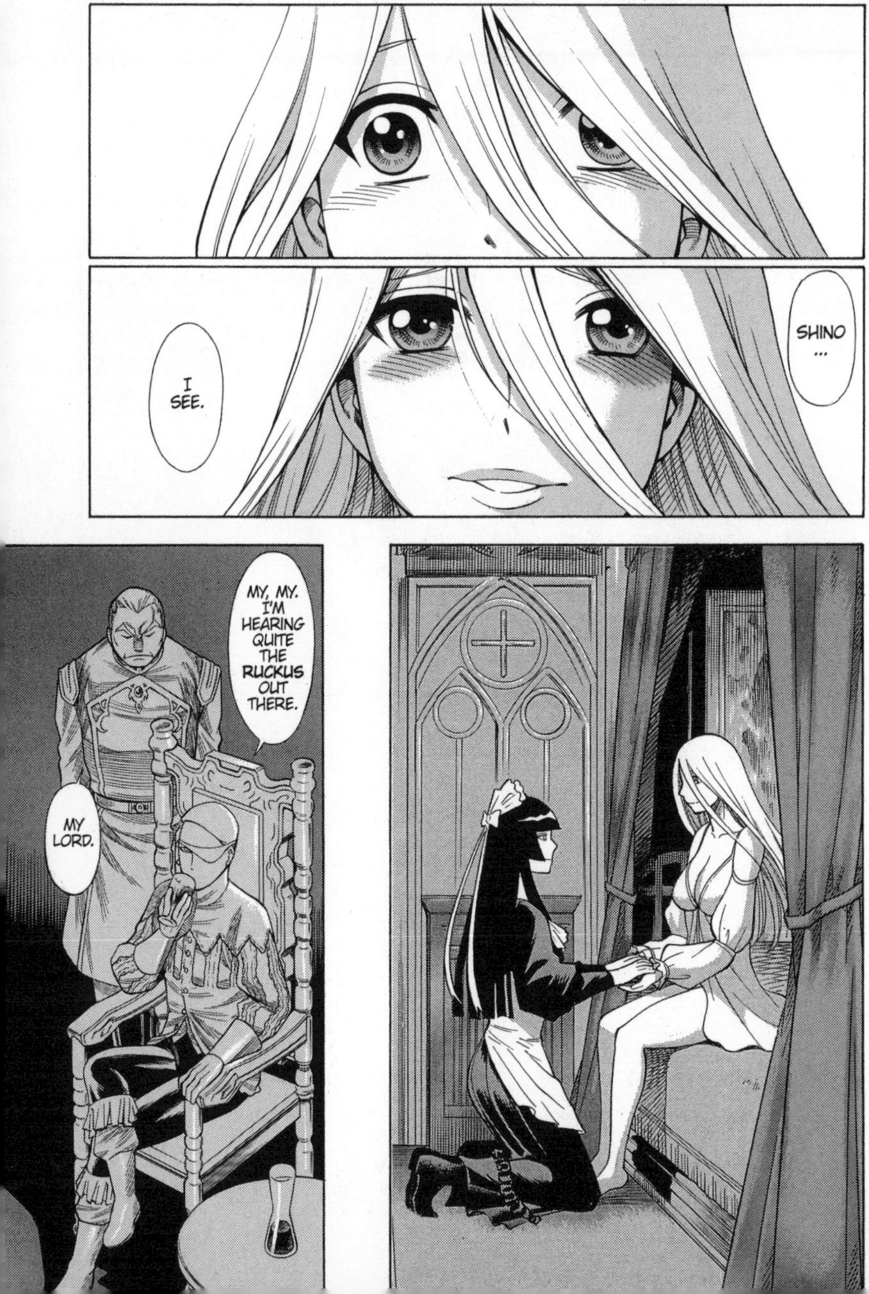
SHINO ...
I SEE.
MY, MY. I'M HEARING QUITE THE RUCKUS OUT THERE.
MY LORD.

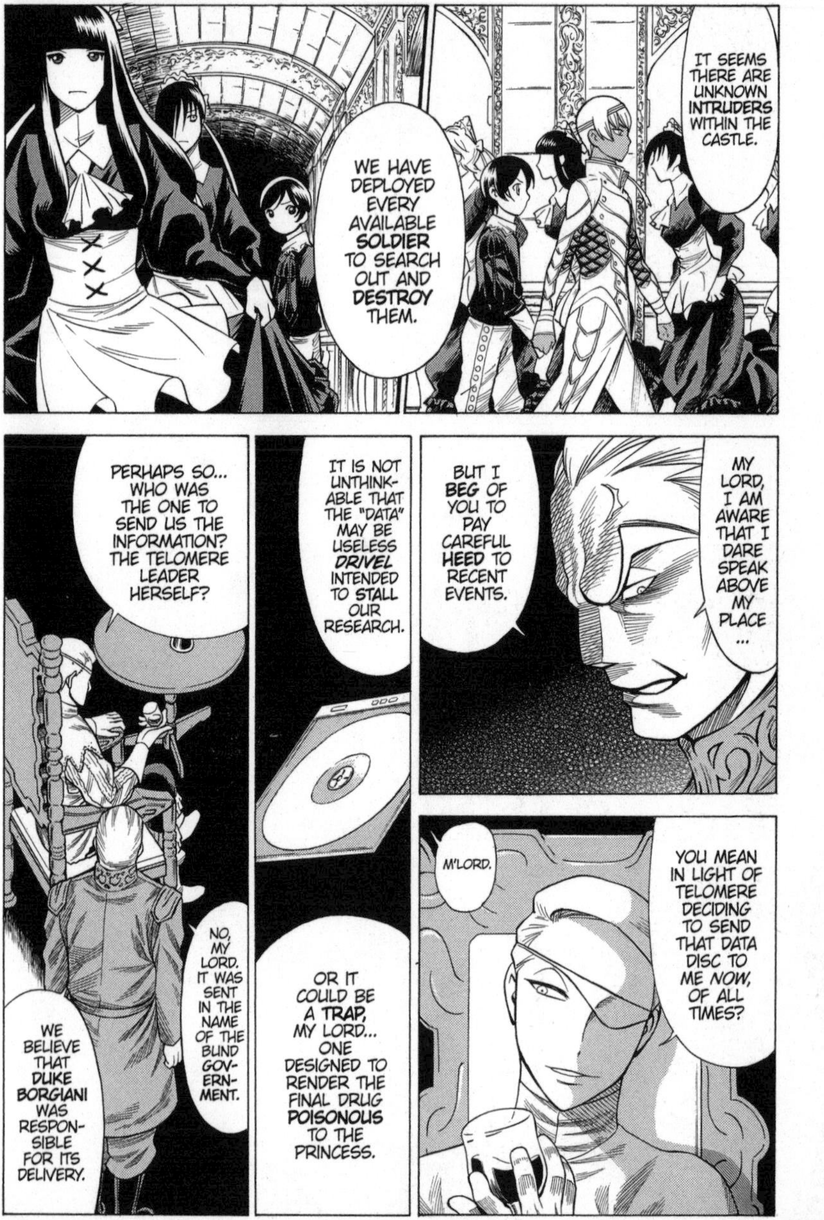
IT SEEMS THERE ARE UNKNOWN INTRUDERS WITHIN THE CASTLE.
WE HAVE DEPLOYED EVERY AVAILABLE SOLDIER TO SEARCH OUT AND DESTROY THEM.
MY LORD, I AM AWARE THAT I DARE SPEAK ABOVE MY PLACE...
BUT I BEG OF YOU TO PAY CAREFUL HEED TO RECENT EVENTS.
YOU MEAN IN LIGHT OF TELOMERE DECIDING TO SEND THAT DATA DISC TO ME NOW, OF ALL TIMES?
M'LORD.
IT IS NOT UNTHINKABLE THAT THE "DATA" MAY BE USELESS DRIVEL INTENDED TO STALL OUR RESEARCH.
OR IT COULD BE A TRAP, MY LORD... ONE DESIGNED TO RENDER THE FINAL DRUG POISONOUS TO THE PRINCESS.
PERHAPS SO... WHO WAS THE ONE TO SEND US THE INFORMATION? THE TELOMERE LEADER HERSELF?
NO, MY LORD. IT WAS SENT IN THE NAME OF THE BUND GOVERNMENT.
WE BELIEVE THAT DUKE BORGIANI WAS RESPONSIBLE FOR ITS DELIVERY.

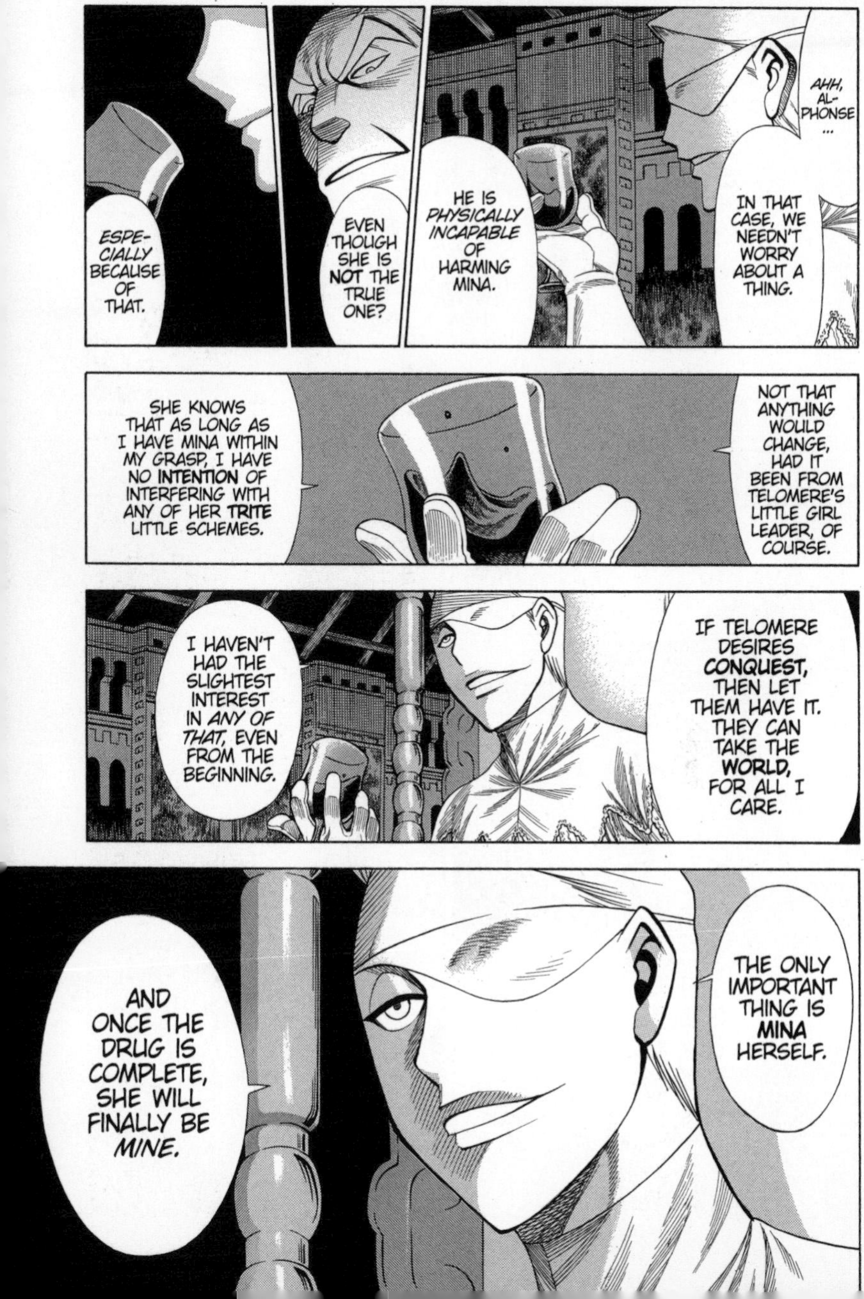
AHH, ALPHONSE ...
IN THAT CASE, WE NEEDN'T WORRY ABOUT A THING.
HE IS PHYSICALLY INCAPABLE OF HARMING MINA.
EVEN THOUGH SHE IS NOT THE TRUE ONE?
ESPECIALLY BECAUSE OF THAT.
NOT THAT ANYTHING WOULD CHANGE, HAD IT BEEN FROM TELOMERE'S LITTLE GIRL LEADER, OF COURSE.
SHE KNOWS THAT AS LONG AS I HAVE MINA WITHIN MY GRASP, I HAVE NO INTENTION OF INTERFERING WITH ANY OF HER TRITE LITTLE SCHEMES.
IF TELOMERE DESIRES CONQUEST, THEN LET THEM HAVE IT. THEY CAN TAKE THE WORLD, FOR ALL I CARE.
I HAVEN'T HAD THE SLIGHTEST INTEREST IN ANY OF THAT, EVEN FROM THE BEGINNING.
THE ONLY IMPORTANT THING IS MINA HERSELF.
AND ONCE THE DRUG IS COMPLETE, SHE WILL FINALLY BE MINE.

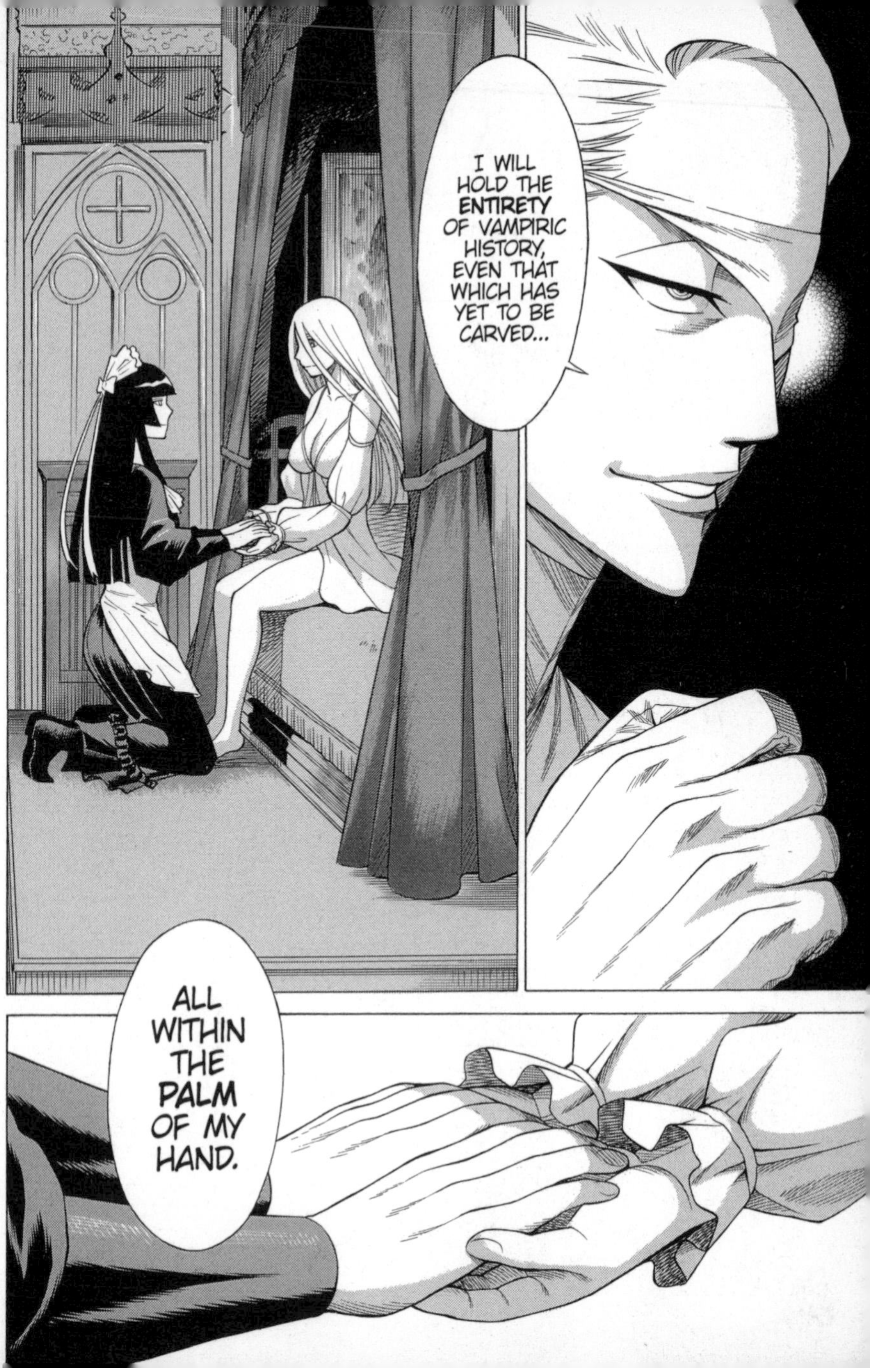
I WILL HOLD THE **ENTIRETY** OF VAMPIRIC HISTORY, EVEN THAT WHICH HAS YET TO BE CARVED...
ALL WITHIN THE PALM OF MY HAND.

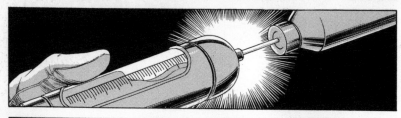

IF YOU WOULD PLEASE JOIN US.

YOUR MAJESTY.

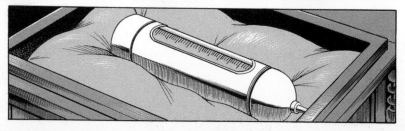

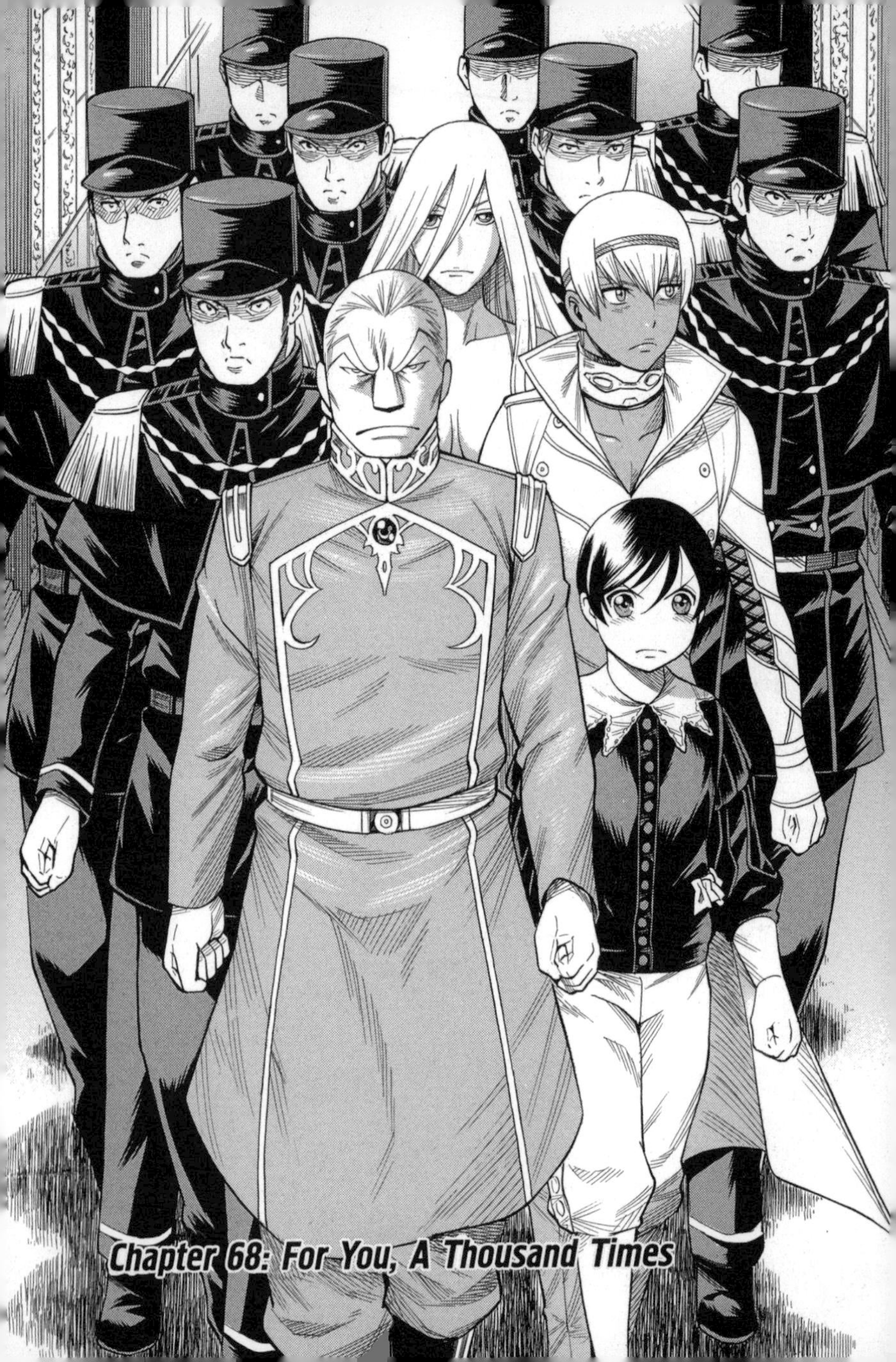
Chapter 68: For You, A Thousand Times

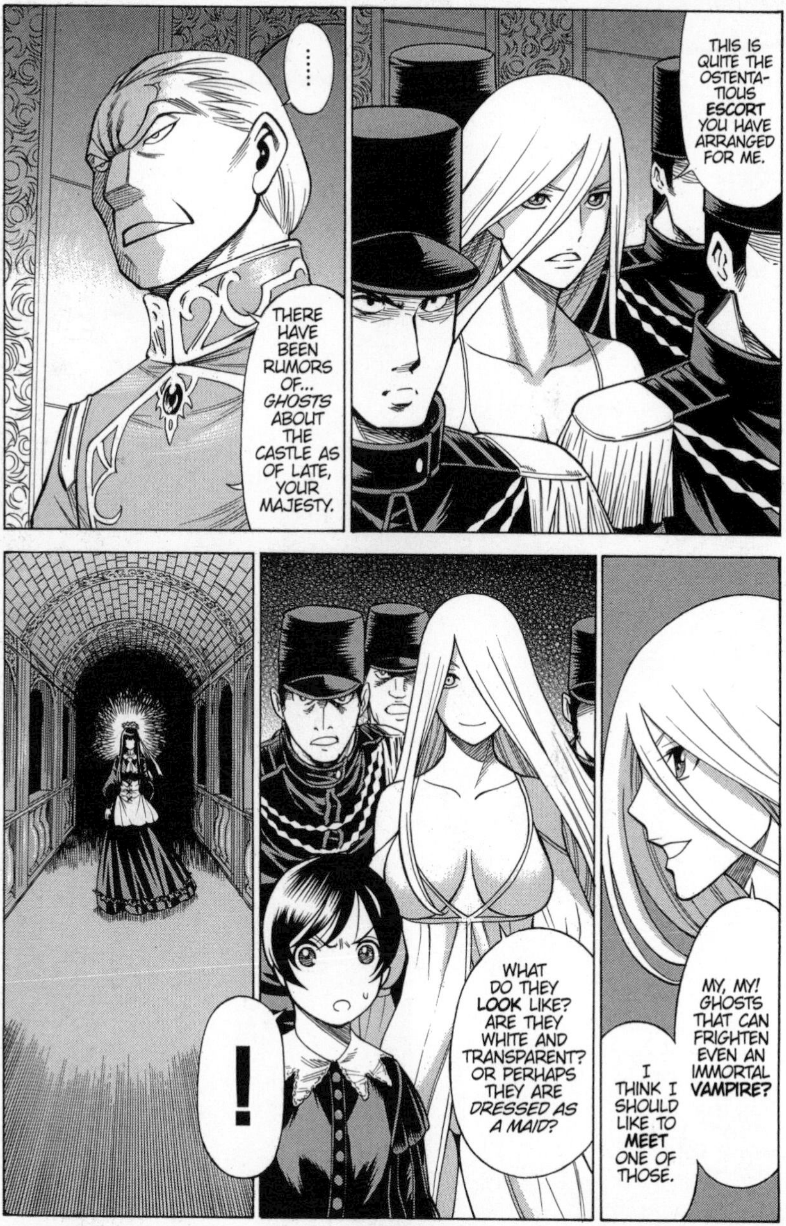
THIS IS QUITE THE OSTENTATIOUS ESCORT YOU HAVE ARRANGED FOR ME.
......
THERE HAVE BEEN RUMORS OF... GHOSTS ABOUT THE CASTLE AS OF LATE, YOUR MAJESTY.
MY, MY! GHOSTS THAT CAN FRIGHTEN EVEN AN IMMORTAL VAMPIRE?
I THINK I SHOULD LIKE TO MEET ONE OF THOSE.
WHAT DO THEY LOOK LIKE? ARE THEY WHITE AND TRANSPARENT? OR PERHAPS THEY ARE DRESSED AS A MAID?
!

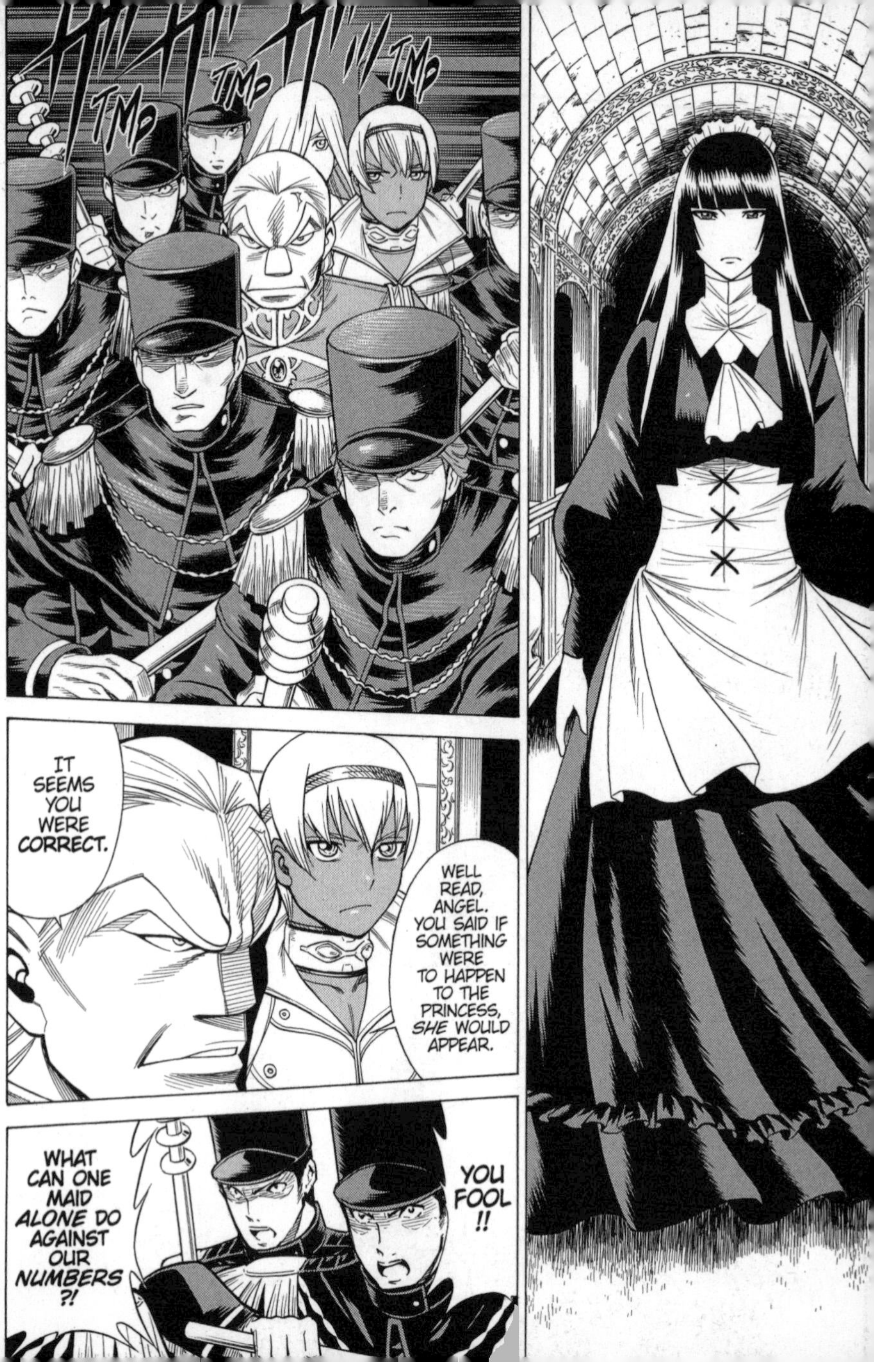
TMP
TMP
TMP
TMP
WELL READ, ANGEL. YOU SAID IF SOMETHING WERE TO HAPPEN TO THE PRINCESS, *SHE* WOULD APPEAR.
IT SEEMS YOU WERE CORRECT.
YOU FOOL!!
WHAT CAN ONE MAID *ALONE* DO AGAINST OUR *NUMBERS*?!

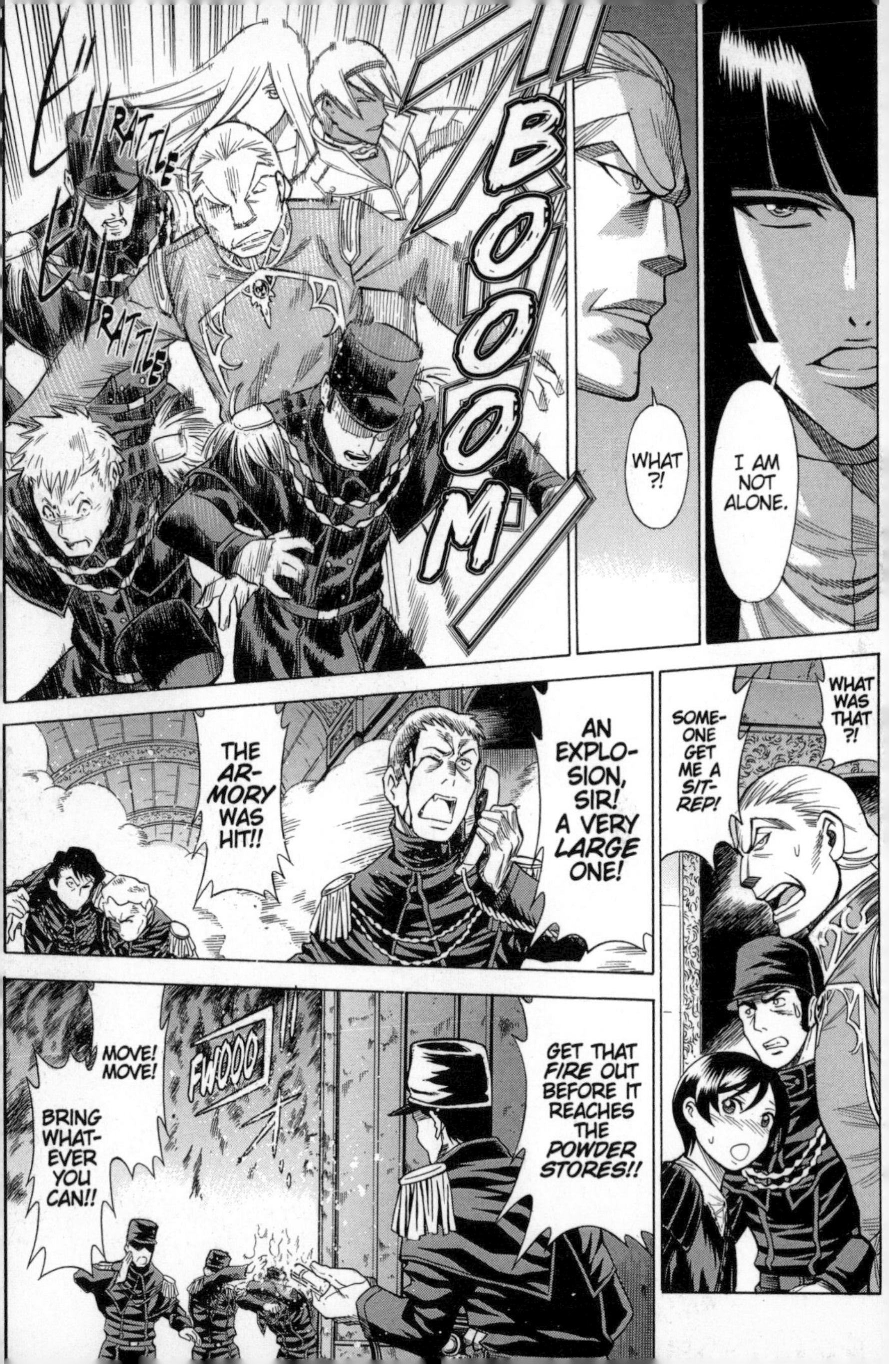
I AM NOT ALONE.
WHAT ?!
BOOOOM
RATTLE
RATTLE
RATTLE
WHAT WAS THAT ?!
SOME-ONE GET ME A SIT-REP!
AN EXPLOSION, SIR! A VERY LARGE ONE!
THE ARMORY WAS HIT!!
GET THAT FIRE OUT BEFORE IT REACHES THE POWDER STORES!!
FWOOO
MOVE! MOVE!
BRING WHATEVER YOU CAN!!

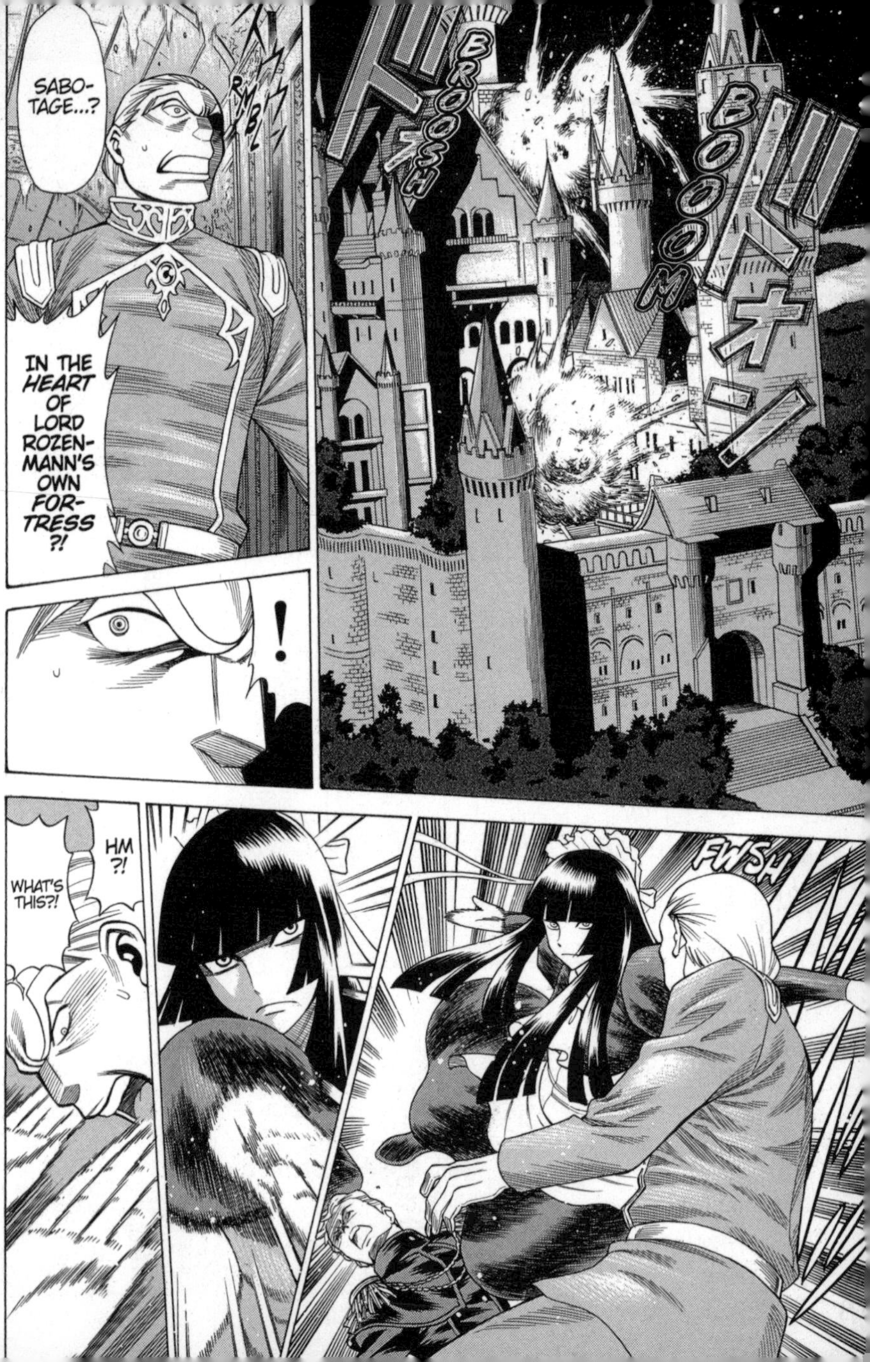

BOOOOM
BROOOSH
RMBL
SABO-TAGE...?
IN THE HEART OF LORD ROZEN-MANN'S OWN FOR-TRESS?!
!
FWSH
HM ?!
WHAT'S THIS?!

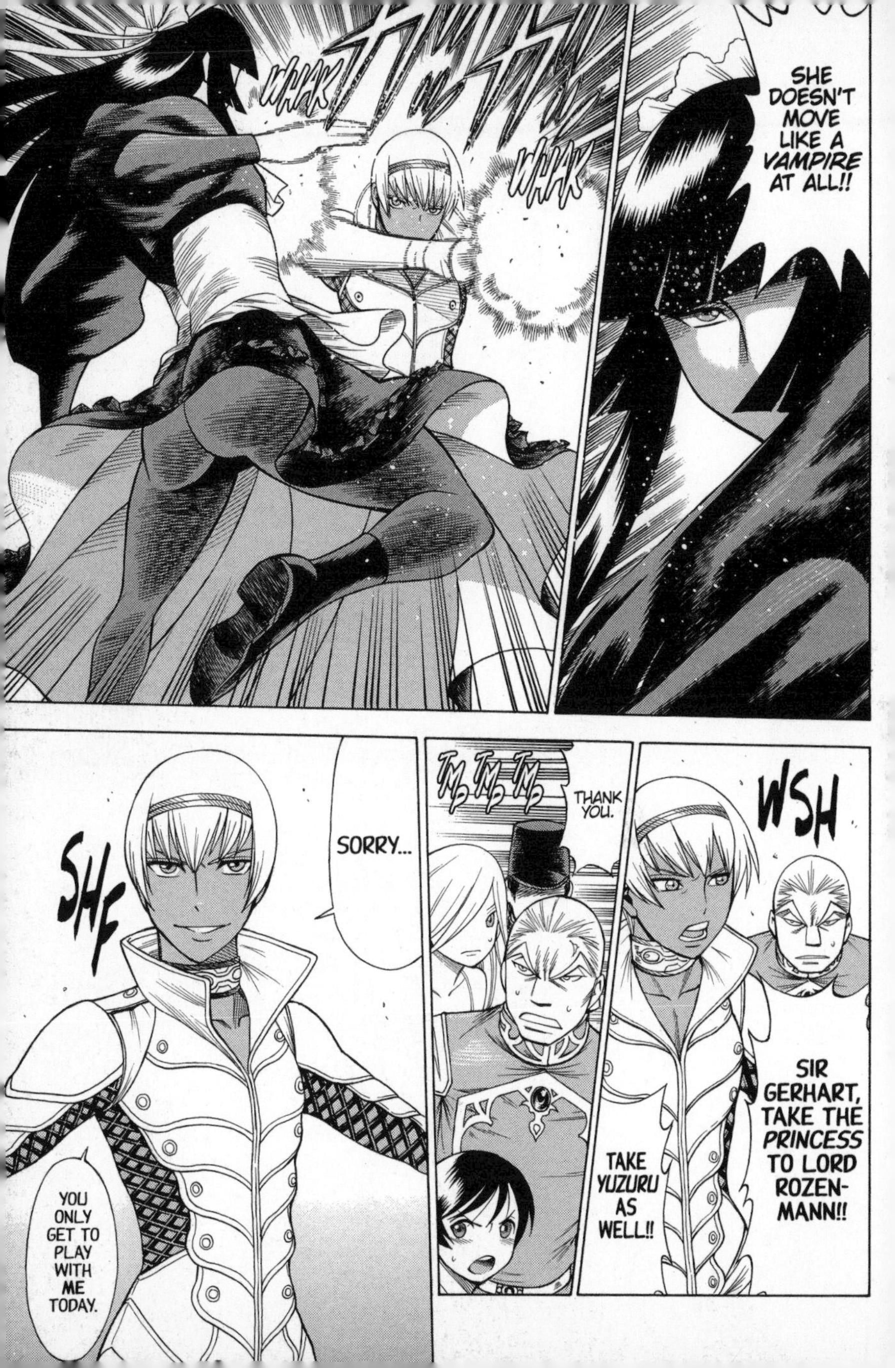
SHE DOESN'T MOVE LIKE A VAMPIRE AT ALL!!
WHAK
WHAK
WSH
SIR GERHART, TAKE THE PRINCESS TO LORD ROZEN-MANN!!
TAKE YUZURU AS WELL!!
TMP TMP TMP
THANK YOU.
SORRY...
SHF
YOU ONLY GET TO PLAY WITH ME TODAY.

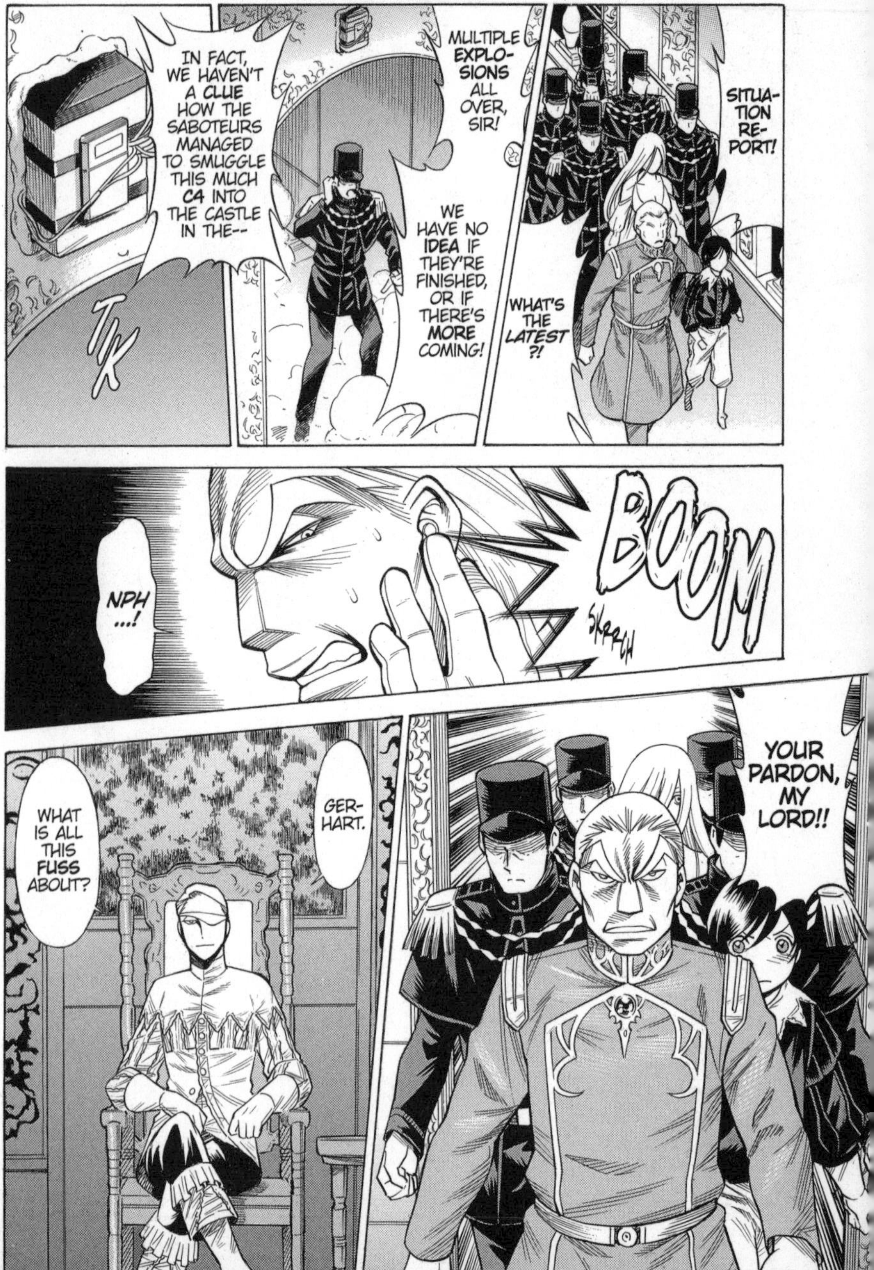
SITUATION REPORT!
WHAT'S THE LATEST?!
MULTIPLE EXPLOSIONS ALL OVER, SIR!
WE HAVE NO IDEA IF THEY'RE FINISHED, OR IF THERE'S MORE COMING!
IN FACT, WE HAVEN'T A CLUE HOW THE SABOTEURS MANAGED TO SMUGGLE THIS MUCH C4 INTO THE CASTLE IN THE--
TIK
BOOM
SKRRCH
NPH ...!
YOUR PARDON, MY LORD!!
GERHART.
WHAT IS ALL THIS FUSS ABOUT?

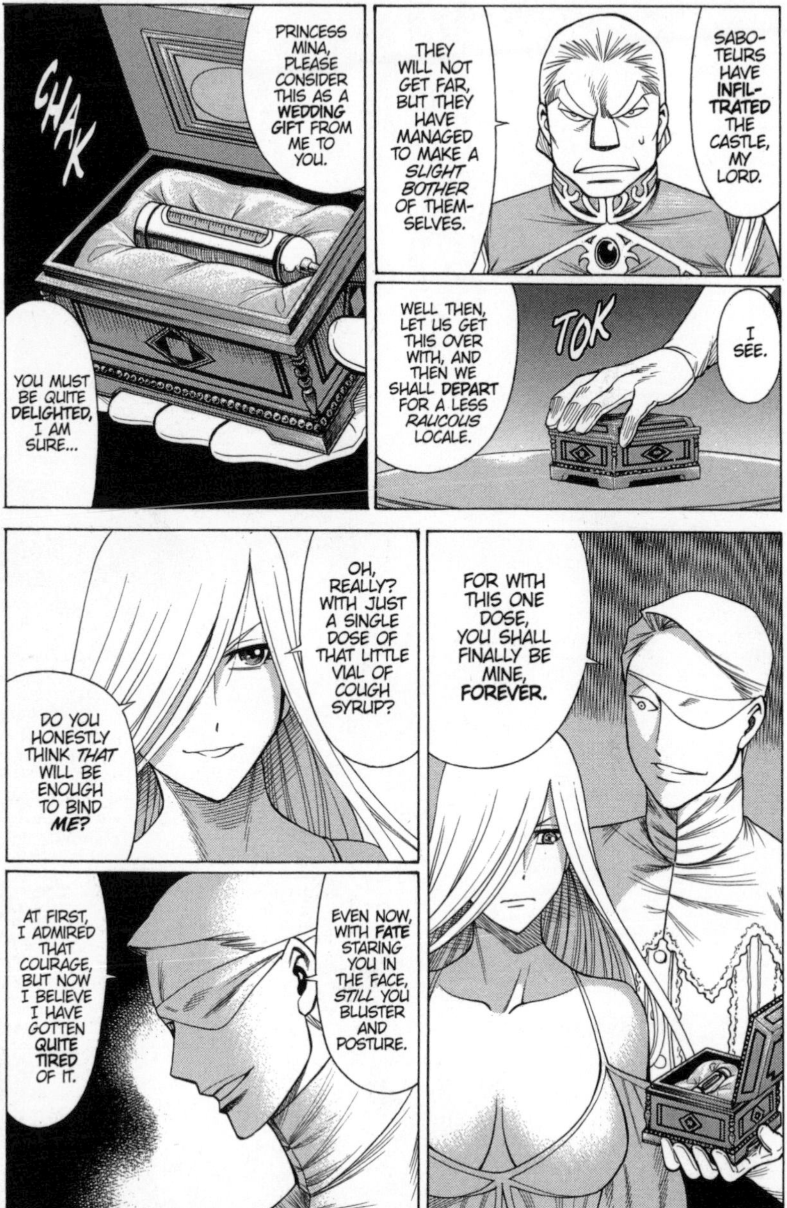
SABOTEURS HAVE INFILTRATED THE CASTLE, MY LORD.
THEY WILL NOT GET FAR, BUT THEY HAVE MANAGED TO MAKE A SLIGHT BOTHER OF THEMSELVES.
I SEE.
TOK
WELL THEN, LET US GET THIS OVER WITH, AND THEN WE SHALL DEPART FOR A LESS RAUCOUS LOCALE.
PRINCESS MINA, PLEASE CONSIDER THIS AS A WEDDING GIFT FROM ME TO YOU.
CHAK
YOU MUST BE QUITE DELIGHTED, I AM SURE...
FOR WITH THIS ONE DOSE, YOU SHALL FINALLY BE MINE, FOREVER.
OH, REALLY? WITH JUST A SINGLE DOSE OF THAT LITTLE VIAL OF COUGH SYRUP?
DO YOU HONESTLY THINK THAT WILL BE ENOUGH TO BIND ME?
EVEN NOW, WITH FATE STARING YOU IN THE FACE, STILL YOU BLUSTER AND POSTURE.
AT FIRST, I ADMIRED THAT COURAGE, BUT NOW I BELIEVE I HAVE GOTTEN QUITE TIRED OF IT.

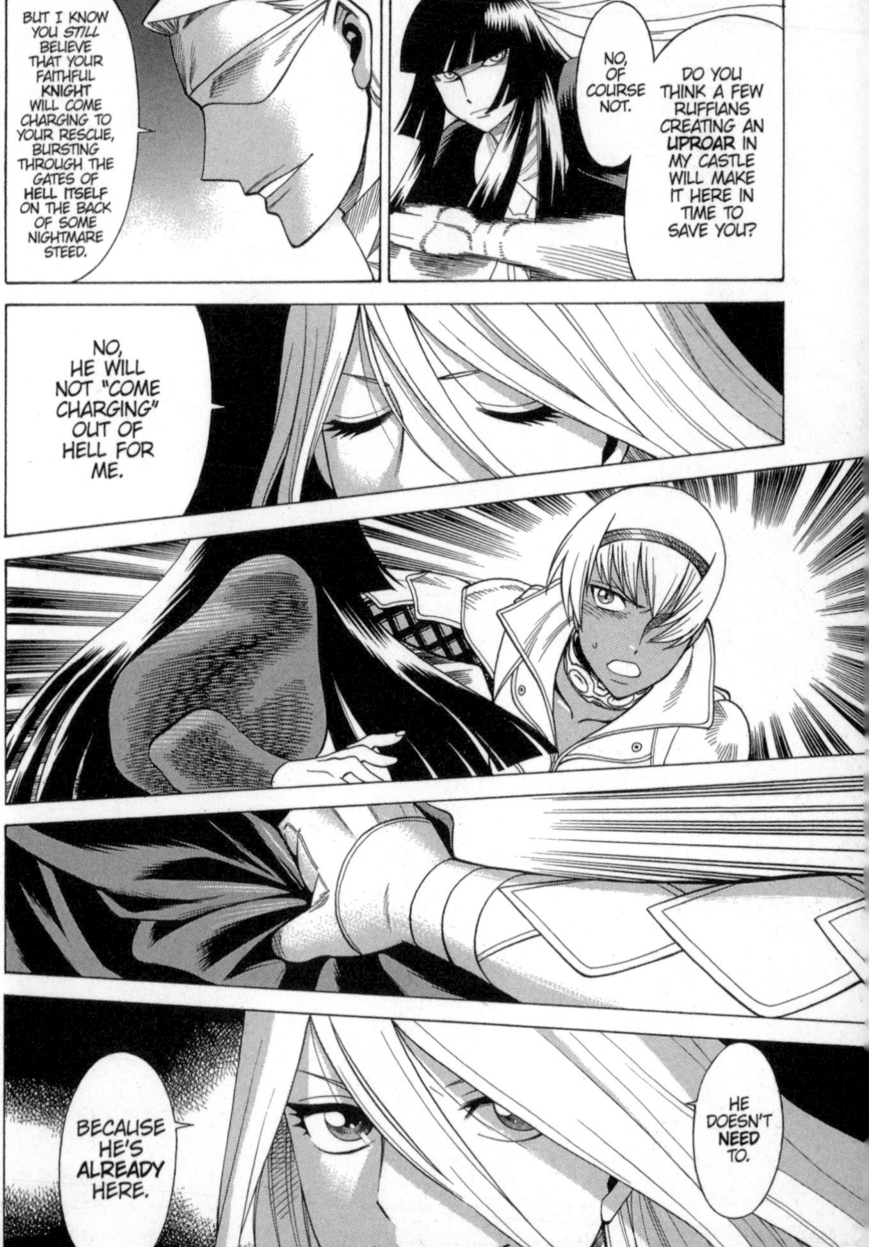
DO YOU THINK A FEW RUFFIANS CREATING AN **UPROAR** IN MY CASTLE WILL MAKE IT HERE IN TIME TO SAVE YOU?
NO, OF COURSE NOT.
BUT I KNOW YOU *STILL* BELIEVE THAT YOUR FAITHFUL **KNIGHT** WILL COME CHARGING TO YOUR RESCUE, BURSTING THROUGH THE GATES OF **HELL ITSELF** ON THE BACK OF SOME NIGHTMARE STEED.
NO, HE WILL NOT "COME CHARGING" OUT OF HELL FOR ME.
HE DOESN'T **NEED** TO.
BECAUSE HE'S **ALREADY** HERE.

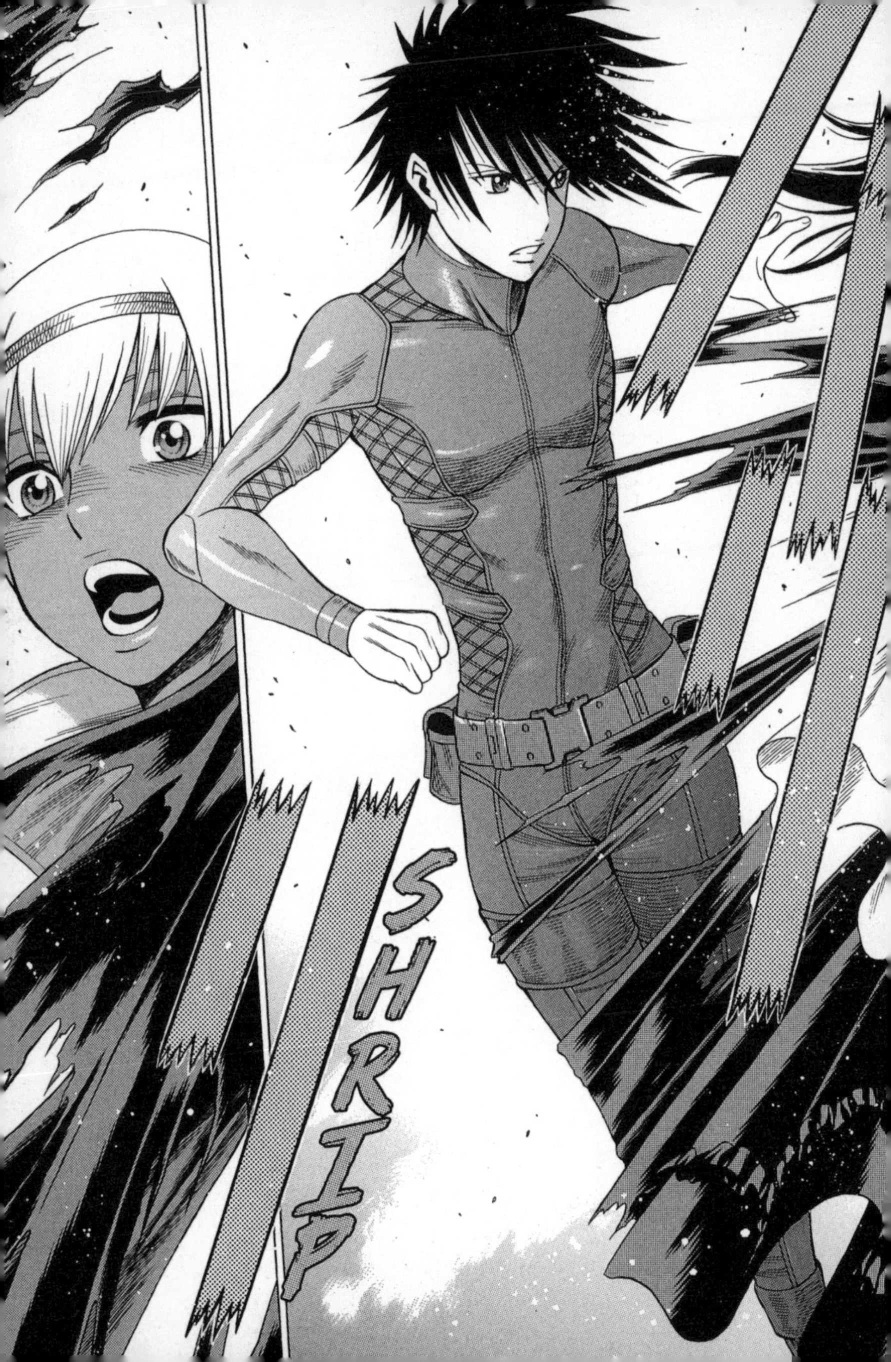
SHRIP

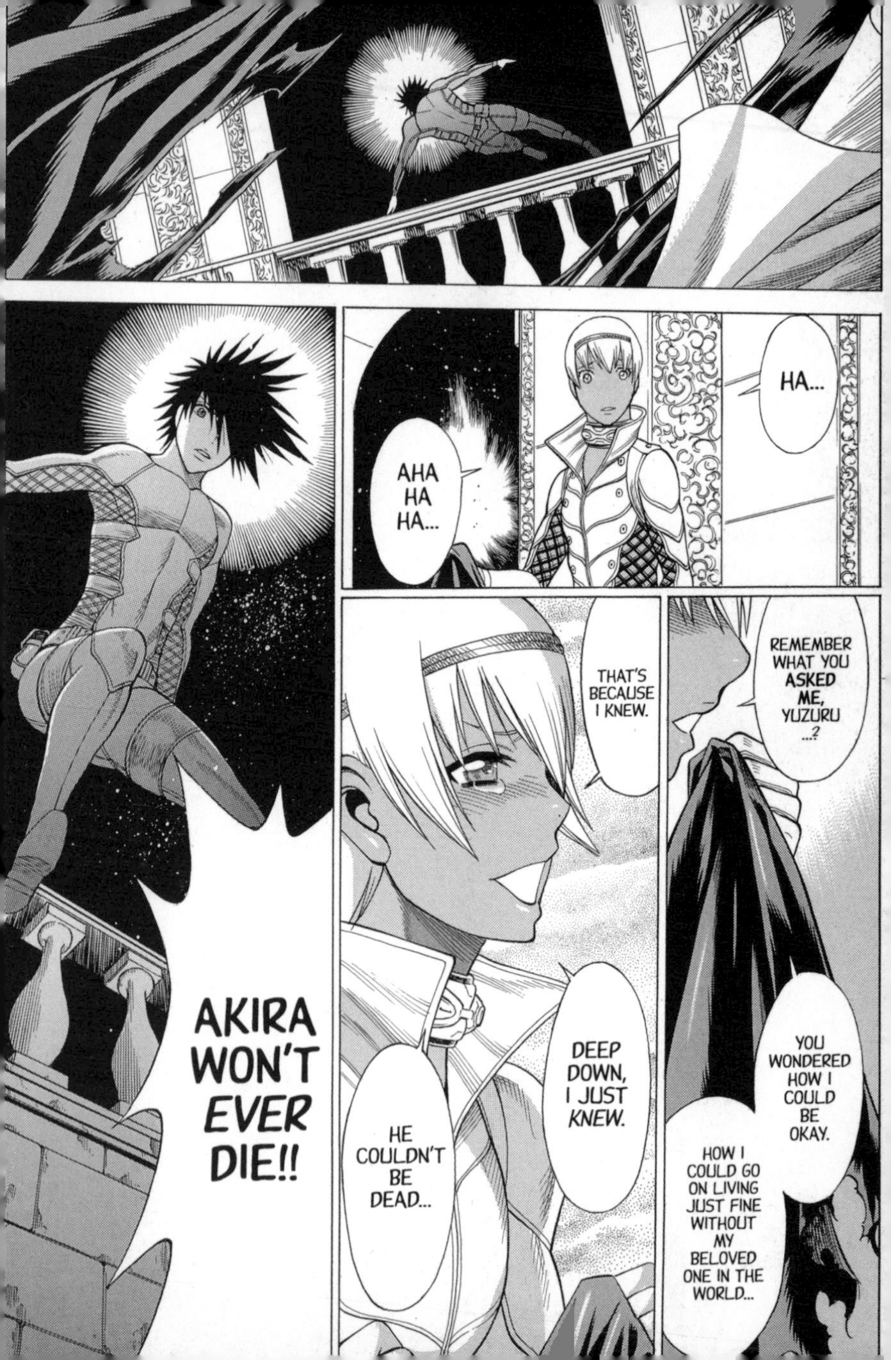
HA...
AHA HA HA...
REMEMBER WHAT YOU ASKED ME, YUZURU...?
YOU WONDERED HOW I COULD BE OKAY.
HOW I COULD GO ON LIVING JUST FINE WITHOUT MY BELOVED ONE IN THE WORLD...
THAT'S BECAUSE I KNEW.
DEEP DOWN, I JUST KNEW.
HE COULDN'T BE DEAD...
AKIRA WON'T EVER DIE!!

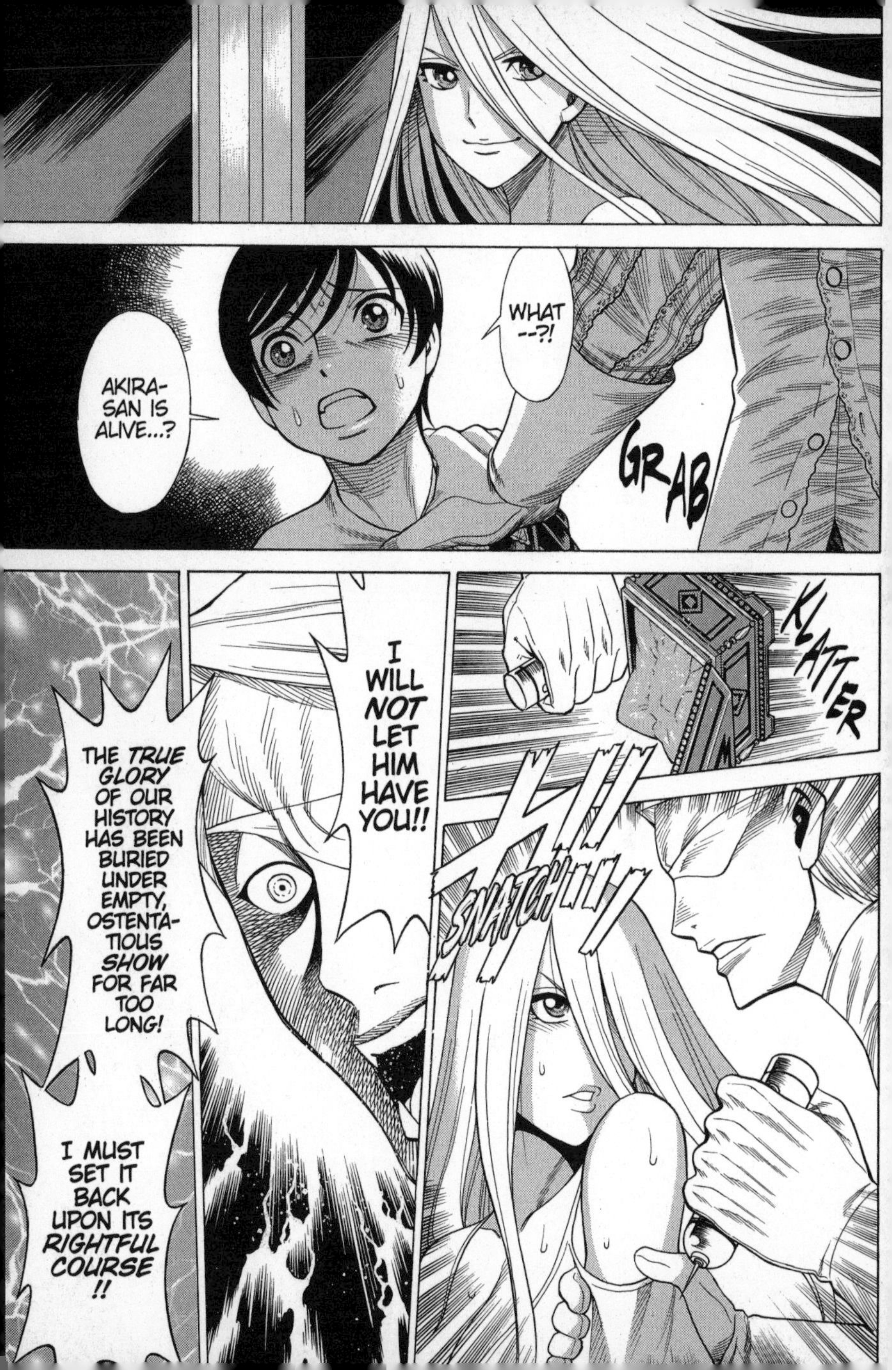
WHAT --?!
AKIRA-SAN IS ALIVE...?
GRAB
KLATTER
SNATCH!!
I WILL NOT LET HIM HAVE YOU!!
THE TRUE GLORY OF OUR HISTORY HAS BEEN BURIED UNDER EMPTY, OSTENTATIOUS SHOW FOR FAR TOO LONG!
I MUST SET IT BACK UPON ITS RIGHTFUL COURSE !!

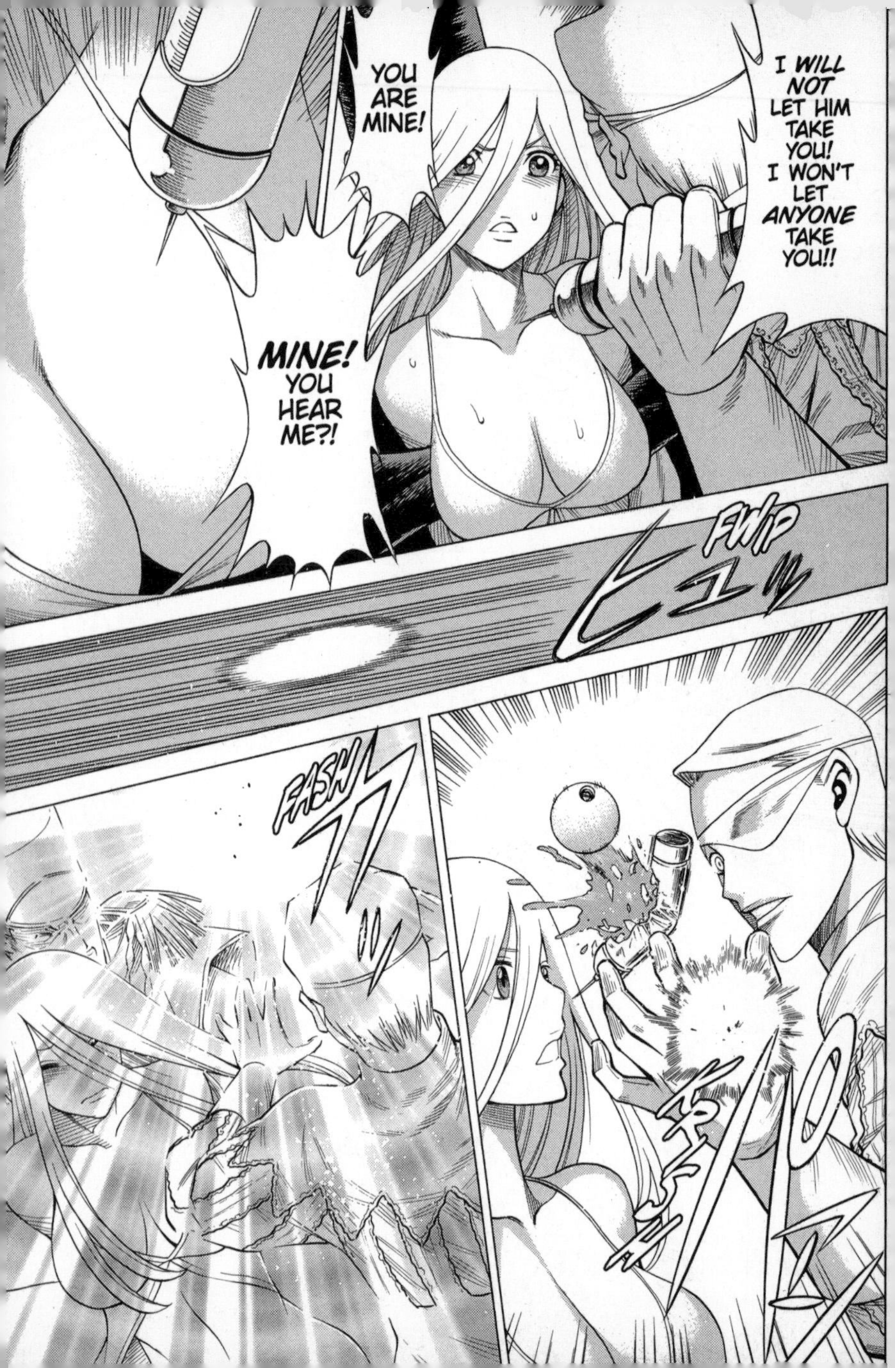

I WILL NOT LET HIM TAKE YOU! I WON'T LET ANYONE TAKE YOU!!
YOU ARE MINE!
MINE! YOU HEAR ME?!
FWIP
FLASH

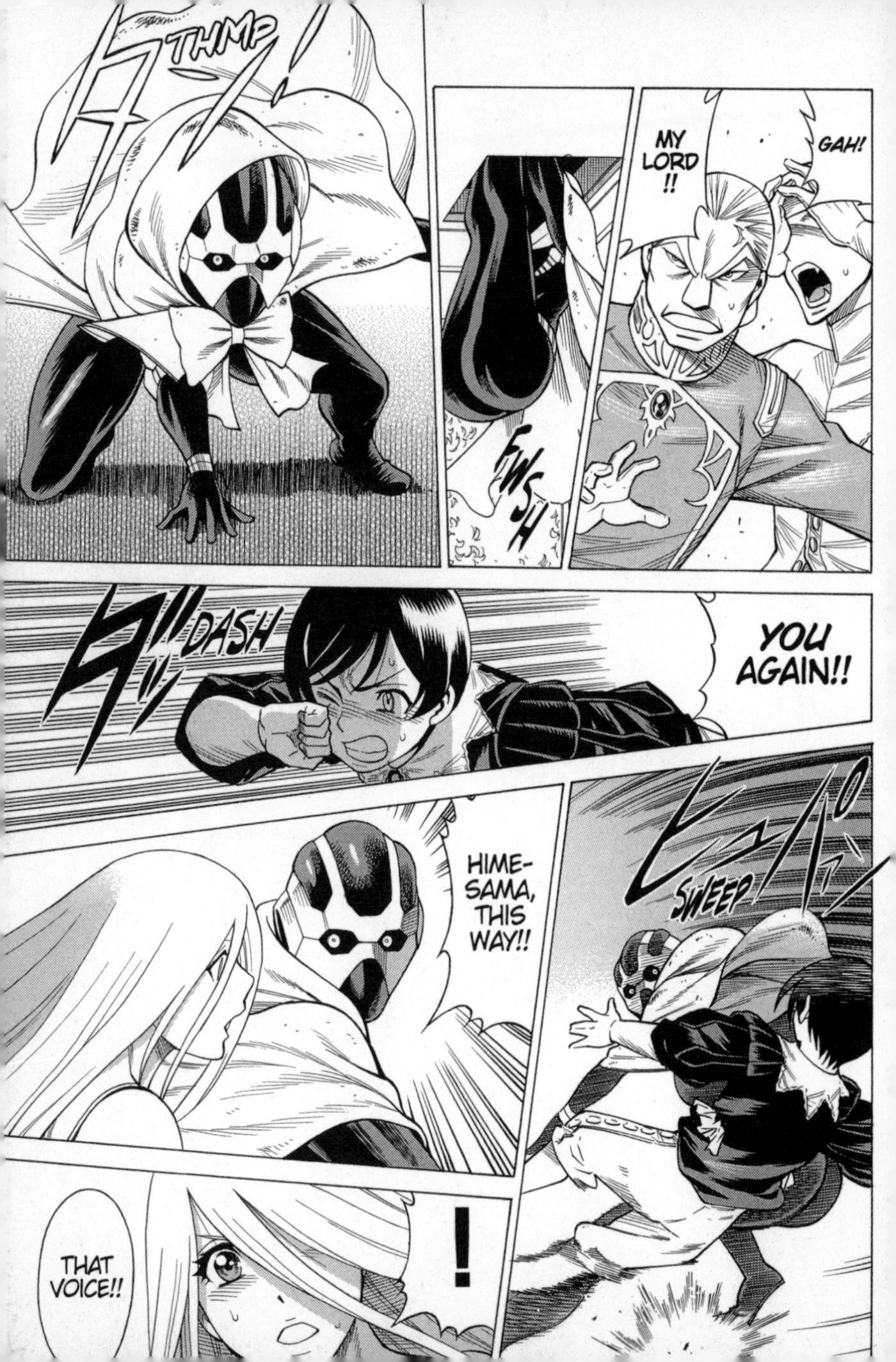
GAH!
MY LORD !!
FWSH
THMP!
YOU AGAIN!!
DASH
SWEEP
HIME-SAMA, THIS WAY!!
!
THAT VOICE!!

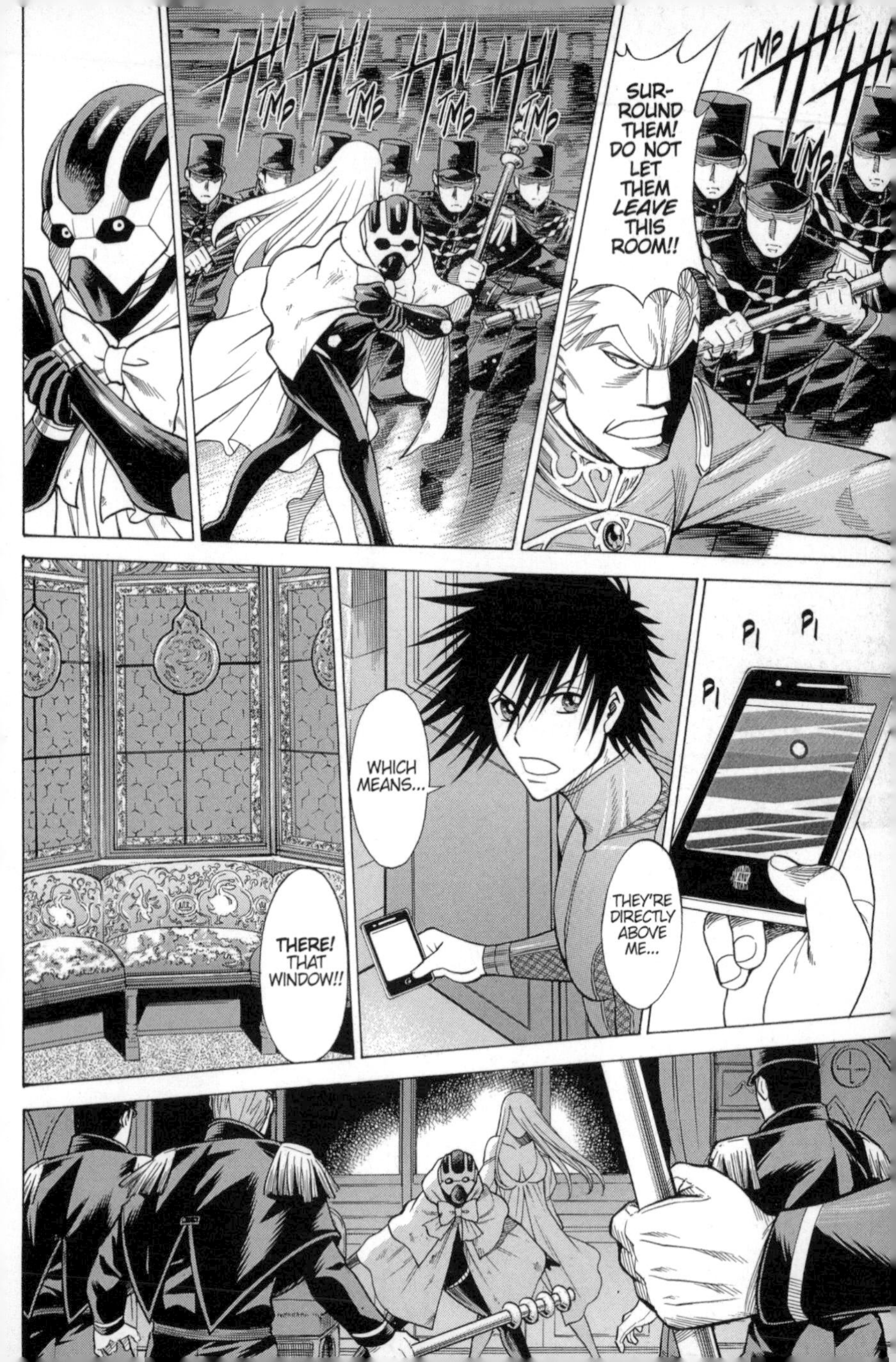
TMP
TMP
SUR-ROUND THEM! DO NOT LET THEM LEAVE THIS ROOM!!
TMP
TMP
TMP
TMP
PI PI PI
THEY'RE DIRECTLY ABOVE ME...
WHICH MEANS...
THERE! THAT WINDOW!!

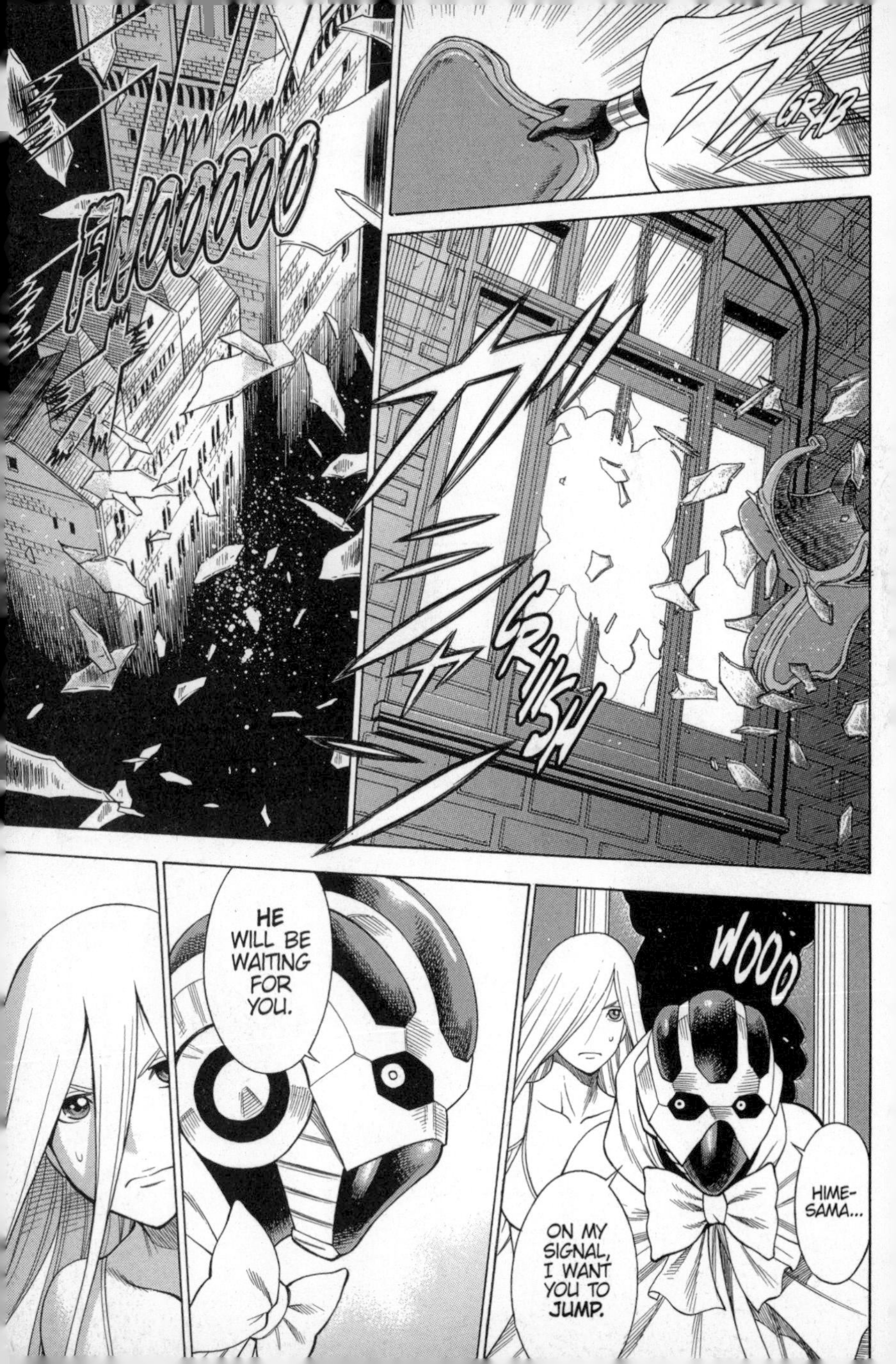
GRAB
CRUSH
FWOOOOO
WOOO
HIME-SAMA...
ON MY SIGNAL, I WANT YOU TO JUMP.
HE WILL BE WAITING FOR YOU.

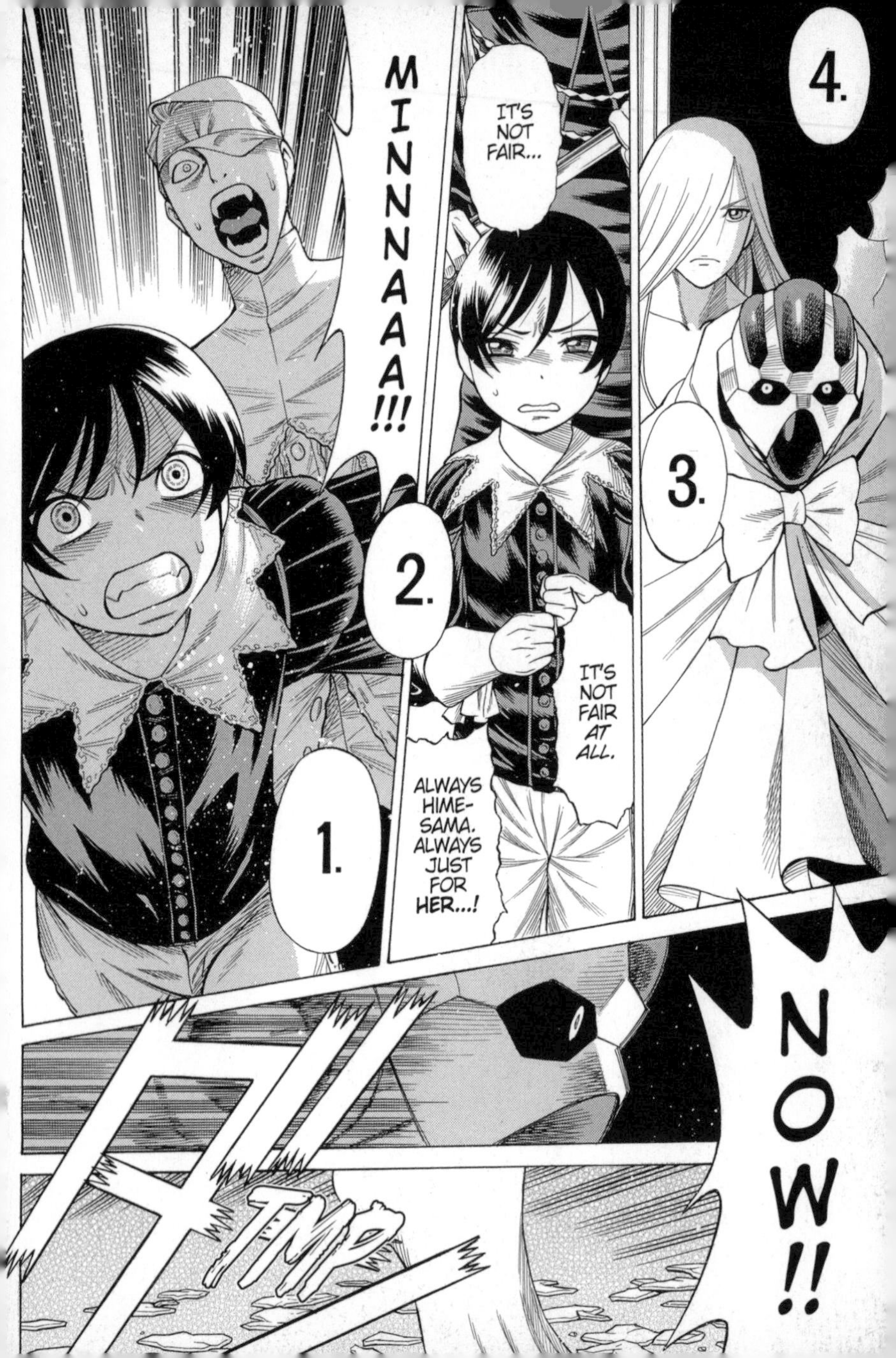

4.
3.
IT'S NOT FAIR...
2.
IT'S NOT FAIR AT ALL.
ALWAYS HIME-SAMA. ALWAYS JUST FOR HER...!
MINNNAAAA!!!
1.
NOW!!
TMP

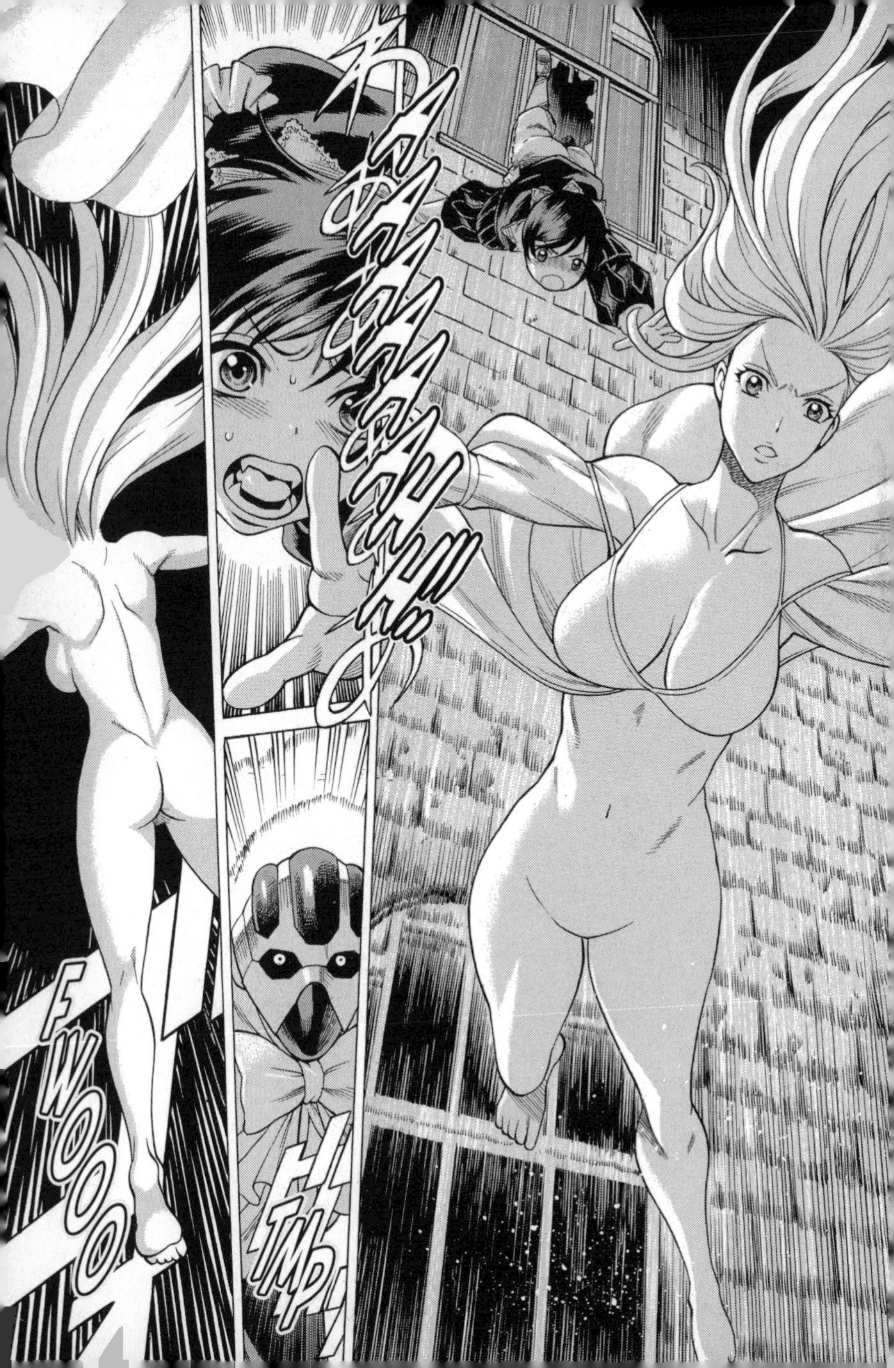
KYAAAAAAHHH!!
HTMP!
FWOOO

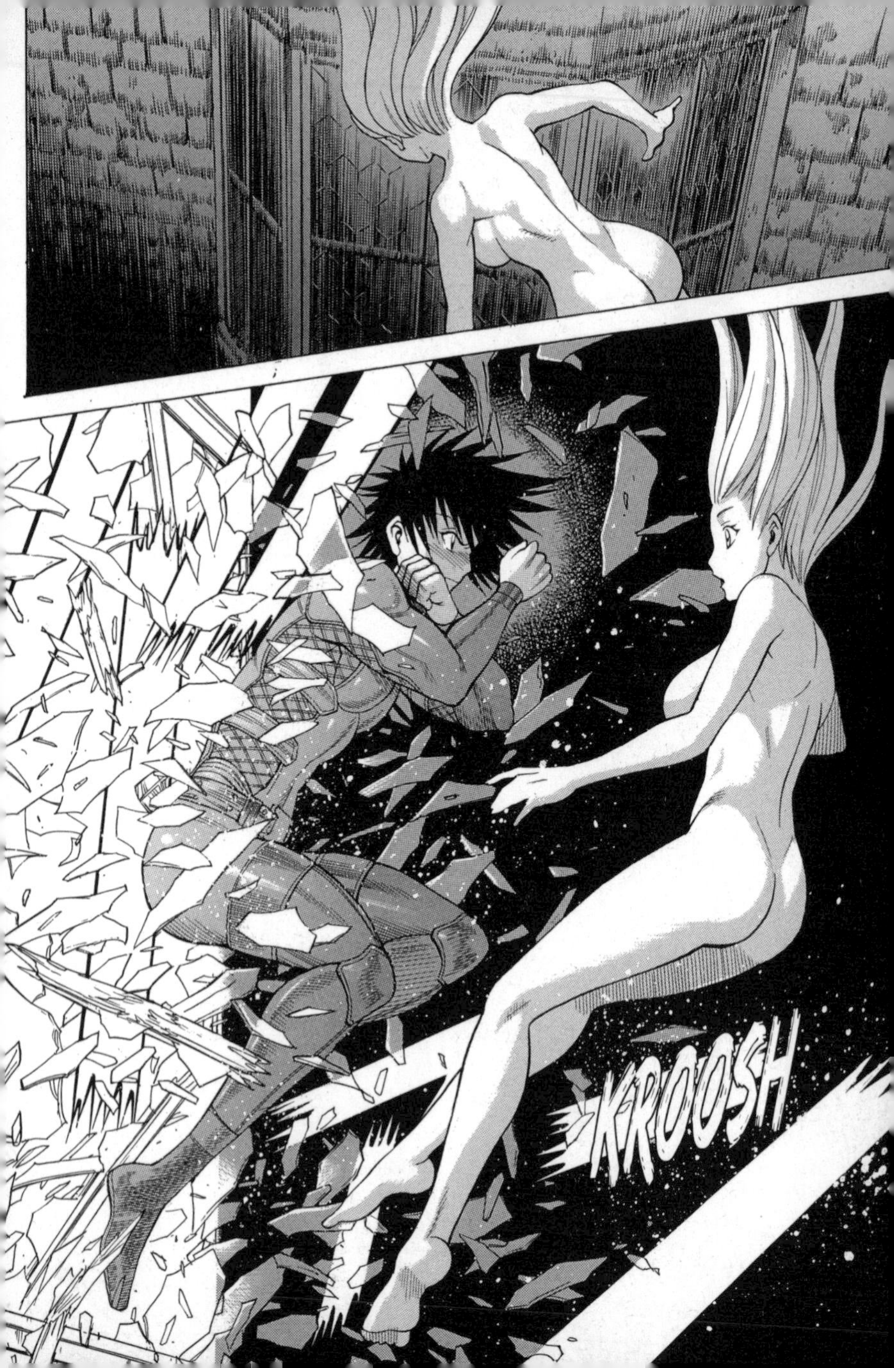
KROOSH

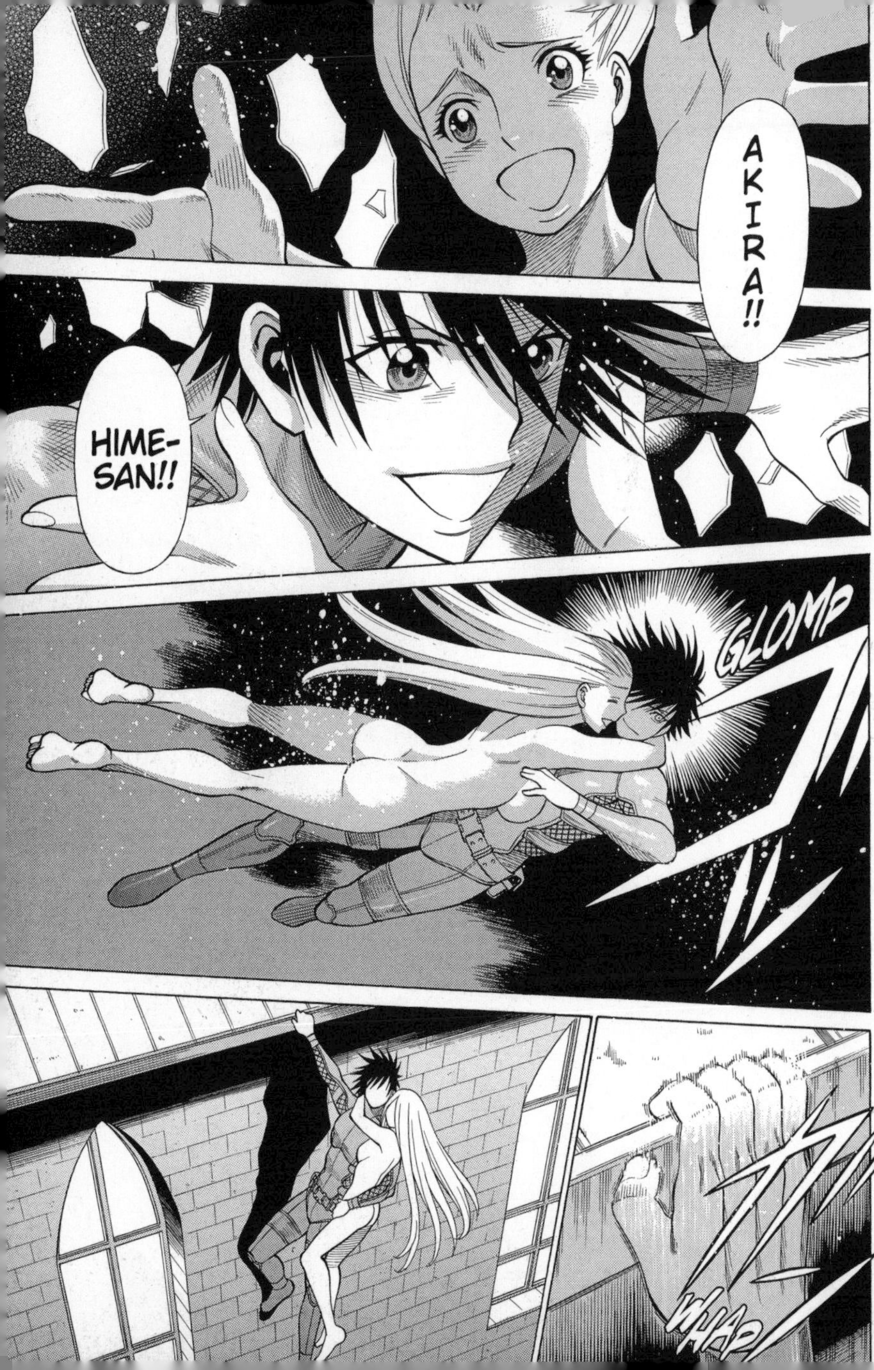
AKIRA!!
HIME-SAN!!
GLOMP
WHAP

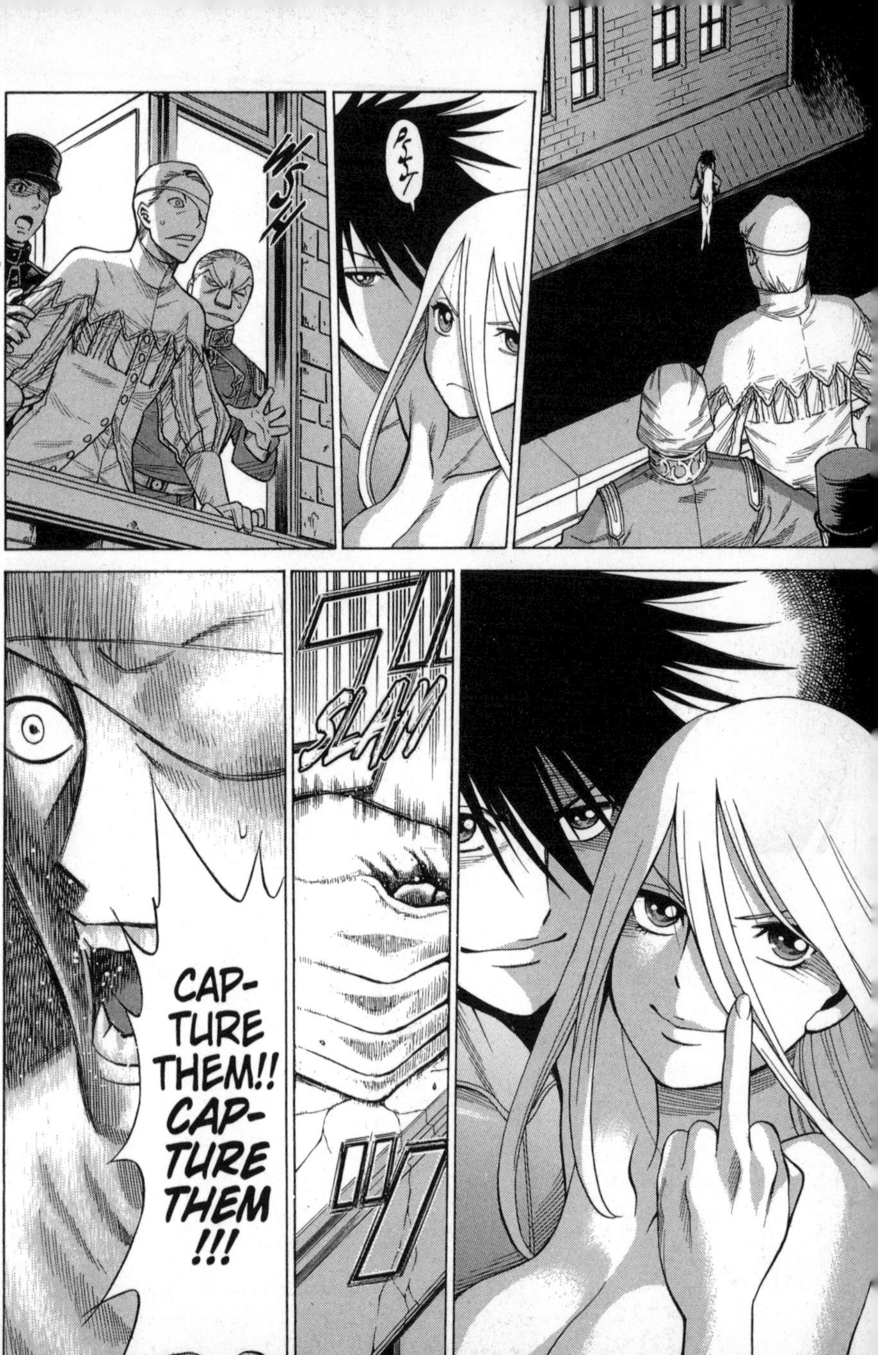
WSHH
SLAM
CAP-
TURE
THEM!!
CAP-
TURE
THEM
!!!

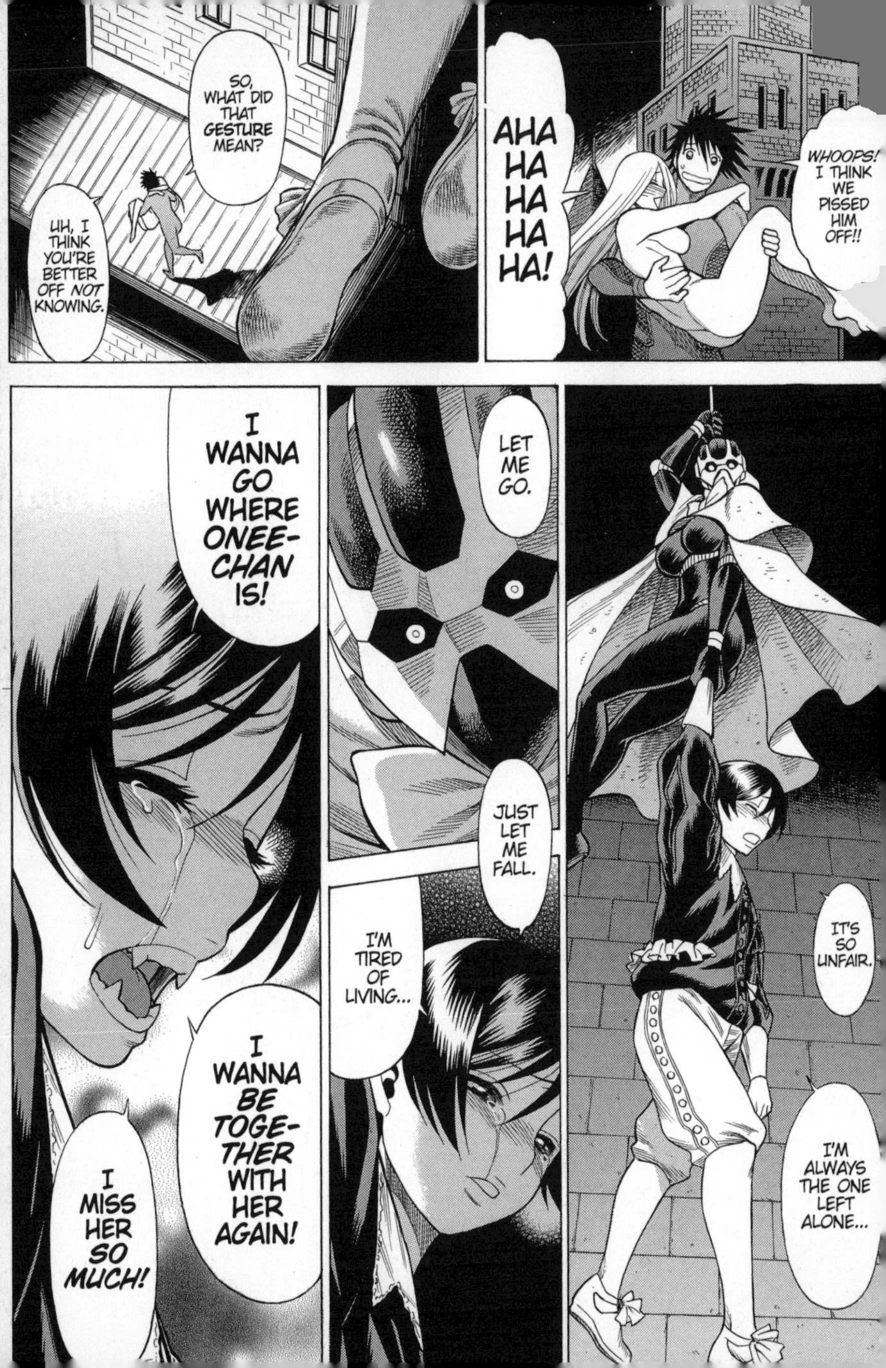
WHOOPS! I THINK WE PISSED HIM OFF!!
AHA HA HA HA HA!
SO, WHAT DID THAT GESTURE MEAN?
UH, I THINK YOU'RE BETTER OFF *NOT* KNOWING.
IT'S SO UNFAIR.
I'M ALWAYS THE ONE LEFT ALONE...
LET ME GO.
JUST LET ME FALL.
I'M TIRED OF LIVING...
I WANNA GO WHERE ONEE-CHAN IS!
I WANNA *BE TOGETHER* WITH HER AGAIN!
I MISS HER *SO MUCH!*

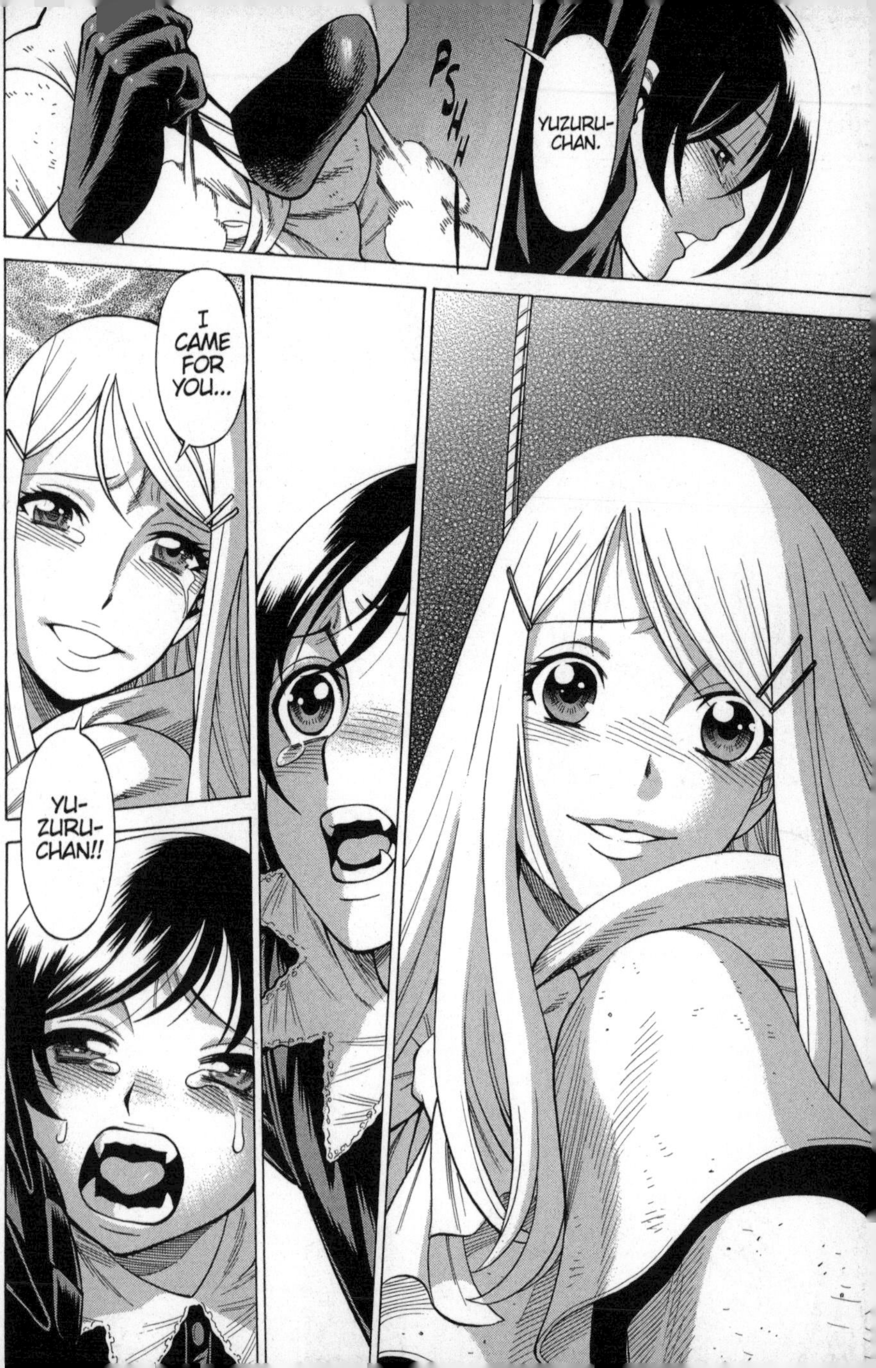
YUZURU-CHAN.
PSHH
I CAME FOR YOU...
YU-ZURU-CHAN!!

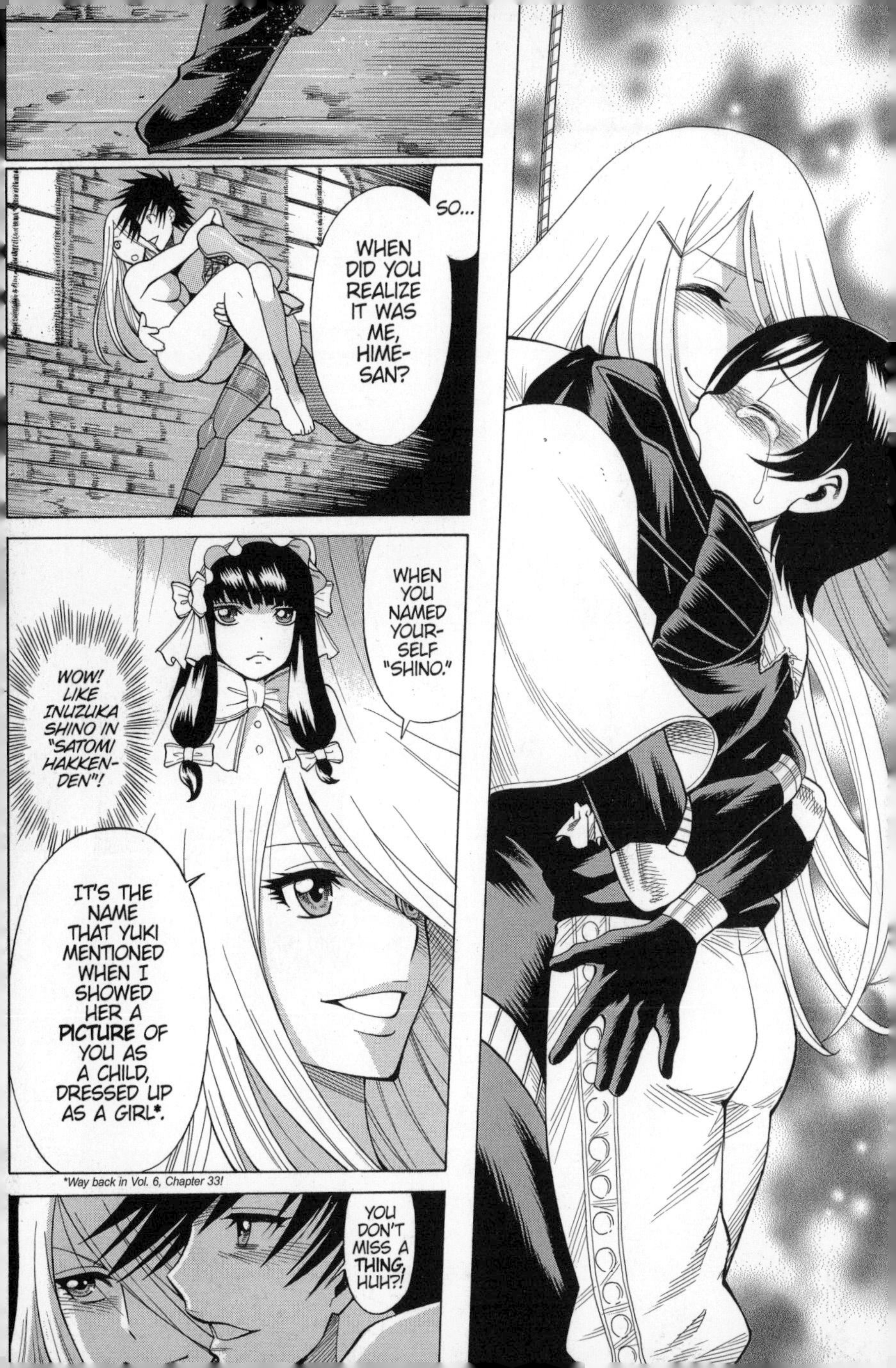
SO...
WHEN DID YOU REALIZE IT WAS ME, HIME-SAN?
WHEN YOU NAMED YOURSELF "SHINO."
WOW! LIKE INUZUKA SHINO IN "SATOMI HAKKENDEN"!
IT'S THE NAME THAT YUKI MENTIONED WHEN I SHOWED HER A **PICTURE** OF YOU AS A CHILD, DRESSED UP AS A GIRL*.
YOU DON'T MISS A THING, HUH?!
*Way back in Vol. 6, Chapter 33!

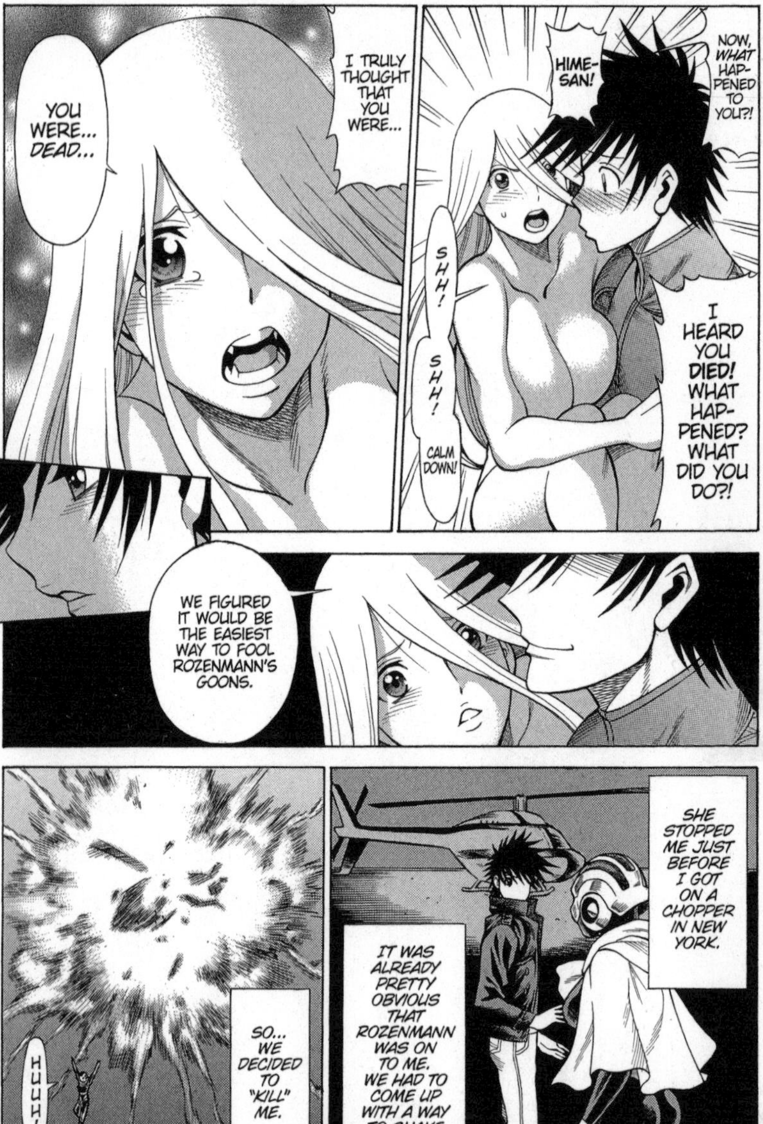
NOW, WHAT HAP-PENED TO YOU?!
HIME-SAN!
I HEARD YOU DIED! WHAT HAP-PENED? WHAT DID YOU DO?!
SHH! SHH!
CALM DOWN!
I TRULY THOUGHT THAT YOU WERE...
YOU WERE... DEAD...
WE FIGURED IT WOULD BE THE EASIEST WAY TO FOOL ROZENMANN'S GOONS.
SHE STOPPED ME JUST BEFORE I GOT ON A CHOPPER IN NEW YORK.
IT WAS ALREADY PRETTY OBVIOUS THAT ROZENMANN WAS ON TO ME. WE HAD TO COME UP WITH A WAY TO SHAKE 'EM.
SO... WE DECIDED TO "KILL" ME.
HUUH!

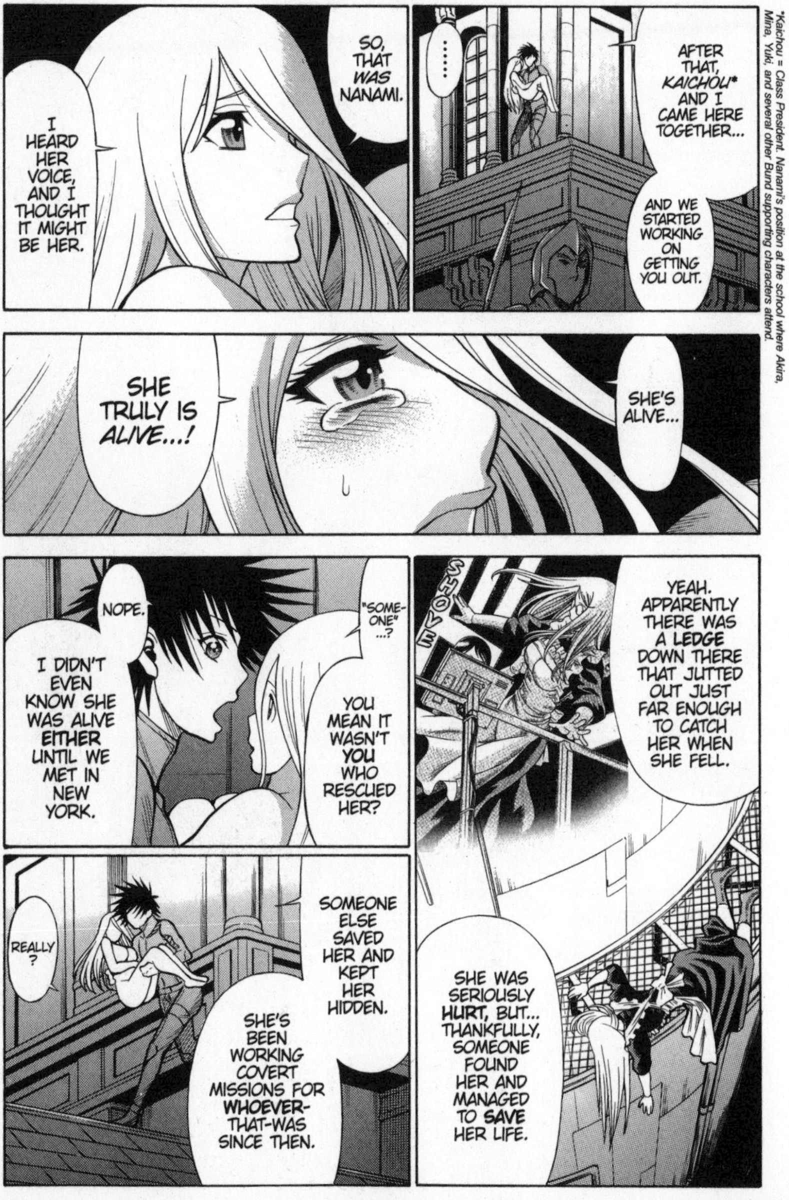
AFTER THAT, KAICHOU* AND I CAME HERE TOGETHER...
AND WE STARTED WORKING ON GETTING YOU OUT.
......
SO, THAT WAS NANAMI.
I HEARD HER VOICE, AND I THOUGHT IT MIGHT BE HER.
SHE'S ALIVE...
SHE TRULY IS ALIVE...!
YEAH. APPARENTLY THERE WAS A LEDGE DOWN THERE THAT JUTTED OUT JUST FAR ENOUGH TO CATCH HER WHEN SHE FELL.
SHOVE
SHE WAS SERIOUSLY HURT, BUT... THANKFULLY, SOMEONE FOUND HER AND MANAGED TO SAVE HER LIFE.
"SOME-ONE" ...?
YOU MEAN IT WASN'T YOU WHO RESCUED HER?
NOPE.
I DIDN'T EVEN KNOW SHE WAS ALIVE EITHER UNTIL WE MET IN NEW YORK.
SOMEONE ELSE SAVED HER AND KEPT HER HIDDEN.
SHE'S BEEN WORKING COVERT MISSIONS FOR WHOEVER-THAT-WAS SINCE THEN.
REALLY?

*Kaichou = Class President. Nanami's position at the school where Akira, Mina, Yuki, and several other Bund supporting characters attend.

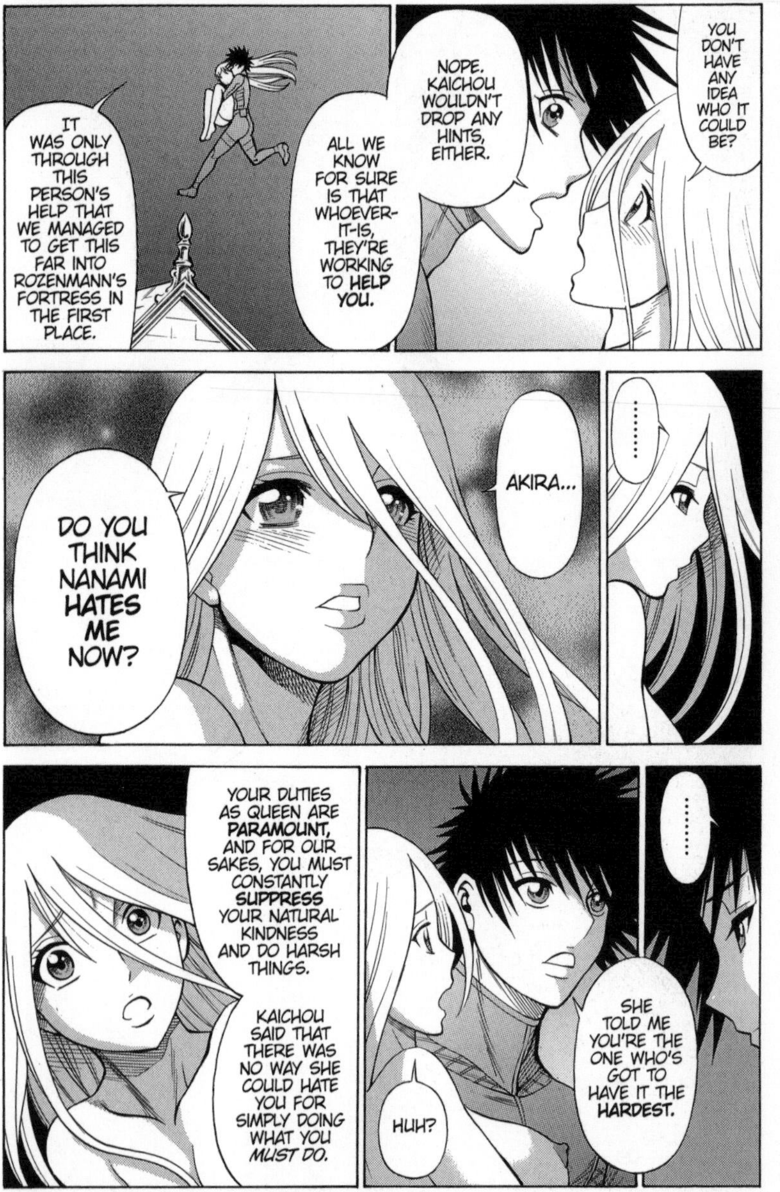
YOU DON'T HAVE ANY IDEA WHO IT COULD BE?
NOPE. KAICHOU WOULDN'T DROP ANY HINTS, EITHER.
ALL WE KNOW FOR SURE IS THAT WHOEVER-IT-IS, THEY'RE WORKING TO **HELP YOU.**
IT WAS ONLY THROUGH THIS PERSON'S HELP THAT WE MANAGED TO GET THIS FAR INTO ROZENMANN'S FORTRESS IN THE FIRST PLACE.
......
AKIRA...
DO YOU THINK NANAMI **HATES** ME NOW?
......
SHE TOLD ME YOU'RE THE ONE WHO'S GOT TO HAVE IT THE **HARDEST.**
HUH?
YOUR DUTIES AS QUEEN ARE **PARAMOUNT,** AND FOR OUR SAKES, YOU MUST CONSTANTLY **SUPPRESS** YOUR NATURAL KINDNESS AND DO HARSH THINGS.
KAICHOU SAID THAT THERE WAS NO WAY SHE COULD HATE YOU FOR SIMPLY DOING WHAT YOU *MUST DO.*

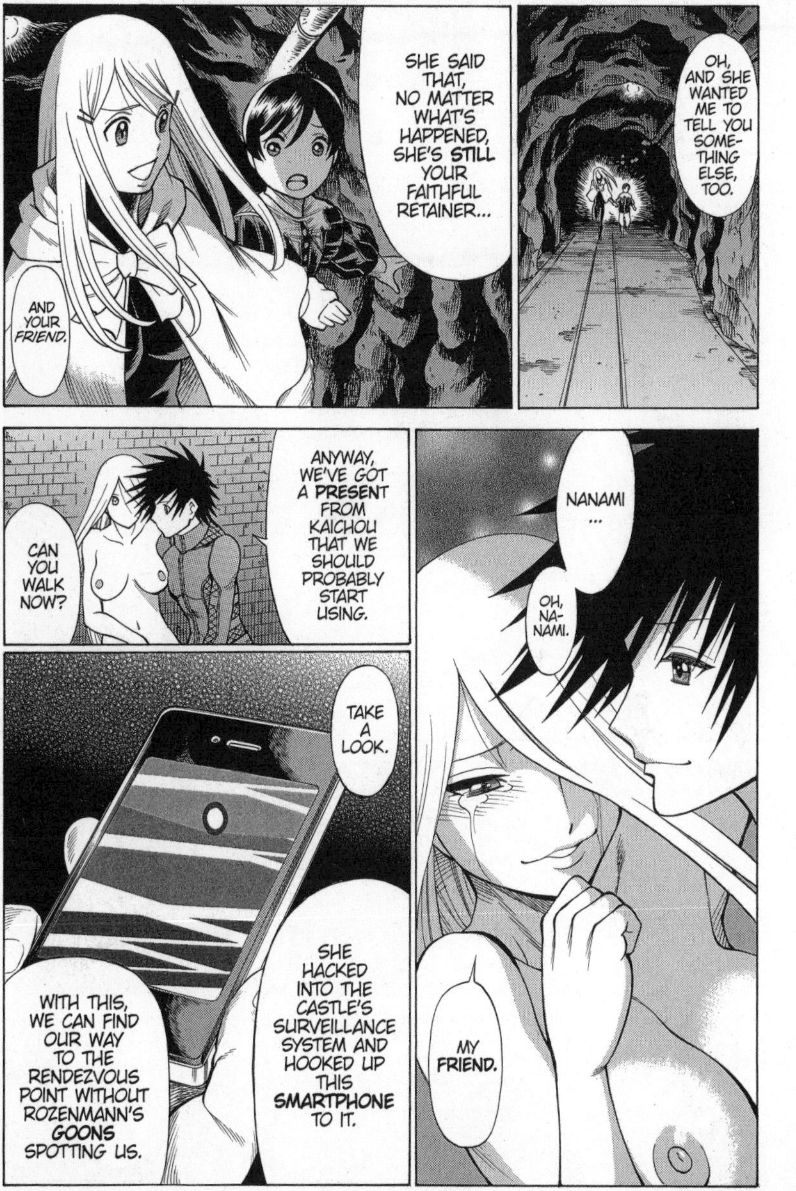
OH, AND SHE WANTED ME TO TELL YOU SOME-THING ELSE, TOO.
SHE SAID THAT, NO MATTER WHAT'S HAPPENED, SHE'S **STILL** YOUR FAITHFUL RETAINER...
AND YOUR FRIEND.
NANAMI ...
OH, NA-NAMI.
MY **FRIEND.**
ANYWAY, WE'VE GOT A **PRESENT** FROM KAICHOU THAT WE SHOULD PROBABLY START USING.
CAN YOU WALK NOW?
TAKE A LOOK.
SHE HACKED INTO THE CASTLE'S SURVEILLANCE SYSTEM AND HOOKED UP THIS **SMARTPHONE** TO IT.
WITH THIS, WE CAN FIND OUR WAY TO THE RENDEZVOUS POINT WITHOUT ROZENMANN'S **GOONS** SPOTTING US.

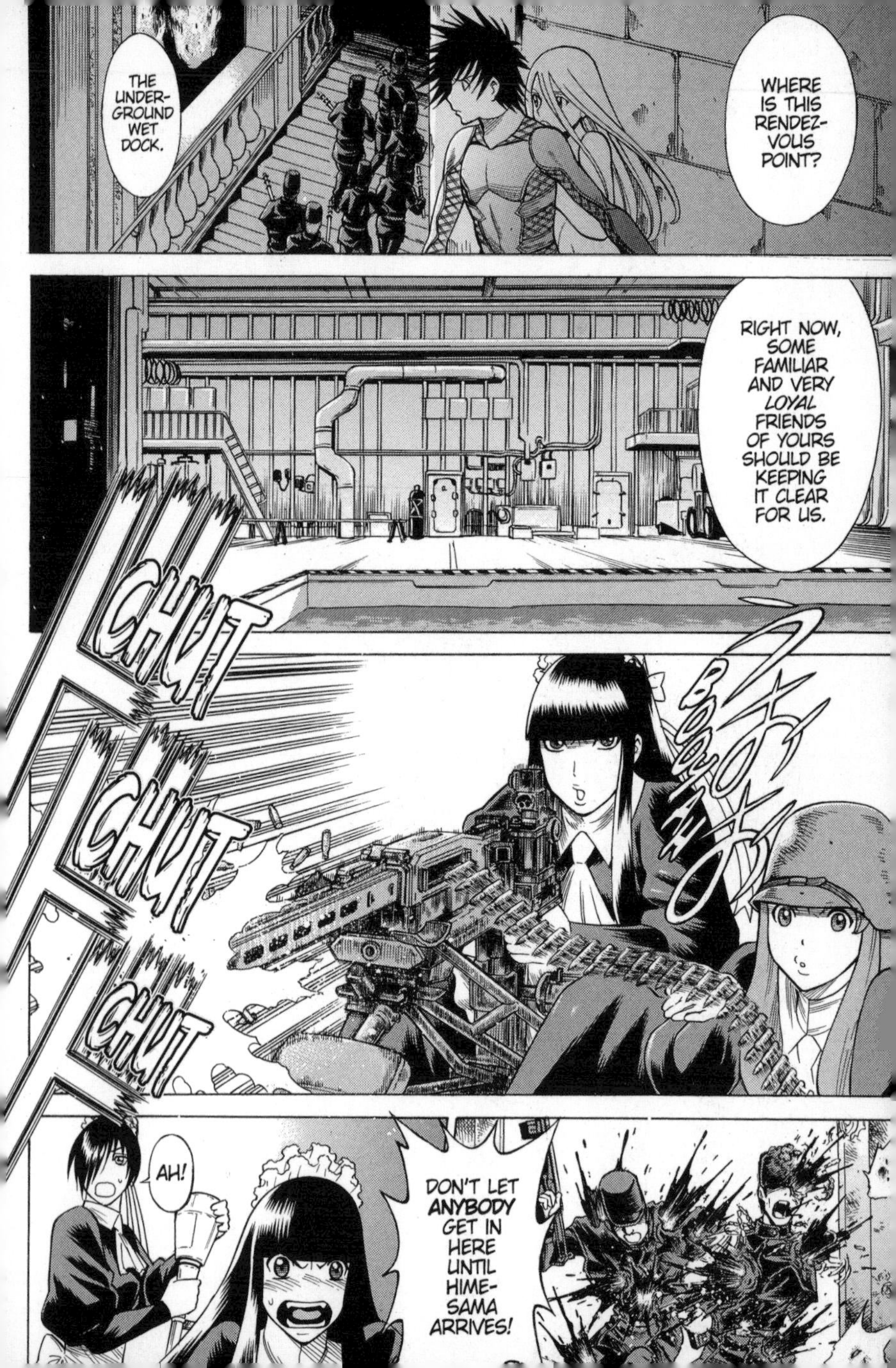
WHERE IS THIS RENDEZ-VOUS POINT?
THE UNDER-GROUND WET DOCK.
RIGHT NOW, SOME FAMILIAR AND VERY *LOYAL* FRIENDS OF YOURS SHOULD BE KEEPING IT CLEAR FOR US.
CHUT
CHUT
CHUT
CHUT
DON'T LET **ANYBODY** GET IN HERE UNTIL HIME-SAMA ARRIVES!
AH!

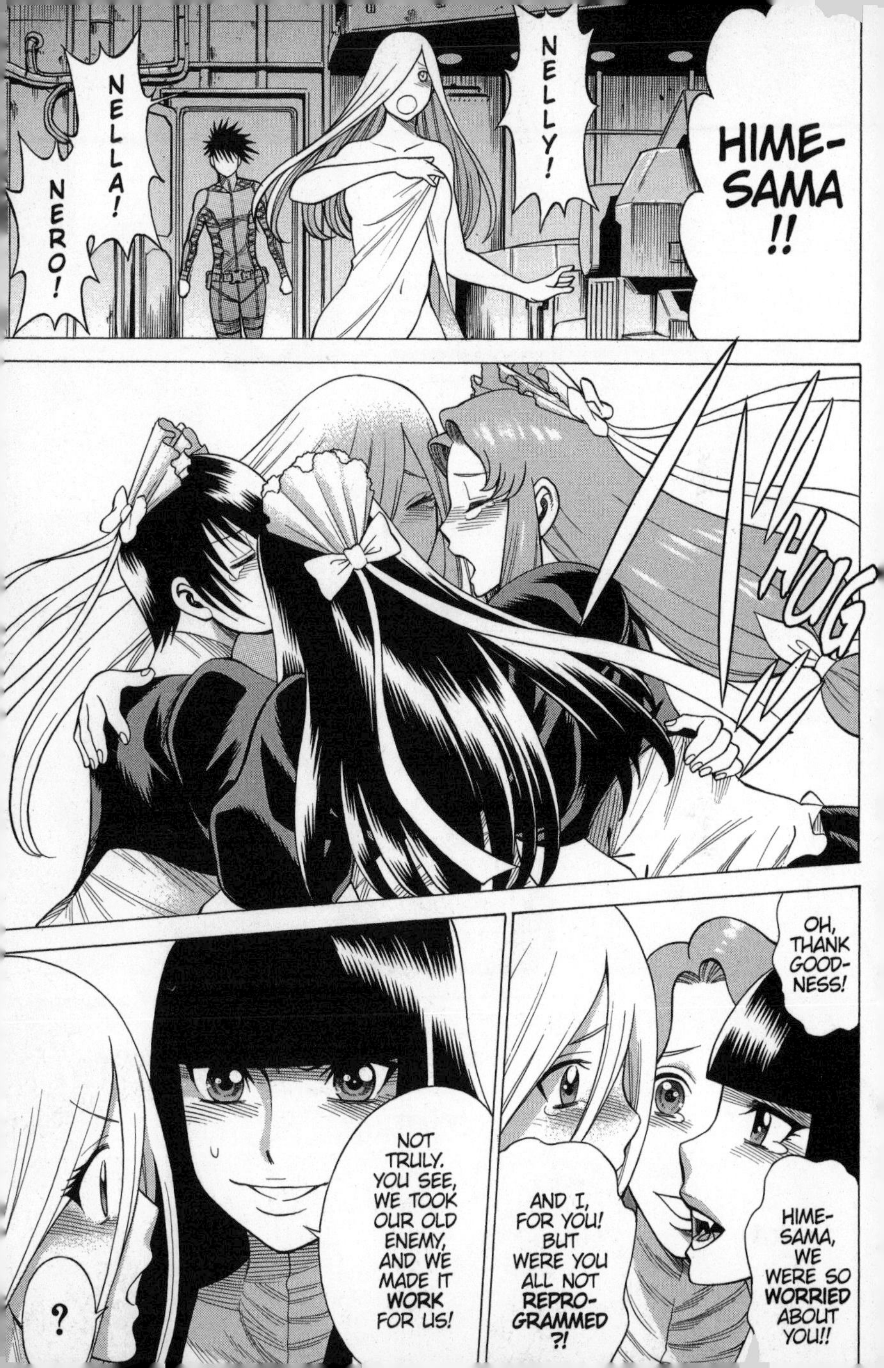
HIME-SAMA!!
NELLY!
NELLA!
NERO!
HUG
OH, THANK GOODNESS!
HIME-SAMA, WE WERE SO WORRIED ABOUT YOU!!
AND I, FOR YOU! BUT WERE YOU ALL NOT REPROGRAMMED?!
NOT TRULY. YOU SEE, WE TOOK OUR OLD ENEMY, AND WE MADE IT WORK FOR US!
?

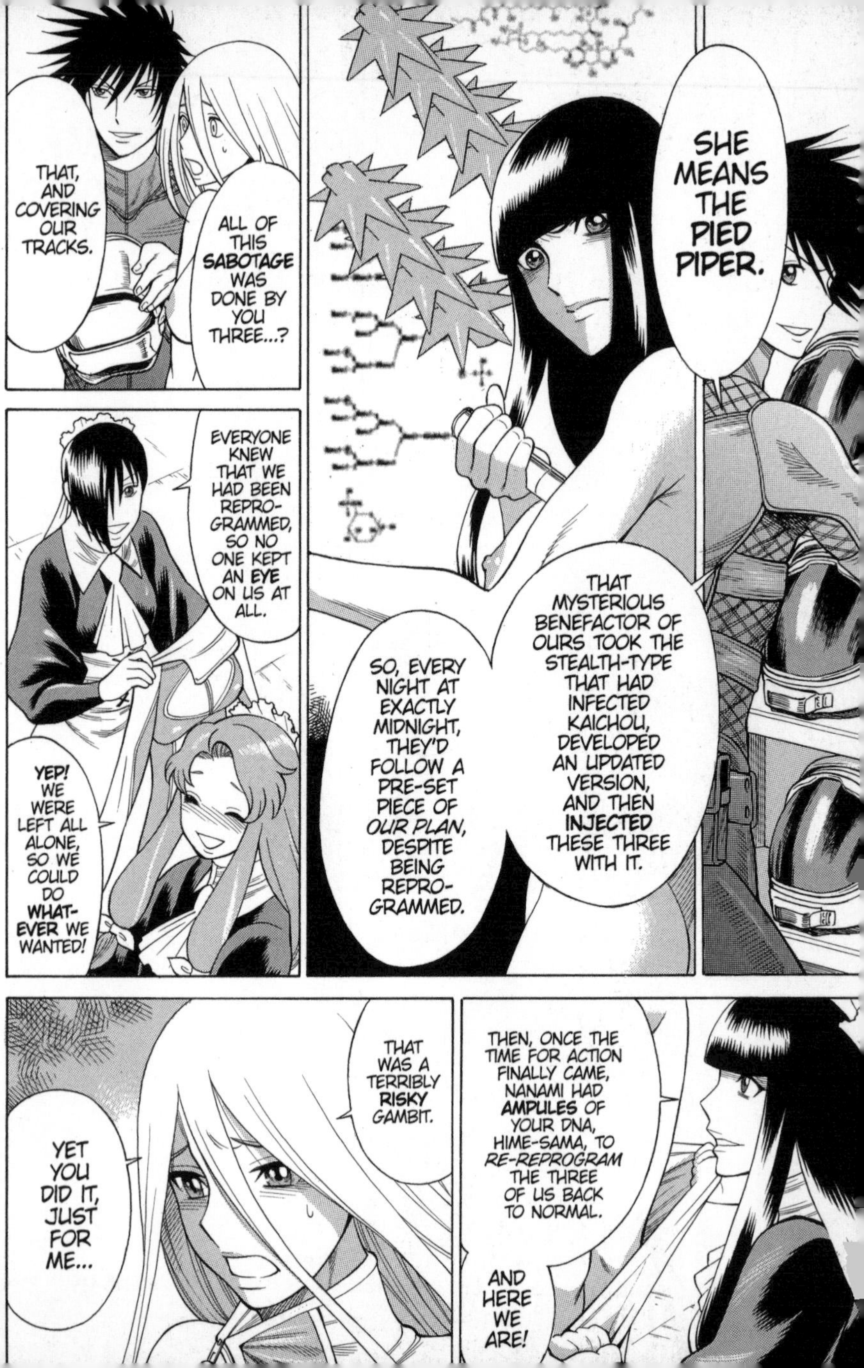
SHE MEANS THE PIED PIPER.
THAT MYSTERIOUS BENEFACTOR OF OURS TOOK THE STEALTH-TYPE THAT HAD INFECTED KAICHOU, DEVELOPED AN UPDATED VERSION, AND THEN INJECTED THESE THREE WITH IT.
SO, EVERY NIGHT AT EXACTLY MIDNIGHT, THEY'D FOLLOW A PRE-SET PIECE OF OUR PLAN, DESPITE BEING REPRO-GRAMMED.
ALL OF THIS SABOTAGE WAS DONE BY YOU THREE...?
THAT, AND COVERING OUR TRACKS.
EVERYONE KNEW THAT WE HAD BEEN REPRO-GRAMMED, SO NO ONE KEPT AN EYE ON US AT ALL.
YEP! WE WERE LEFT ALL ALONE, SO WE COULD DO WHAT-EVER WE WANTED!
THEN, ONCE THE TIME FOR ACTION FINALLY CAME, NANAMI HAD AMPULES OF YOUR DNA, HIME-SAMA, TO RE-REPROGRAM THE THREE OF US BACK TO NORMAL.
AND HERE WE ARE!
THAT WAS A TERRIBLY RISKY GAMBIT.
YET YOU DID IT, JUST FOR ME...

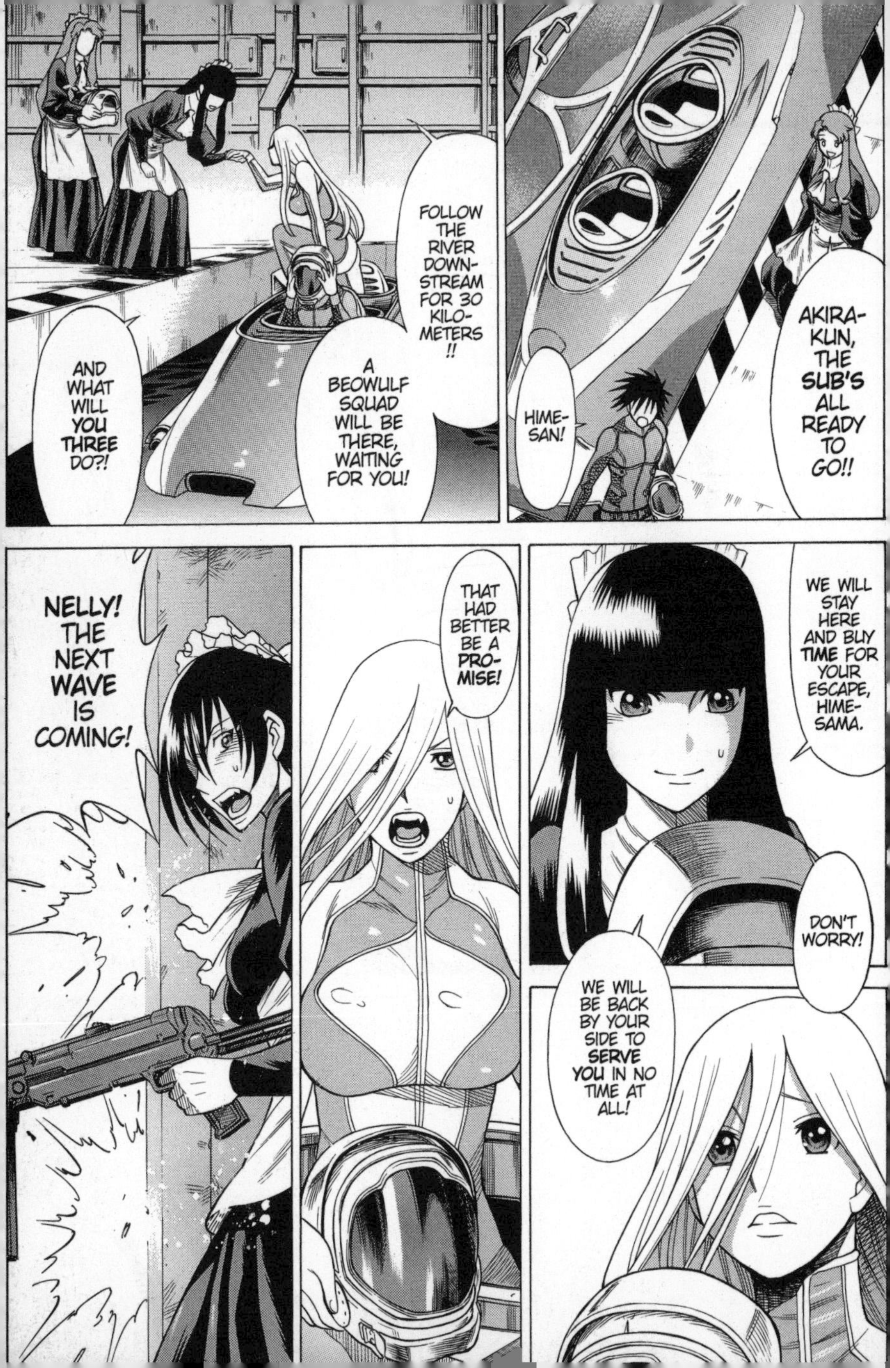
AKIRA-KUN, THE SUB'S ALL READY TO GO!!
HIME-SAN!
FOLLOW THE RIVER DOWN-STREAM FOR 30 KILO-METERS!!
A BEOWULF SQUAD WILL BE THERE, WAITING FOR YOU!
AND WHAT WILL YOU THREE DO?!
WE WILL STAY HERE AND BUY TIME FOR YOUR ESCAPE, HIME-SAMA.
DON'T WORRY!
WE WILL BE BACK BY YOUR SIDE TO SERVE YOU IN NO TIME AT ALL!
THAT HAD BETTER BE A PRO-MISE!
NELLY! THE NEXT WAVE IS COMING!

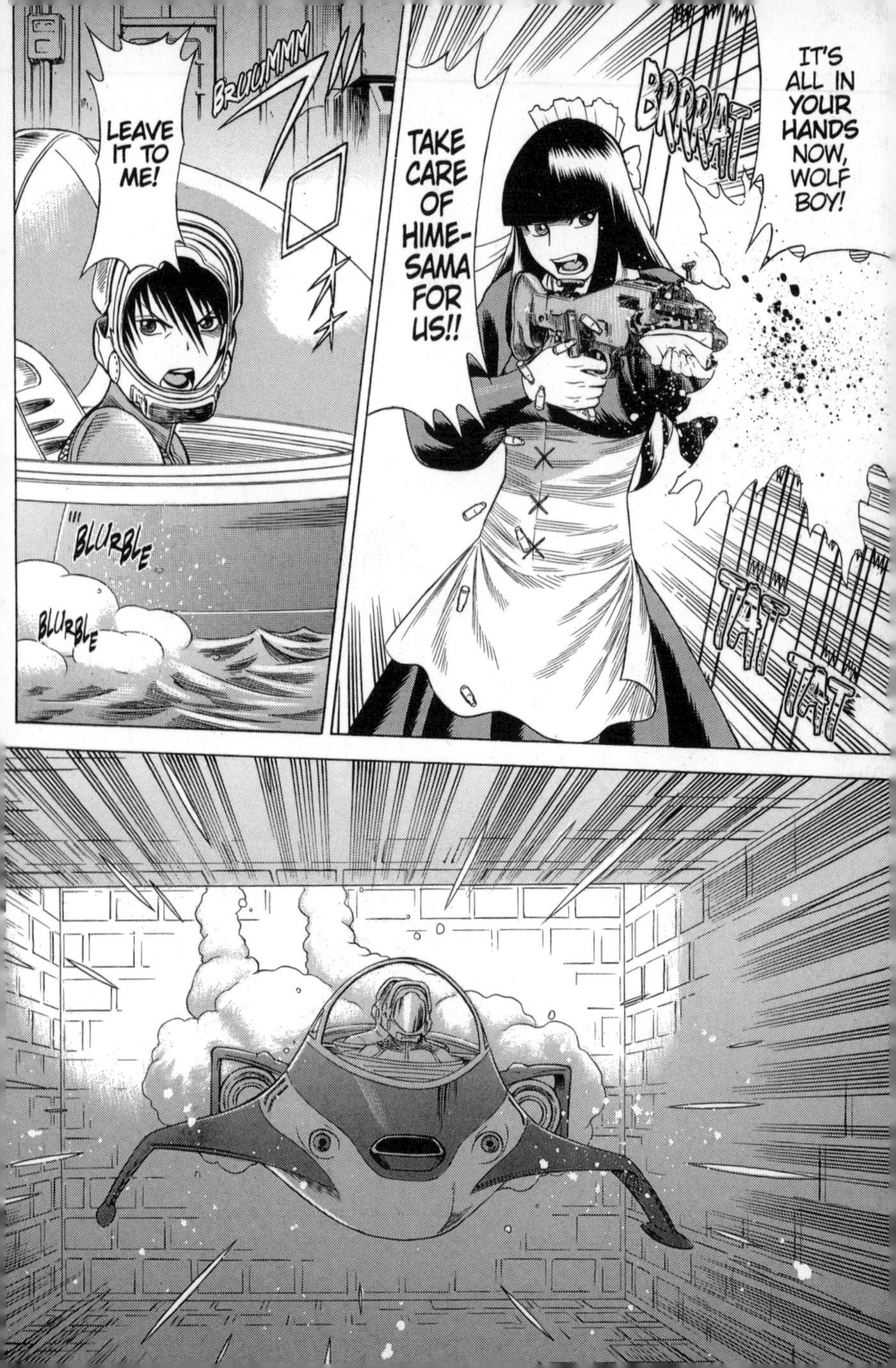
IT'S ALL IN YOUR HANDS NOW, WOLF BOY!
BRRRAT
TAKE CARE OF HIME-SAMA FOR US!!
TAT TAT
BRUUMMM
LEAVE IT TO ME!
BLURBLE
BLURBLE

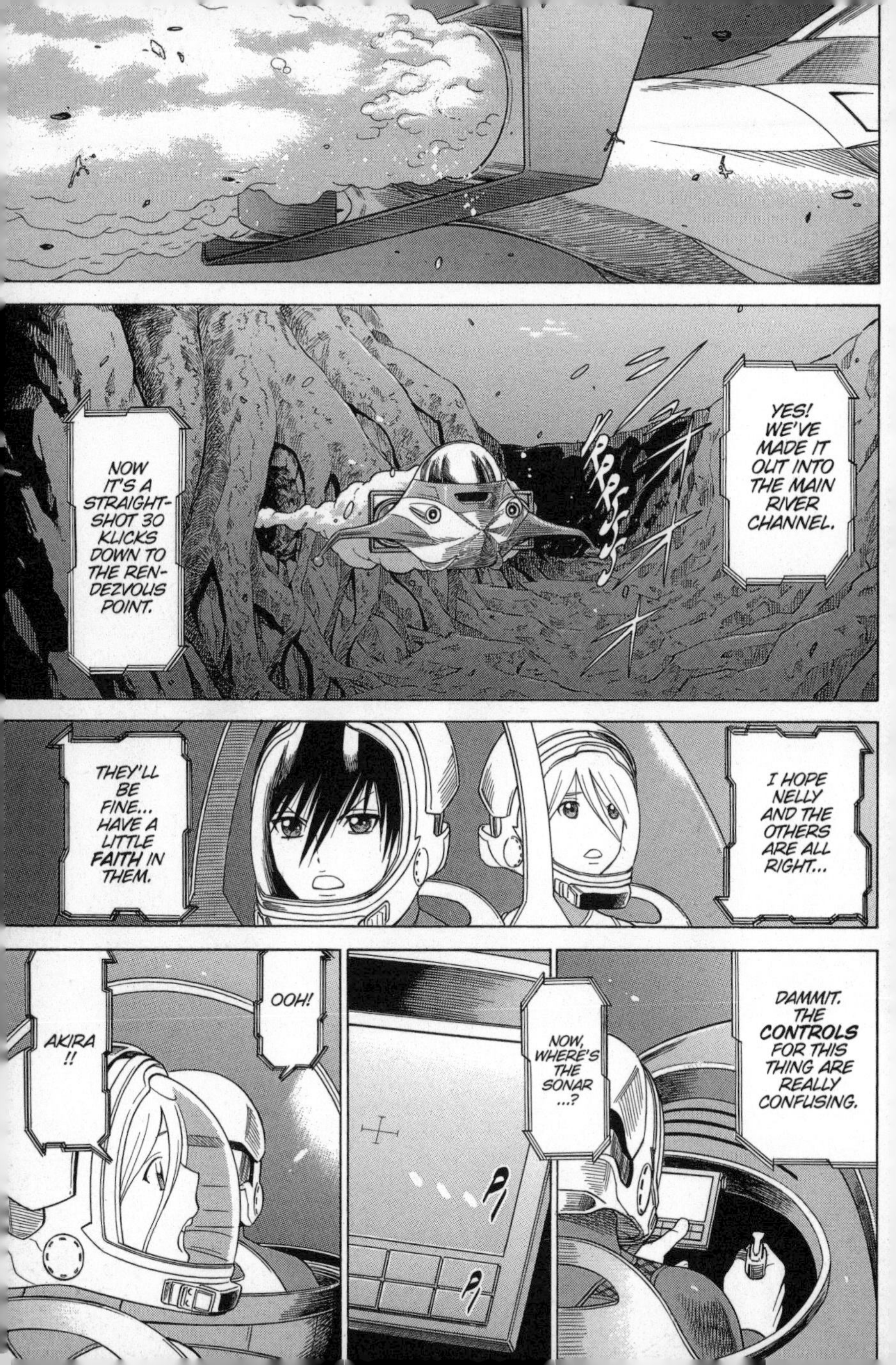
YES! WE'VE MADE IT OUT INTO THE MAIN RIVER CHANNEL.
NOW IT'S A STRAIGHT-SHOT 30 KLICKS DOWN TO THE REN-DEZVOUS POINT.
I HOPE NELLY AND THE OTHERS ARE ALL RIGHT...
THEY'LL BE FINE... HAVE A LITTLE FAITH IN THEM.
DAMMIT. THE CONTROLS FOR THIS THING ARE REALLY CONFUSING.
NOW, WHERE'S THE SONAR ...?
OOH!
AKIRA !!

Chapter 69: Escape From the Tiger's Lair

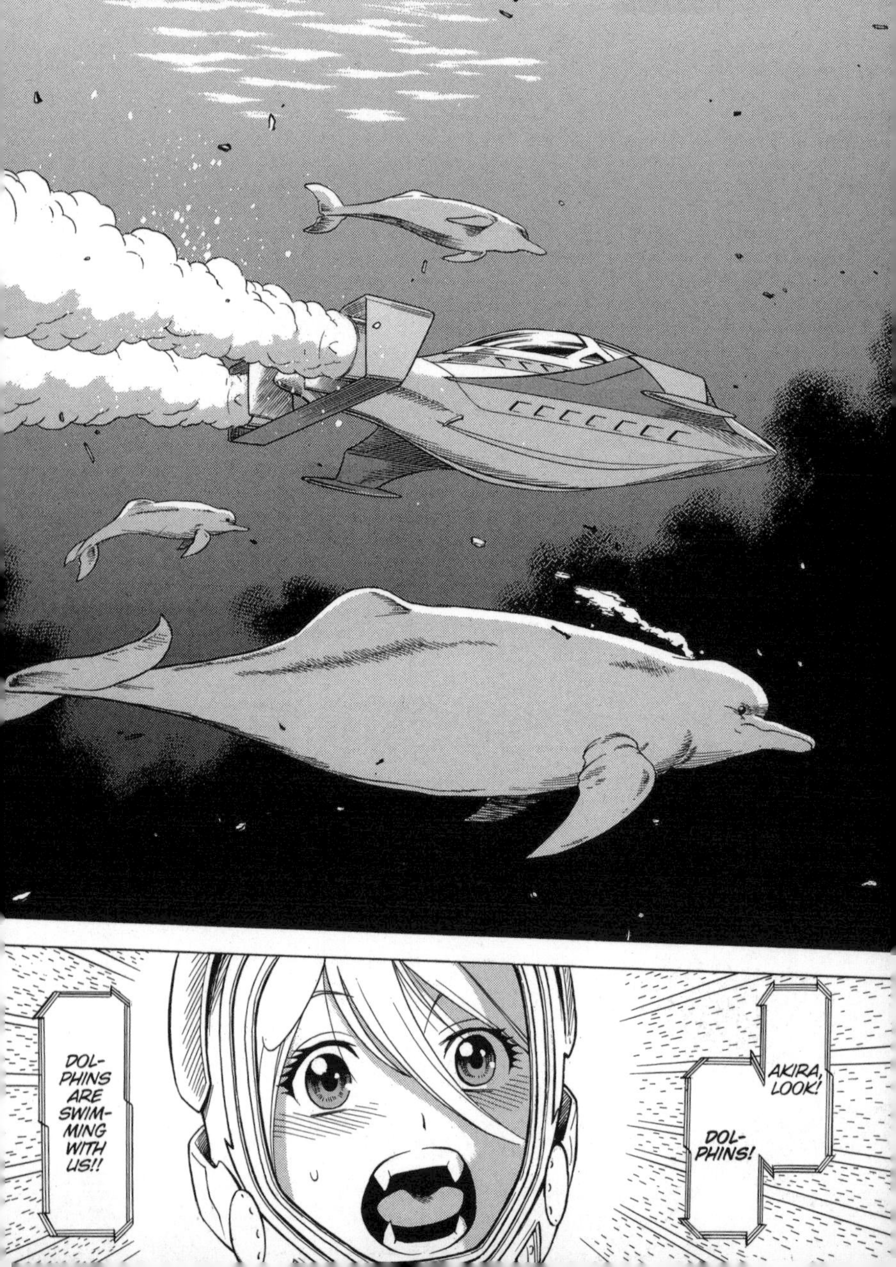
AKIRA, LOOK!
DOLPHINS!
DOLPHINS ARE SWIMMING WITH US!!

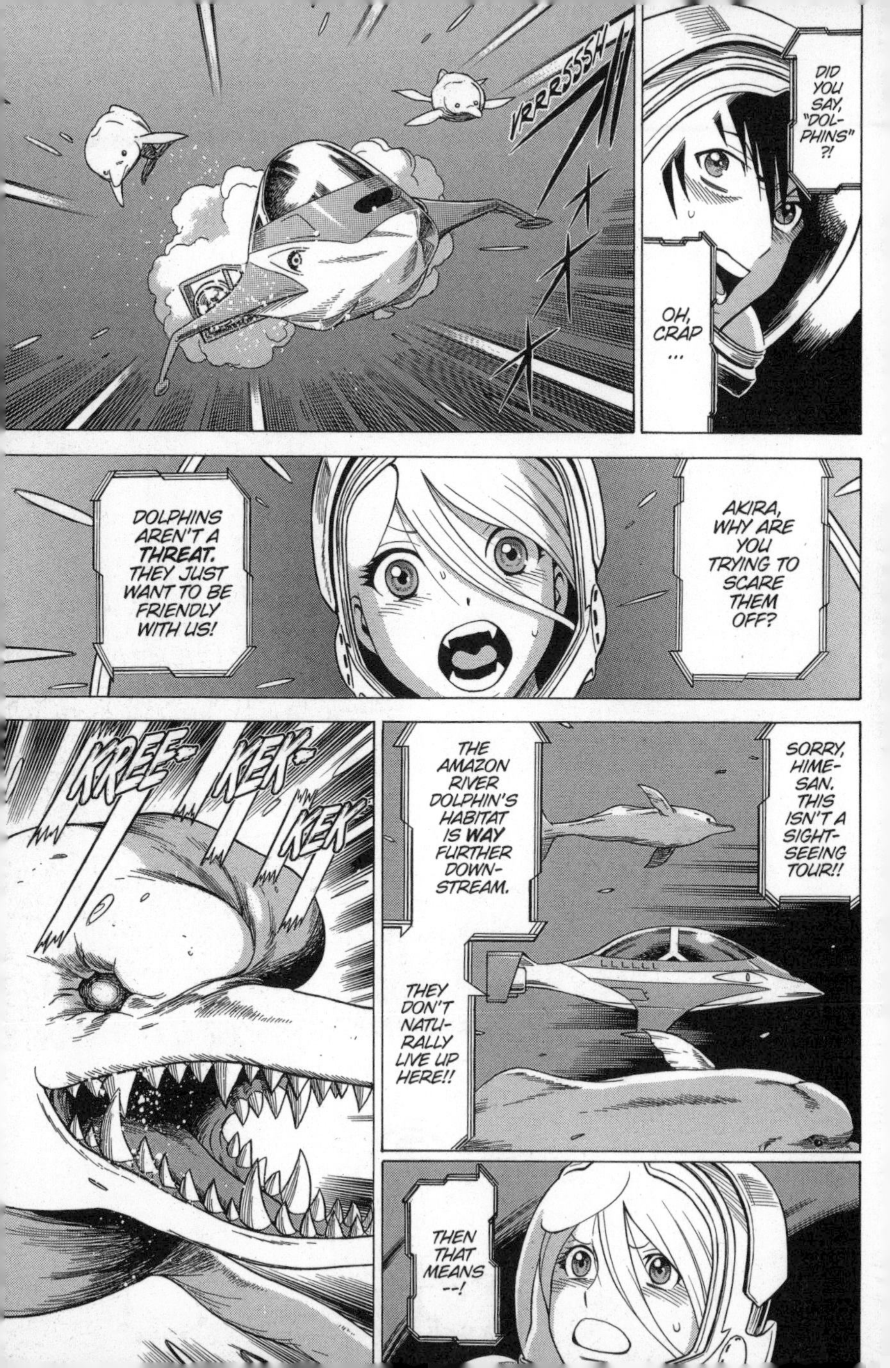
DID YOU SAY, "DOLPHINS"?!
OH, CRAP ...
VRRRSSSH--
AKIRA, WHY ARE YOU TRYING TO SCARE THEM OFF?
DOLPHINS AREN'T A **THREAT.** THEY JUST WANT TO BE FRIENDLY WITH US!
SORRY, HIME-SAN. THIS ISN'T A SIGHTSEEING TOUR!!
THE AMAZON RIVER DOLPHIN'S HABITAT IS **WAY** FURTHER DOWNSTREAM.
THEY DON'T NATURALLY LIVE UP HERE!!
THEN THAT MEANS --!
KREE-KEK-KEK

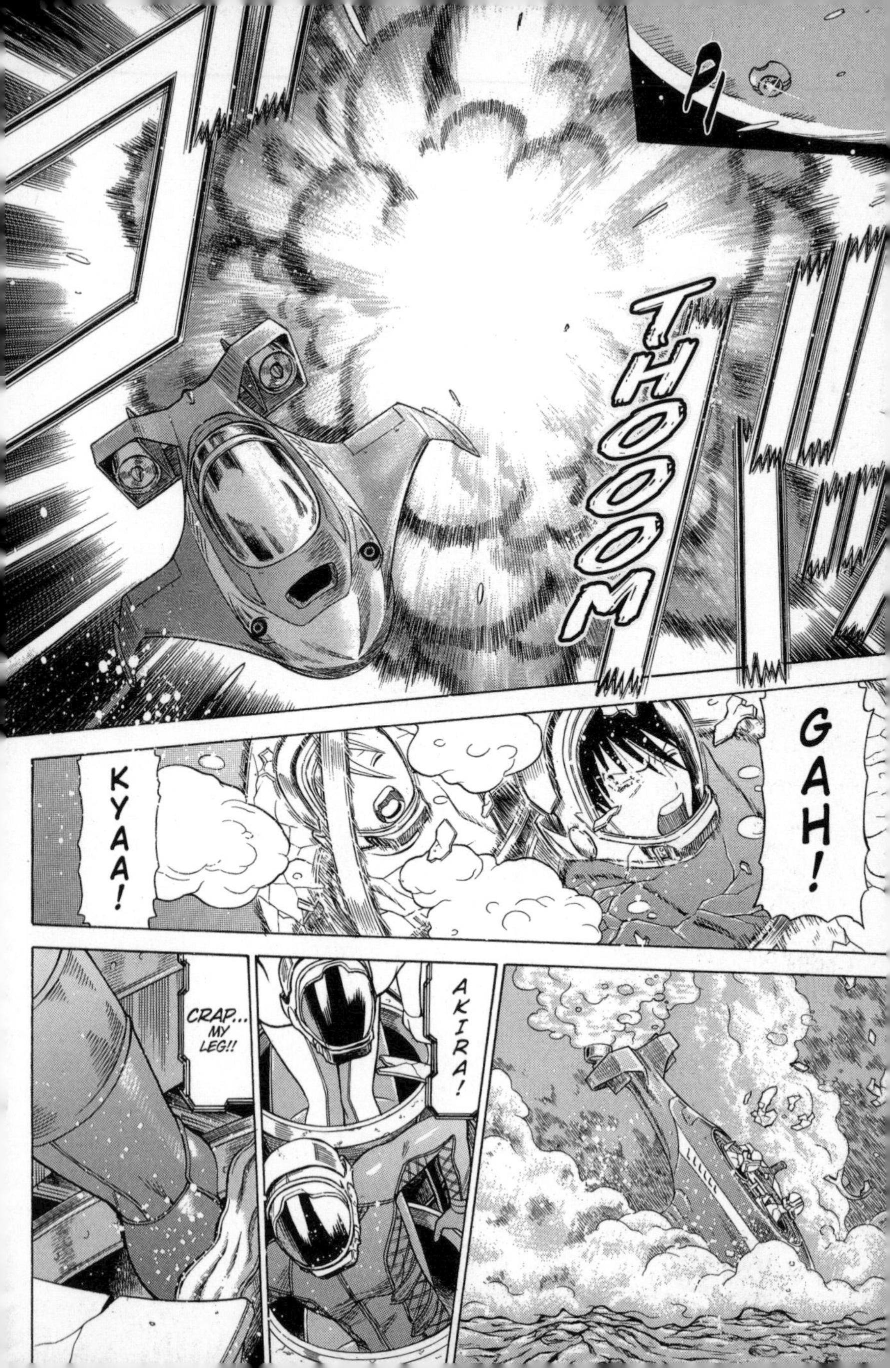
THOOOOM
GAH!
KYAA!
AKIRA!
CRAP... MY LEG!!

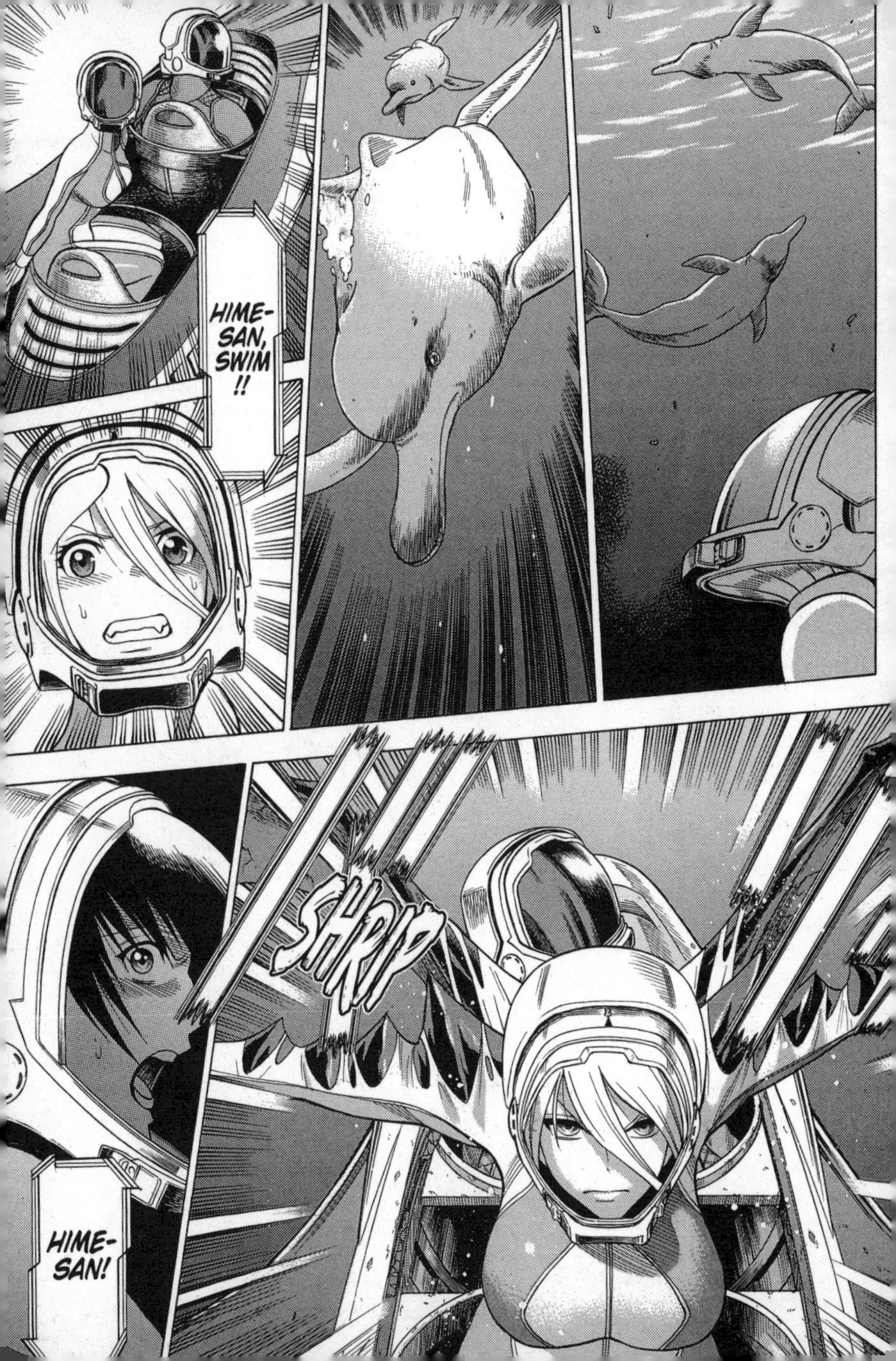
HIME-SAN, SWIM!!
SHRIP
HIME-SAN!

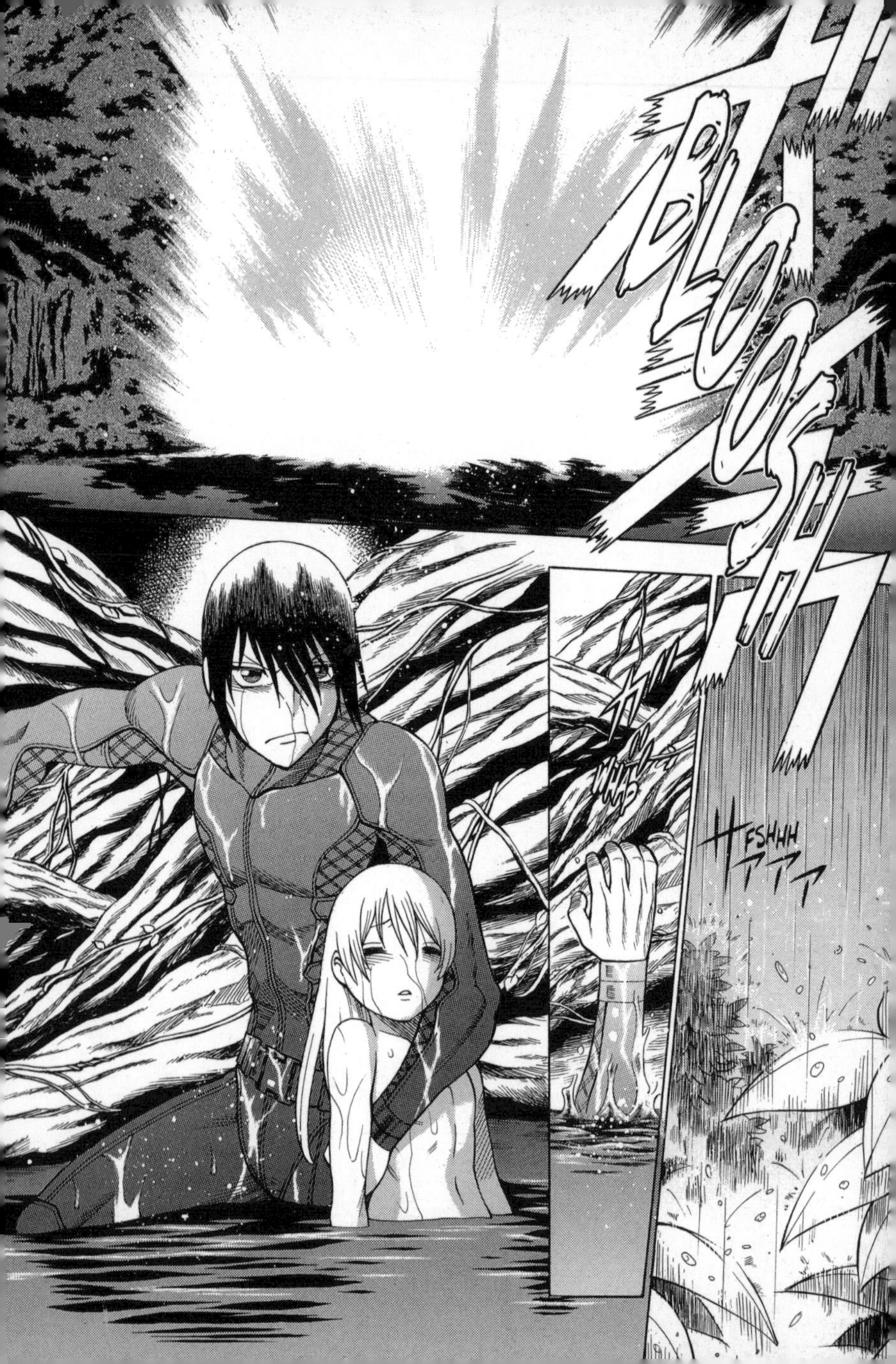
BLOOSHH
WHAP
FSHHH

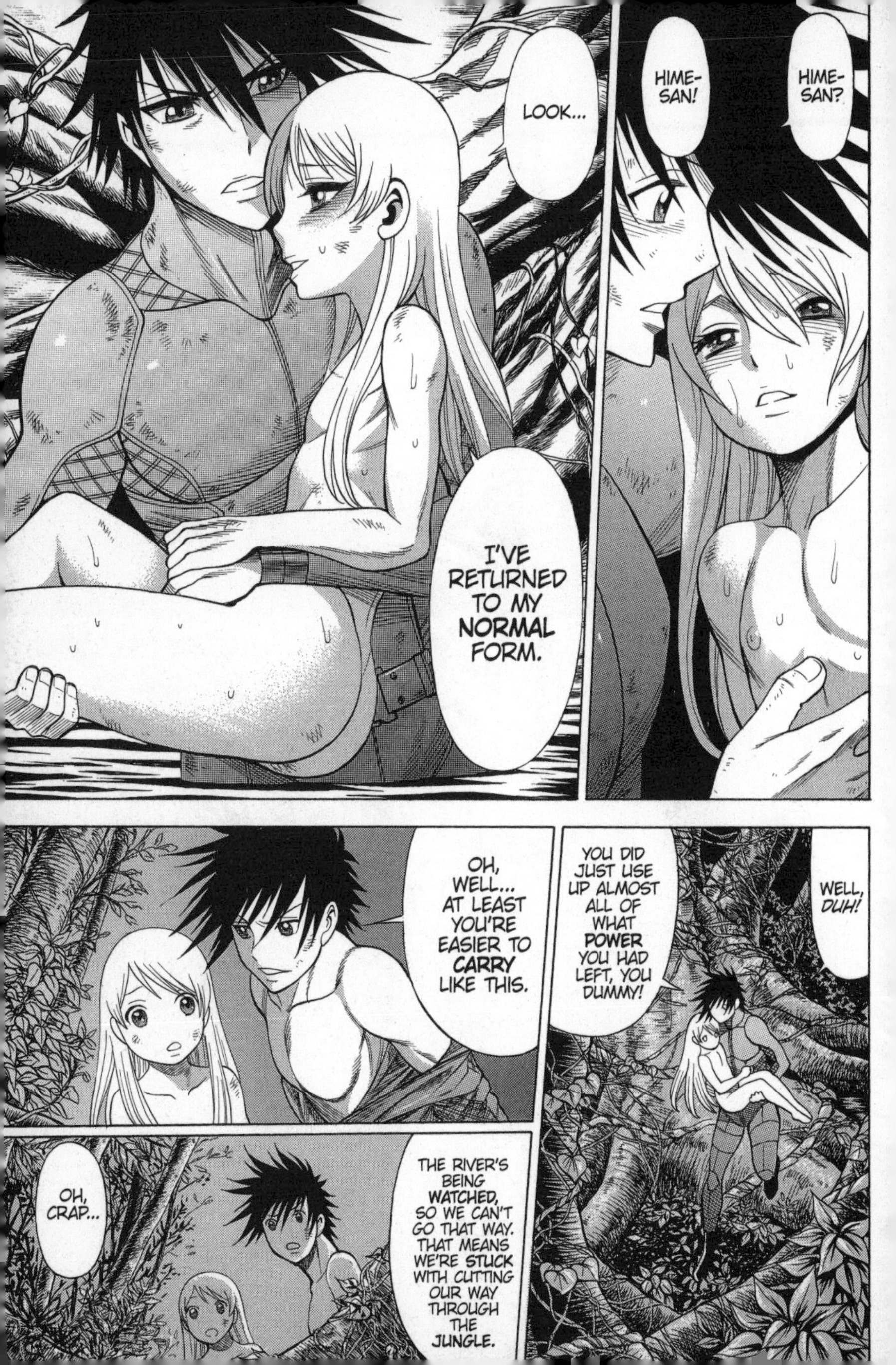
HIME-SAN?
HIME-SAN!
LOOK...
I'VE RETURNED TO MY NORMAL FORM.
WELL, DUH!
YOU DID JUST USE UP ALMOST ALL OF WHAT POWER YOU HAD LEFT, YOU DUMMY!
OH, WELL... AT LEAST YOU'RE EASIER TO CARRY LIKE THIS.
THE RIVER'S BEING WATCHED, SO WE CAN'T GO THAT WAY. THAT MEANS WE'RE STUCK WITH CUTTING OUR WAY THROUGH THE JUNGLE.
OH, CRAP...

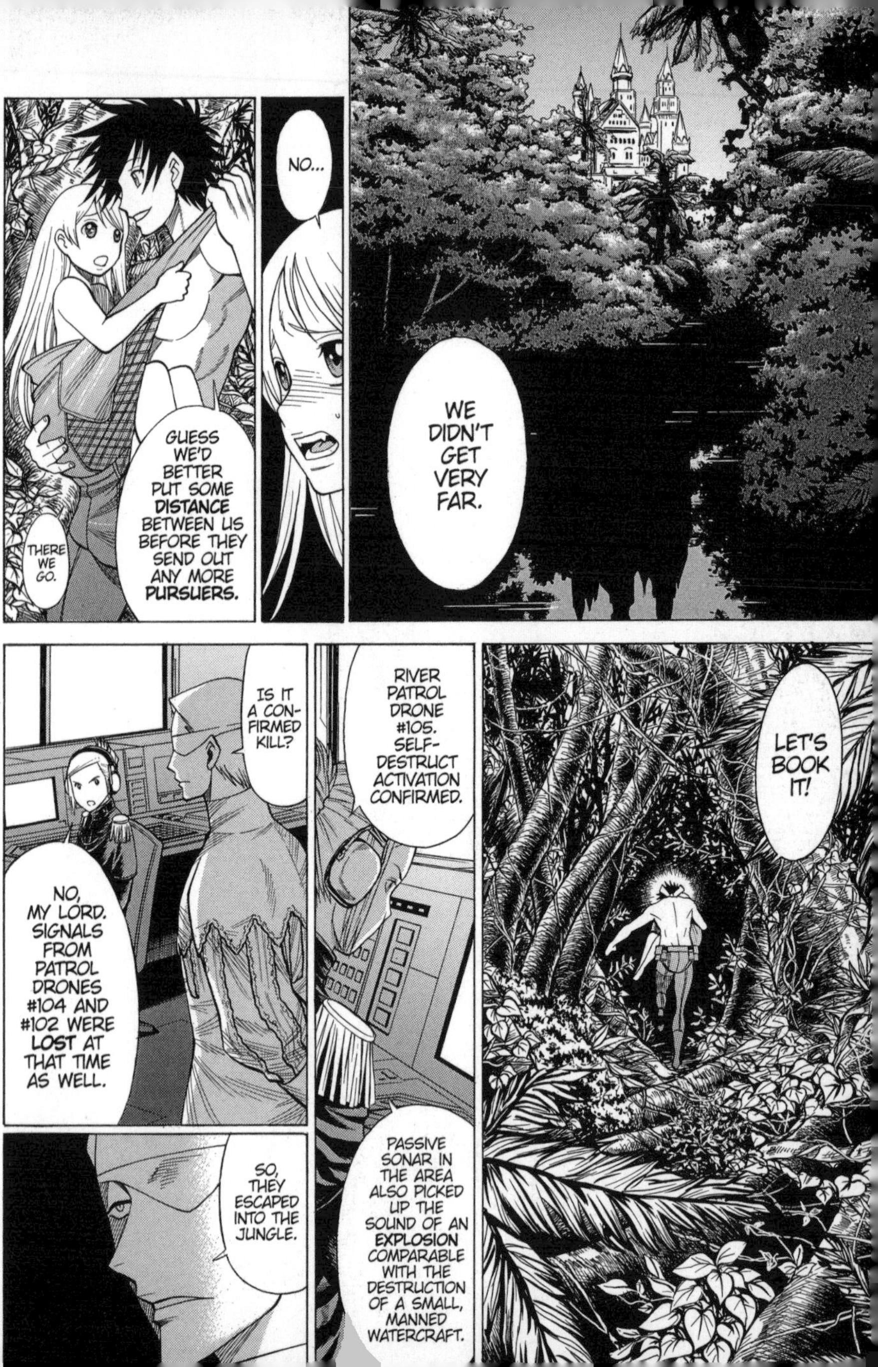
WE DIDN'T GET VERY FAR.
NO...
GUESS WE'D BETTER PUT SOME **DISTANCE** BETWEEN US BEFORE THEY SEND OUT ANY MORE **PURSUERS.**
THERE WE GO.
LET'S BOOK IT!
RIVER PATROL DRONE #105. SELF-DESTRUCT ACTIVATION CONFIRMED.
PASSIVE SONAR IN THE AREA ALSO PICKED UP THE SOUND OF AN **EXPLOSION** COMPARABLE WITH THE DESTRUCTION OF A SMALL, MANNED WATERCRAFT.
IS IT A CON-FIRMED KILL?
NO, MY LORD. SIGNALS FROM PATROL DRONES #104 AND #102 WERE **LOST** AT THAT TIME AS WELL.
SO, THEY ESCAPED INTO THE JUNGLE.

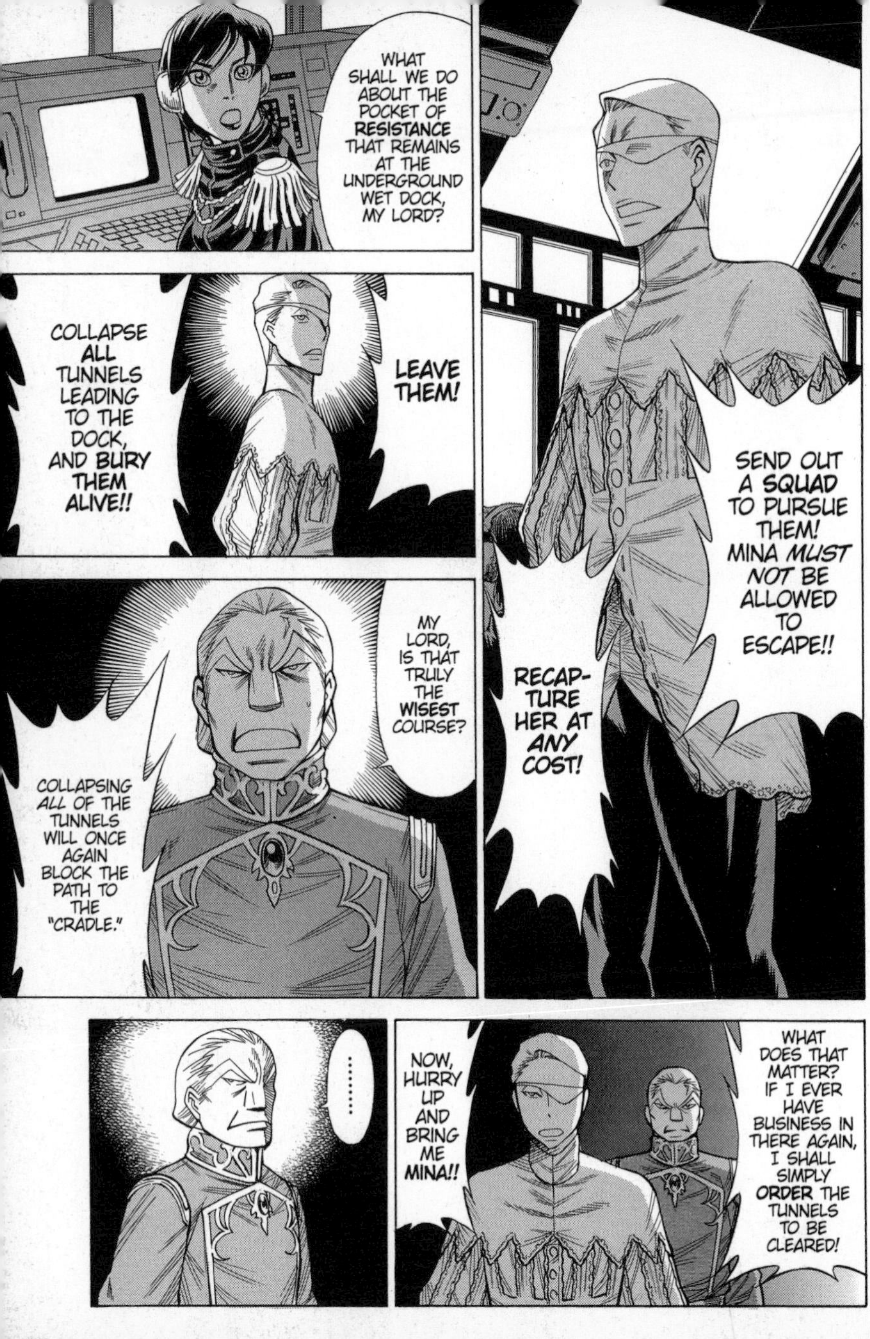
WHAT SHALL WE DO ABOUT THE POCKET OF RESISTANCE THAT REMAINS AT THE UNDERGROUND WET DOCK, MY LORD?
LEAVE THEM!
COLLAPSE ALL TUNNELS LEADING TO THE DOCK, AND BURY THEM ALIVE!!
MY LORD, IS THAT TRULY THE WISEST COURSE?
COLLAPSING ALL OF THE TUNNELS WILL ONCE AGAIN BLOCK THE PATH TO THE "CRADLE."
SEND OUT A SQUAD TO PURSUE THEM! MINA MUST NOT BE ALLOWED TO ESCAPE!!
RECAP-TURE HER AT ANY COST!
WHAT DOES THAT MATTER? IF I EVER HAVE BUSINESS IN THERE AGAIN, I SHALL SIMPLY ORDER THE TUNNELS TO BE CLEARED!
NOW, HURRY UP AND BRING ME MINA!!
....

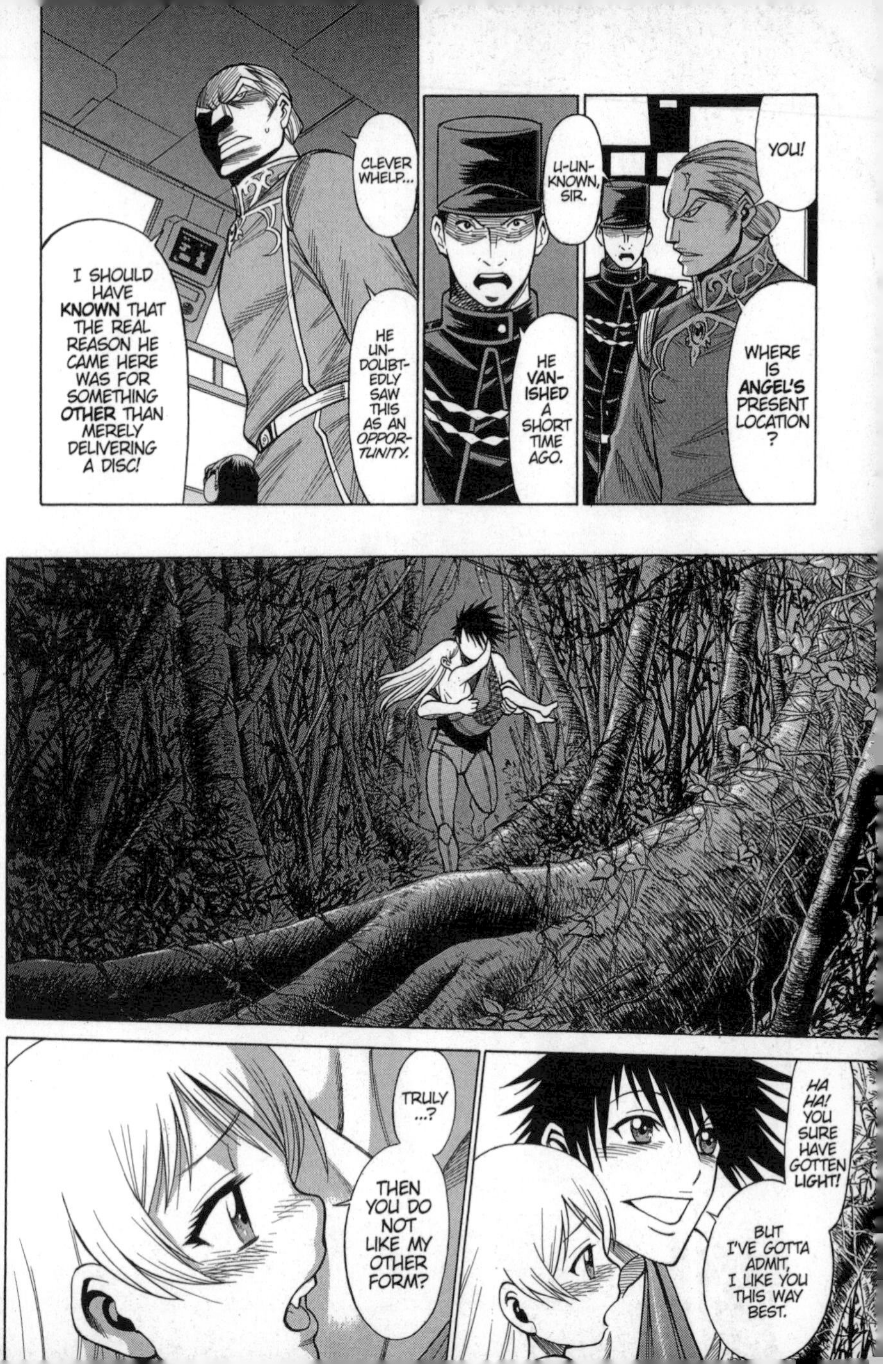
YOU!
WHERE IS ANGEL'S PRESENT LOCATION?
U-UNKNOWN, SIR.
HE VANISHED A SHORT TIME AGO.
CLEVER WHELP...
HE UNDOUBTEDLY SAW THIS AS AN OPPORTUNITY.
I SHOULD HAVE KNOWN THAT THE REAL REASON HE CAME HERE WAS FOR SOMETHING OTHER THAN MERELY DELIVERING A DISC!
HA HA! YOU SURE HAVE GOTTEN LIGHT!
BUT I'VE GOTTA ADMIT, I LIKE YOU THIS WAY BEST.
TRULY ...?
THEN YOU DO NOT LIKE MY OTHER FORM?

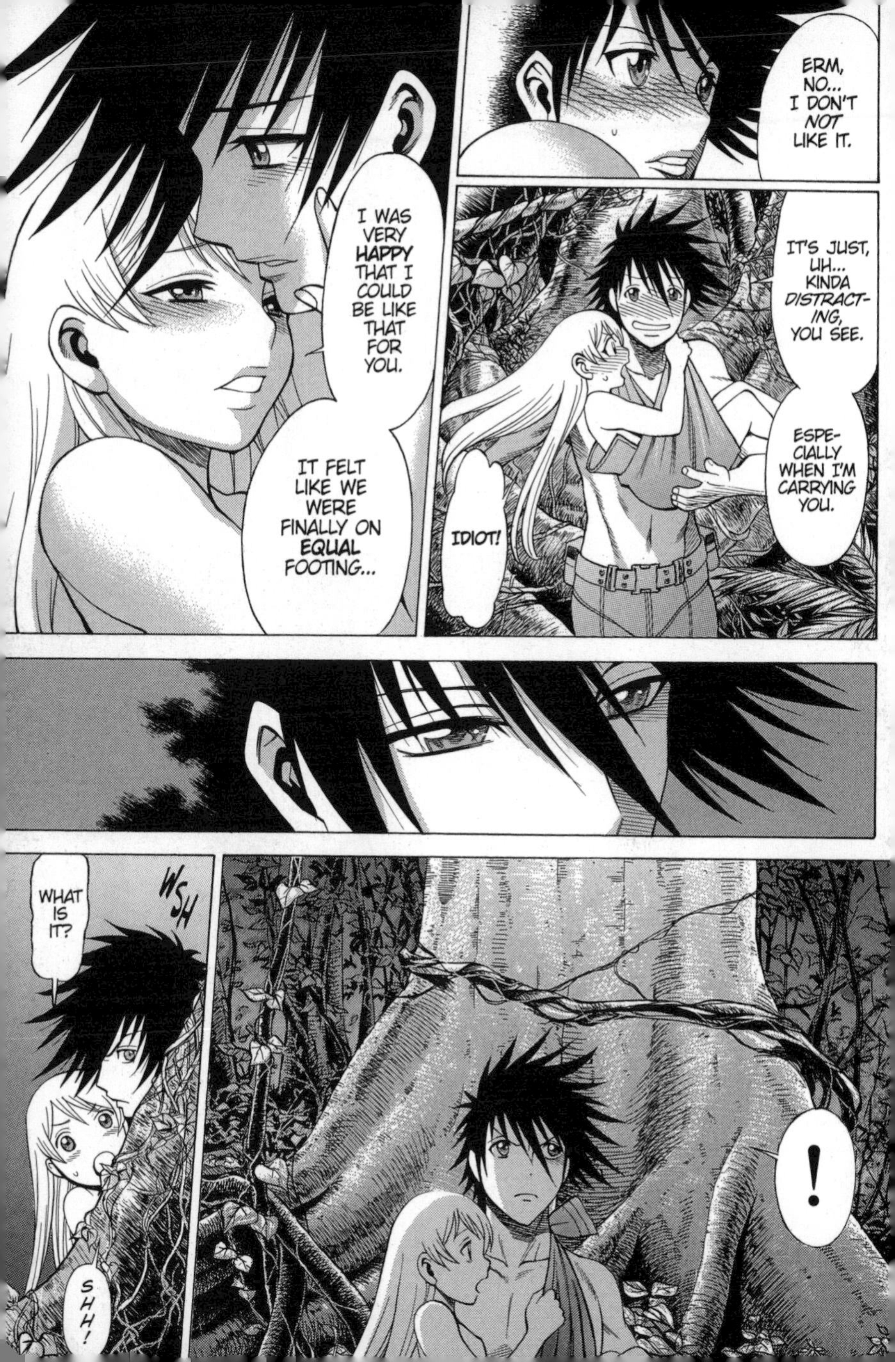
ERM, NO... I DON'T *NOT* LIKE IT.
IT'S JUST, UH... KINDA *DISTRACTING*, YOU SEE.
ESPECIALLY WHEN I'M CARRYING YOU.
IDIOT!
I WAS VERY **HAPPY** THAT I COULD BE LIKE THAT FOR YOU.
IT FELT LIKE WE WERE FINALLY ON **EQUAL** FOOTING...
!
WHAT IS IT?
WSH
SHH!

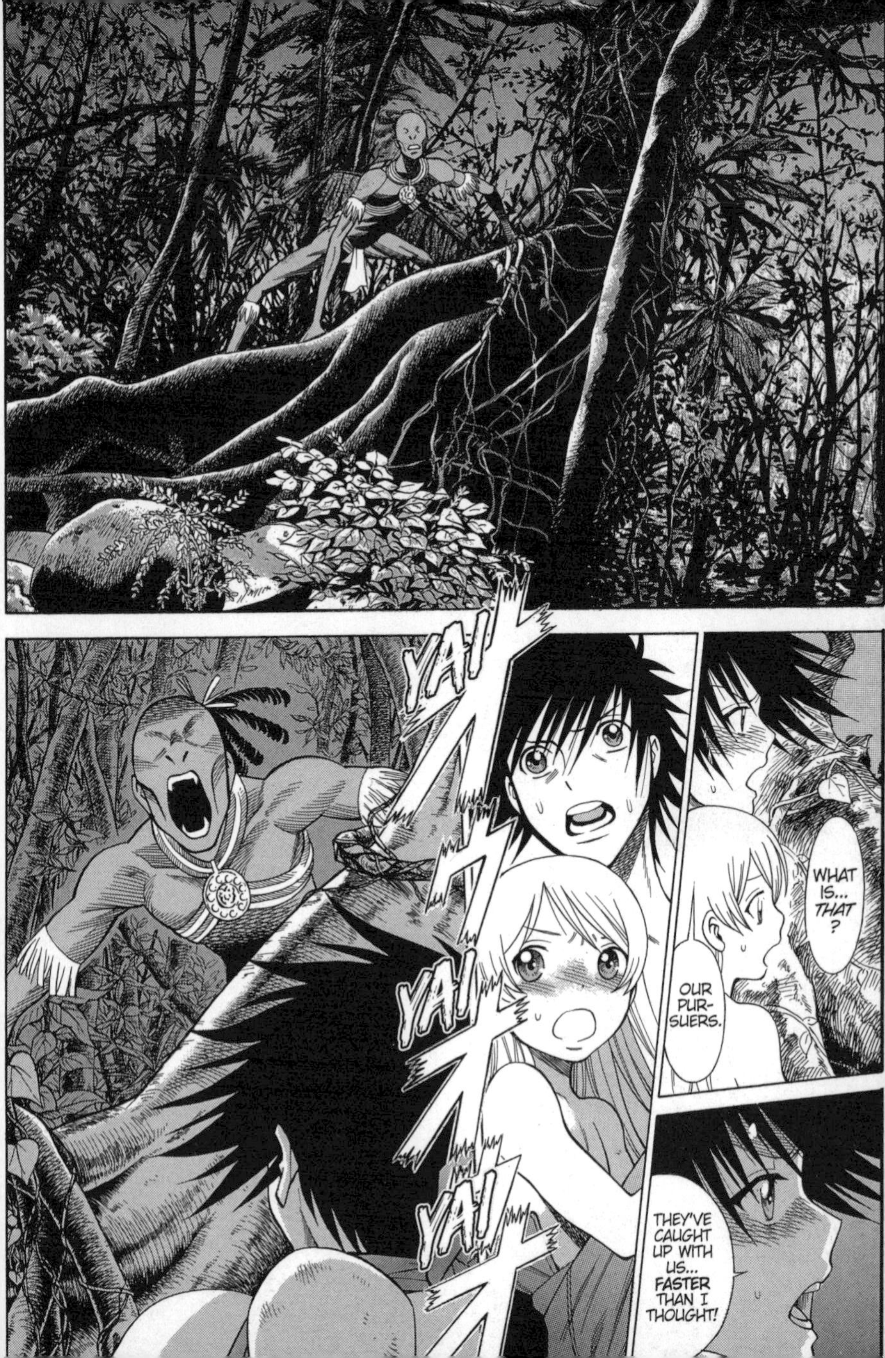
WHAT IS... THAT?
OUR PURSUERS.
THEY'VE CAUGHT UP WITH US... FASTER THAN I THOUGHT!
YA!
YA!
YA!

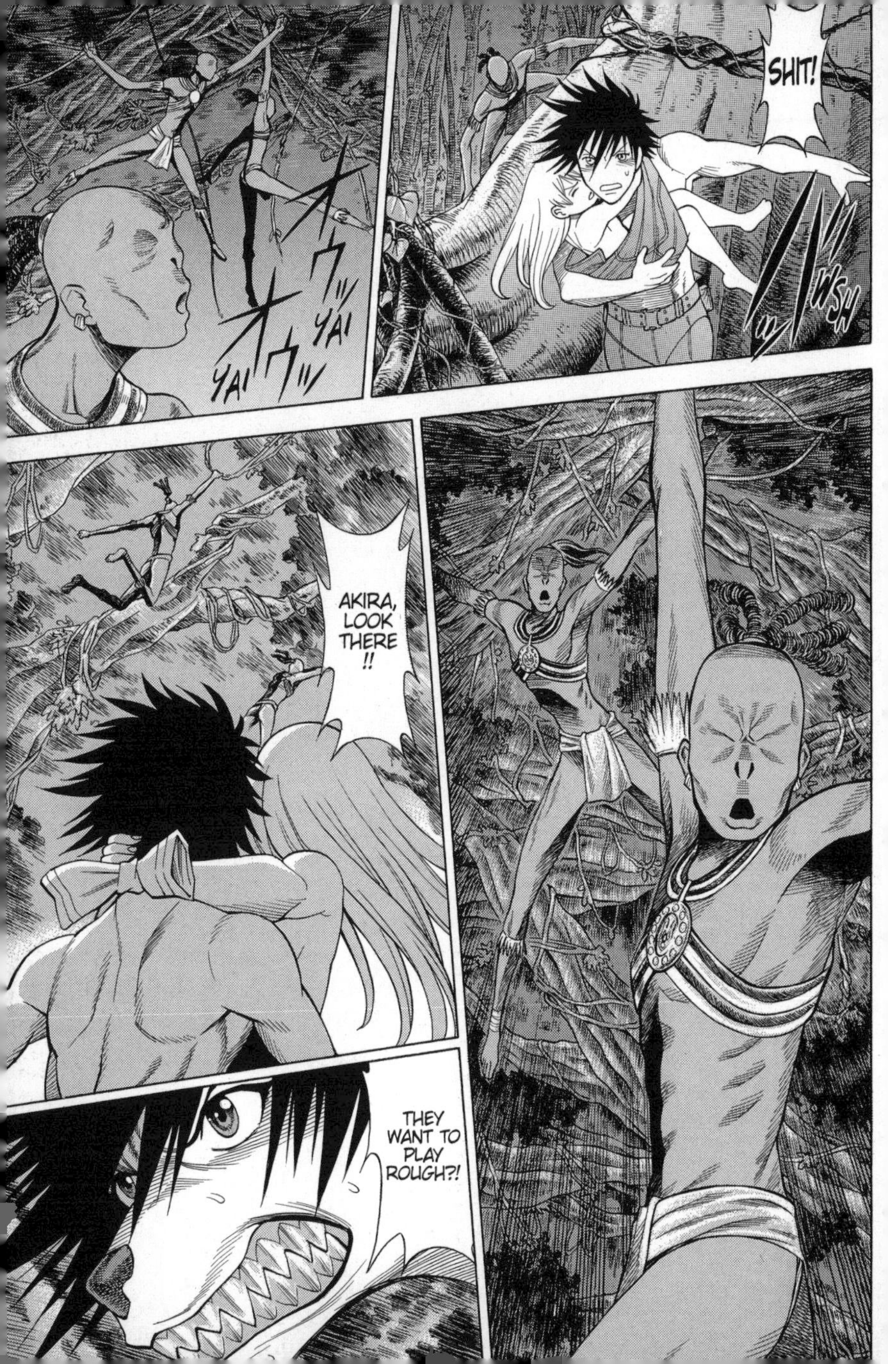

SHIT!
WSH
YAI
YAI
AKIRA, LOOK THERE!!
THEY WANT TO PLAY ROUGH?!

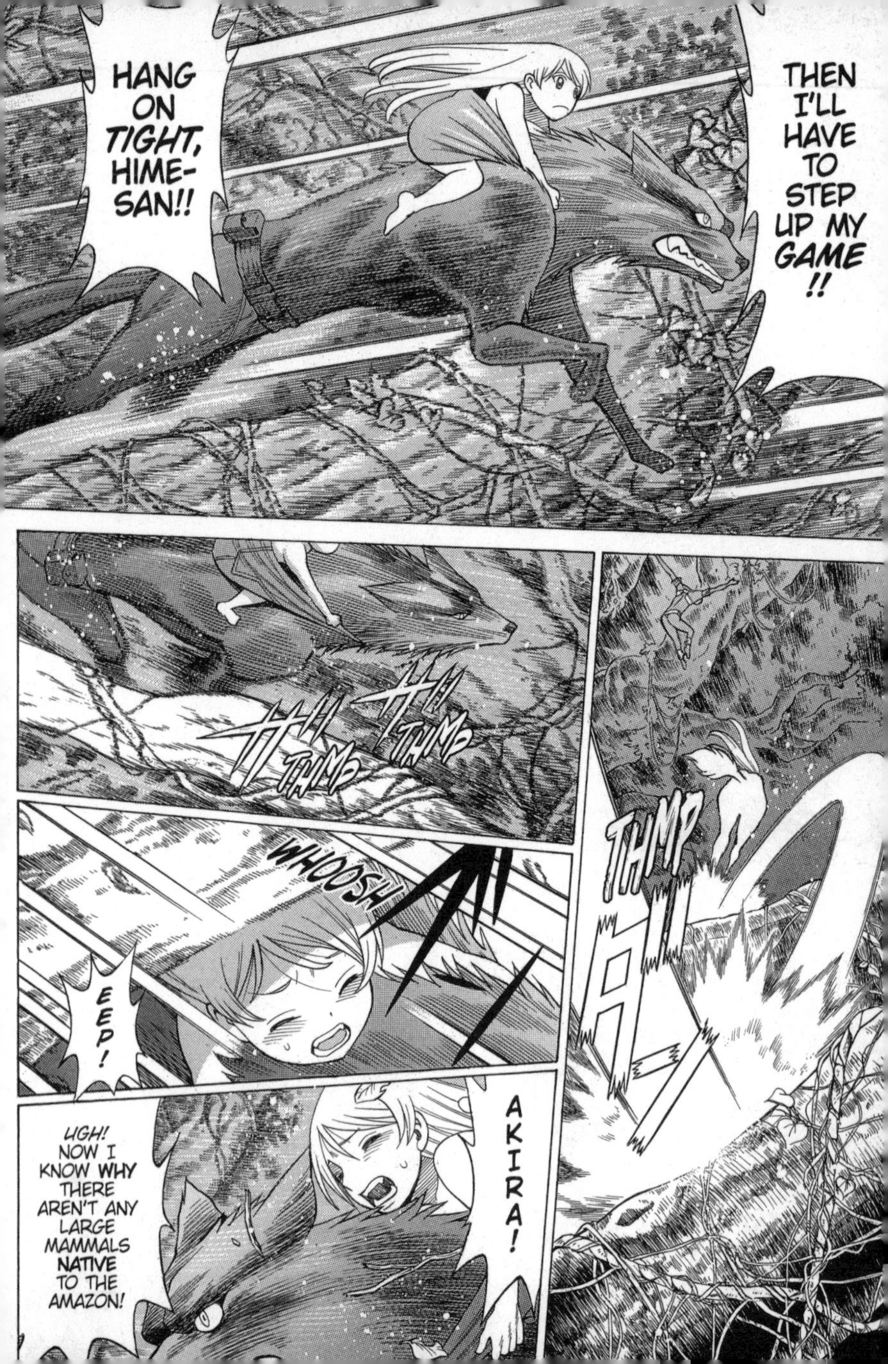
THEN I'LL HAVE TO STEP UP MY GAME!!
HANG ON TIGHT, HIME-SAN!!
THMP
THMP
THMP
WHOOSH
EEP!
AKIRA!
UGH! NOW I KNOW WHY THERE AREN'T ANY LARGE MAMMALS NATIVE TO THE AMAZON!

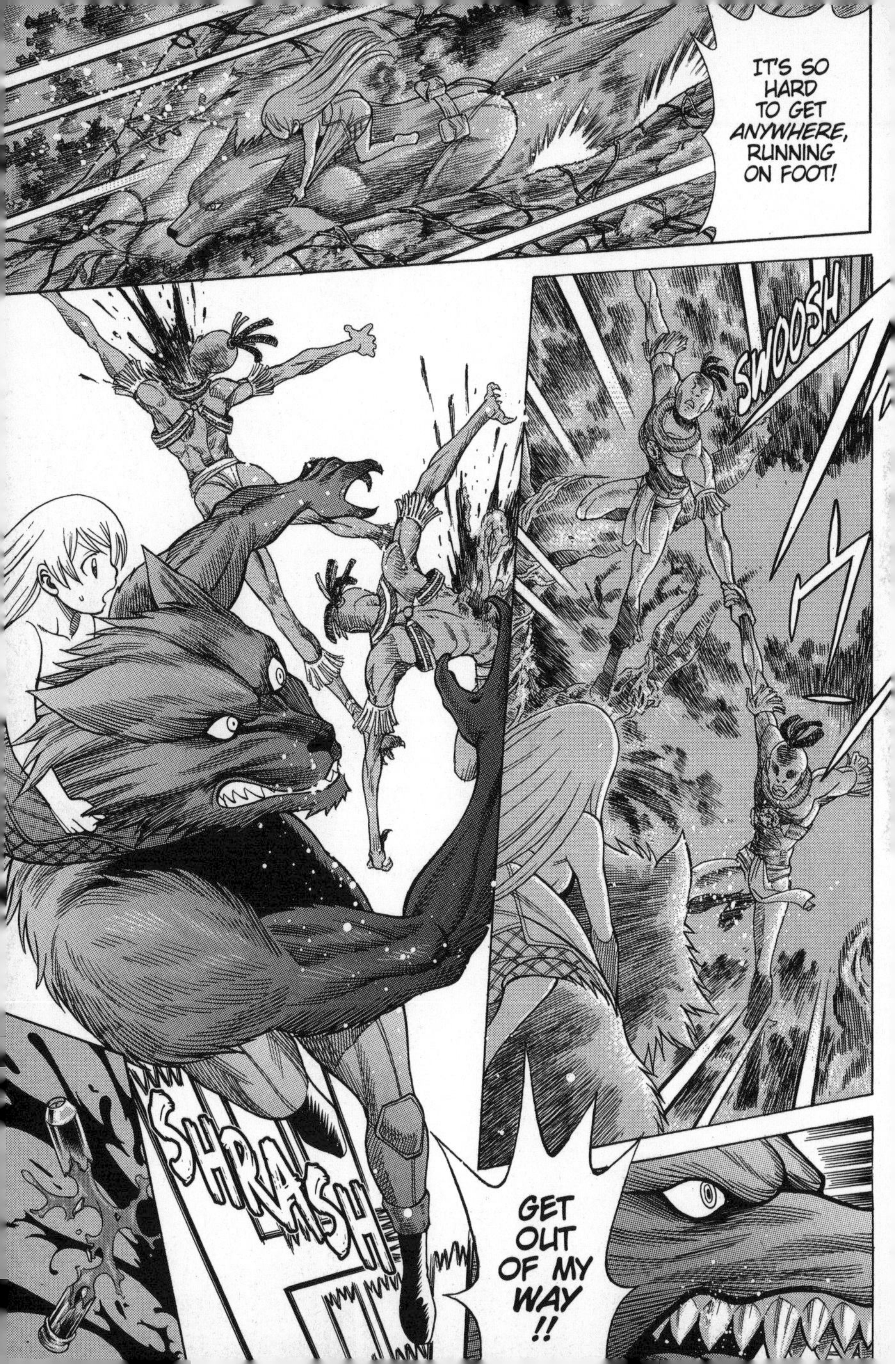
IT'S SO HARD TO GET ANYWHERE, RUNNING ON FOOT!
SWOOSH
SHRASH
GET OUT OF MY WAY!!

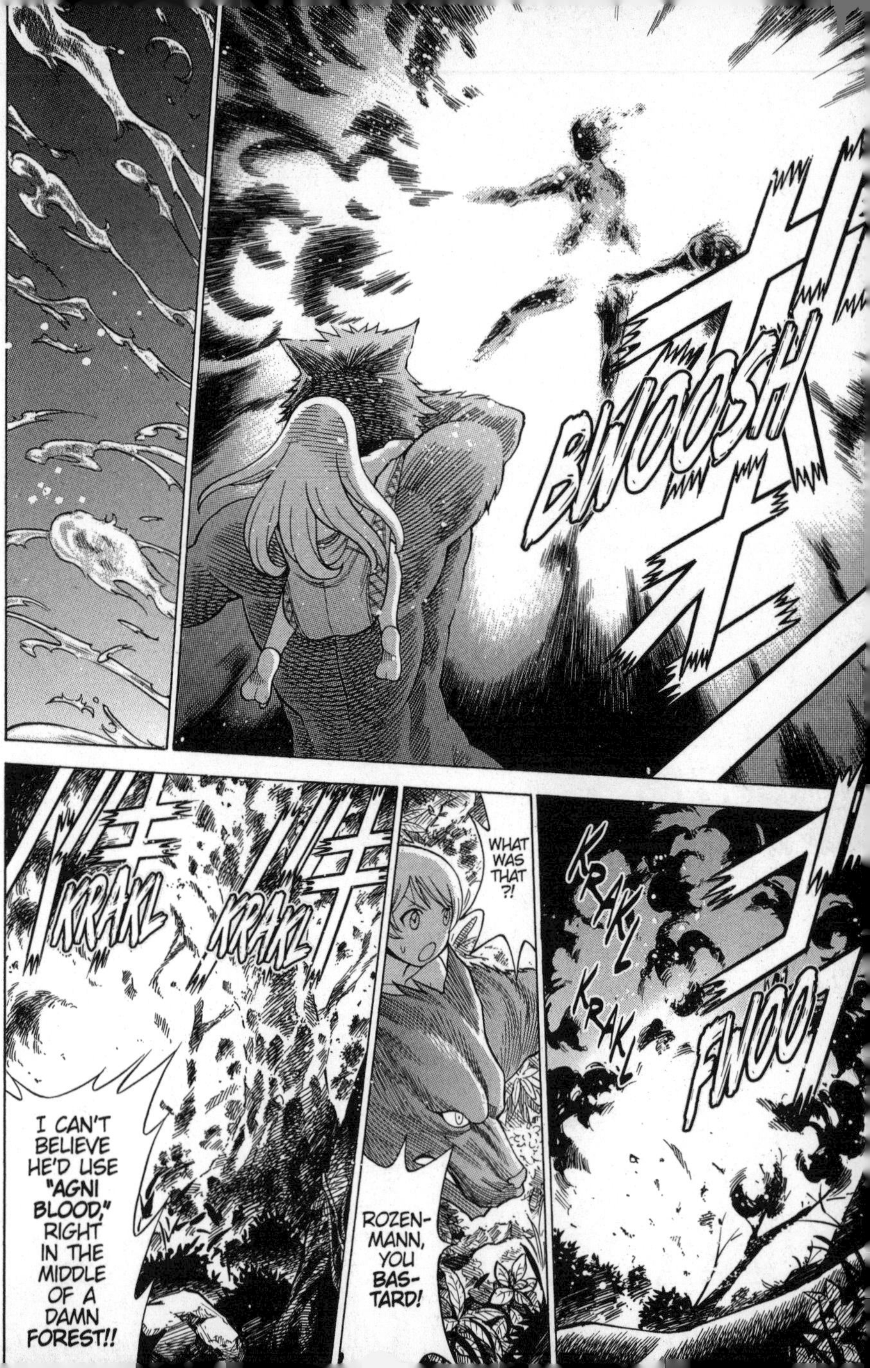
BWOOSH
KRAKL KRAKL
FWOO
WHAT WAS THAT?!
ROZEN-MANN, YOU BAS-TARD!
KRAKL
KRAKL
I CAN'T BELIEVE HE'D USE "AGNI BLOOD," RIGHT IN THE MIDDLE OF A DAMN FOREST!!

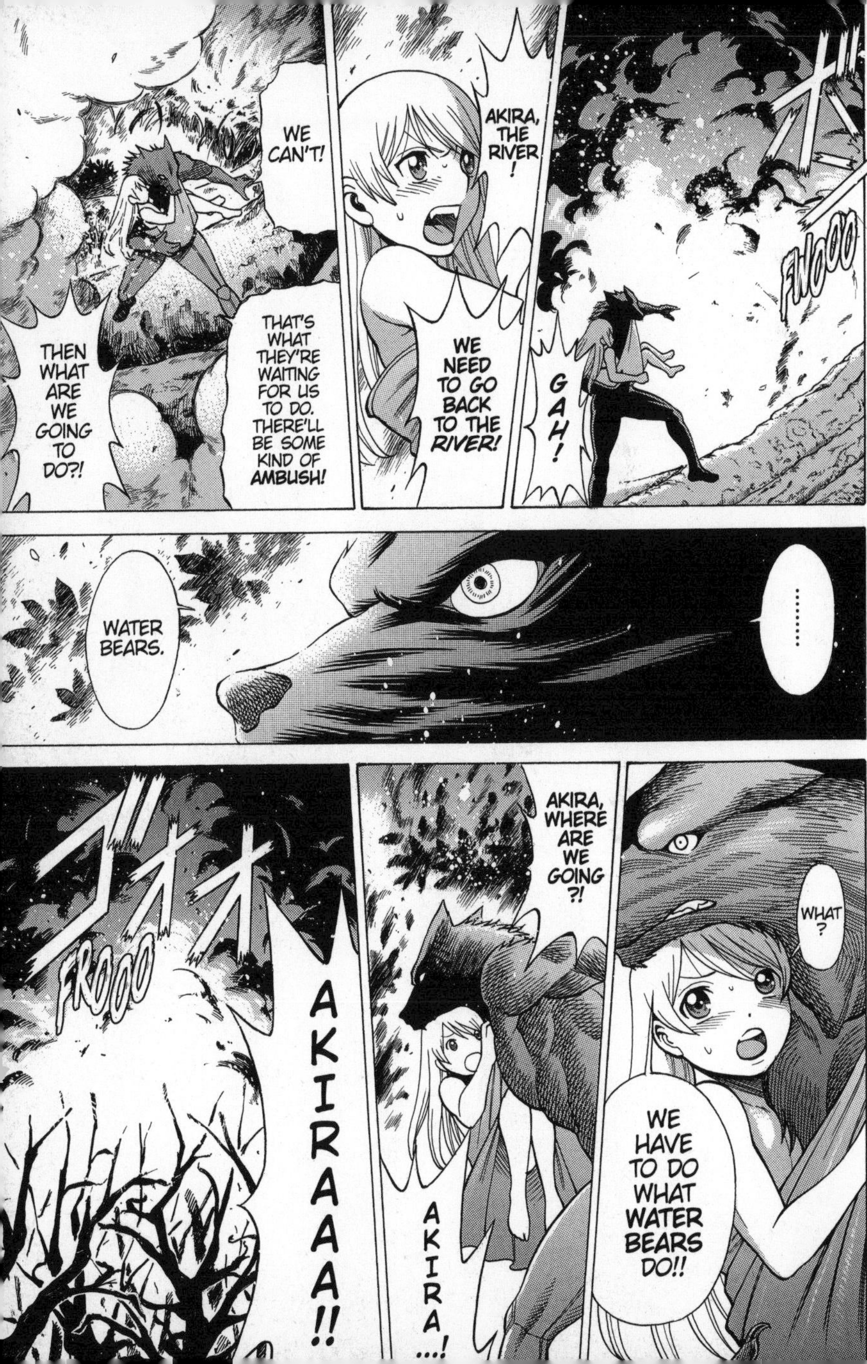
FWOOO
GAH!
AKIRA, THE RIVER!
WE NEED TO GO BACK TO THE RIVER!
WE CAN'T!
THAT'S WHAT THEY'RE WAITING FOR US TO DO. THERE'LL BE SOME KIND OF AMBUSH!
THEN WHAT ARE WE GOING TO DO?!
......
WATER BEARS.
WHAT?
WE HAVE TO DO WHAT WATER BEARS DO!!
AKIRA, WHERE ARE WE GOING?!
AKIRA...!
FROOO
AKIRAAAA!!

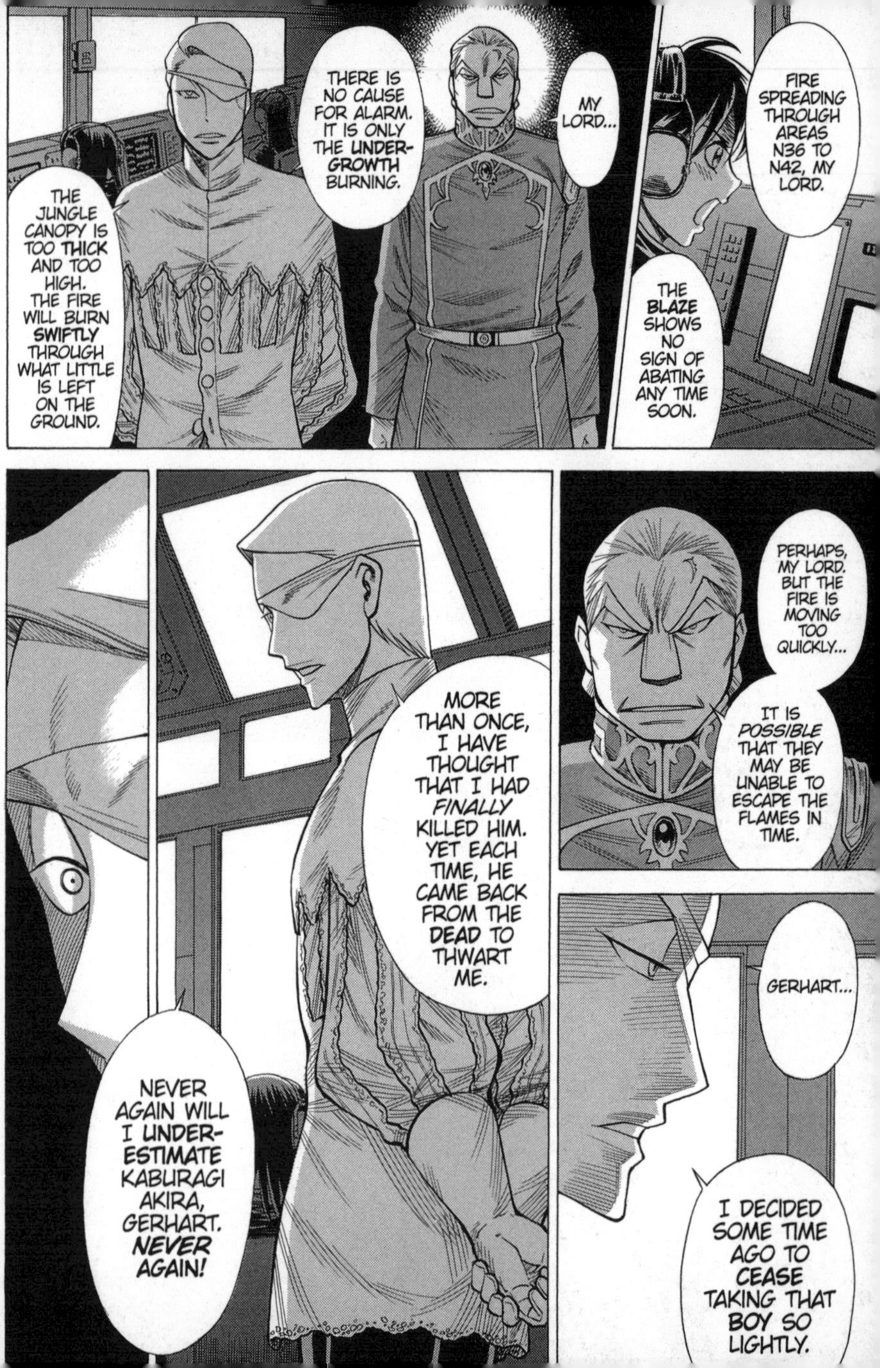
FIRE SPREADING THROUGH AREAS N36 TO N42, MY LORD.
THE BLAZE SHOWS NO SIGN OF ABATING ANY TIME SOON.
MY LORD...
THERE IS NO CAUSE FOR ALARM. IT IS ONLY THE UNDER-GROWTH BURNING.
THE JUNGLE CANOPY IS TOO THICK AND TOO HIGH. THE FIRE WILL BURN SWIFTLY THROUGH WHAT LITTLE IS LEFT ON THE GROUND.
PERHAPS, MY LORD. BUT THE FIRE IS MOVING TOO QUICKLY...
IT IS POSSIBLE THAT THEY MAY BE UNABLE TO ESCAPE THE FLAMES IN TIME.
GERHART...
I DECIDED SOME TIME AGO TO CEASE TAKING THAT BOY SO LIGHTLY.
MORE THAN ONCE, I HAVE THOUGHT THAT I HAD FINALLY KILLED HIM. YET EACH TIME, HE CAME BACK FROM THE DEAD TO THWART ME.
NEVER AGAIN WILL I UNDER-ESTIMATE KABURAGI AKIRA, GERHART. NEVER AGAIN!

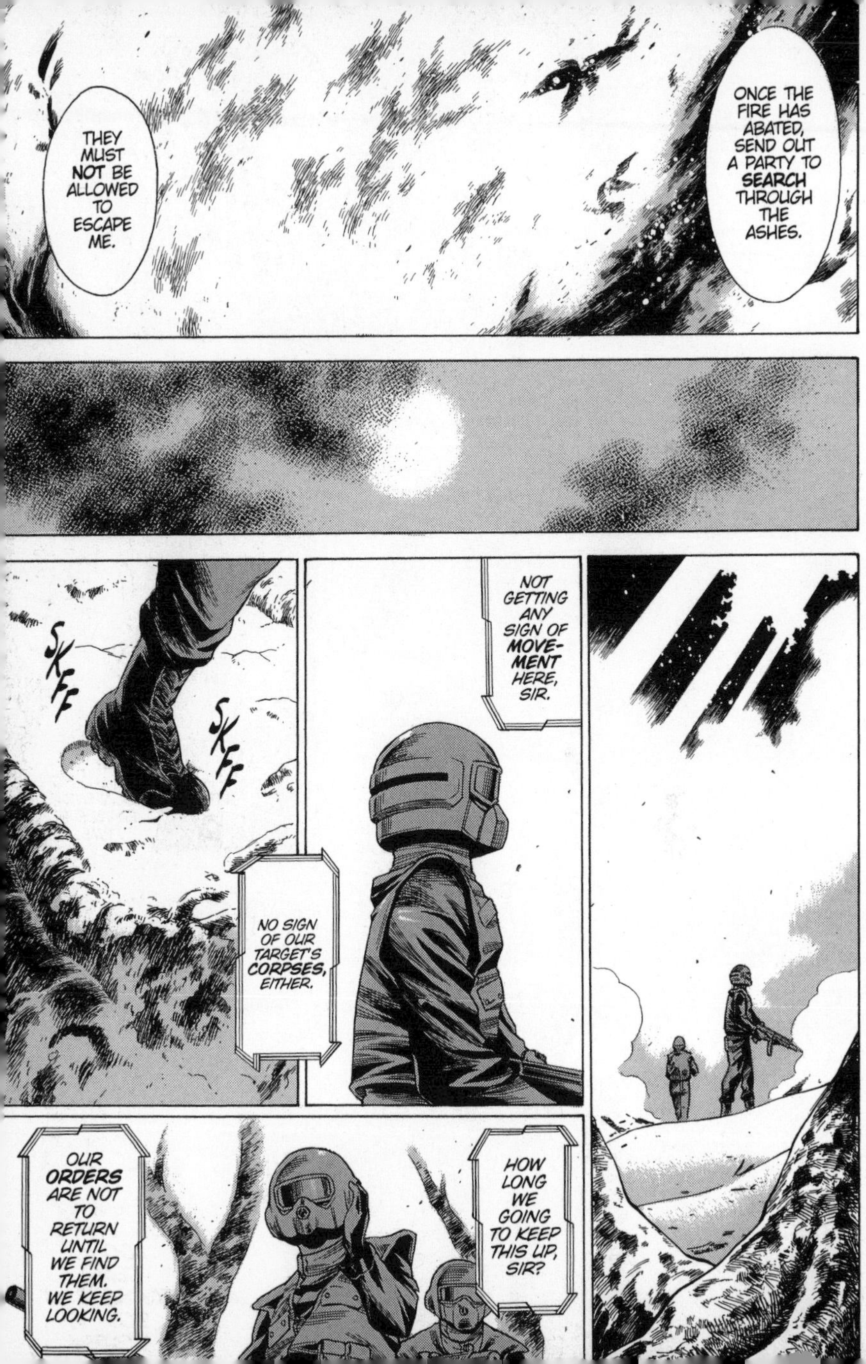
ONCE THE FIRE HAS ABATED, SEND OUT A PARTY TO SEARCH THROUGH THE ASHES.
THEY MUST NOT BE ALLOWED TO ESCAPE ME.
NOT GETTING ANY SIGN OF MOVEMENT HERE, SIR.
NO SIGN OF OUR TARGET'S CORPSES, EITHER.
SKFF
SKFF
HOW LONG WE GOING TO KEEP THIS UP, SIR?
OUR ORDERS ARE NOT TO RETURN UNTIL WE FIND THEM. WE KEEP LOOKING.

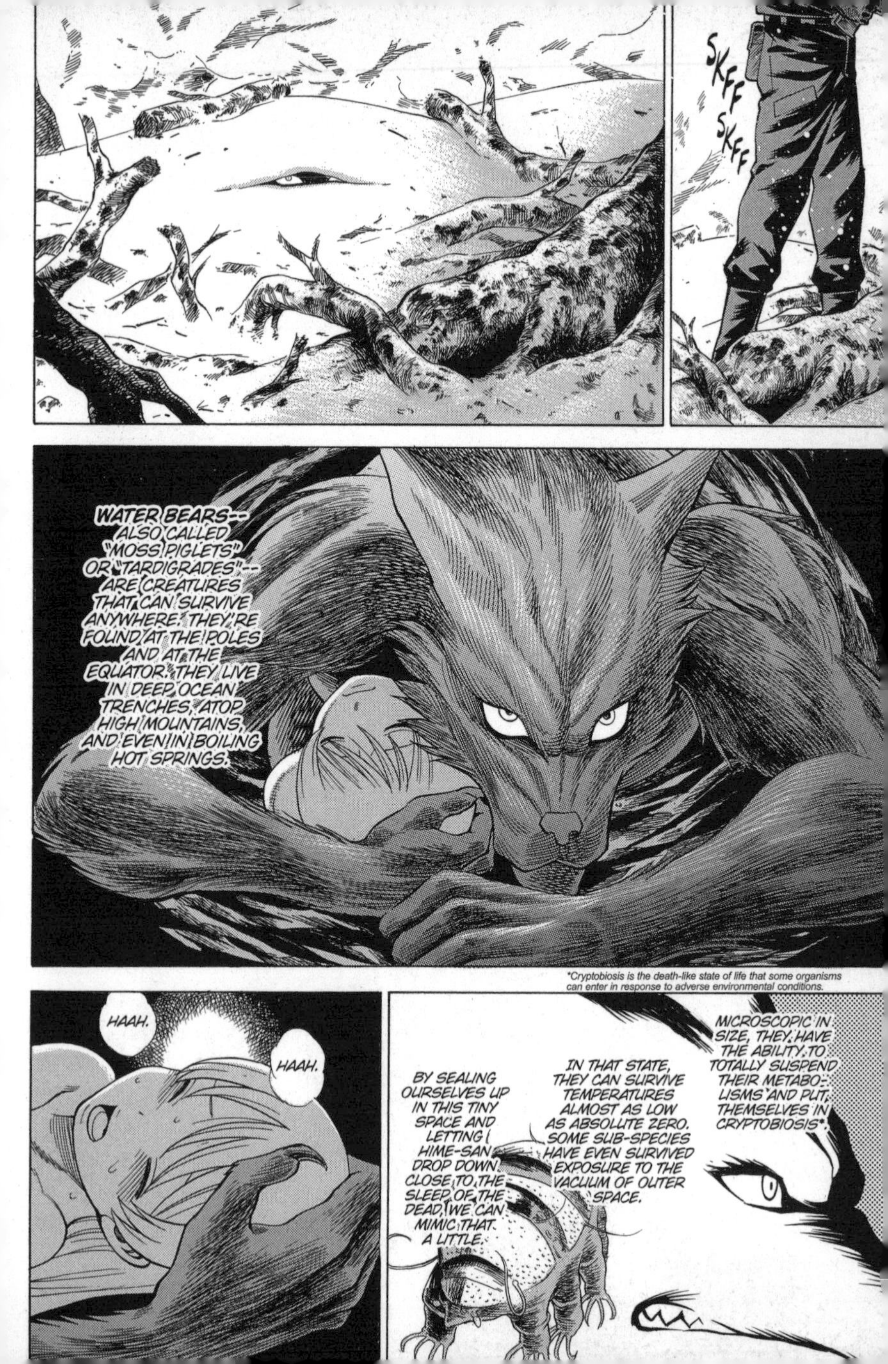
SKFF SKFF
WATER BEARS-- ALSO CALLED "MOSS PIGLETS" OR "TARDIGRADES"-- ARE CREATURES THAT CAN SURVIVE ANYWHERE. THEY'RE FOUND AT THE POLES AND AT THE EQUATOR. THEY LIVE IN DEEP OCEAN TRENCHES, ATOP HIGH MOUNTAINS, AND EVEN IN BOILING HOT SPRINGS.
MICROSCOPIC IN SIZE, THEY HAVE THE ABILITY TO TOTALLY SUSPEND THEIR METABO-LISMS AND PUT THEMSELVES IN CRYPTOBIOSIS*.
IN THAT STATE, THEY CAN SURVIVE TEMPERATURES ALMOST AS LOW AS ABSOLUTE ZERO. SOME SUB-SPECIES HAVE EVEN SURVIVED EXPOSURE TO THE VACUUM OF OUTER SPACE.
BY SEALING OURSELVES UP IN THIS TINY SPACE AND LETTING HIME-SAN DROP DOWN CLOSE TO THE SLEEP OF THE DEAD, WE CAN MIMIC THAT A LITTLE.
HAAH.
HAAH.

*Cryptobiosis is the death-like state of life that some organisms can enter in response to adverse environmental conditions.

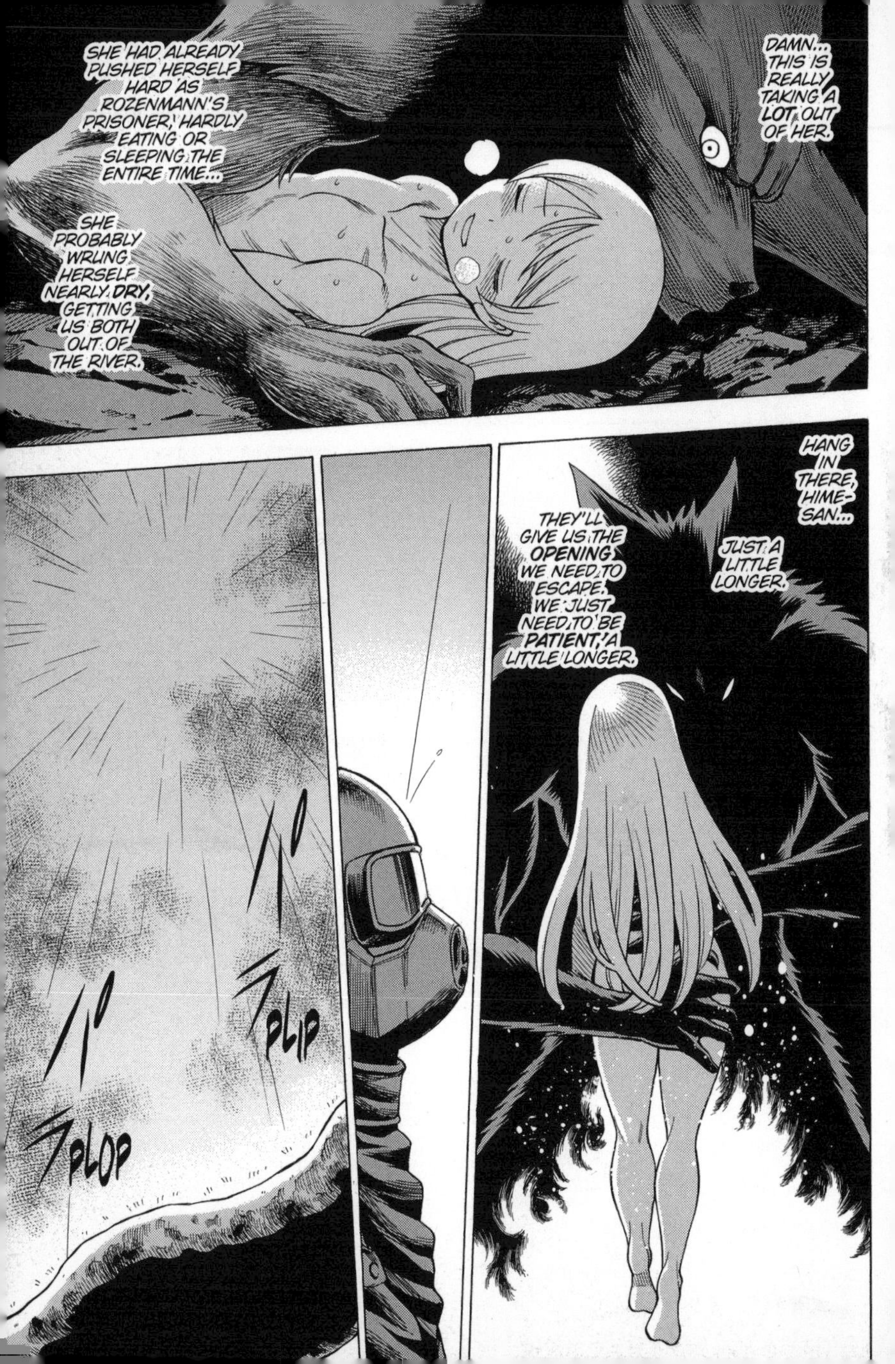
DAMN... THIS IS REALLY TAKING A LOT OUT OF HER.
SHE HAD ALREADY PUSHED HERSELF HARD AS ROZENMANN'S PRISONER, HARDLY EATING OR SLEEPING THE ENTIRE TIME...
SHE PROBABLY WRUNG HERSELF NEARLY DRY, GETTING US BOTH OUT OF THE RIVER.
HANG IN THERE, HIME-SAN...
JUST A LITTLE LONGER.
THEY'LL GIVE US THE OPENING WE NEED TO ESCAPE. WE JUST NEED TO BE PATIENT, A LITTLE LONGER.
PLIP
PLOP

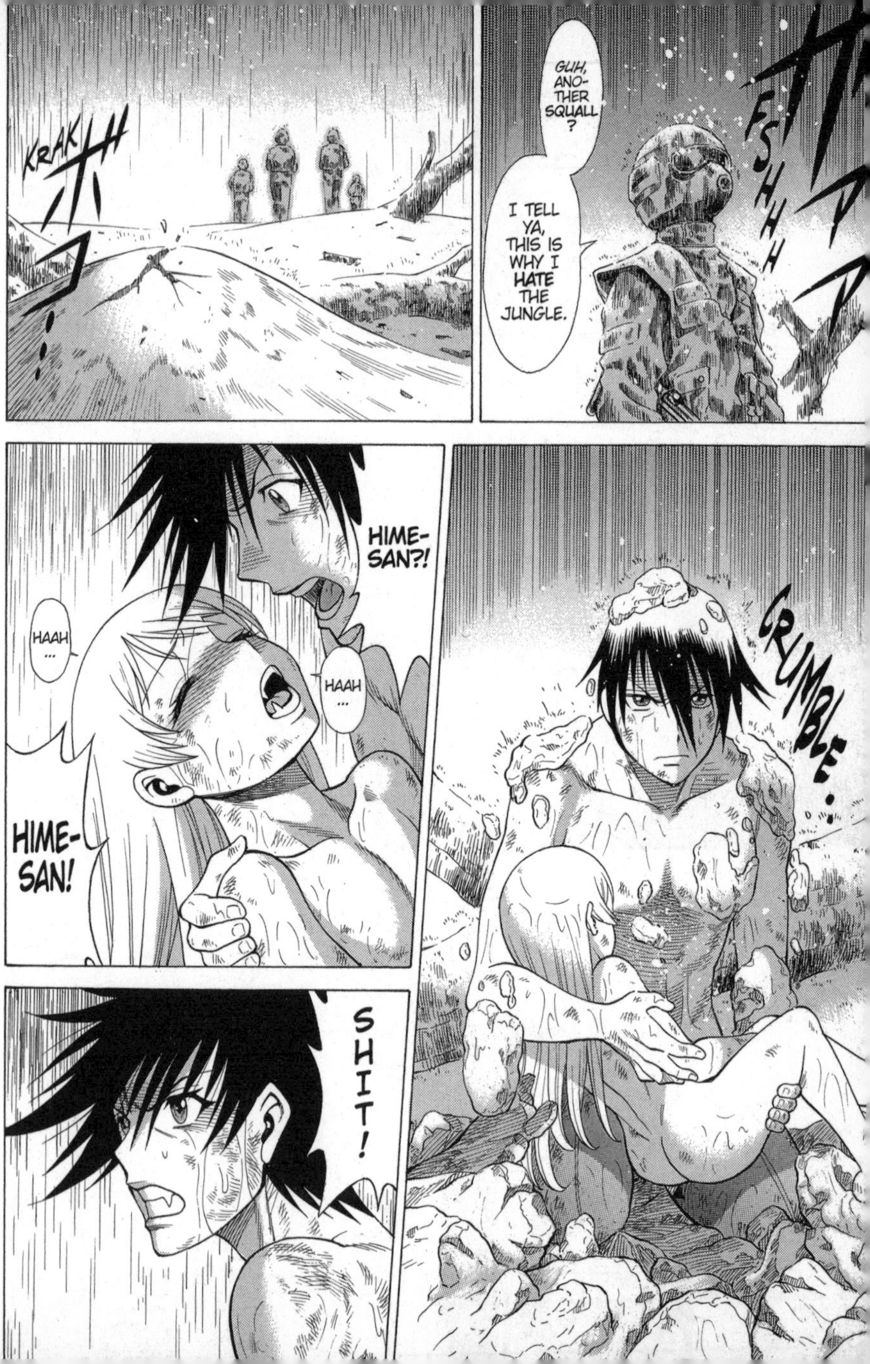
FSHHH
GUH, ANOTHER SQUALL?
I TELL YA, THIS IS WHY I HATE THE JUNGLE.
KRAK
CRUMBLE..
HIME-SAN?!
HAAH ...
HAAH ...
HIME-SAN!
SHIT!

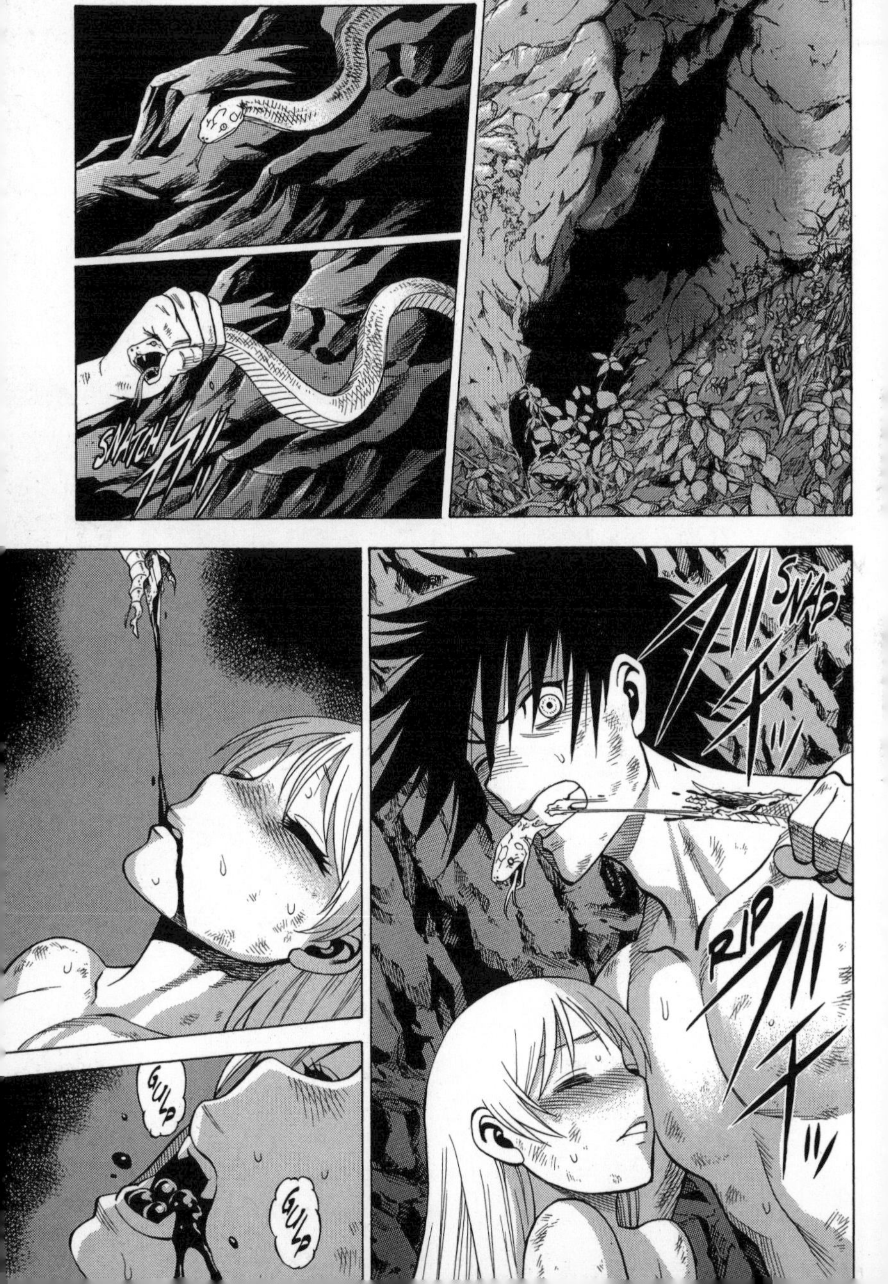
SNATCH
SNAP
RIP
GULP
GULP

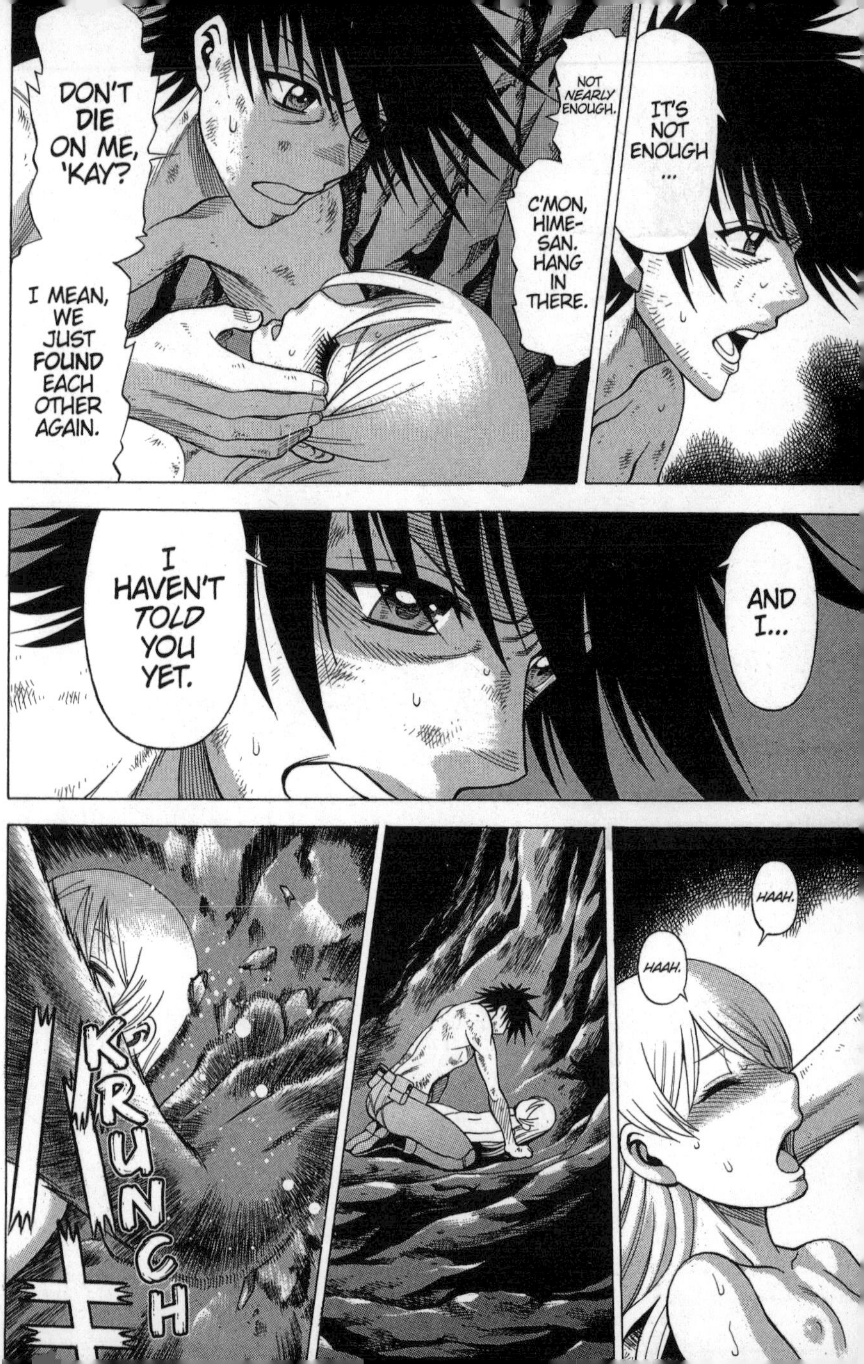
IT'S NOT ENOUGH ...
NOT NEARLY ENOUGH.
C'MON, HIME-SAN. HANG IN THERE.
DON'T DIE ON ME, 'KAY?
I MEAN, WE JUST FOUND EACH OTHER AGAIN.
AND I...
I HAVEN'T TOLD YOU YET.
HAAH.
HAAH.
KRUNCH

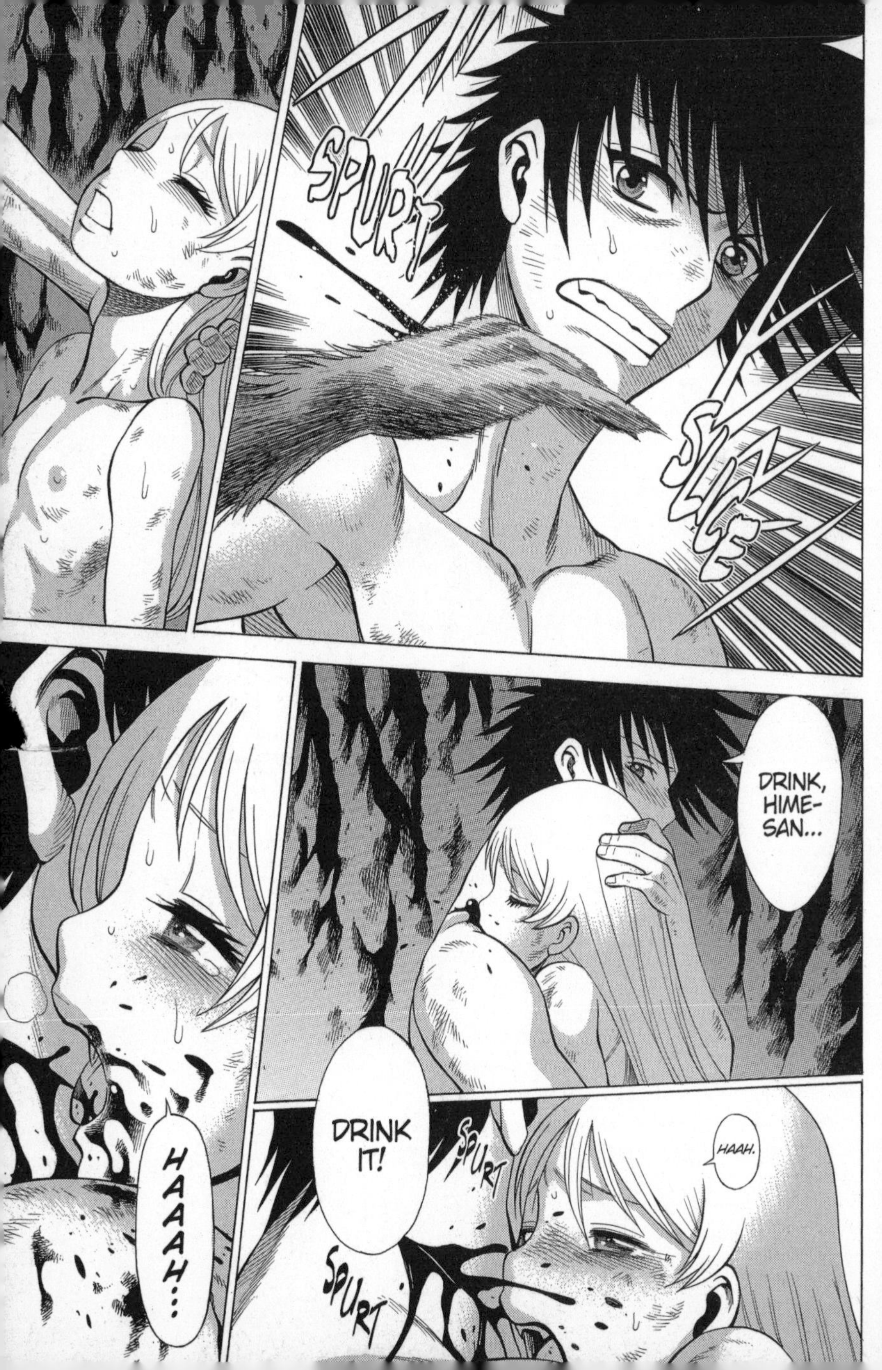
SLICE
SPURT
DRINK, HIME-SAN...
HAAH.
SPURT
DRINK IT!
SPURT
HAAAH...

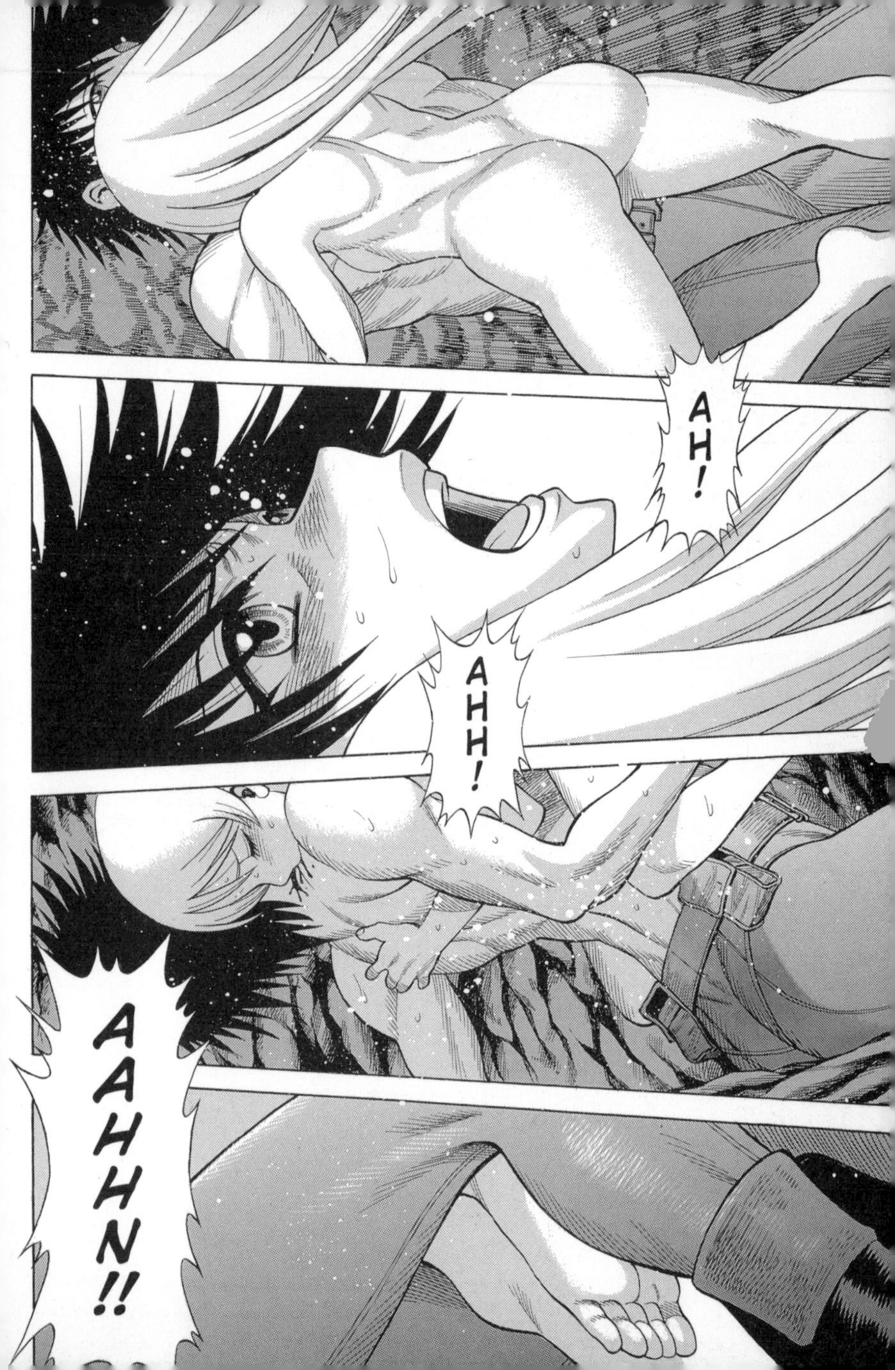
AH!
AHH!
AAHHN!!

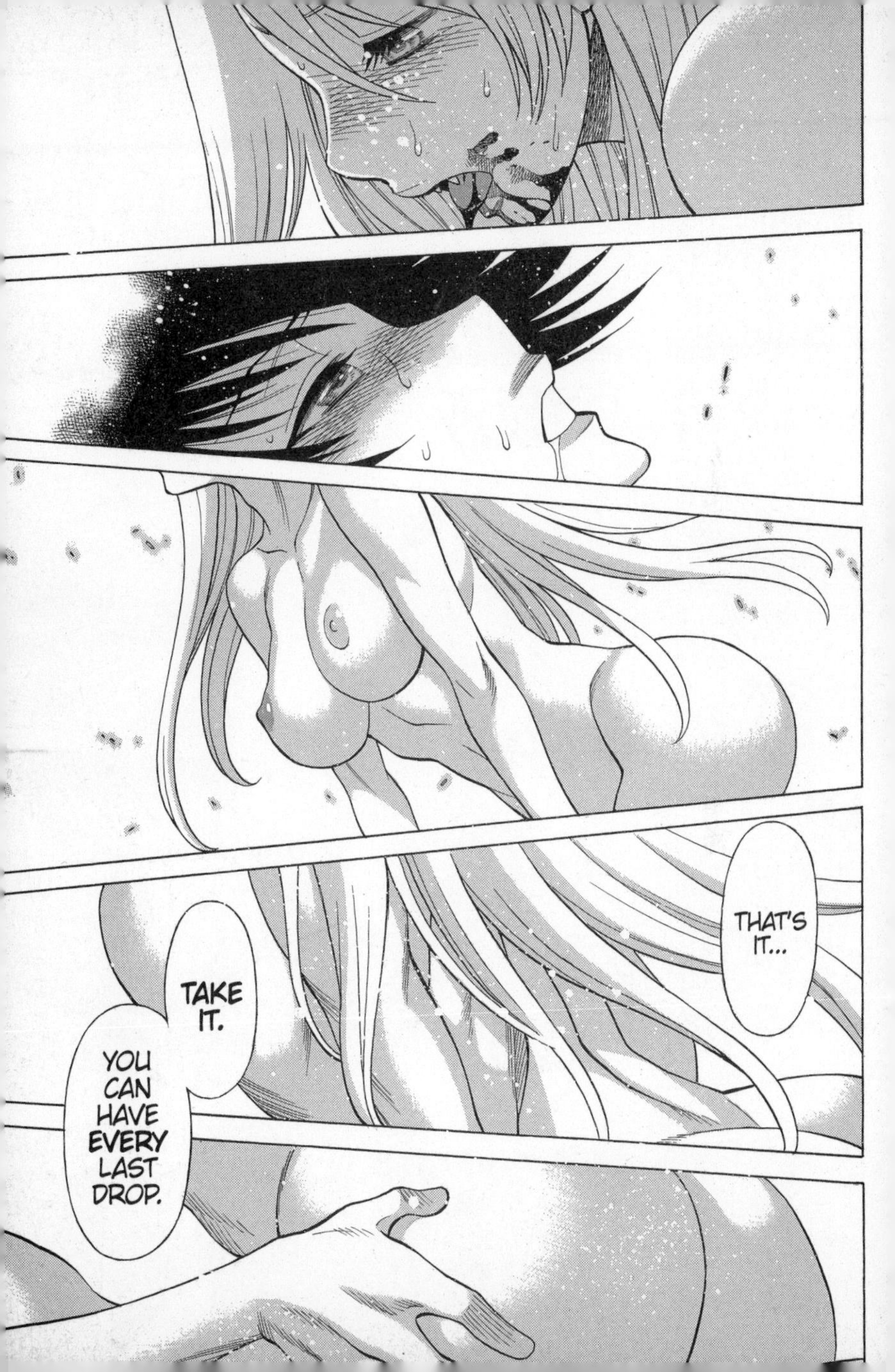
THAT'S IT...
TAKE IT.
YOU CAN HAVE EVERY LAST DROP.

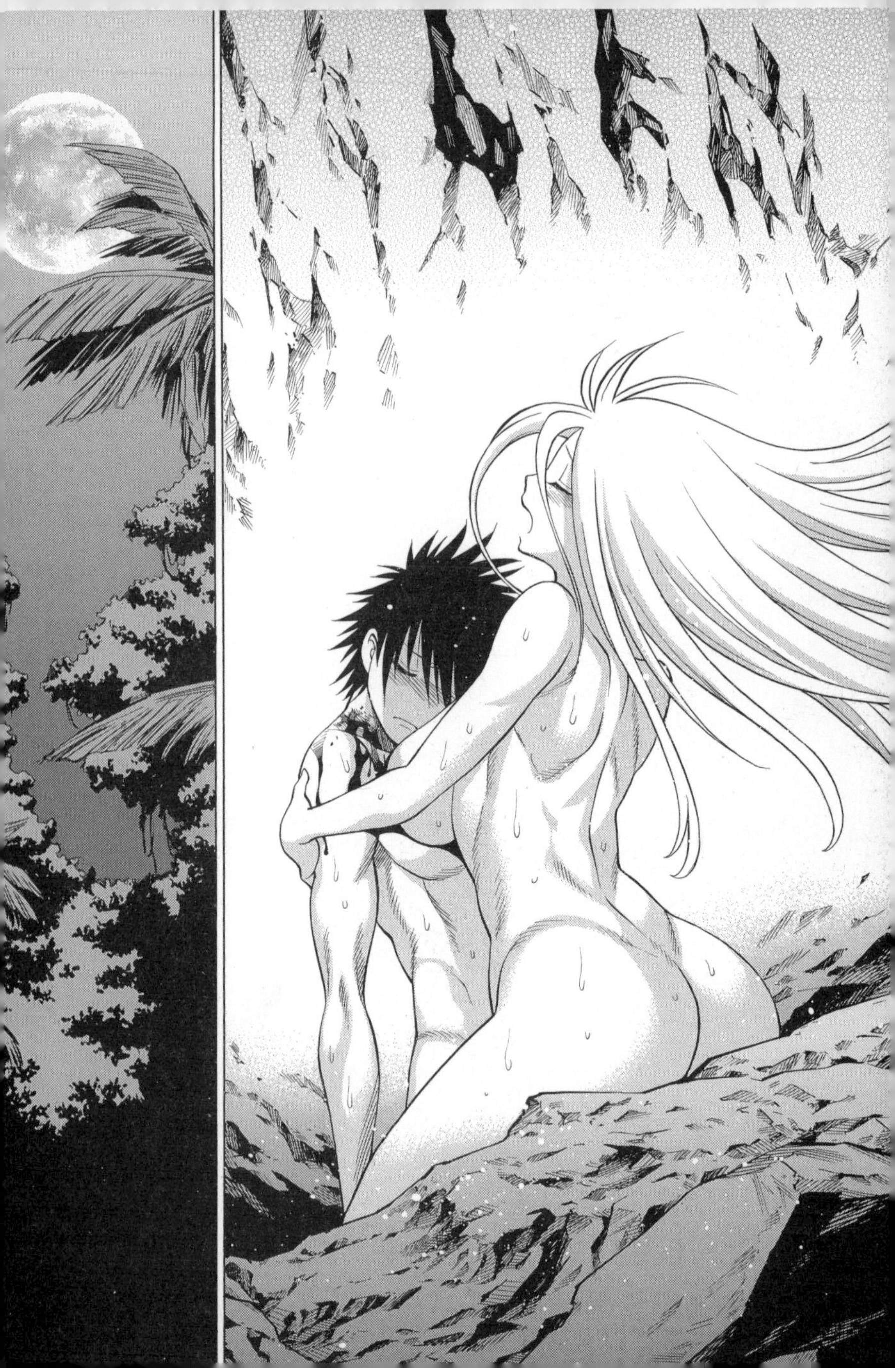

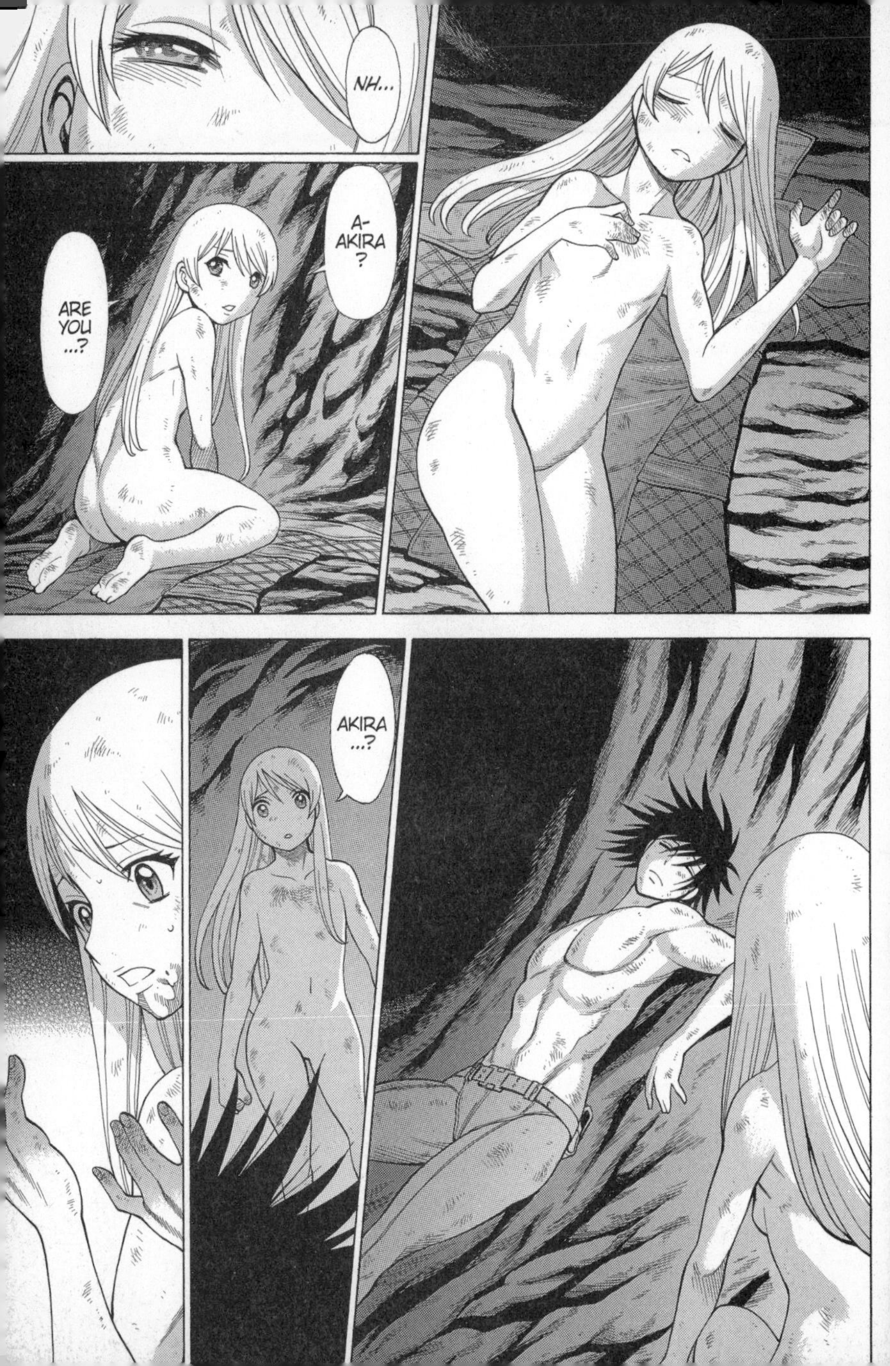
NH...
A-AKIRA?
ARE YOU...?
AKIRA...?

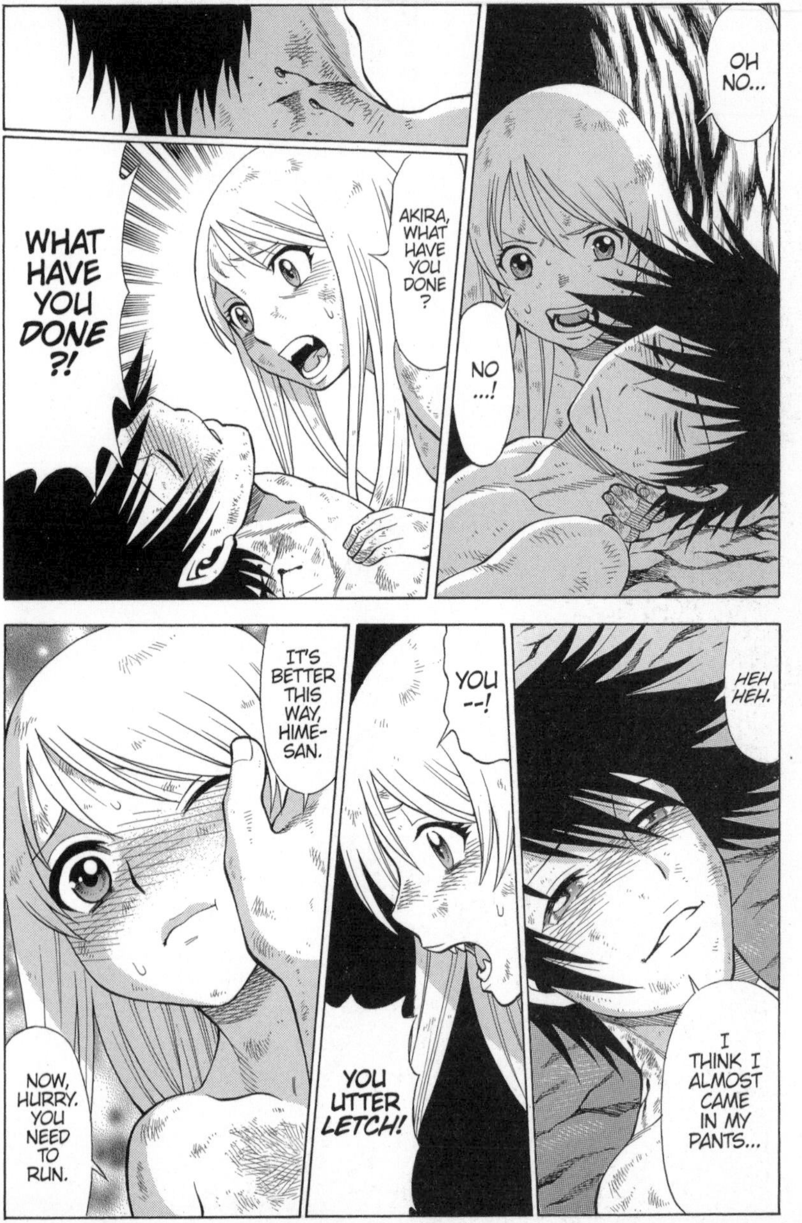
OH NO...
NO ...!
AKIRA, WHAT HAVE YOU DONE?
WHAT HAVE YOU DONE?!
HEH HEH.
I THINK I ALMOST CAME IN MY PANTS...
YOU --!
YOU UTTER LETCH!
IT'S BETTER THIS WAY, HIME-SAN.
NOW, HURRY. YOU NEED TO RUN.

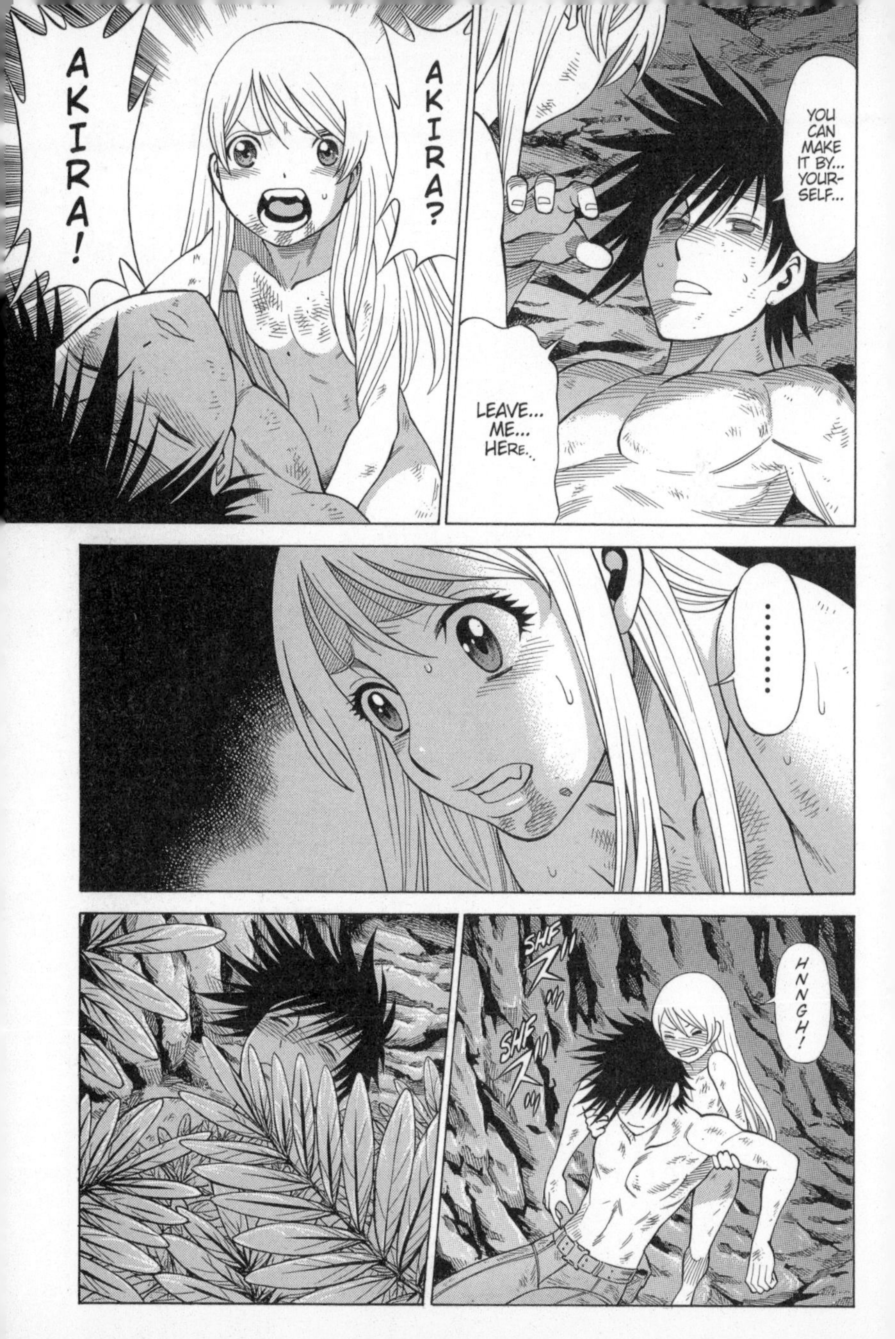
YOU CAN MAKE IT BY... YOUR-SELF...
LEAVE... ME... HERE...
AKIRA?
AKIRA!
......
HNNGH!
SHF
SHF

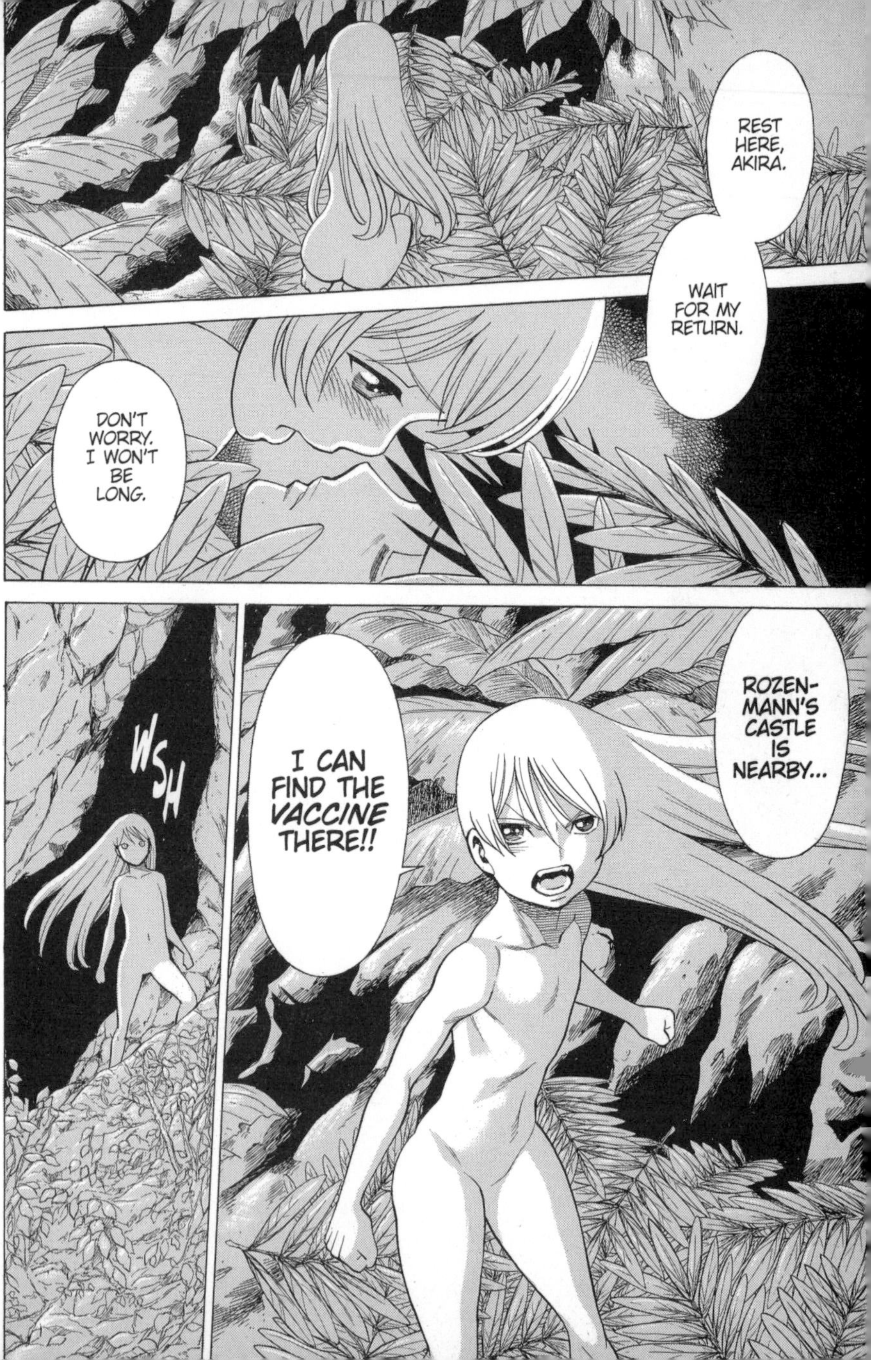
REST HERE, AKIRA.
WAIT FOR MY RETURN.
DON'T WORRY. I WON'T BE LONG.
ROZEN-MANN'S CASTLE IS NEARBY...
I CAN FIND THE *VACCINE* THERE!!
WSH

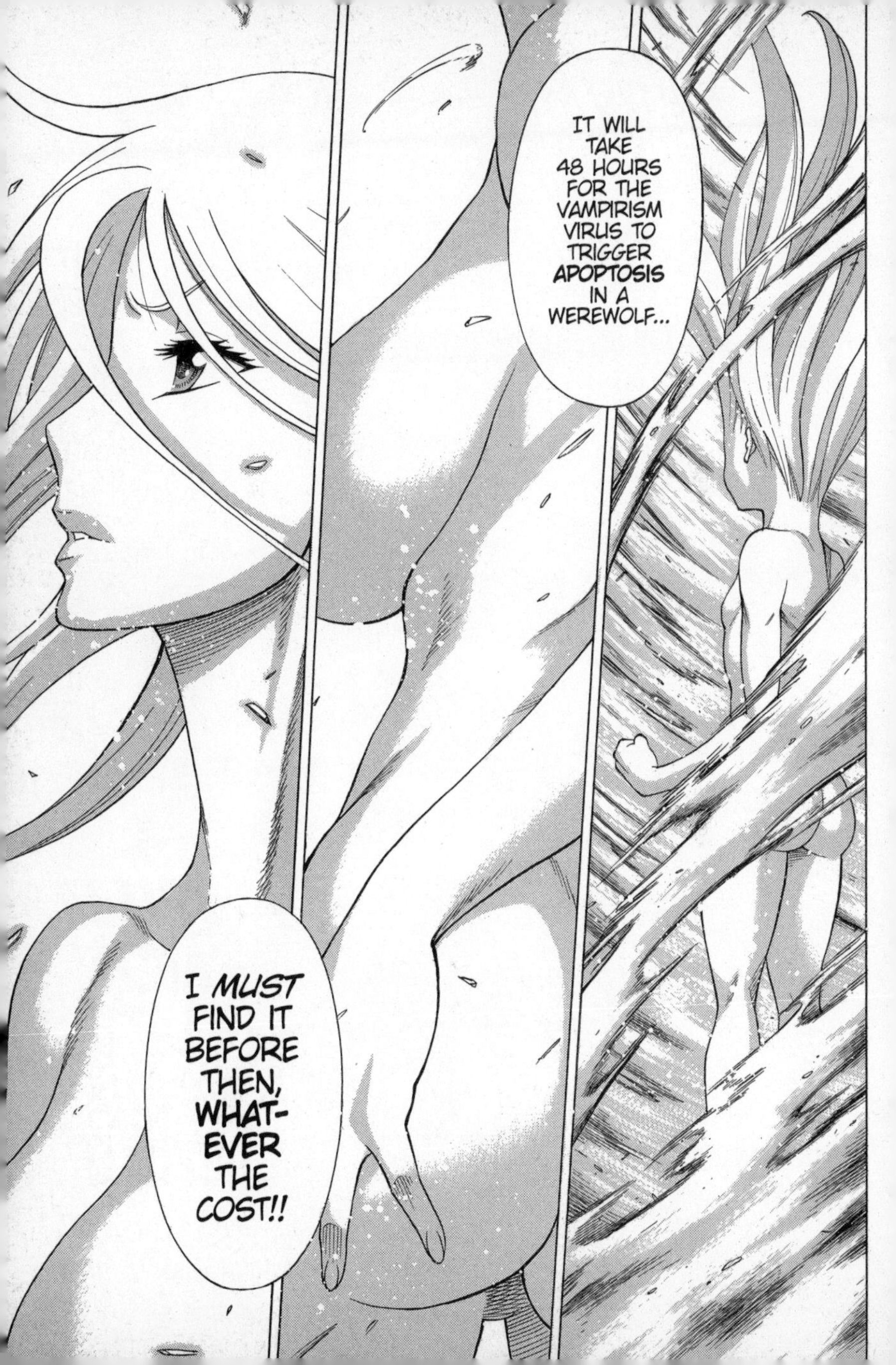
IT WILL TAKE 48 HOURS FOR THE VAMPIRISM VIRUS TO TRIGGER APOPTOSIS IN A WEREWOLF...
I MUST FIND IT BEFORE THEN, WHAT-EVER THE COST!!

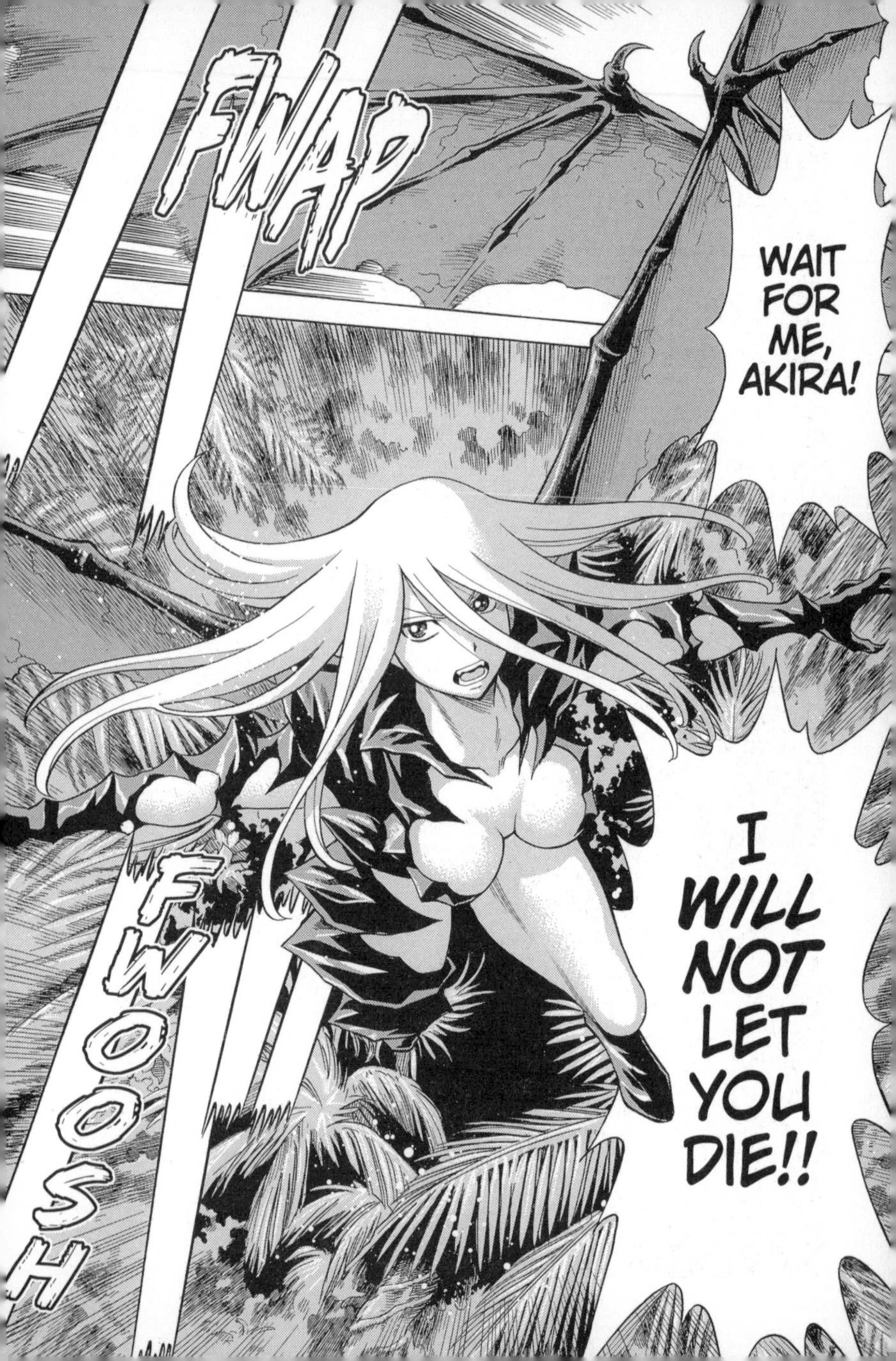
WAIT FOR ME, AKIRA!
FWAP
I WILL NOT LET YOU DIE!!
FWOOSH

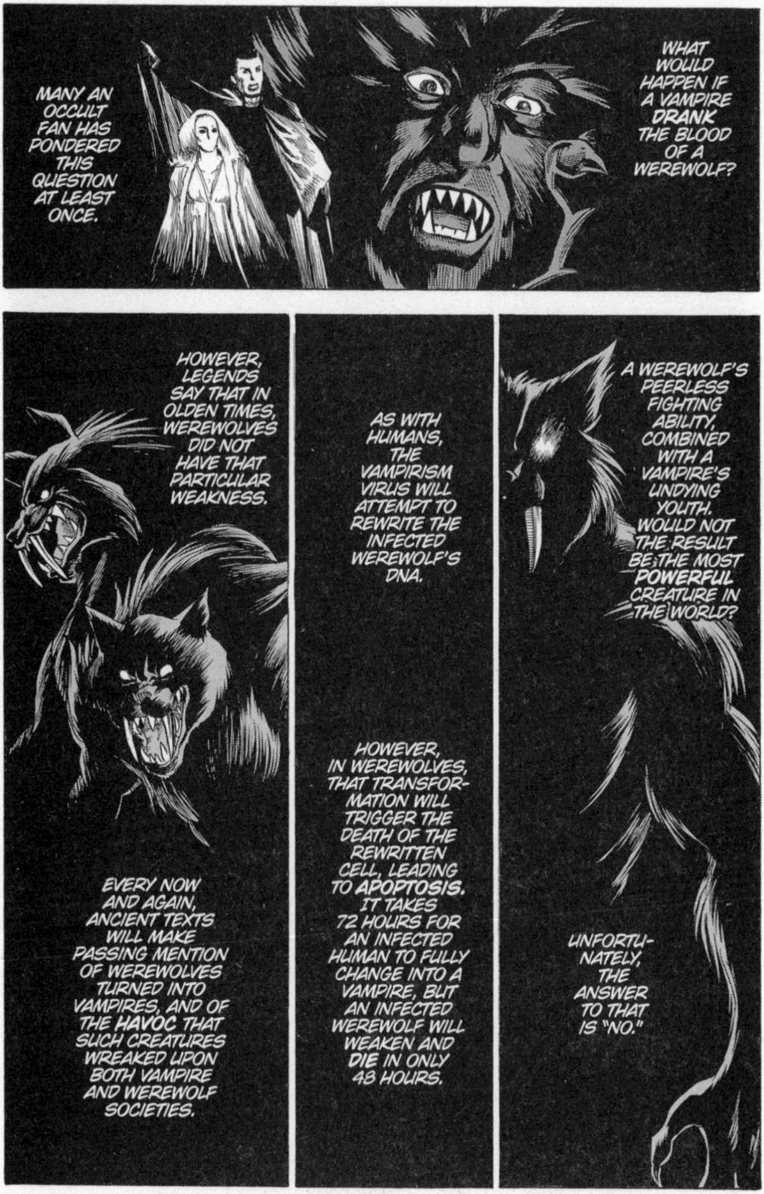
WHAT WOULD HAPPEN IF A VAMPIRE **DRANK** THE BLOOD OF A WEREWOLF?
MANY AN OCCULT FAN HAS PONDERED THIS QUESTION AT LEAST ONCE.
A WEREWOLF'S PEERLESS FIGHTING ABILITY, COMBINED WITH A VAMPIRE'S UNDYING YOUTH. WOULD NOT THE RESULT BE THE MOST **POWERFUL** CREATURE IN THE WORLD?
UNFORTU-NATELY, THE ANSWER TO THAT IS "NO."
AS WITH HUMANS, THE VAMPIRISM VIRUS WILL ATTEMPT TO REWRITE THE INFECTED WEREWOLF'S DNA.
HOWEVER, IN WEREWOLVES, THAT TRANSFOR-MATION WILL TRIGGER THE DEATH OF THE REWRITTEN CELL, LEADING TO **APOPTOSIS.** IT TAKES 72 HOURS FOR AN INFECTED HUMAN TO FULLY CHANGE INTO A VAMPIRE, BUT AN INFECTED WEREWOLF WILL WEAKEN AND **DIE** IN ONLY 48 HOURS.
HOWEVER, LEGENDS SAY THAT IN OLDEN TIMES, WEREWOLVES DID NOT HAVE THAT PARTICULAR WEAKNESS.
EVERY NOW AND AGAIN, ANCIENT TEXTS WILL MAKE PASSING MENTION OF WEREWOLVES TURNED INTO VAMPIRES, AND OF THE **HAVOC** THAT SUCH CREATURES WREAKED UPON BOTH VAMPIRE AND WEREWOLF SOCIETIES.

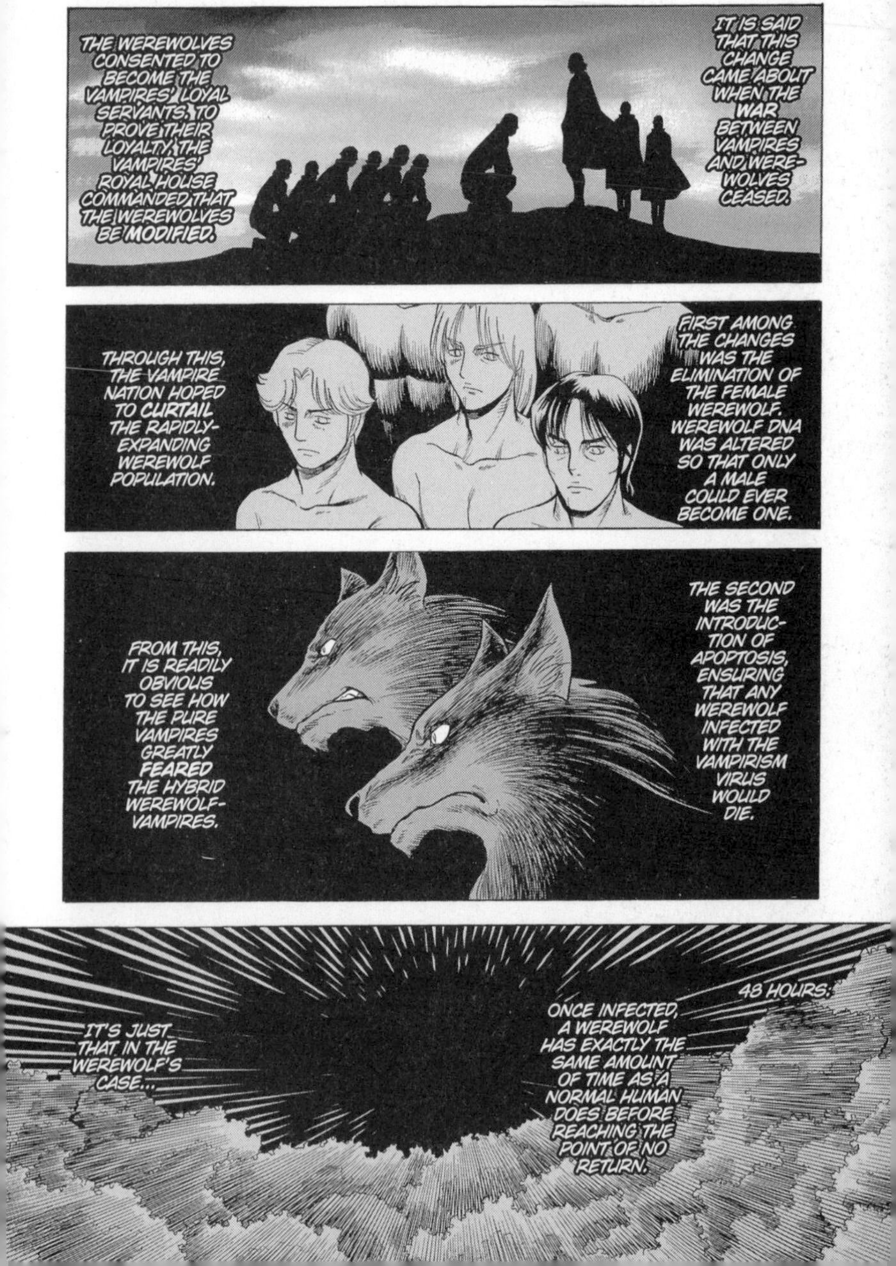
IT IS SAID THAT THIS CHANGE CAME ABOUT WHEN THE WAR BETWEEN VAMPIRES AND WERE-WOLVES CEASED.
THE WEREWOLVES CONSENTED TO BECOME THE VAMPIRES' LOYAL SERVANTS. TO PROVE THEIR LOYALTY, THE VAMPIRES' ROYAL HOUSE COMMANDED THAT THE WEREWOLVES BE MODIFIED.
FIRST AMONG THE CHANGES WAS THE ELIMINATION OF THE FEMALE WEREWOLF. WEREWOLF DNA WAS ALTERED SO THAT ONLY A MALE COULD EVER BECOME ONE.
THROUGH THIS, THE VAMPIRE NATION HOPED TO CURTAIL THE RAPIDLY-EXPANDING WEREWOLF POPULATION.
THE SECOND WAS THE INTRODUC-TION OF APOPTOSIS, ENSURING THAT ANY WEREWOLF INFECTED WITH THE VAMPIRISM VIRUS WOULD DIE.
FROM THIS, IT IS READILY OBVIOUS TO SEE HOW THE PURE VAMPIRES GREATLY FEARED THE HYBRID WEREWOLF-VAMPIRES.
48 HOURS.
ONCE INFECTED, A WEREWOLF HAS EXACTLY THE SAME AMOUNT OF TIME AS A NORMAL HUMAN DOES BEFORE REACHING THE POINT OF NO RETURN.
IT'S JUST THAT IN THE WEREWOLF'S CASE...

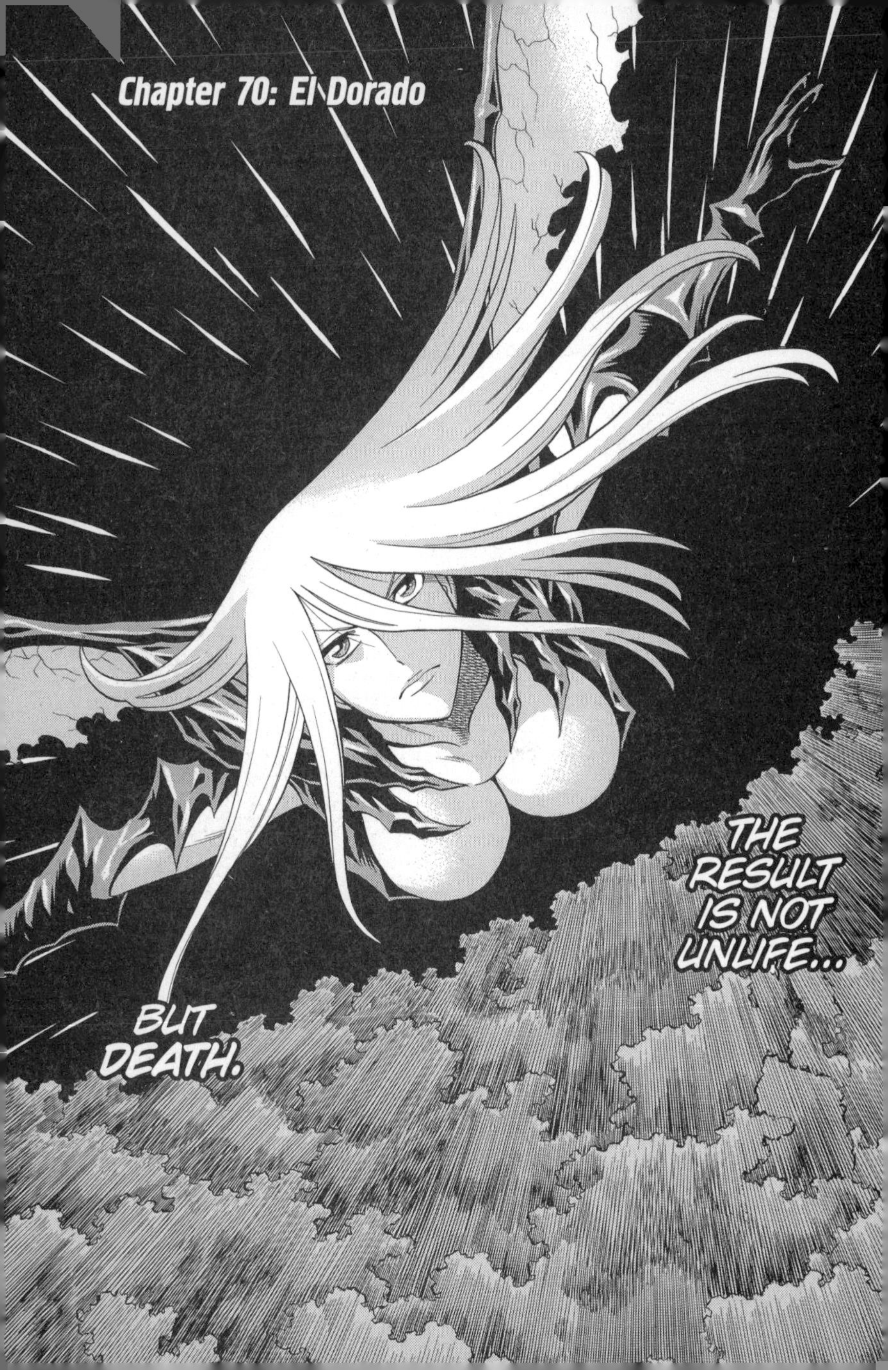
Chapter 70: El Dorado
THE RESULT IS NOT UNLIFE...
BUT DEATH.

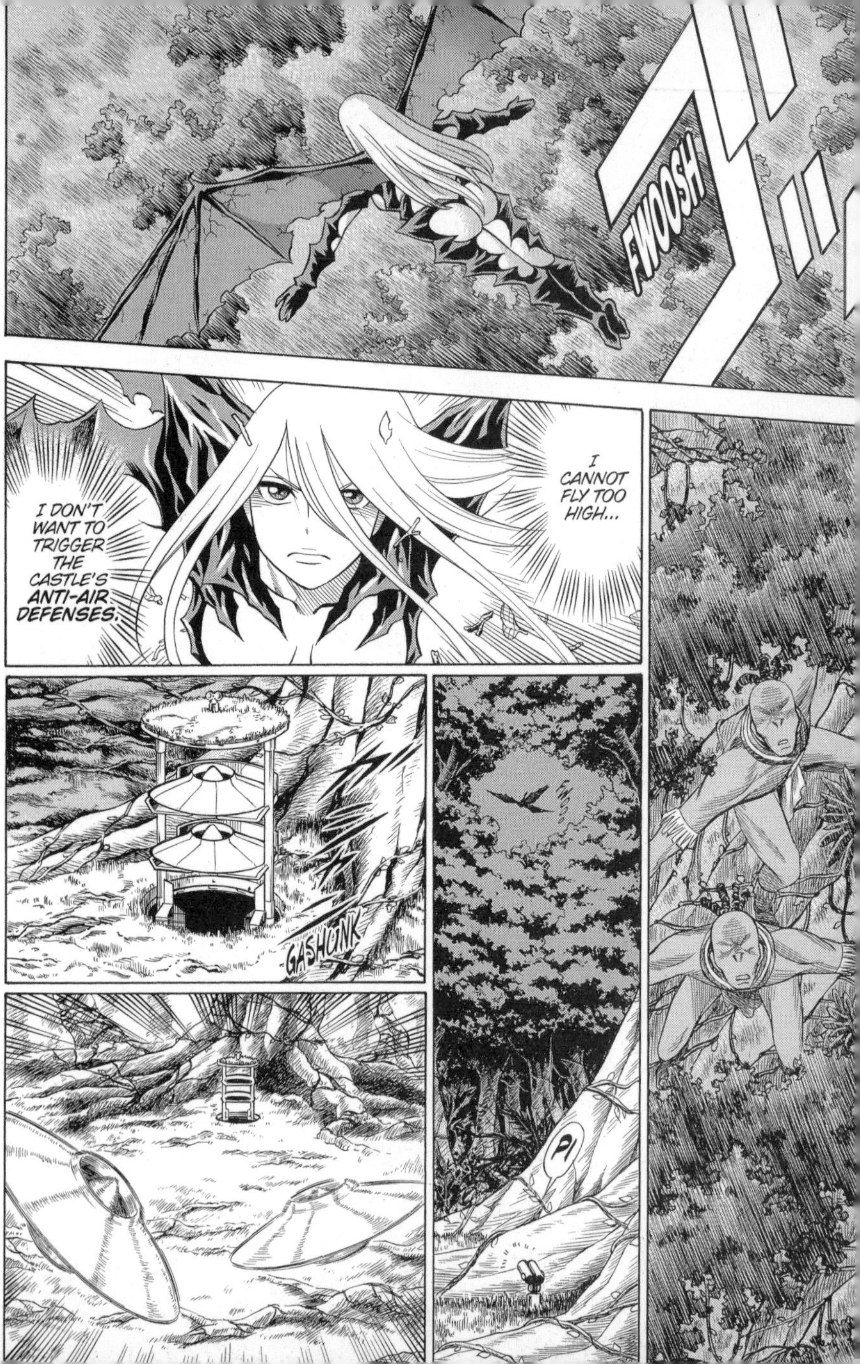
FWOOSH
I CANNOT FLY TOO HIGH...
I DON'T WANT TO TRIGGER THE CASTLE'S ANTI-AIR DEFENSES.
PI
GASHUNK

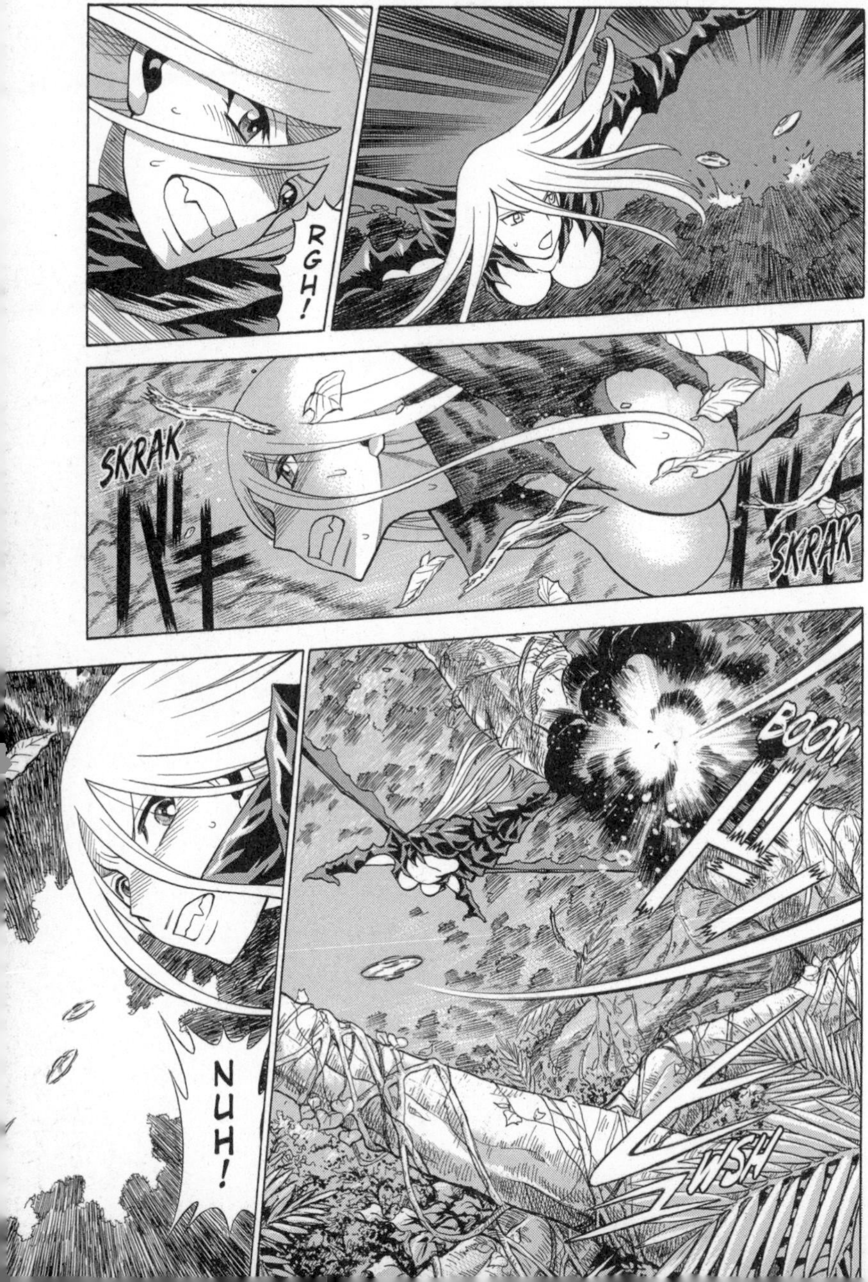
RGH!
SKRAK
SKRAK
BOOM
SWSH
NUH!

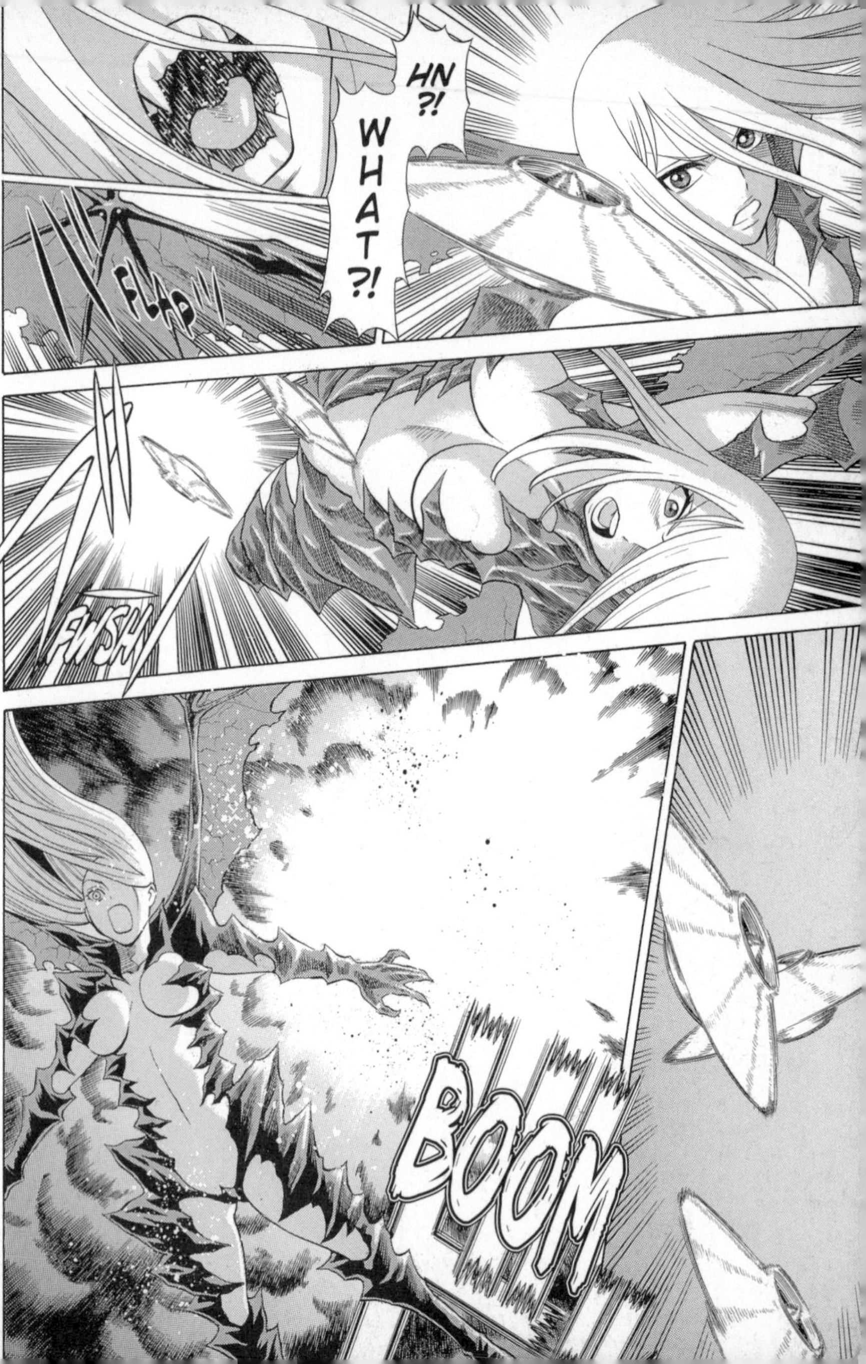
HN ?!
WHAT ?!
FLAP
FWSH
BOOM

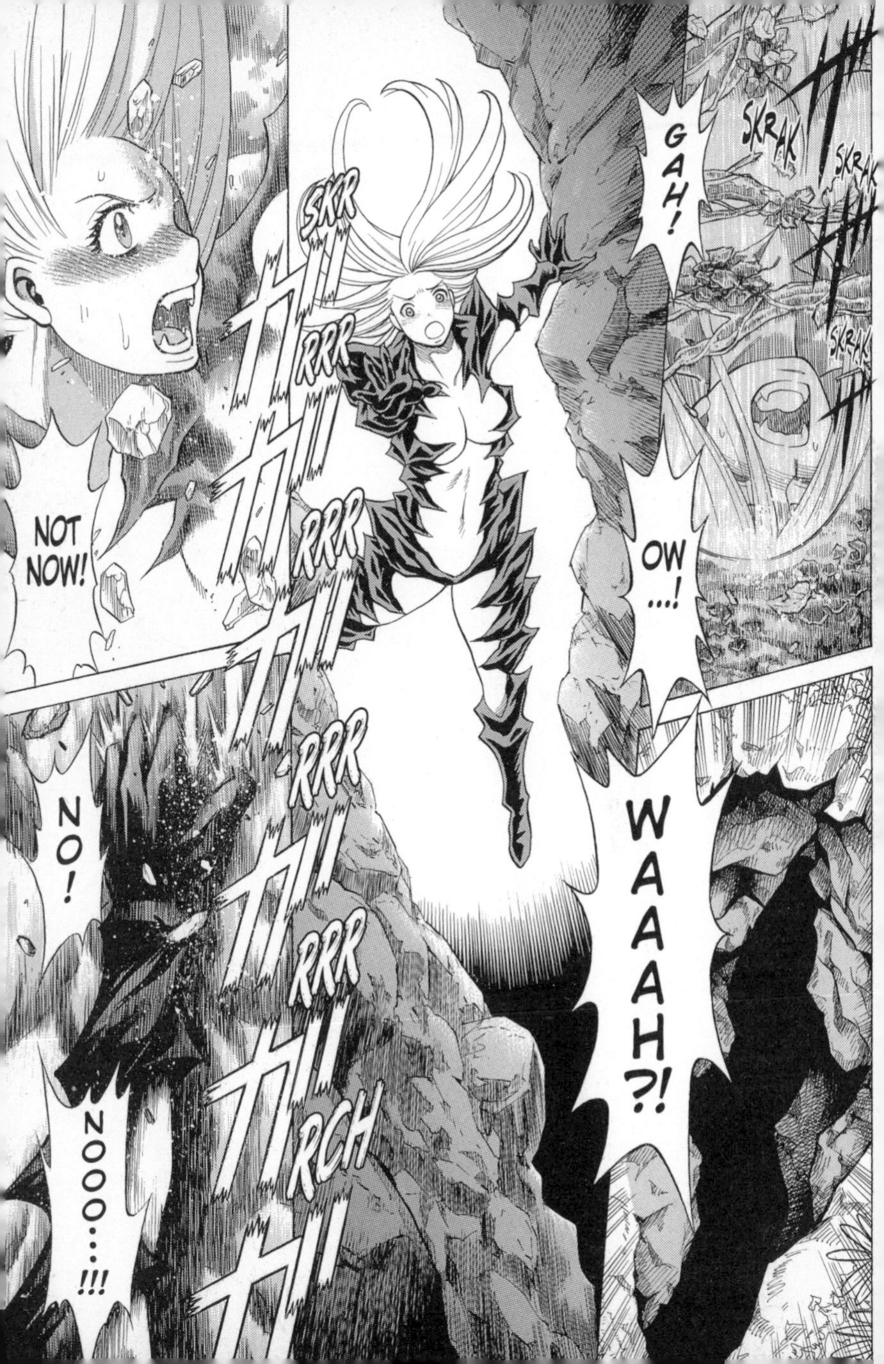
GAH!
SKRAK
SKRAK
SKRAK
OW ...!
SKRRRRRRRRRRRRRRCH
WAAAH?!
NOT NOW!
NO!
NOOOO....!!!

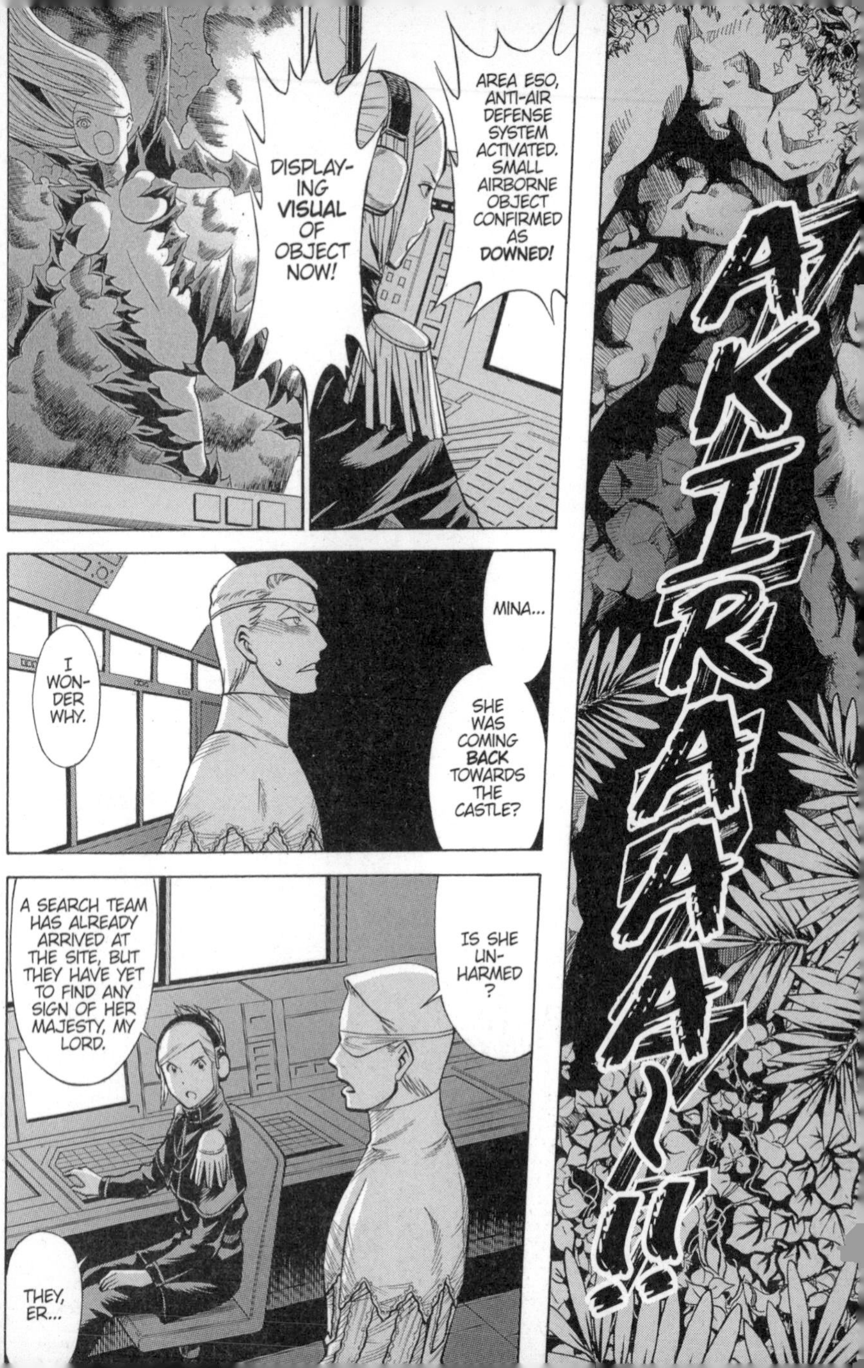
AKIRAAA!!
AREA E50, ANTI-AIR DEFENSE SYSTEM ACTIVATED. SMALL AIRBORNE OBJECT CONFIRMED AS DOWNED!
DISPLAY-ING VISUAL OF OBJECT NOW!
MINA...
SHE WAS COMING BACK TOWARDS THE CASTLE?
I WON-DER WHY.
IS SHE UN-HARMED ?
A SEARCH TEAM HAS ALREADY ARRIVED AT THE SITE, BUT THEY HAVE YET TO FIND ANY SIGN OF HER MAJESTY, MY LORD.
THEY, ER...

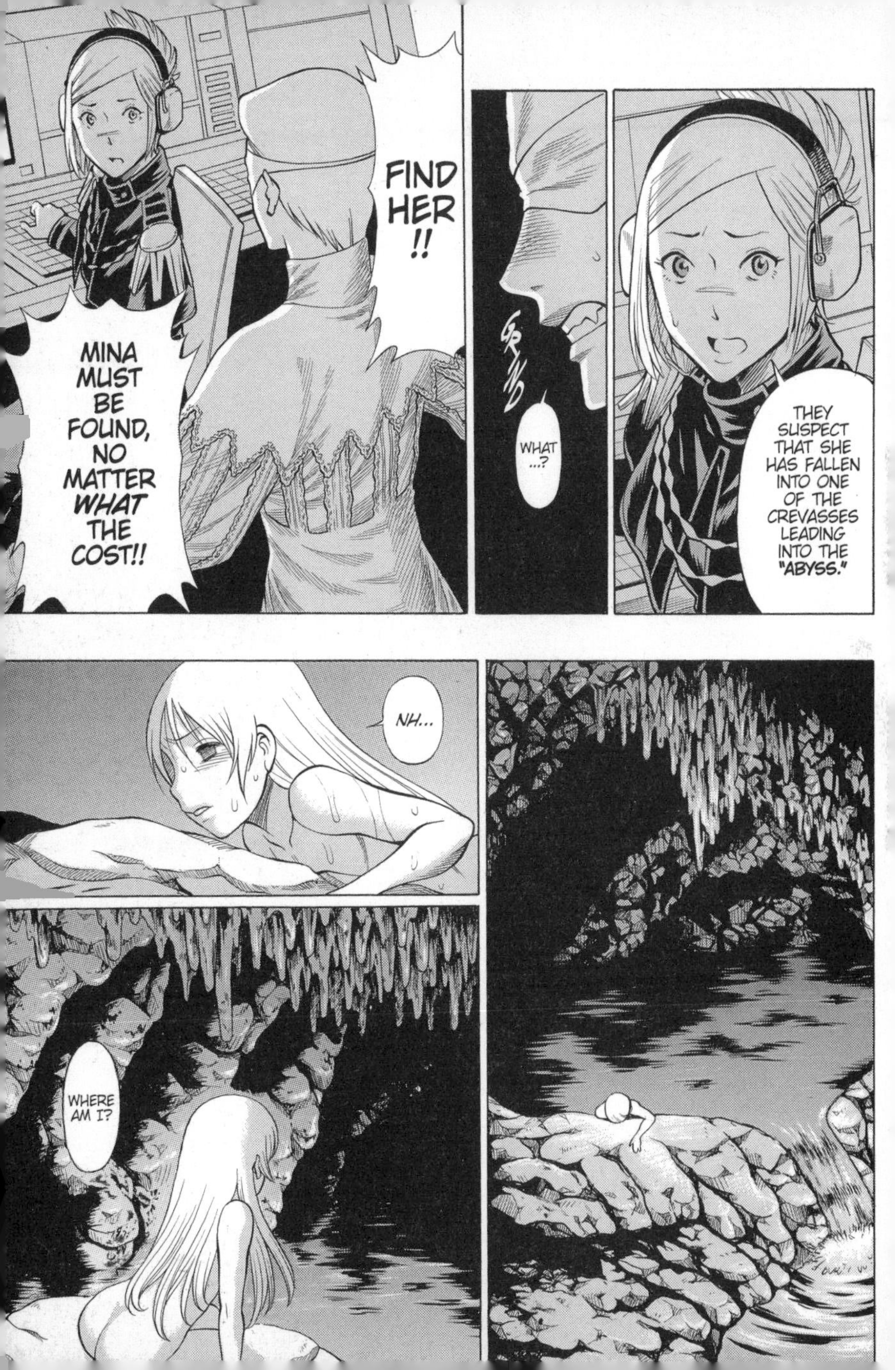
THEY SUSPECT THAT SHE HAS FALLEN INTO ONE OF THE CREVASSES LEADING INTO THE "ABYSS."
GRIND
WHAT ...?
FIND HER !!
MINA MUST BE FOUND, NO MATTER *WHAT* THE COST!!
NH...
WHERE AM I?

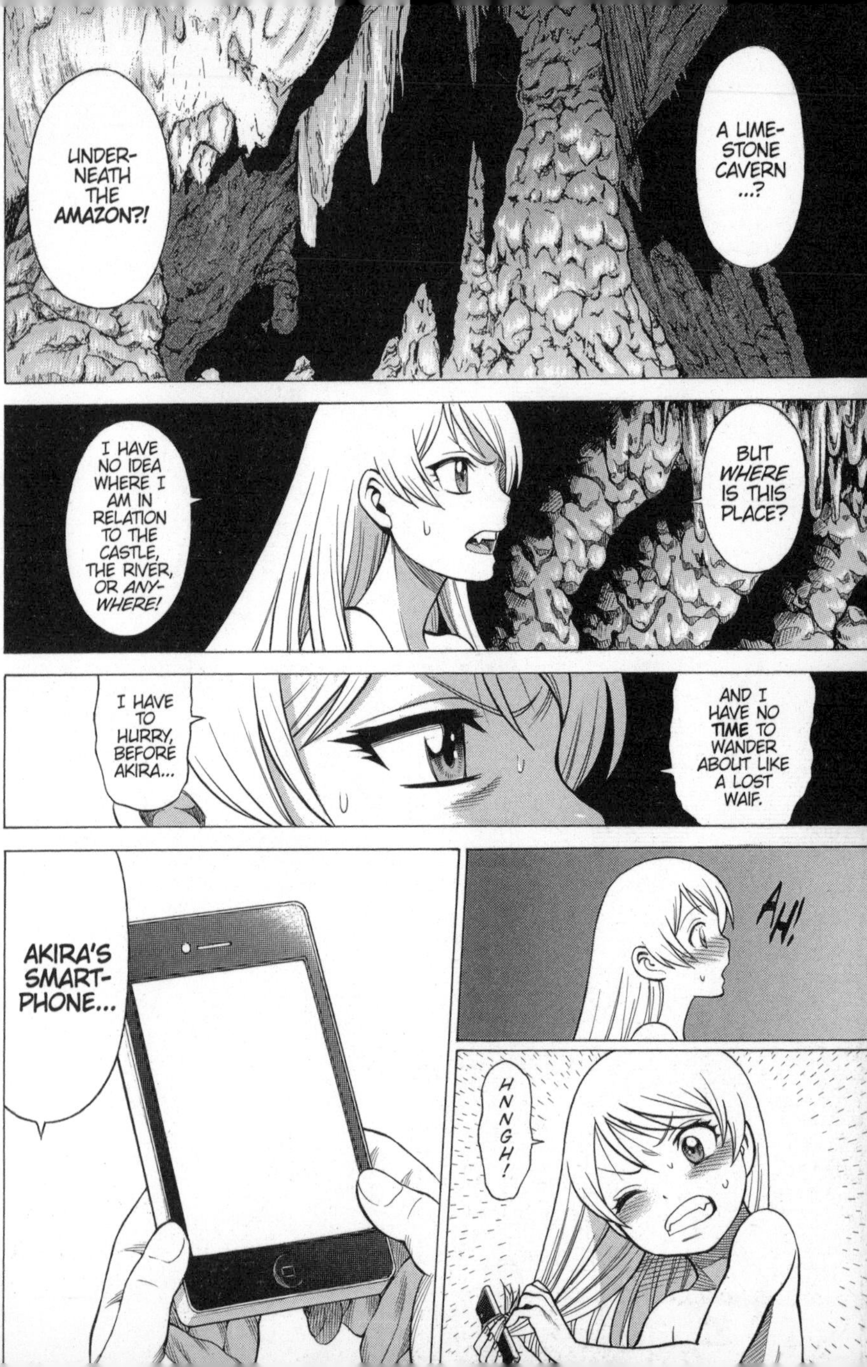
A LIME-STONE CAVERN...?
UNDER-NEATH THE AMAZON?!
BUT WHERE IS THIS PLACE?
I HAVE NO IDEA WHERE I AM IN RELATION TO THE CASTLE, THE RIVER, OR ANY-WHERE!
AND I HAVE NO TIME TO WANDER ABOUT LIKE A LOST WAIF.
I HAVE TO HURRY, BEFORE AKIRA...
AH!
HNNGH!
AKIRA'S SMART-PHONE...

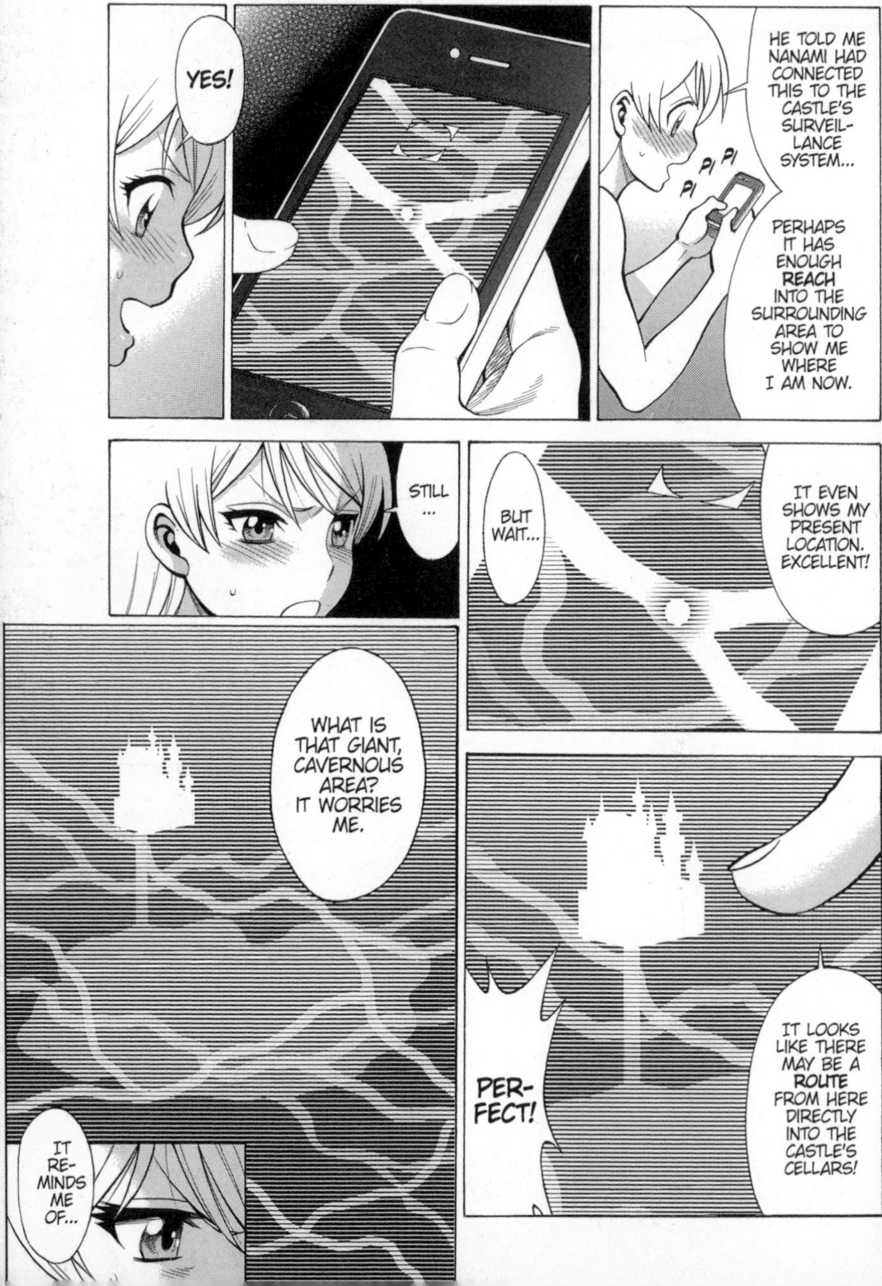
HE TOLD ME NANAMI HAD CONNECTED THIS TO THE CASTLE'S SURVEIL-LANCE SYSTEM...
PI PI PI
PERHAPS IT HAS ENOUGH **REACH** INTO THE SURROUNDING AREA TO SHOW ME WHERE I AM NOW.
YES!
IT EVEN SHOWS MY PRESENT LOCATION. EXCELLENT!
BUT WAIT...
STILL ...
IT LOOKS LIKE THERE MAY BE A **ROUTE** FROM HERE DIRECTLY INTO THE CASTLE'S CELLARS!
PER-FECT!
WHAT IS THAT GIANT, CAVERNOUS AREA? IT WORRIES ME.
IT RE-MINDS ME OF...

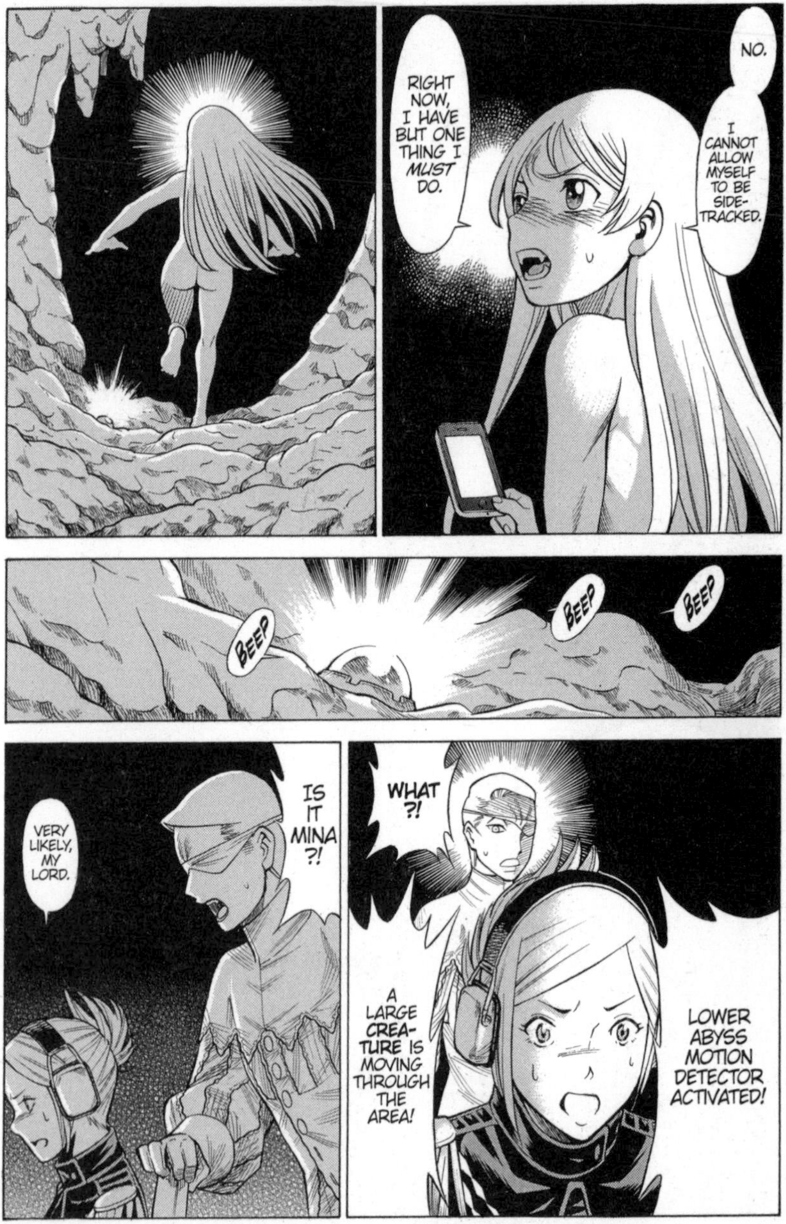
NO.
I CANNOT ALLOW MYSELF TO BE SIDE-TRACKED.
RIGHT NOW, I HAVE BUT ONE THING I *MUST* DO.
BEEP
BEEP
BEEP
WHAT ?!
LOWER ABYSS MOTION DETECTOR ACTIVATED!
A LARGE **CREA-TURE** IS MOVING THROUGH THE AREA!
IS IT MINA ?!
VERY LIKELY, MY LORD.

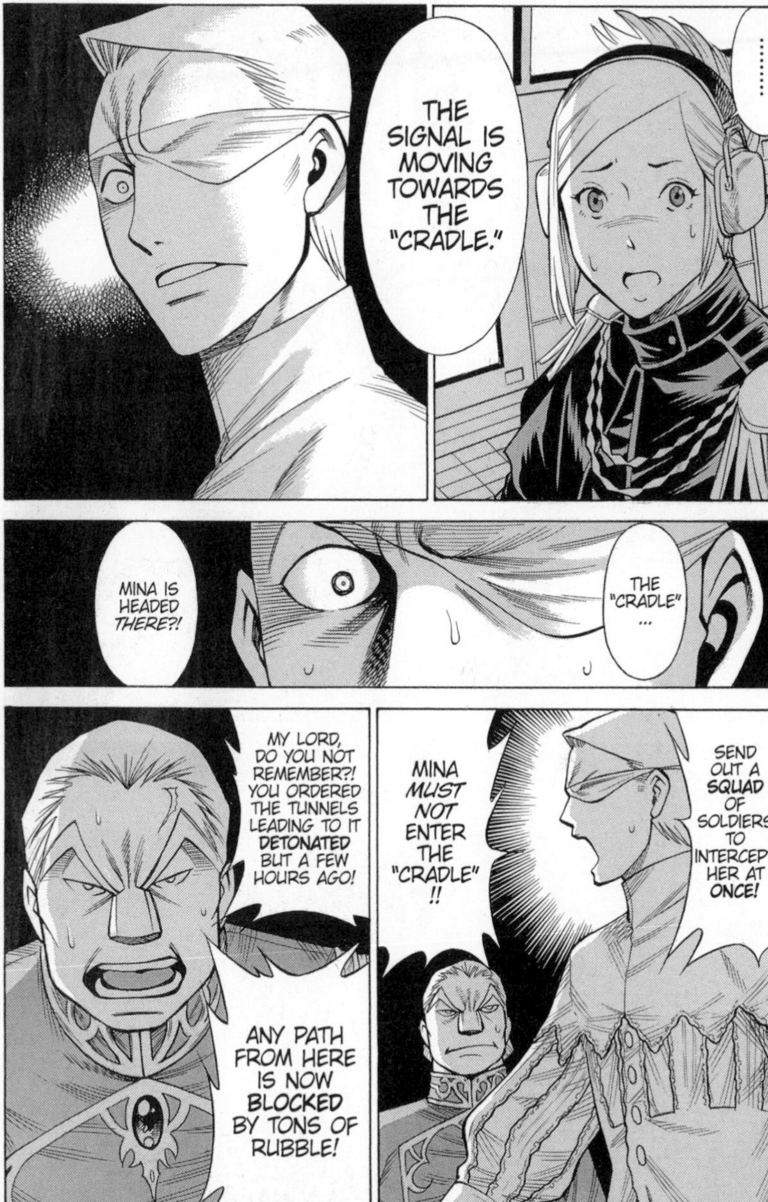
......
THE SIGNAL IS MOVING TOWARDS THE "CRADLE."
THE "CRADLE" ...
MINA IS HEADED THERE?!
SEND OUT A SQUAD OF SOLDIERS TO INTERCEPT HER AT ONCE!
MINA MUST NOT ENTER THE "CRADLE" !!
MY LORD, DO YOU NOT REMEMBER?! YOU ORDERED THE TUNNELS LEADING TO IT DETONATED BUT A FEW HOURS AGO!
ANY PATH FROM HERE IS NOW BLOCKED BY TONS OF RUBBLE!

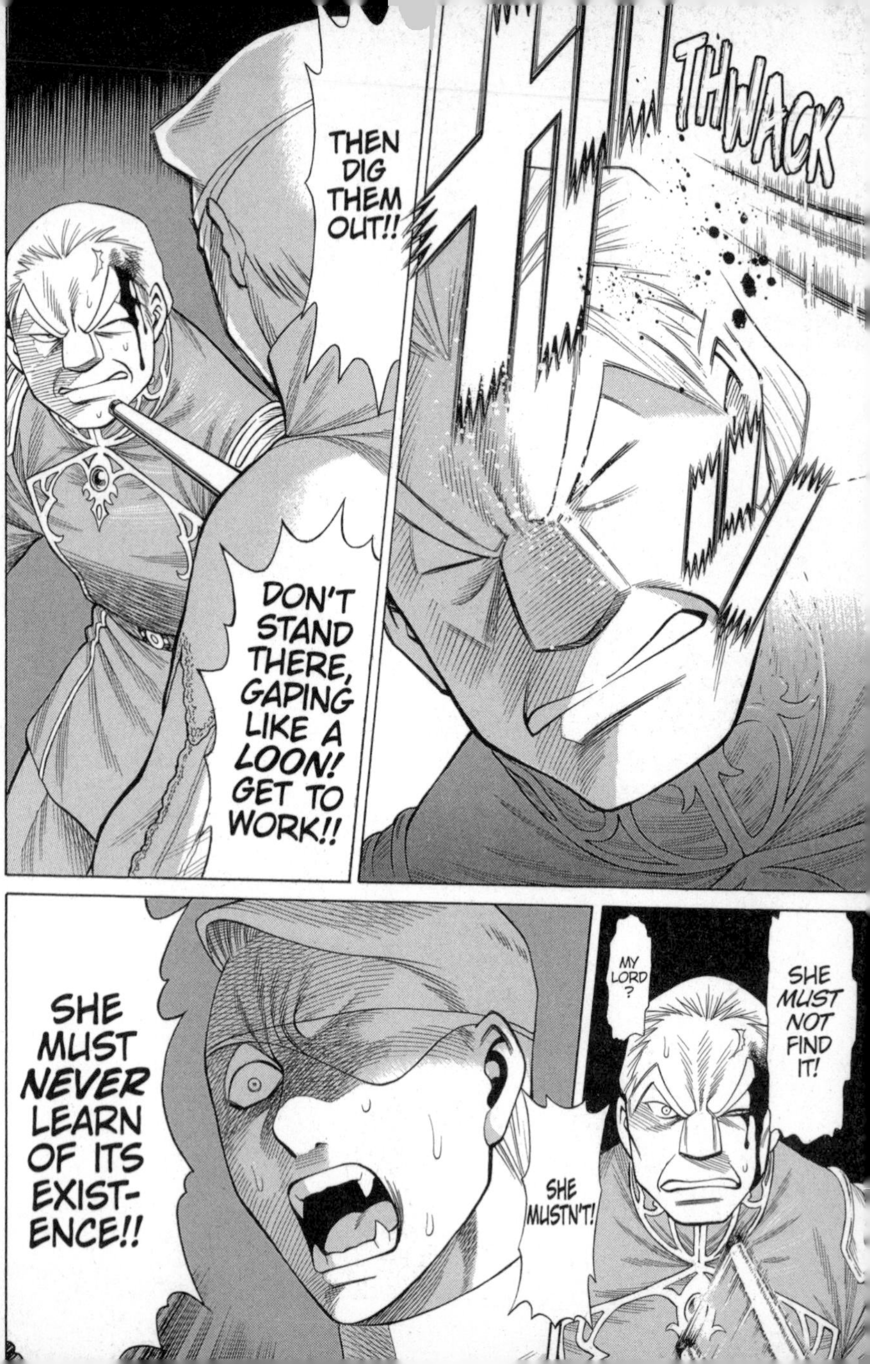
THWACK
THEN DIG THEM OUT!!
DON'T STAND THERE, GAPING LIKE A LOON! GET TO WORK!!
SHE MUST NOT FIND IT!
MY LORD?
SHE MUSTN'T!
SHE MUST NEVER LEARN OF ITS EXISTENCE!!

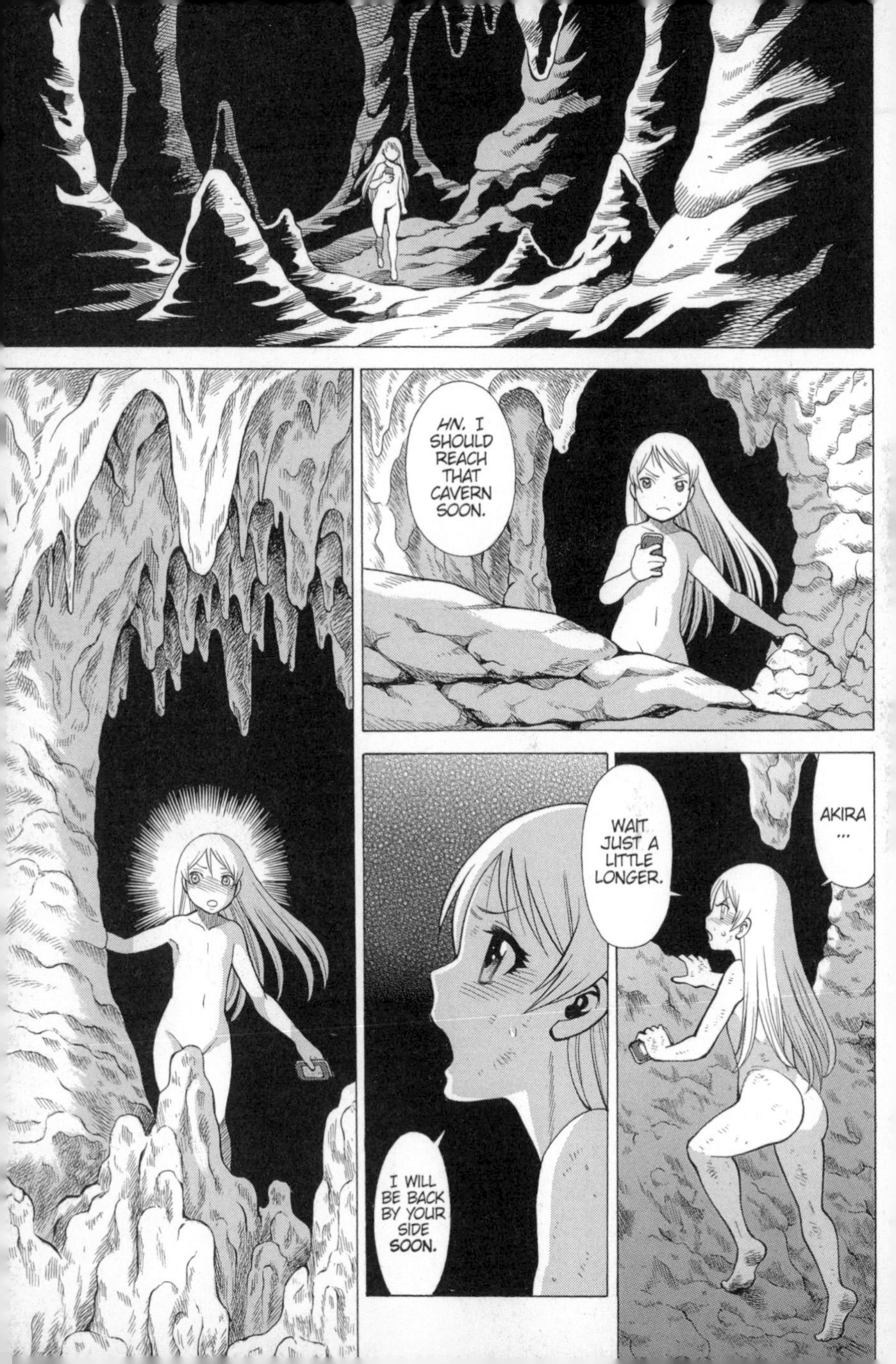

HN. I SHOULD REACH THAT CAVERN SOON.
AKIRA ...
WAIT JUST A LITTLE LONGER.
I WILL BE BACK BY YOUR SIDE SOON.

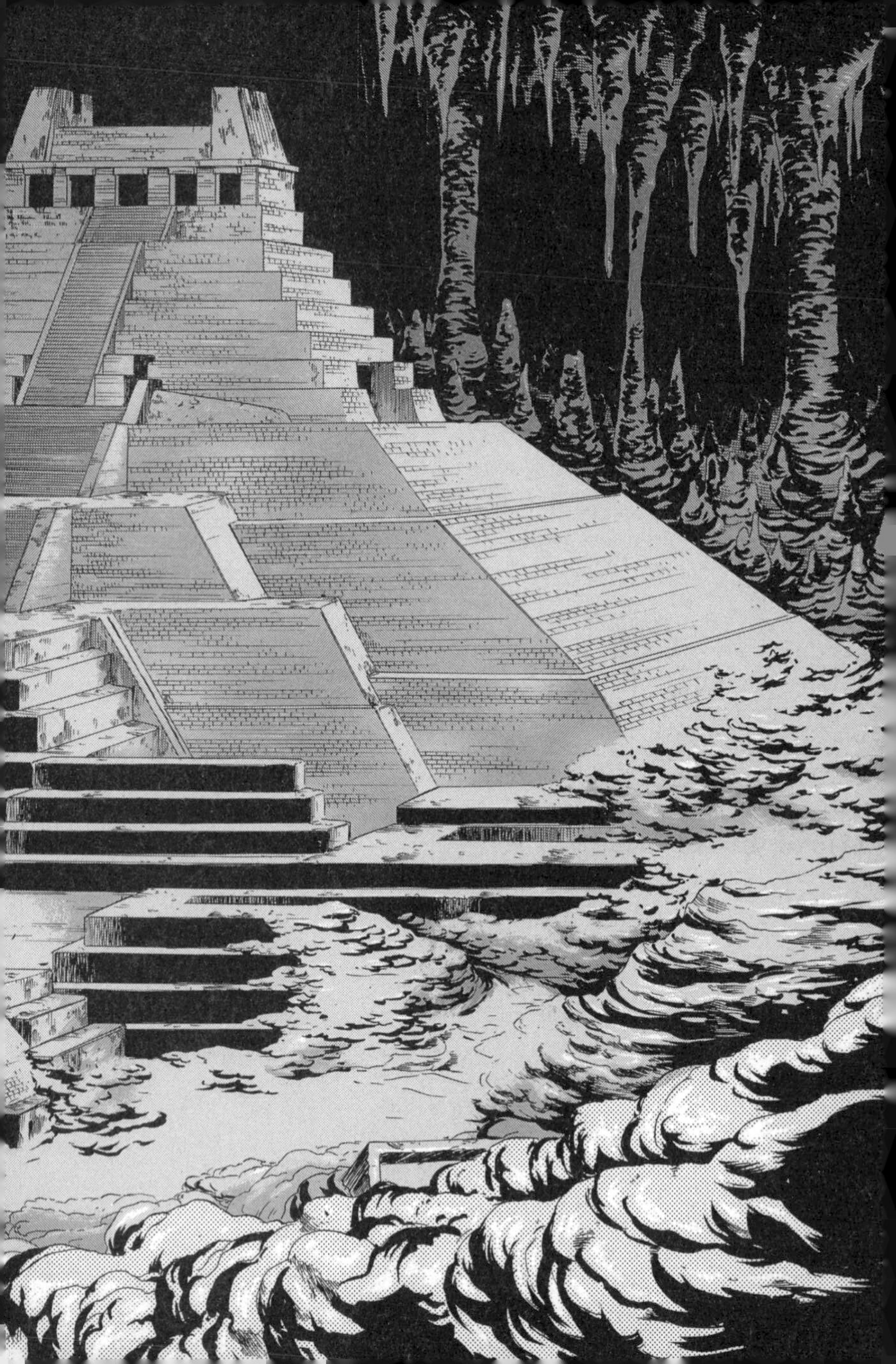

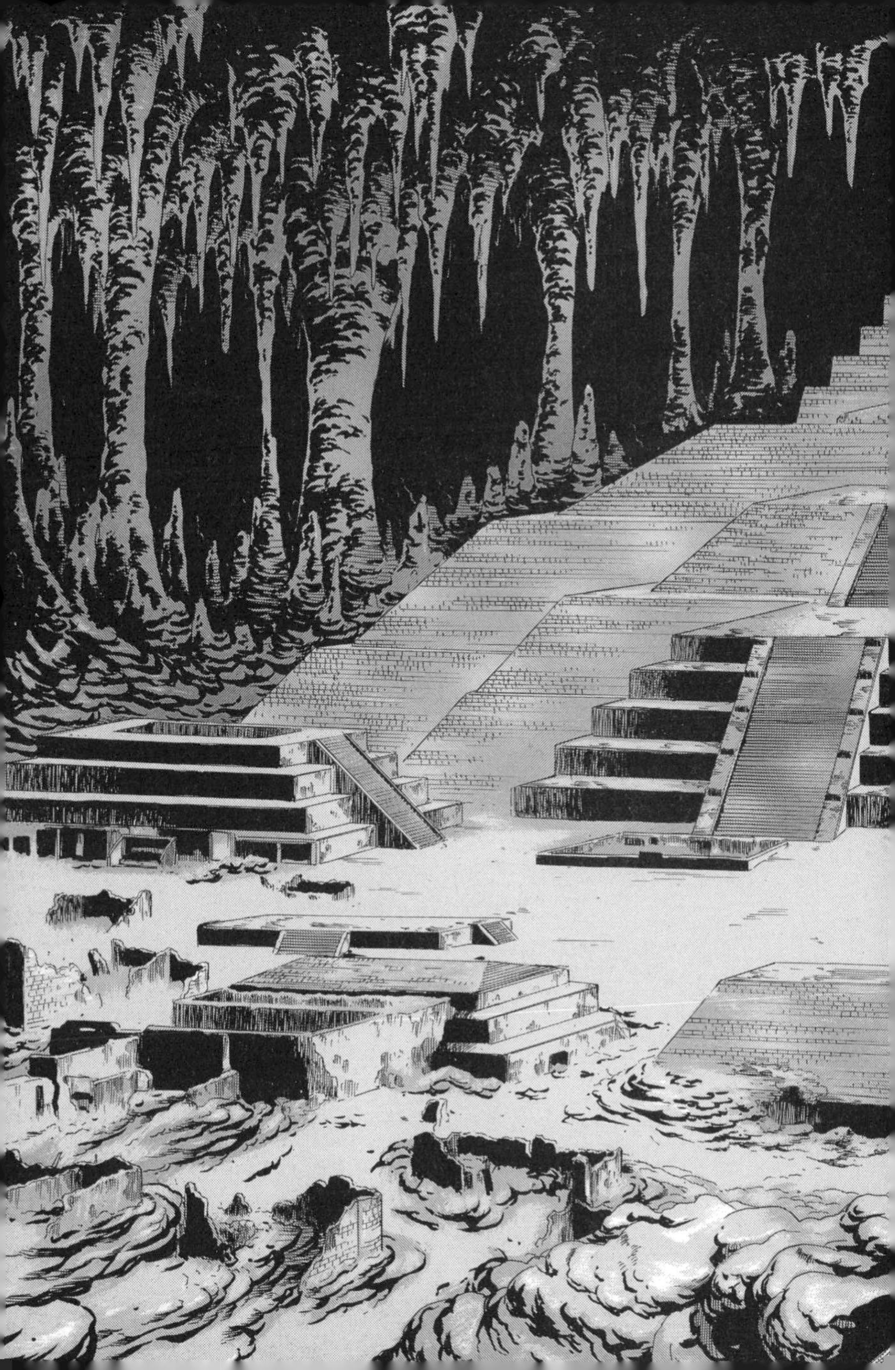

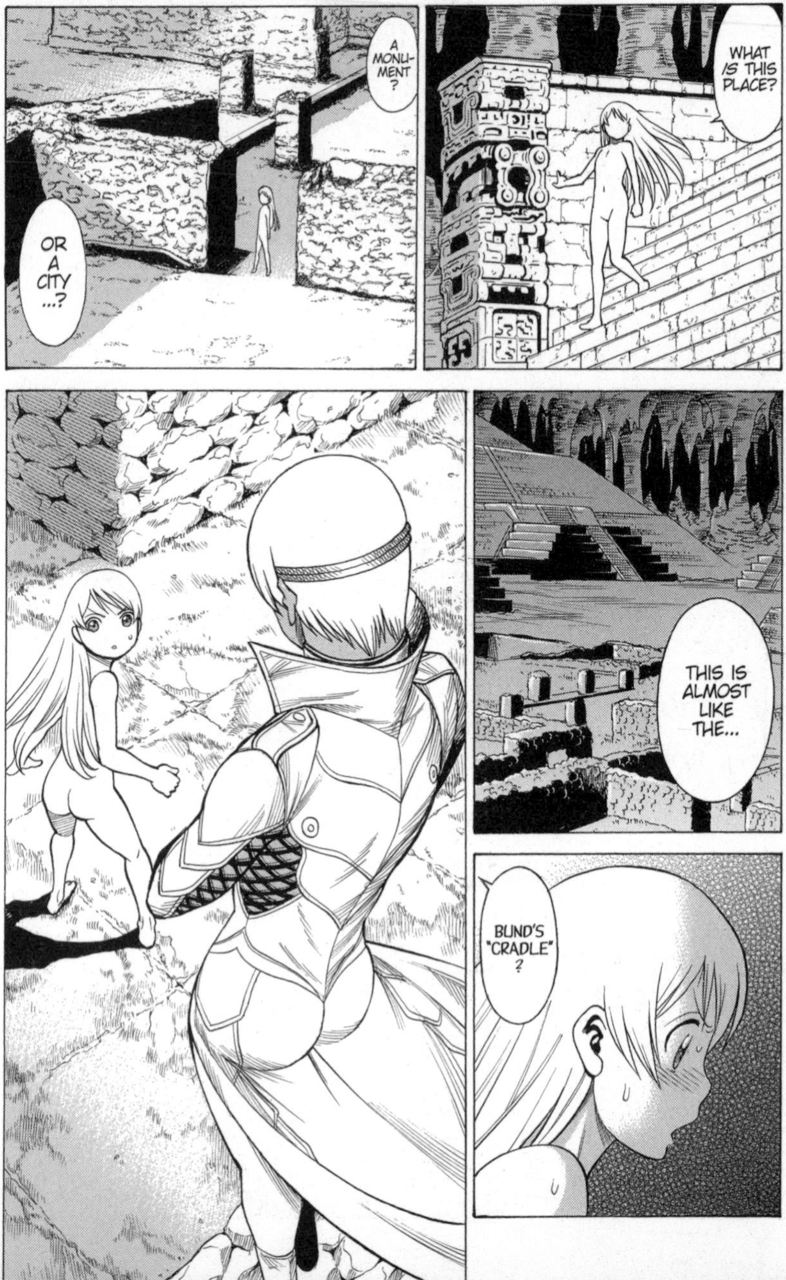
WHAT IS THIS PLACE?
A MONUMENT?
OR A CITY...?
THIS IS ALMOST LIKE THE...
BUND'S "CRADLE"?

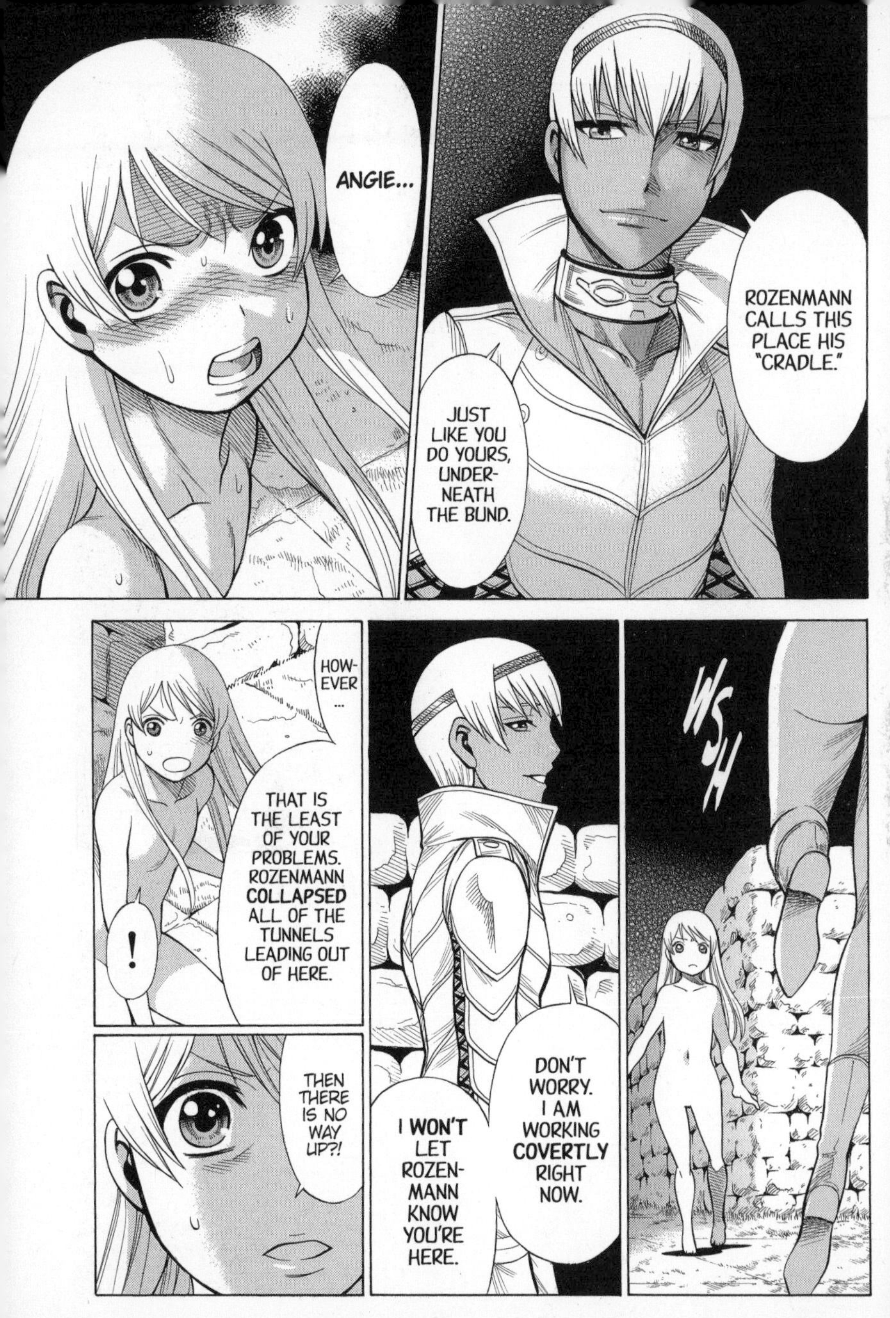
ROZENMANN CALLS THIS PLACE HIS "CRADLE."
JUST LIKE YOU DO YOURS, UNDER-NEATH THE BUND.
ANGIE...
WSH
HOW-EVER ...
THAT IS THE LEAST OF YOUR PROBLEMS. ROZENMANN **COLLAPSED** ALL OF THE TUNNELS LEADING OUT OF HERE.
!
THEN THERE IS NO WAY UP?!
DON'T WORRY. I AM WORKING **COVERTLY** RIGHT NOW.
I **WON'T** LET ROZEN-MANN KNOW YOU'RE HERE.

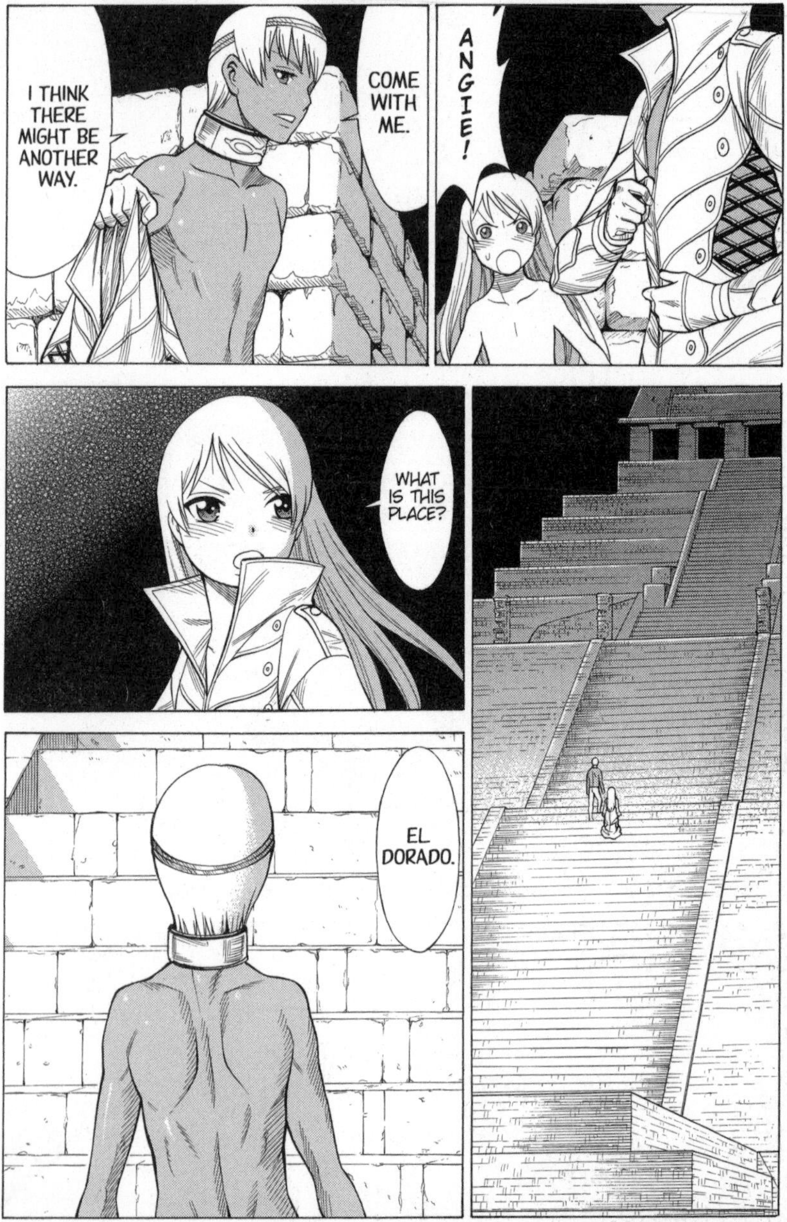
ANGIE!
COME WITH ME.
I THINK THERE MIGHT BE ANOTHER WAY.
WHAT IS THIS PLACE?
EL DORADO.

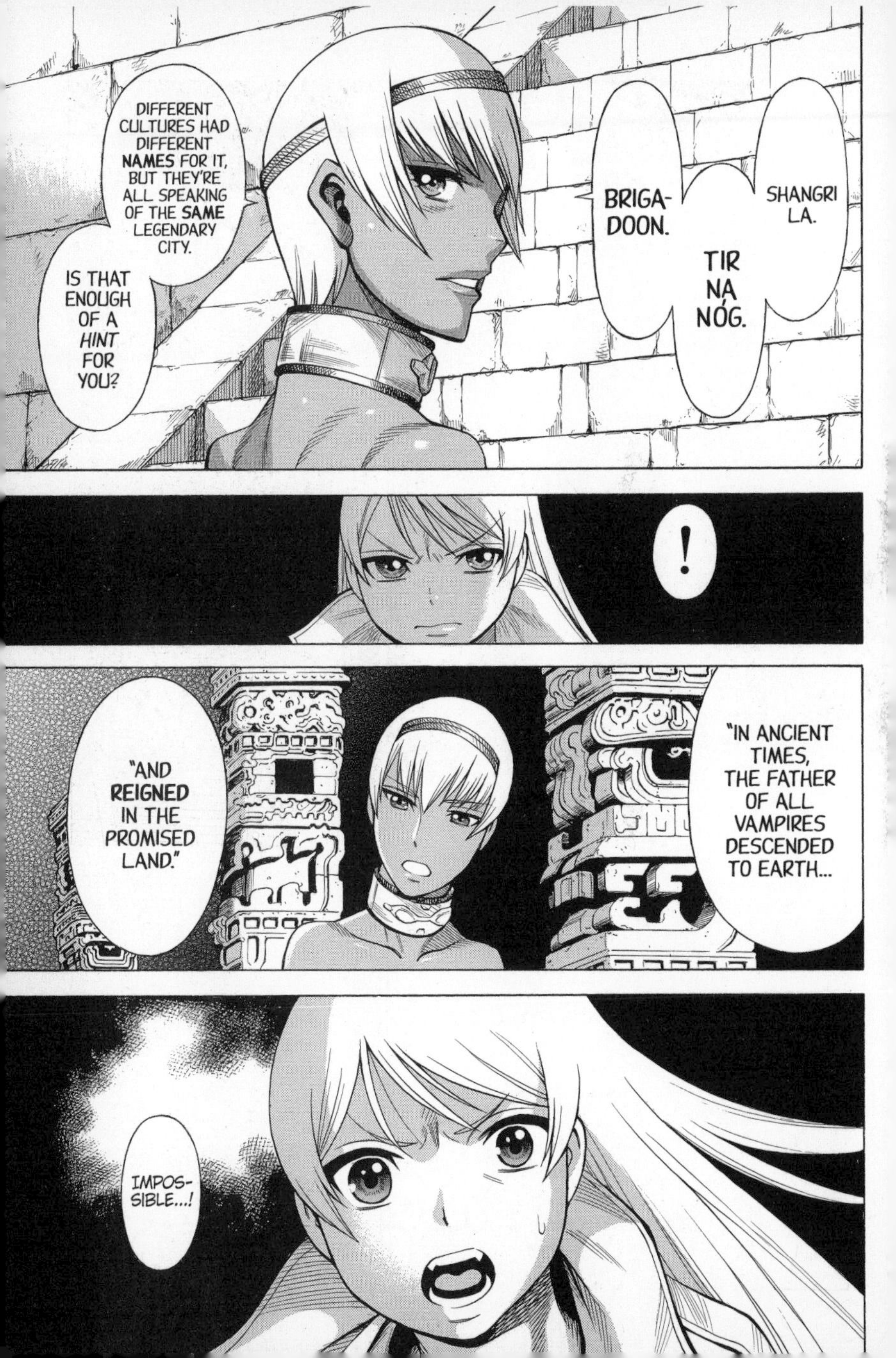
SHANGRI LA.
TIR NA NÓG.
BRIGA-DOON.
DIFFERENT CULTURES HAD DIFFERENT **NAMES** FOR IT, BUT THEY'RE ALL SPEAKING OF THE **SAME** LEGENDARY CITY.
IS THAT ENOUGH OF A *HINT* FOR YOU?
!
"IN ANCIENT TIMES, THE FATHER OF ALL VAMPIRES DESCENDED TO EARTH...
"AND **REIGNED** IN THE PROMISED LAND."
IMPOS-SIBLE...!

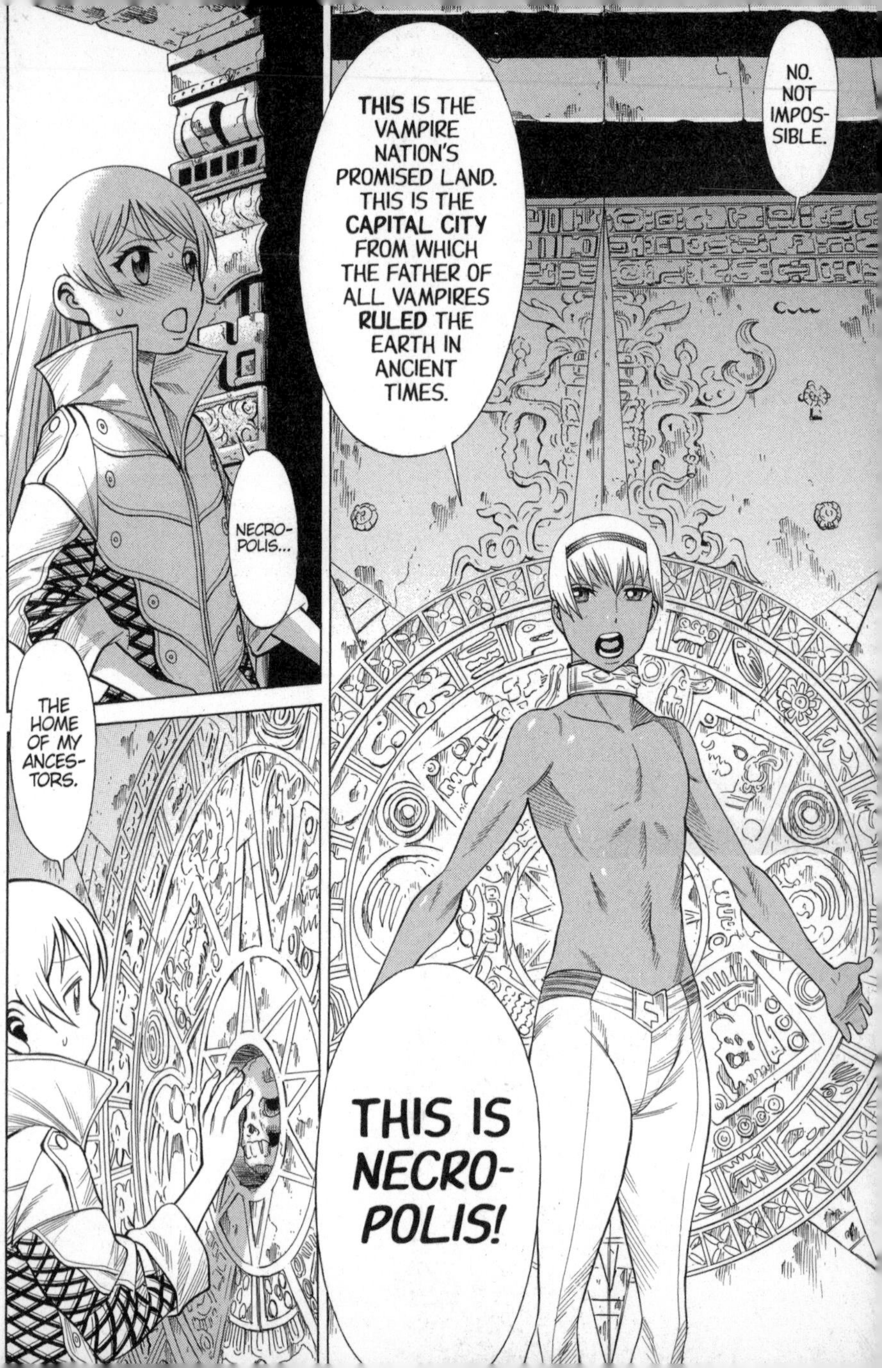
NO. NOT IMPOSSIBLE.
THIS IS THE VAMPIRE NATION'S PROMISED LAND. THIS IS THE CAPITAL CITY FROM WHICH THE FATHER OF ALL VAMPIRES RULED THE EARTH IN ANCIENT TIMES.
THIS IS NECROPOLIS!
NECROPOLIS...
THE HOME OF MY ANCESTORS.

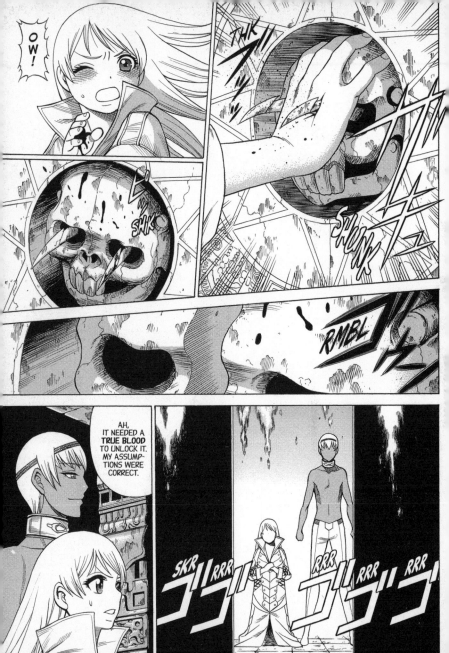

OW!

THK!!

SHK

SHUNK

RMBL

AH, IT NEEDED A **TRUE BLOOD** TO UNLOCK IT. MY ASSUMPTIONS WERE CORRECT.

SKR RRR

RRR

RRR

RRR

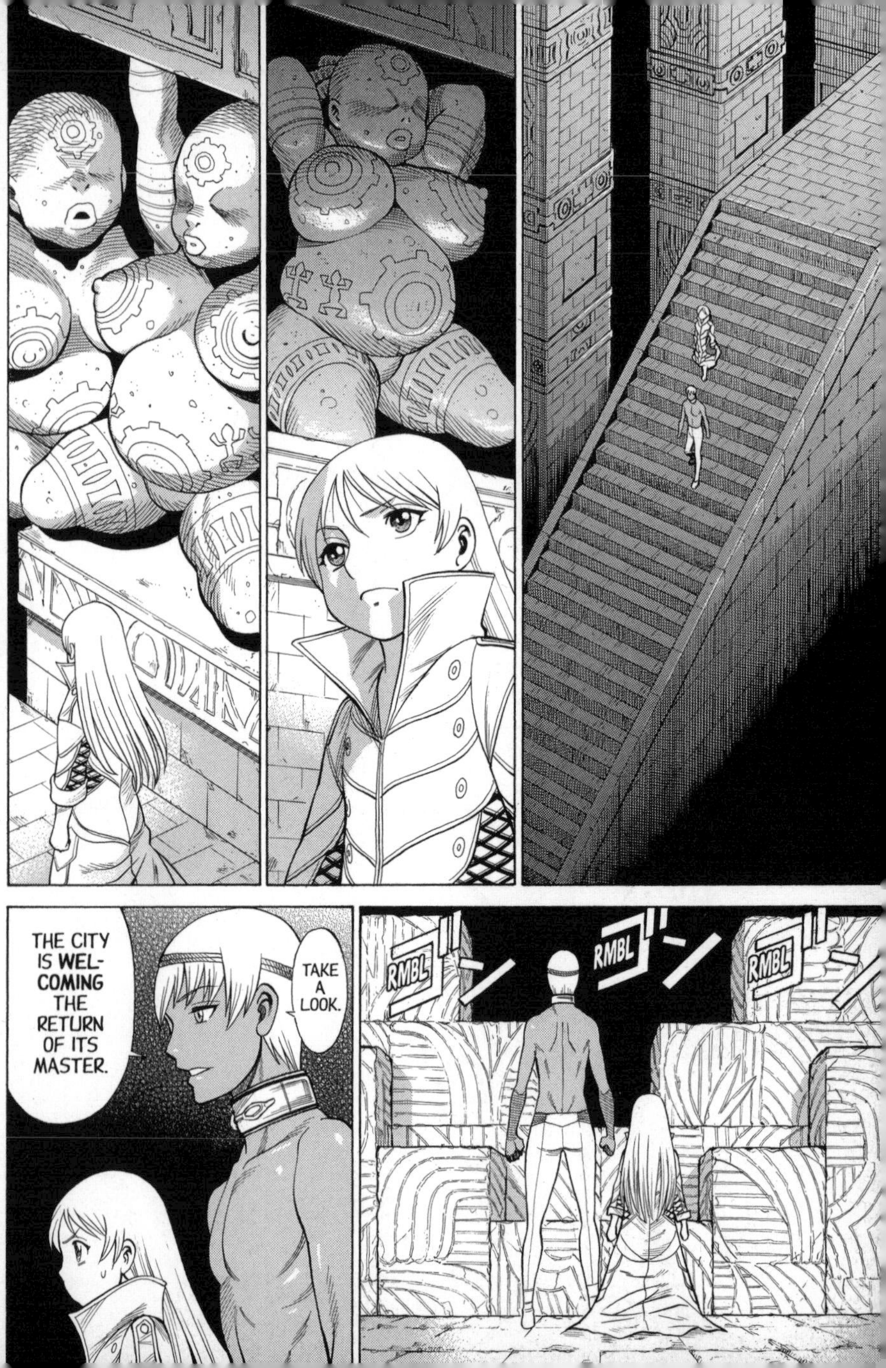
RMBL
RMBL
RMBL
TAKE A LOOK.
THE CITY IS WELCOMING THE RETURN OF ITS MASTER.

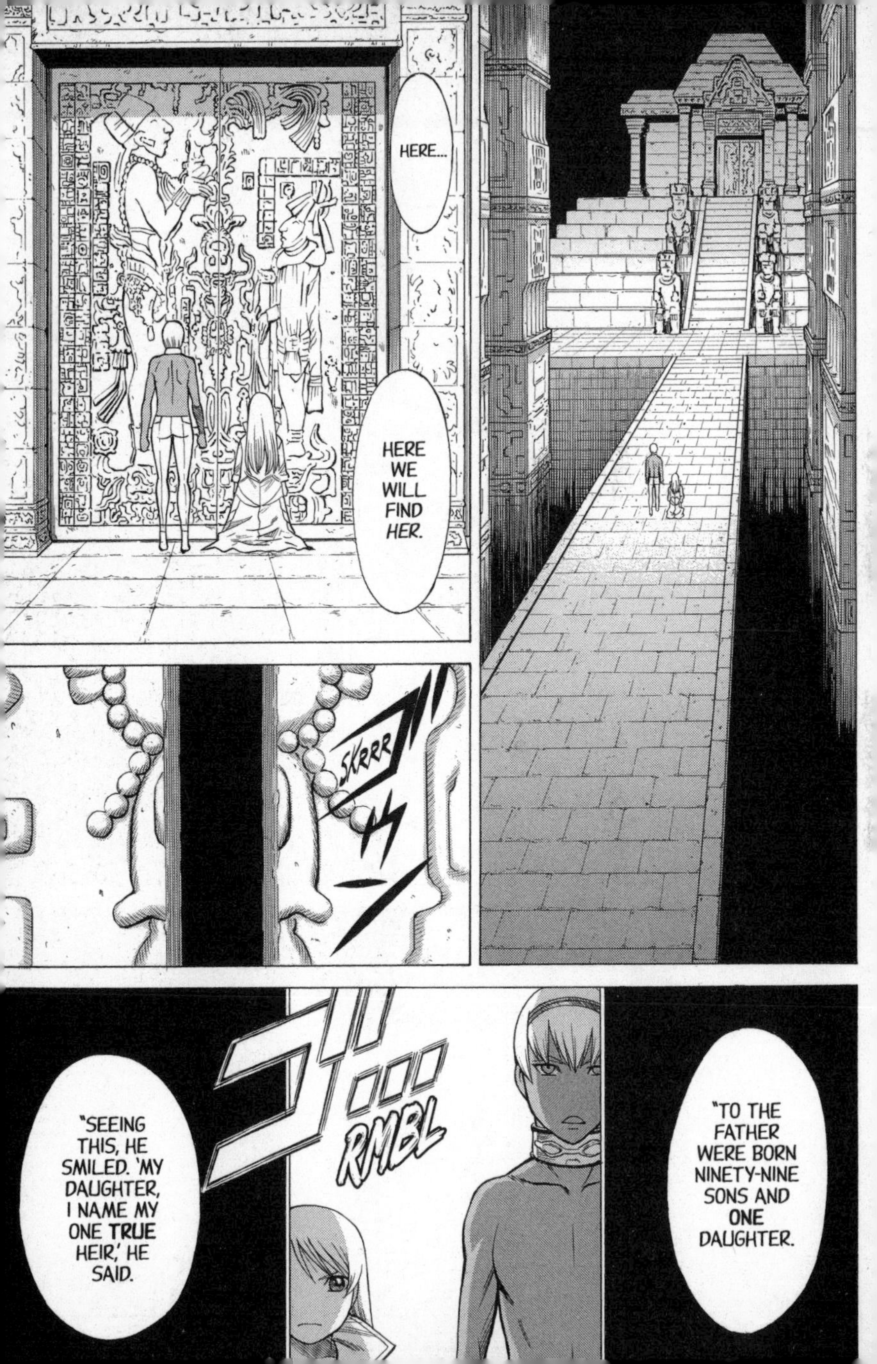
HERE...
HERE WE WILL FIND HER.
SKRRR
"TO THE FATHER WERE BORN NINETY-NINE SONS AND ONE DAUGHTER.
RMBL
"SEEING THIS, HE SMILED. 'MY DAUGHTER, I NAME MY ONE TRUE HEIR,' HE SAID.

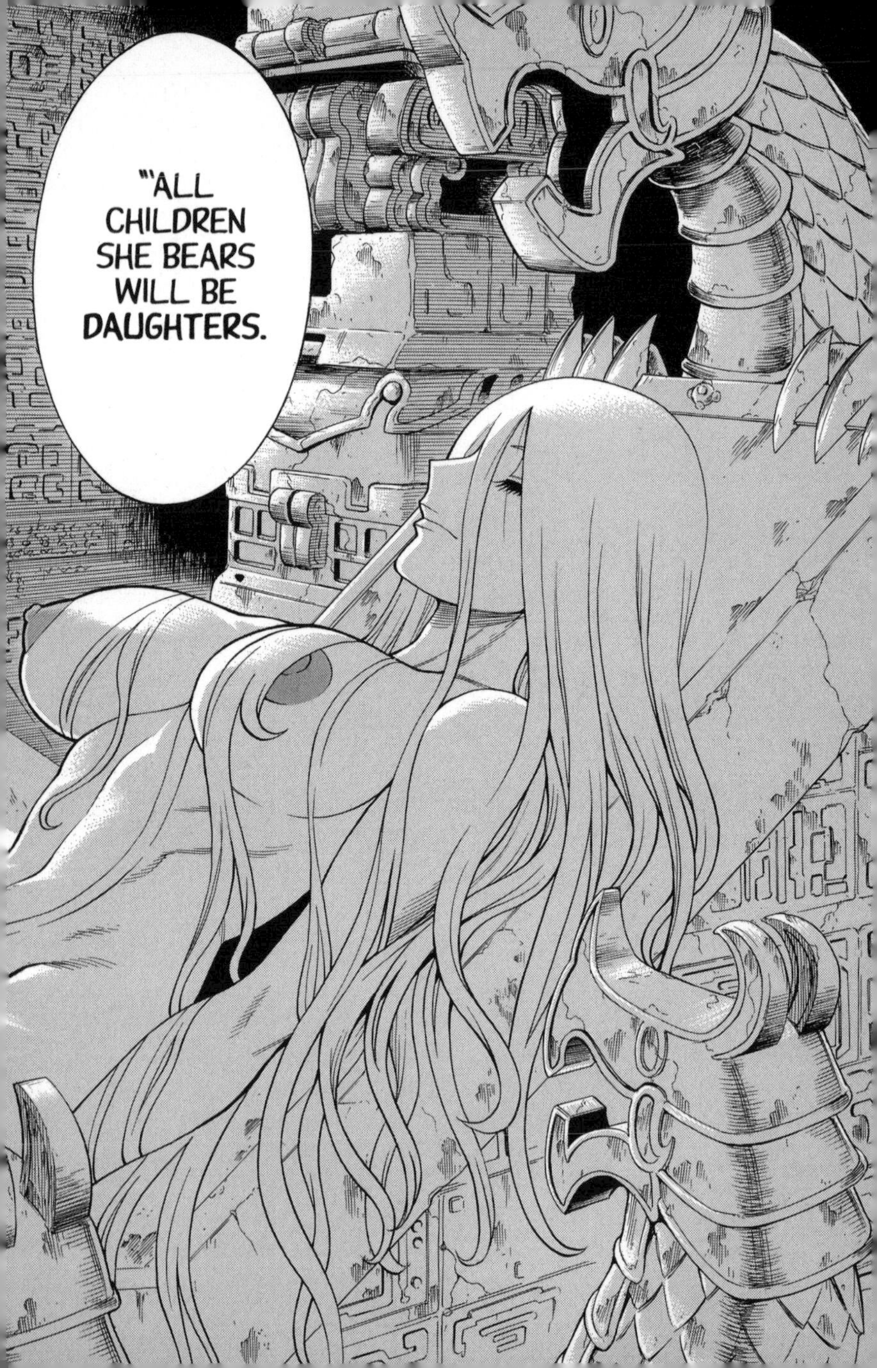
"'ALL CHILDREN SHE BEARS WILL BE DAUGHTERS.

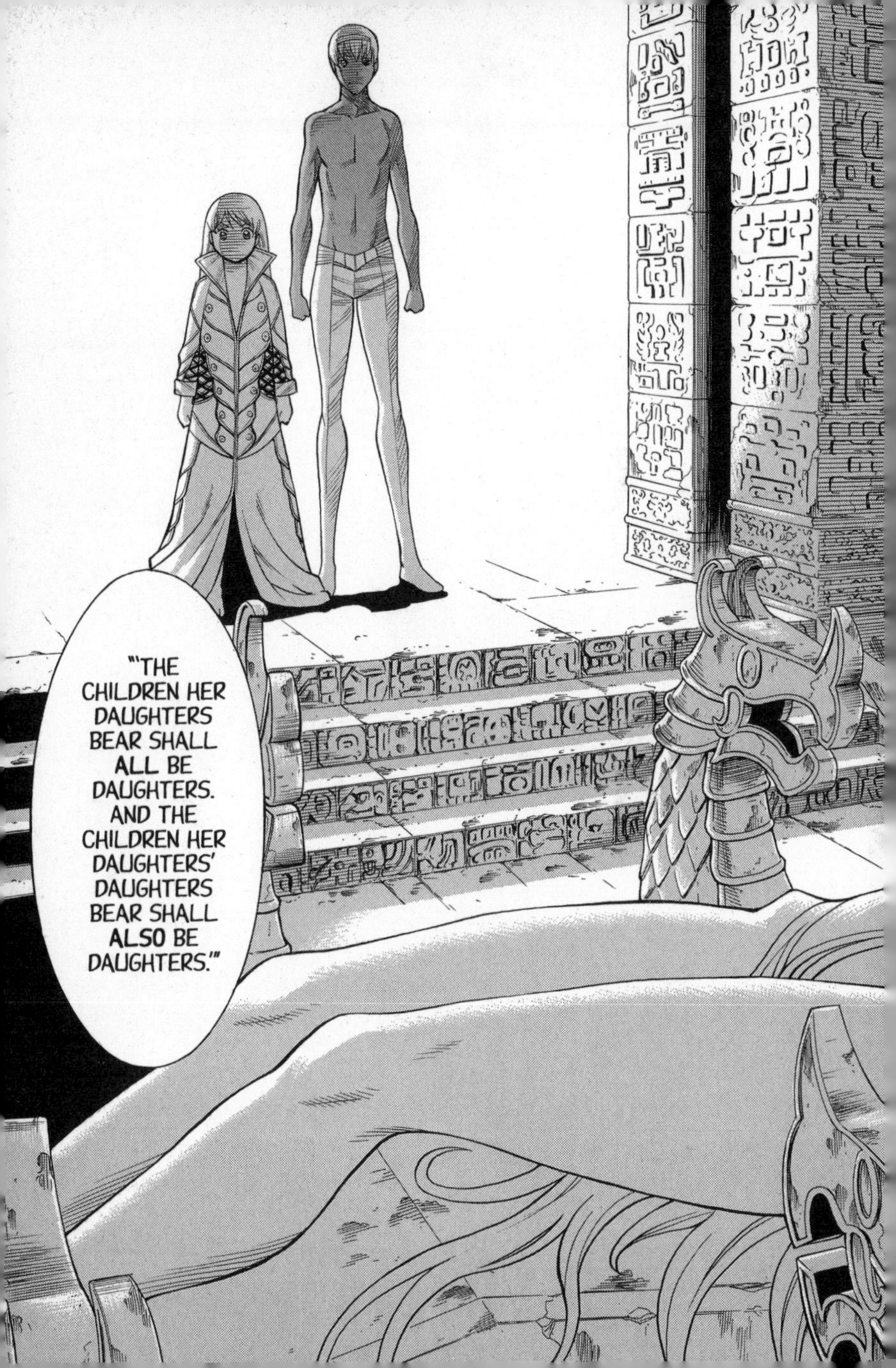
"'THE CHILDREN HER DAUGHTERS BEAR SHALL ALL BE DAUGHTERS. AND THE CHILDREN HER DAUGHTERS' DAUGHTERS BEAR SHALL ALSO BE DAUGHTERS.'"

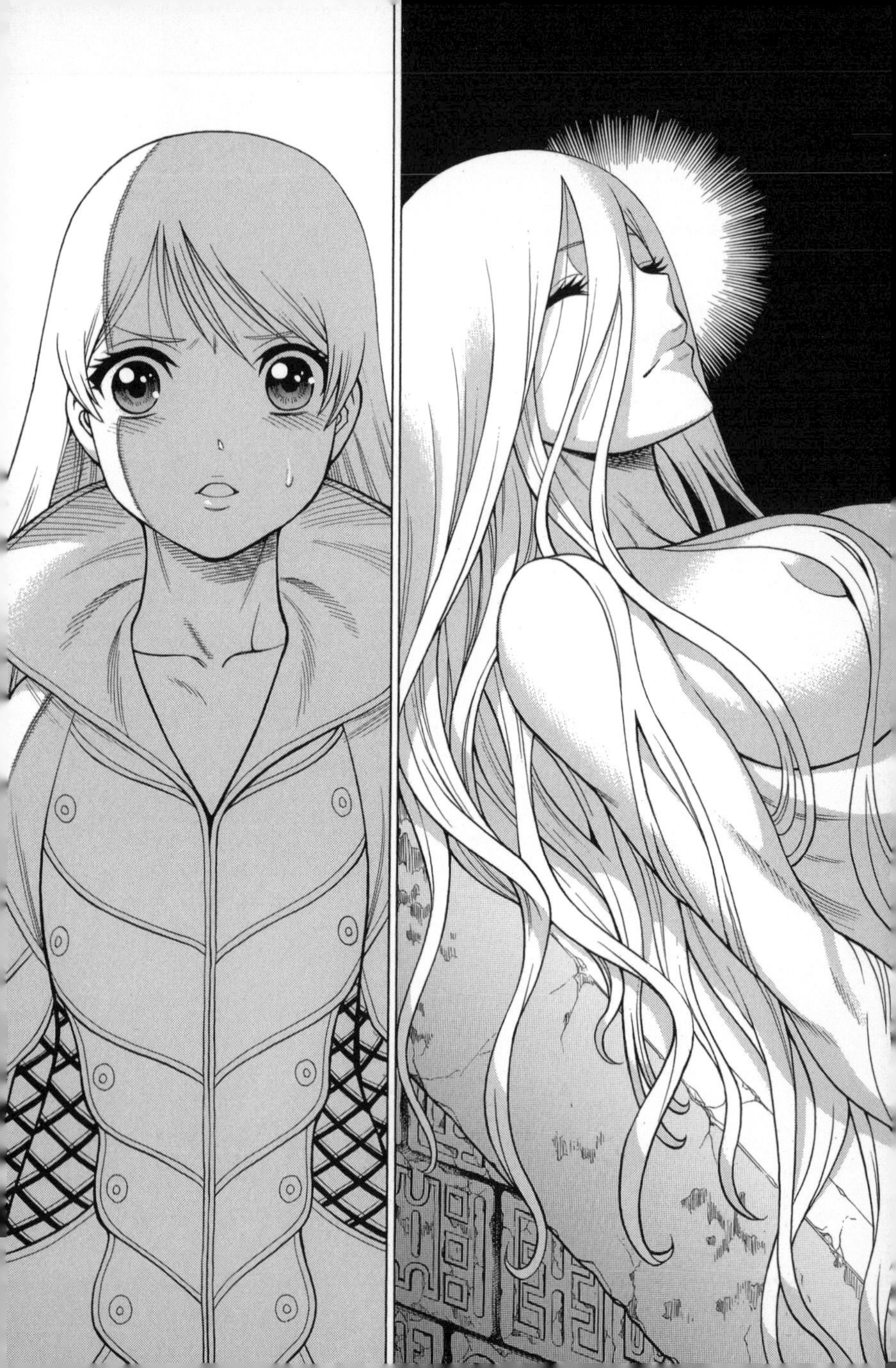

Dance In The Vampire Bund

ダンス イン ザ ヴァンパイア バンド

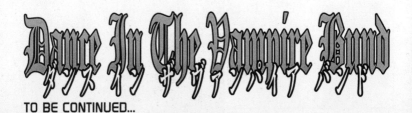

TO BE CONTINUED...

DANCE with the VAMPIRE MAID

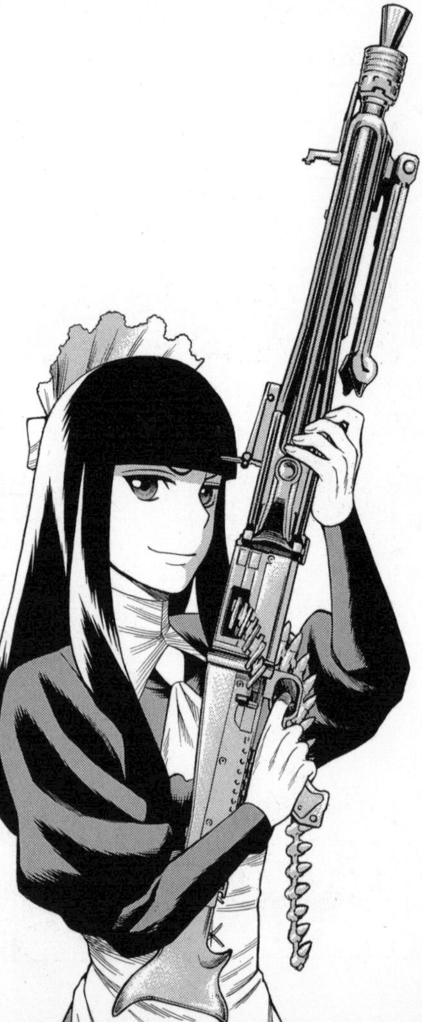

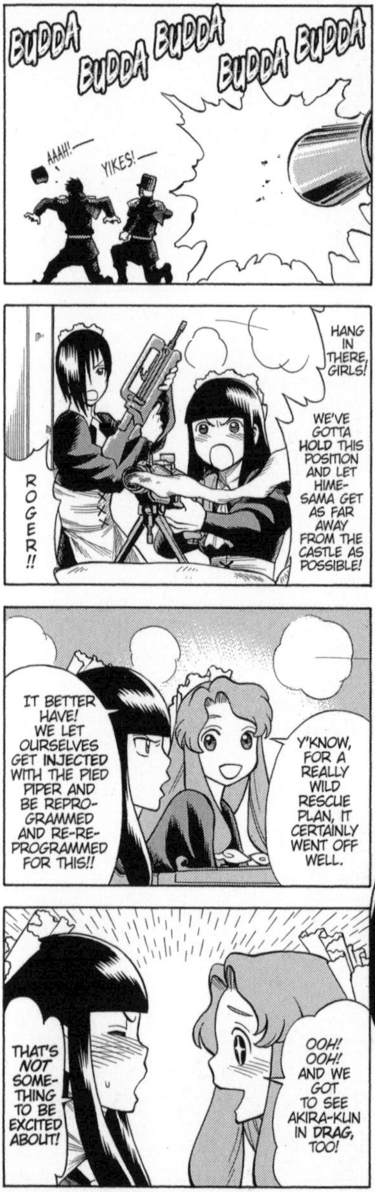
BUDDA BUDDA
BUDDA BUDDA
BUDDA
YIKES!
AAAH!
HANG IN THERE, GIRLS!
WE'VE GOTTA HOLD THIS POSITION AND LET HIME-SAMA GET AS FAR AWAY FROM THE CASTLE AS POSSIBLE!
ROGER!!
Y'KNOW, FOR A REALLY WILD RESCUE PLAN, IT CERTAINLY WENT OFF WELL.
IT BETTER HAVE! WE LET OURSELVES GET INJECTED WITH THE PIED PIPER AND BE REPRO-GRAMMED AND RE-RE-PROGRAMMED FOR THIS!!
OOH! OOH! AND WE GOT TO SEE AKIRA-KUN IN DRAG, TOO!
THAT'S *NOT* SOME-THING TO BE EXCITED ABOUT!

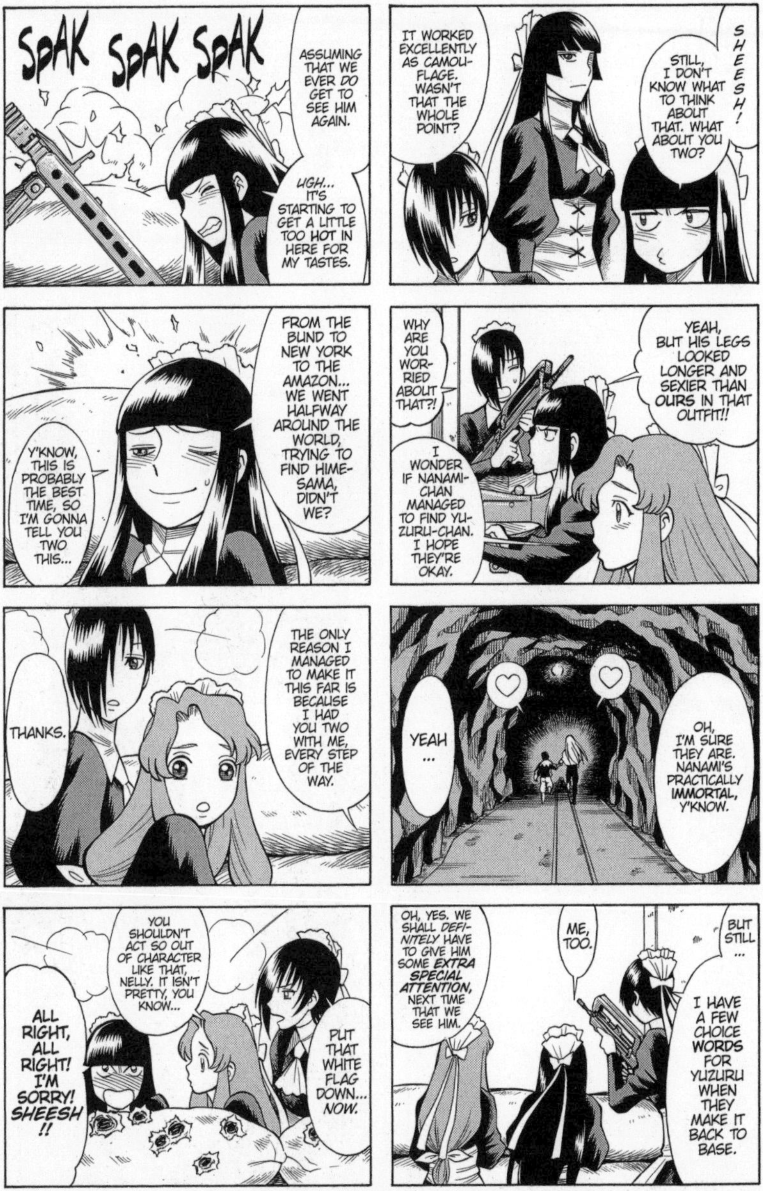
SHEESH!
STILL, I DON'T KNOW WHAT TO THINK ABOUT THAT. WHAT ABOUT YOU TWO?
IT WORKED EXCELLENTLY AS CAMOU-FLAGE. WASN'T THAT THE WHOLE POINT?
YEAH, BUT HIS LEGS LOOKED LONGER AND SEXIER THAN **OURS** IN THAT OUTFIT!!
WHY ARE YOU WOR-RIED ABOUT THAT?!
I WONDER IF NANAMI-CHAN MANAGED TO FIND YU-ZURU-CHAN. I HOPE THEY'RE OKAY.
OH, I'M SURE THEY ARE. NANAMI'S PRACTICALLY **IMMORTAL**, Y'KNOW.
YEAH ...
BUT STILL ...
I HAVE A FEW CHOICE **WORDS** FOR YUZURU WHEN THEY MAKE IT BACK TO BASE.
ME, TOO.
OH, YES. WE SHALL *DEFI-NITELY* HAVE TO GIVE HIM SOME ***EXTRA SPECIAL ATTENTION***, NEXT TIME THAT WE SEE HIM.
ASSUMING THAT WE EVER *DO* GET TO SEE HIM AGAIN.
UGH... IT'S STARTING TO GET A LITTLE TOO **HOT** IN HERE FOR MY TASTES.
SPAK SPAK SPAK
FROM THE BUND TO NEW YORK TO THE AMAZON... WE WENT HALFWAY AROUND THE WORLD, TRYING TO FIND HIME-SAMA, DIDN'T WE?
Y'KNOW, THIS IS PROBABLY THE BEST TIME, SO I'M GONNA TELL YOU TWO THIS...
THE ONLY REASON I MANAGED TO MAKE IT THIS FAR IS BECAUSE I HAD YOU TWO WITH ME, EVERY STEP OF THE WAY.
THANKS.
YOU SHOULDN'T ACT SO OUT OF CHARACTER LIKE THAT, NELLY. IT ISN'T PRETTY, YOU KNOW...
PUT THAT WHITE FLAG DOWN... ***NOW.***
ALL RIGHT, ALL RIGHT! I'M SORRY! *SHEESH* !!

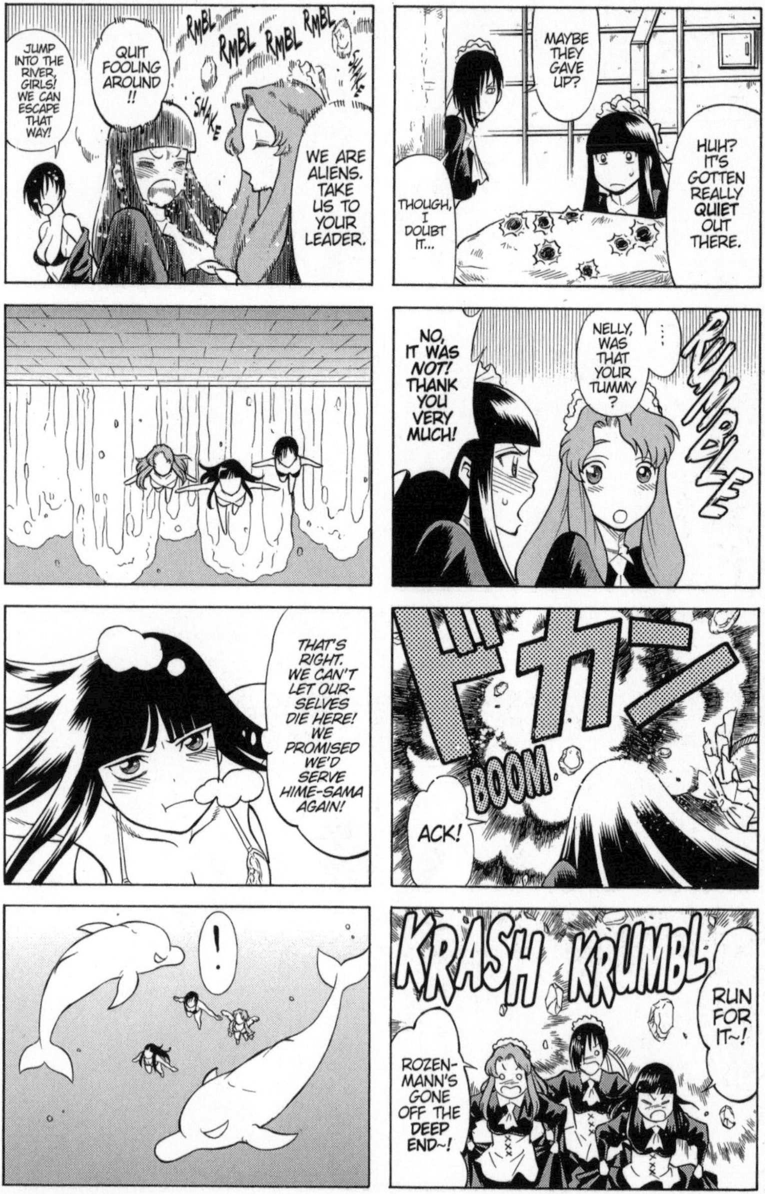
HUH? IT'S GOTTEN REALLY QUIET OUT THERE.
MAYBE THEY GAVE UP?
THOUGH, I DOUBT IT...
RUMMBLE
...
NELLY, WAS THAT YOUR TUMMY?
NO, IT WAS NOT! THANK YOU VERY MUCH!
ドカン
BOOM
ACK!
KRASH KRUMBL
RUN FOR IT~!
ROZEN-MANN'S GONE OFF THE DEEP END~!
RMBL RMBL RMBL RMBL
SHAKE SHAKE
QUIT FOOLING AROUND!!
JUMP INTO THE RIVER, GIRLS! WE CAN ESCAPE THAT WAY!
WE ARE ALIENS. TAKE US TO YOUR LEADER.
THAT'S RIGHT. WE CAN'T LET OURSELVES DIE HERE! WE PROMISED WE'D SERVE HIME-SAMA AGAIN!
!

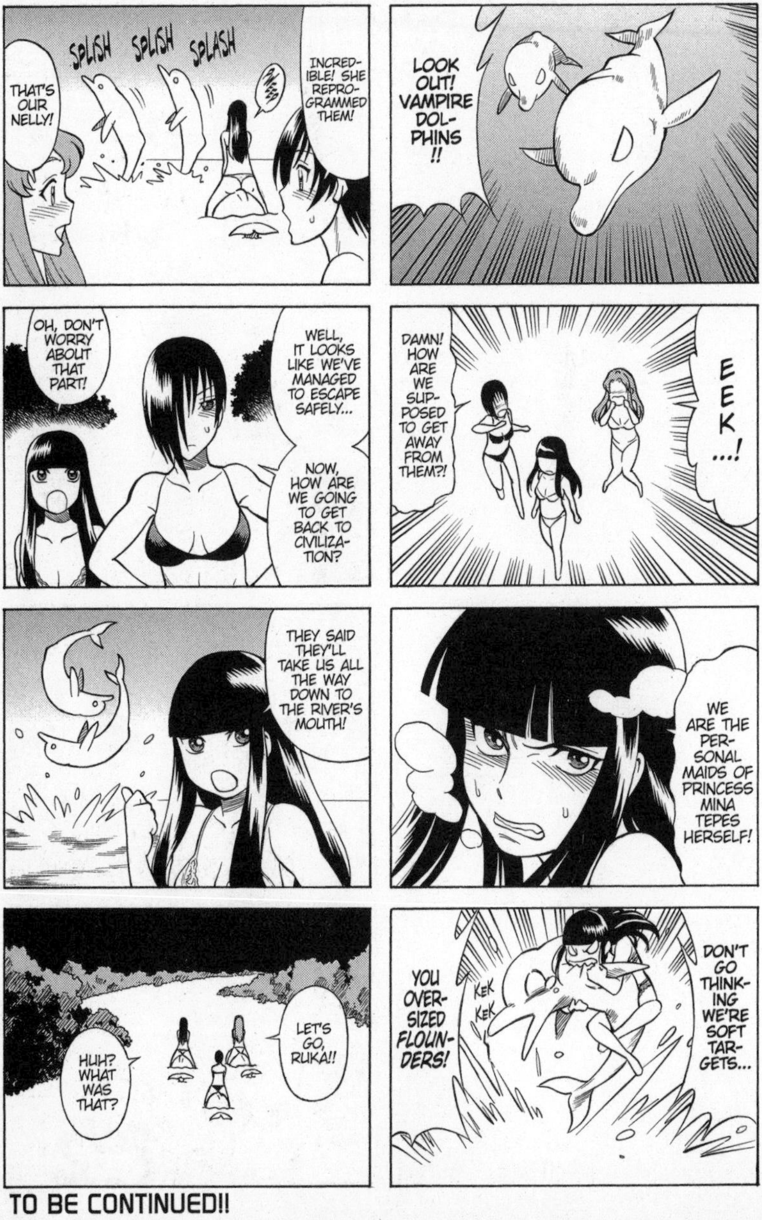
LOOK OUT! VAMPIRE DOLPHINS!!
EEK...!
DAMN! HOW ARE WE SUPPOSED TO GET AWAY FROM THEM?!
WE ARE THE PERSONAL MAIDS OF PRINCESS MINA TEPES HERSELF!
DON'T GO THINKING WE'RE SOFT TARGETS...
KEK KEK
YOU OVERSIZED FLOUNDERS!
INCREDIBLE! SHE REPROGRAMMED THEM!
SPLASH
SPLISH
SPLISH
THAT'S OUR NELLY!
WELL, IT LOOKS LIKE WE'VE MANAGED TO ESCAPE SAFELY...
NOW, HOW ARE WE GOING TO GET BACK TO CIVILIZATION?
OH, DON'T WORRY ABOUT THAT PART!
THEY SAID THEY'LL TAKE US ALL THE WAY DOWN TO THE RIVER'S MOUTH!
LET'S GO, RUKA!!
HUH? WHAT WAS THAT?

TO BE CONTINUED!!

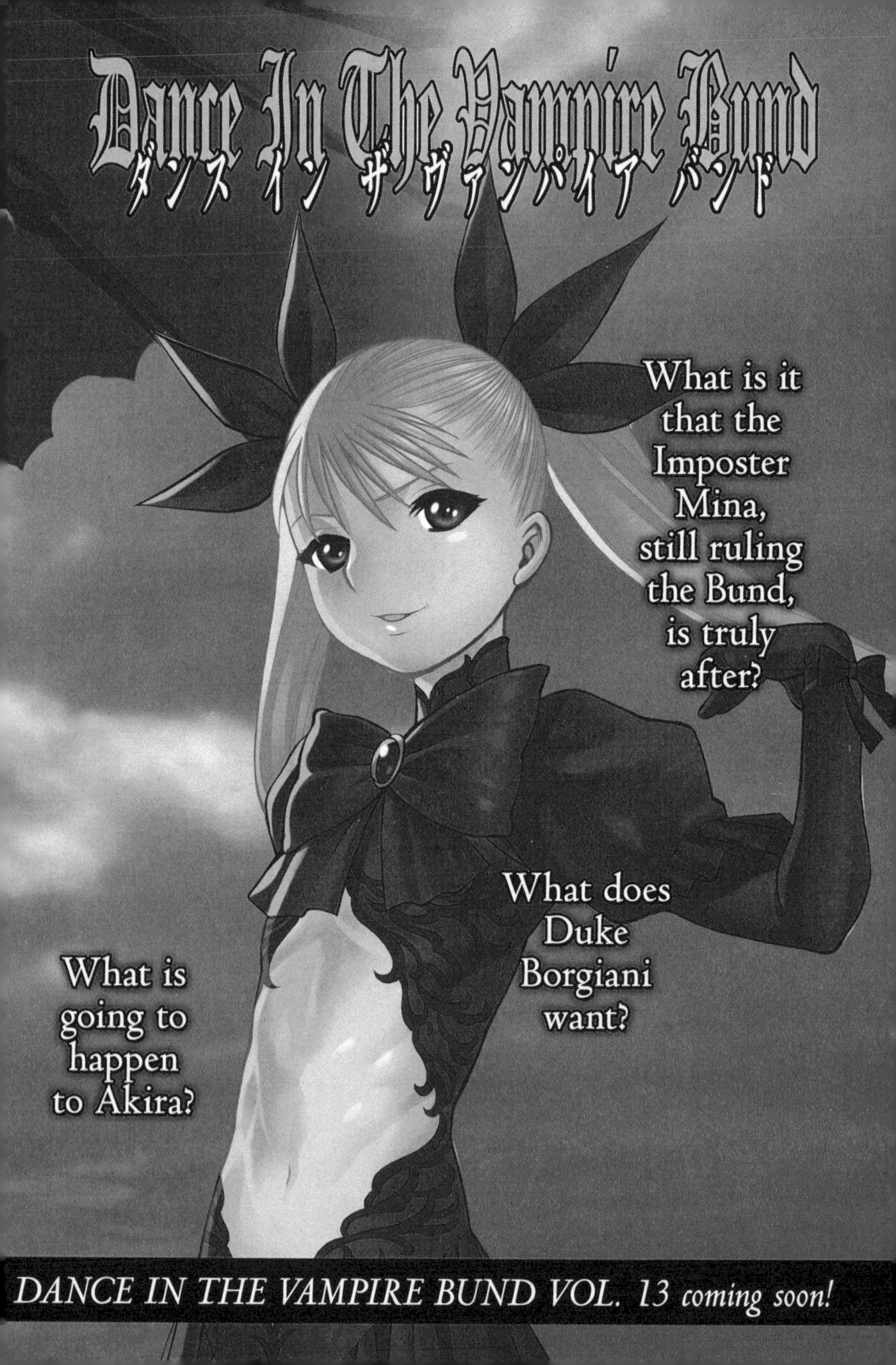

Dance In The Vampire Bund
ダンス イン ザ ヴァンパイア バンド
What is it that the Imposter Mina, still ruling the Bund, is truly after?
What does Duke Borgiani want?
What is going to happen to Akira?
DANCE IN THE VAMPIRE BUND VOL. 13 coming soon!

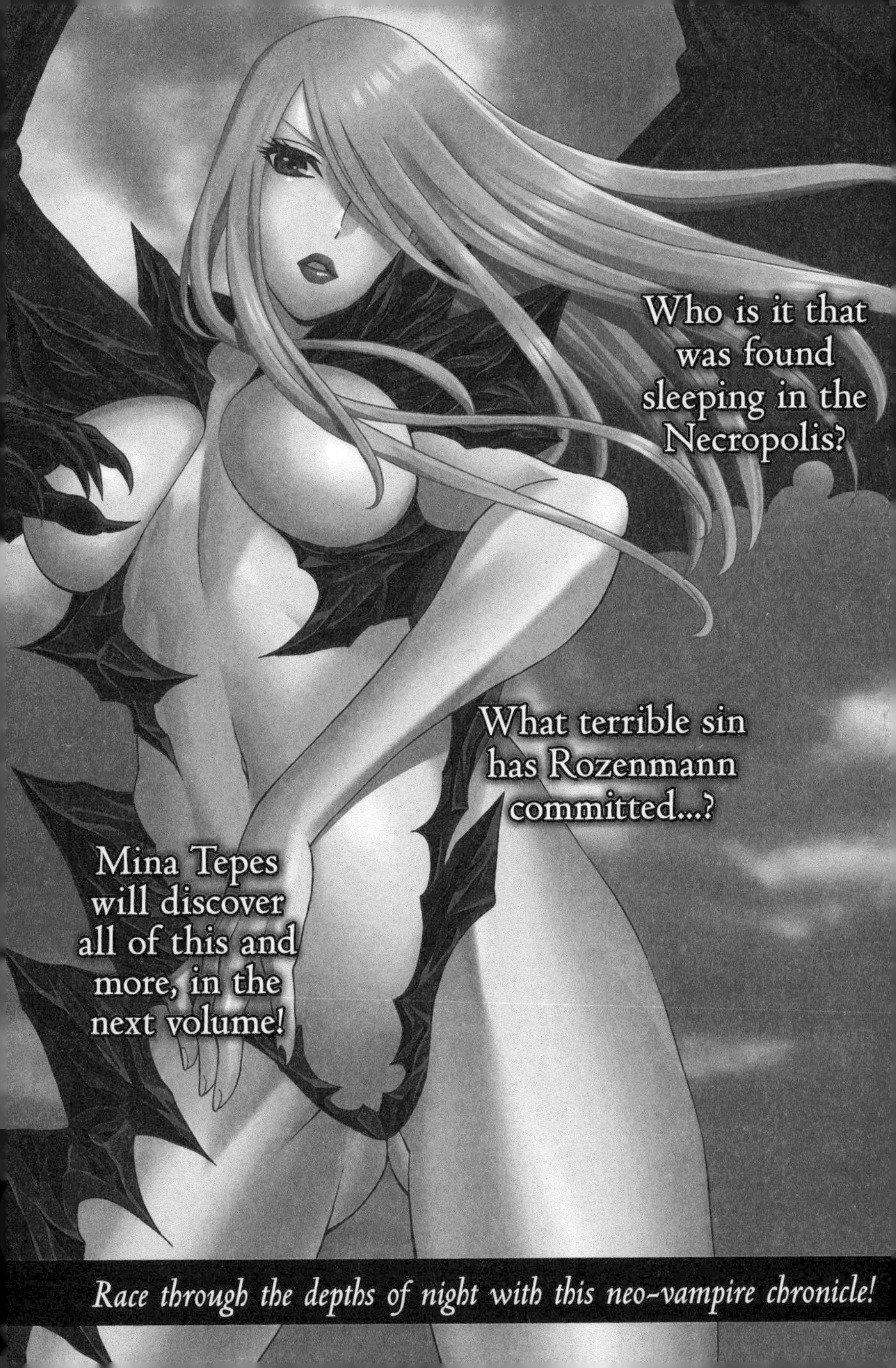
Who is it that was found sleeping in the Necropolis?
What terrible sin has Rozenmann committed...?
Mina Tepes will discover all of this and more, in the next volume!
Race through the depths of night with this neo-vampire chronicle!

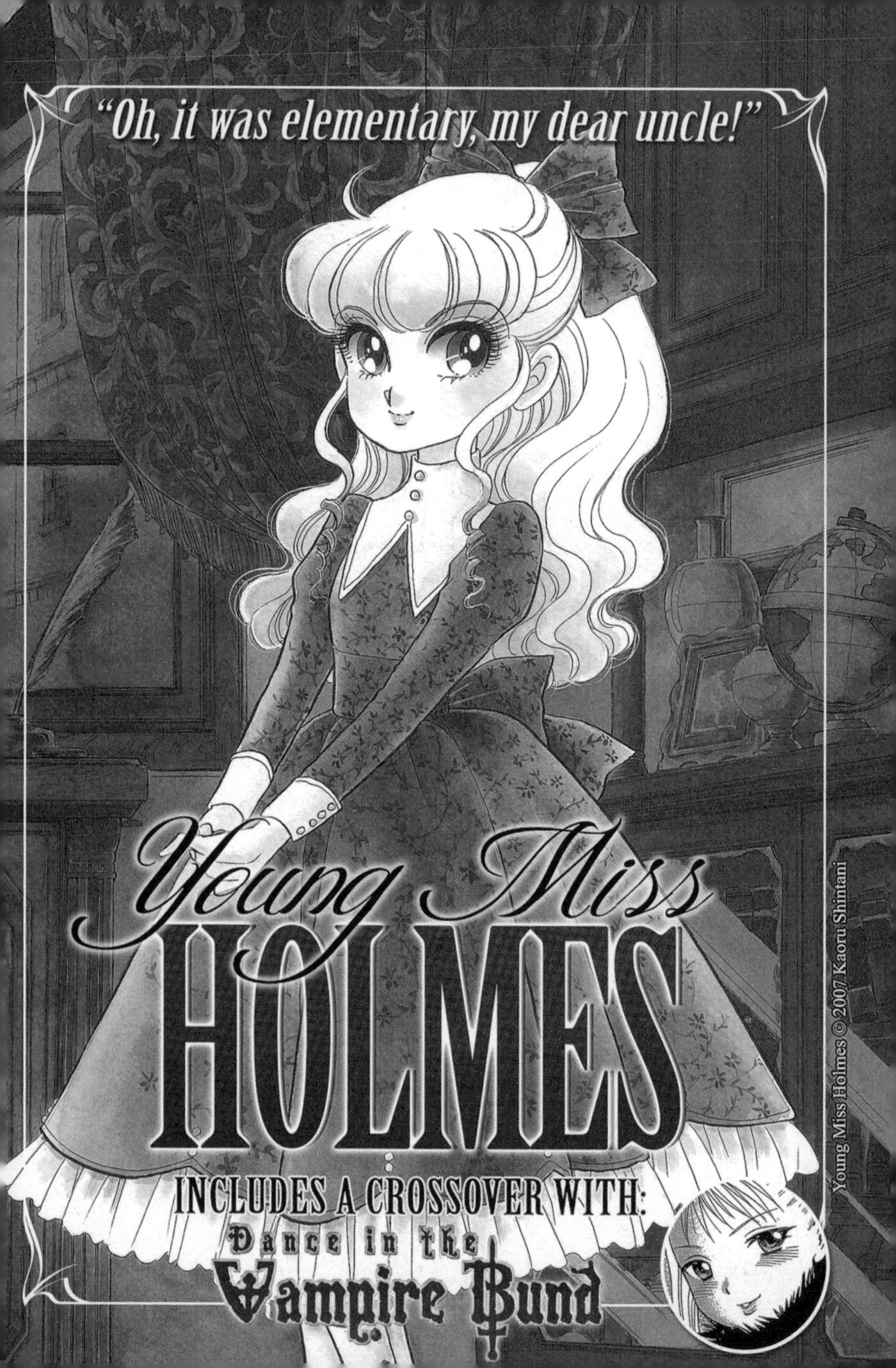

"Oh, it was elementary, my dear uncle!"
Young Miss
HOLMES
INCLUDES A CROSSOVER WITH:
Dance in the
Vampire Bund
Young Miss Holmes © 2007 Kaoru Shintani

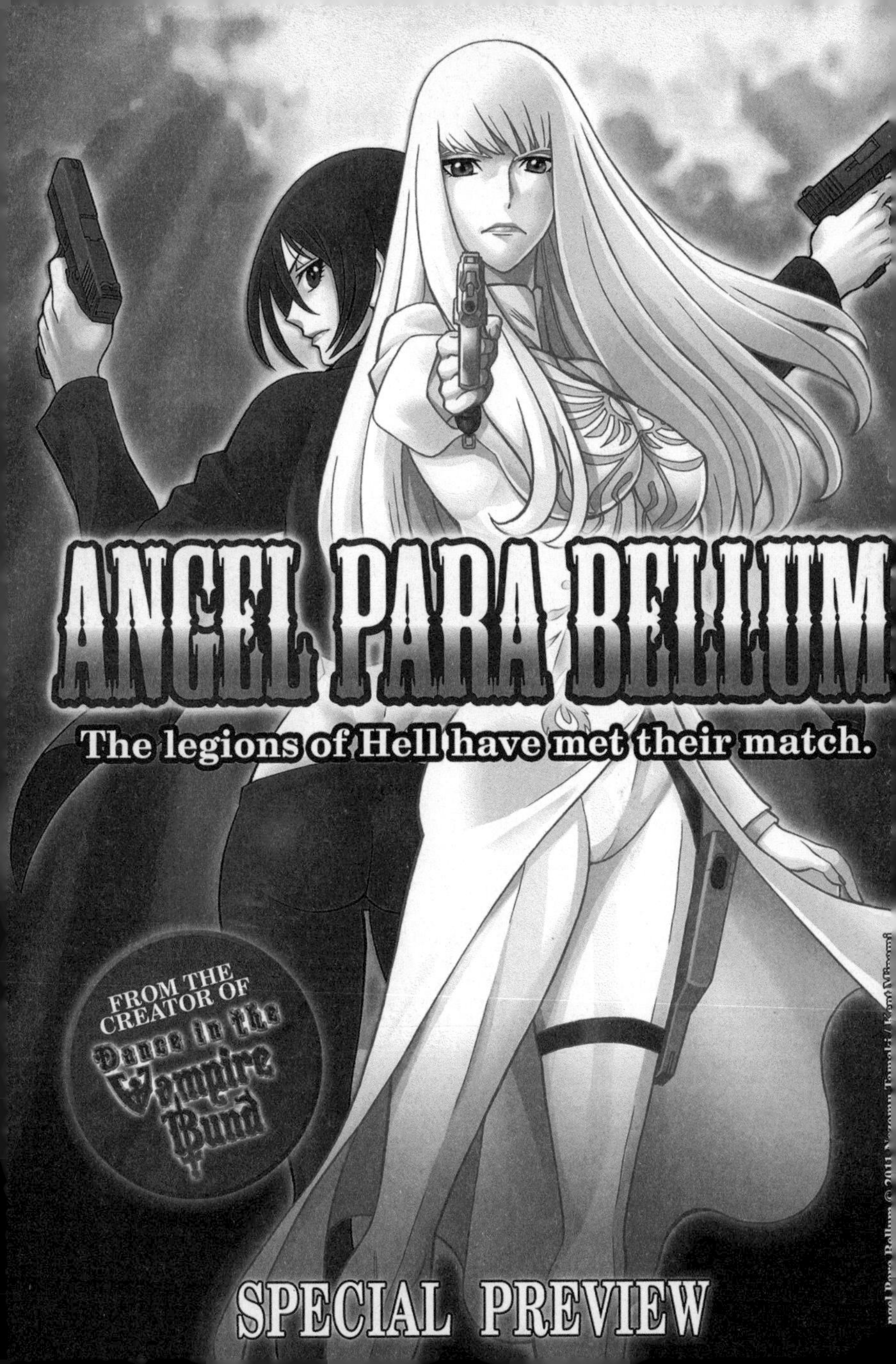
ANGEL PARA BELLUM
The legions of Hell have met their match.
FROM THE CREATOR OF
Dance in the Vampire Bund
SPECIAL PREVIEW

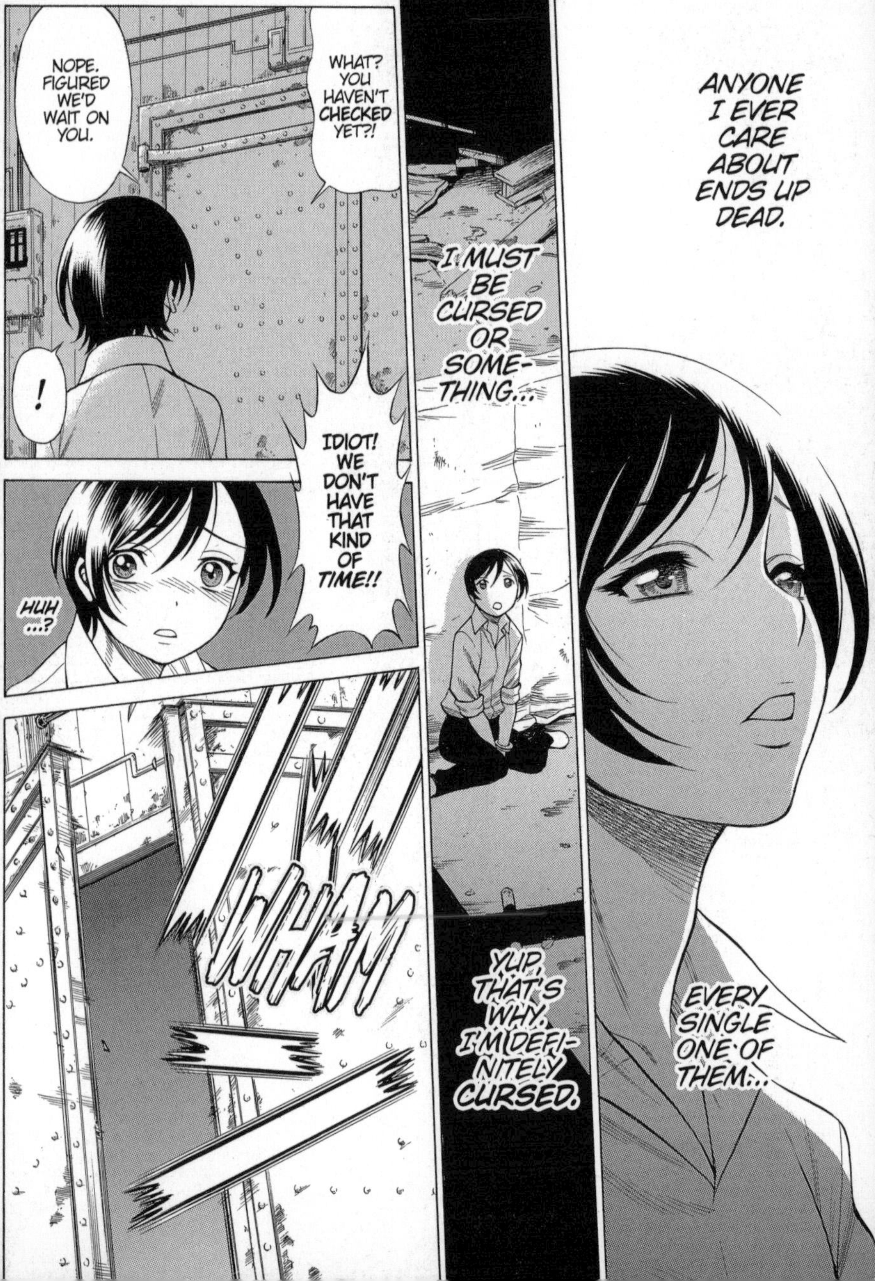
ANYONE I EVER CARE ABOUT ENDS UP DEAD.
EVERY SINGLE ONE OF THEM...
I MUST BE CURSED OR SOMETHING...
YUP, THAT'S WHY. I'M DEFINITELY CURSED.
WHAT? YOU HAVEN'T CHECKED YET?!
NOPE. FIGURED WE'D WAIT ON YOU.
!
IDIOT! WE DON'T HAVE THAT KIND OF TIME!!
HUH ...?
WHAM

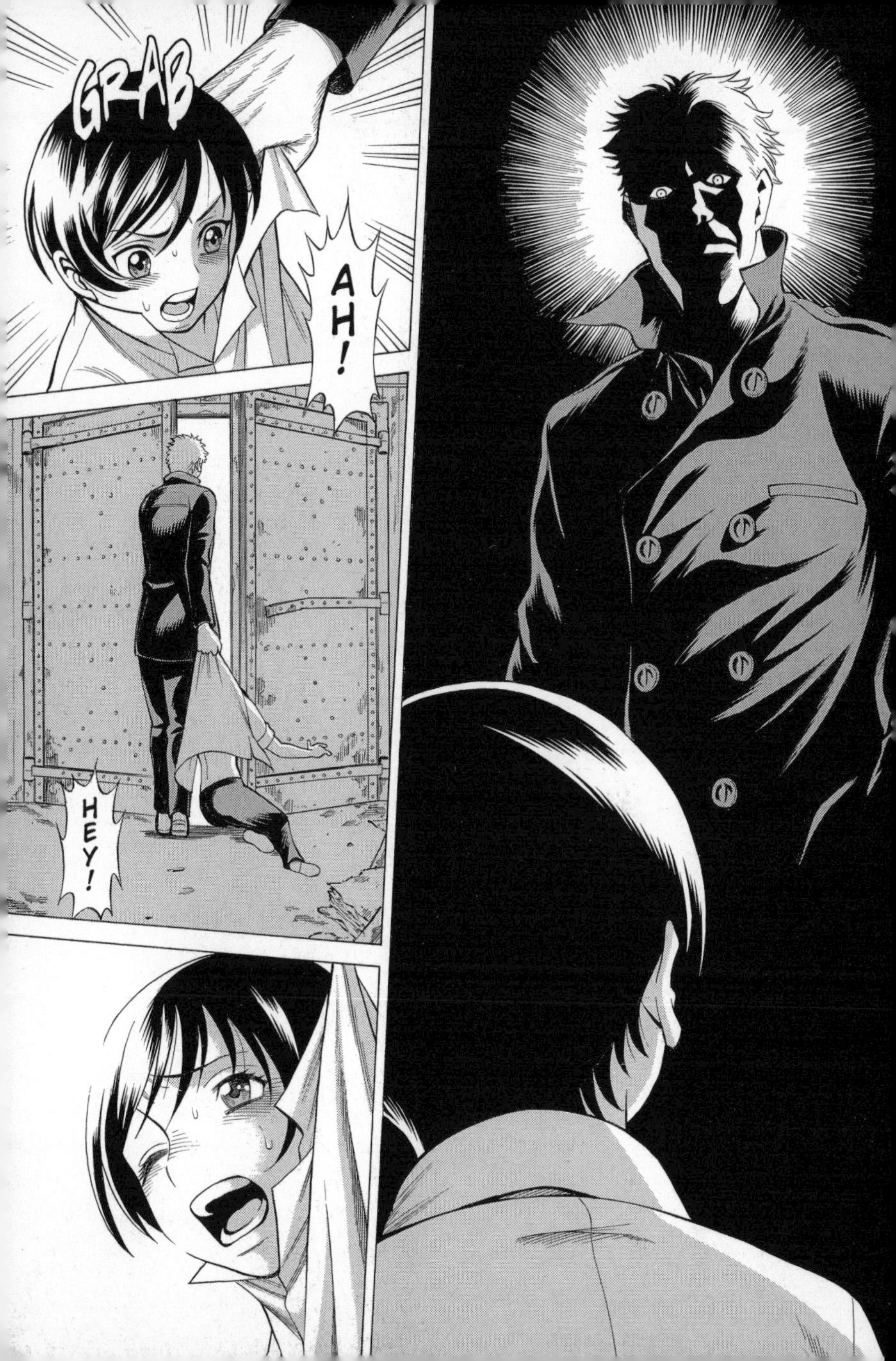
GRAB
AH!
HEY!

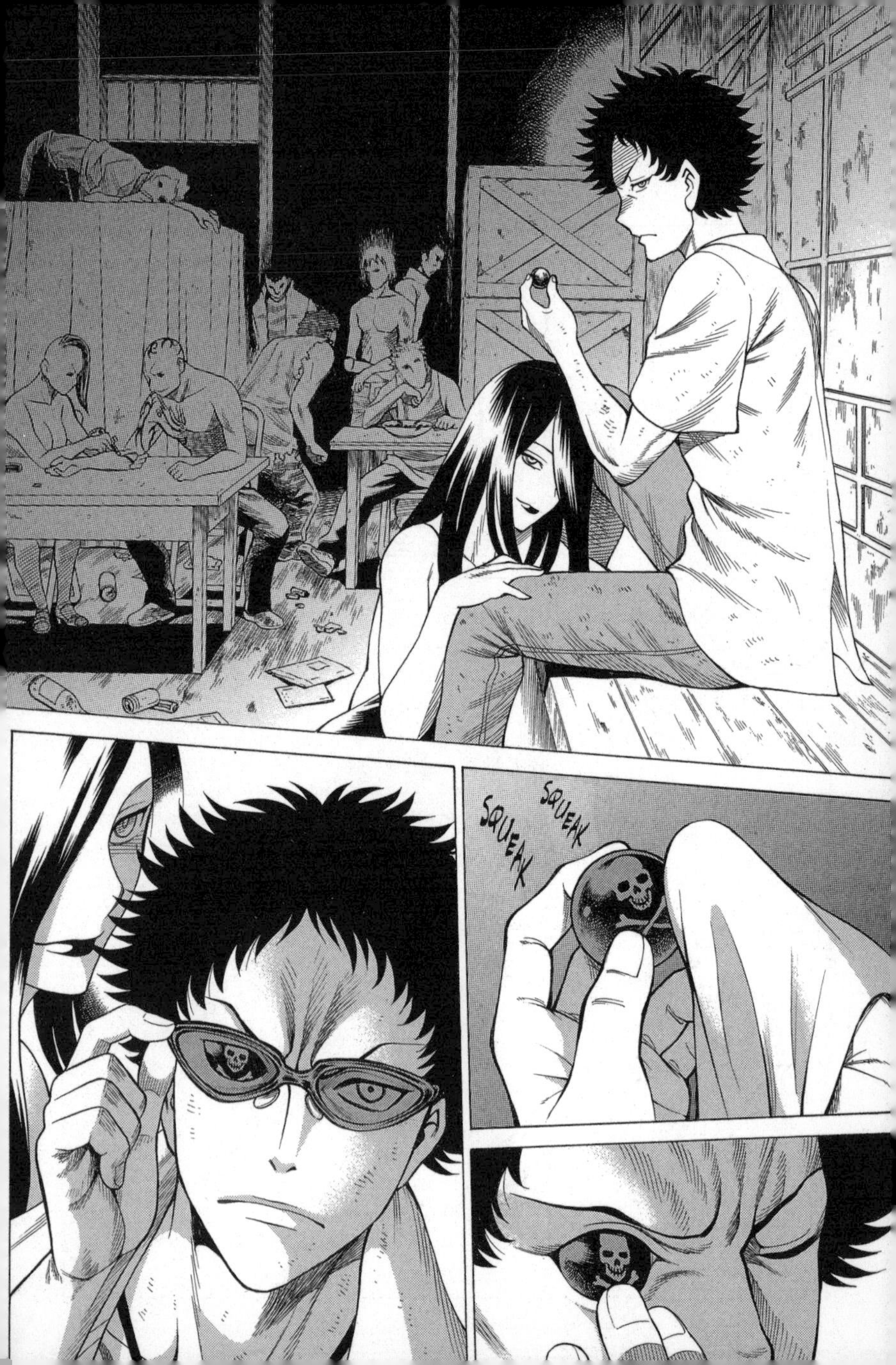
SQUEAK
SQUEAK

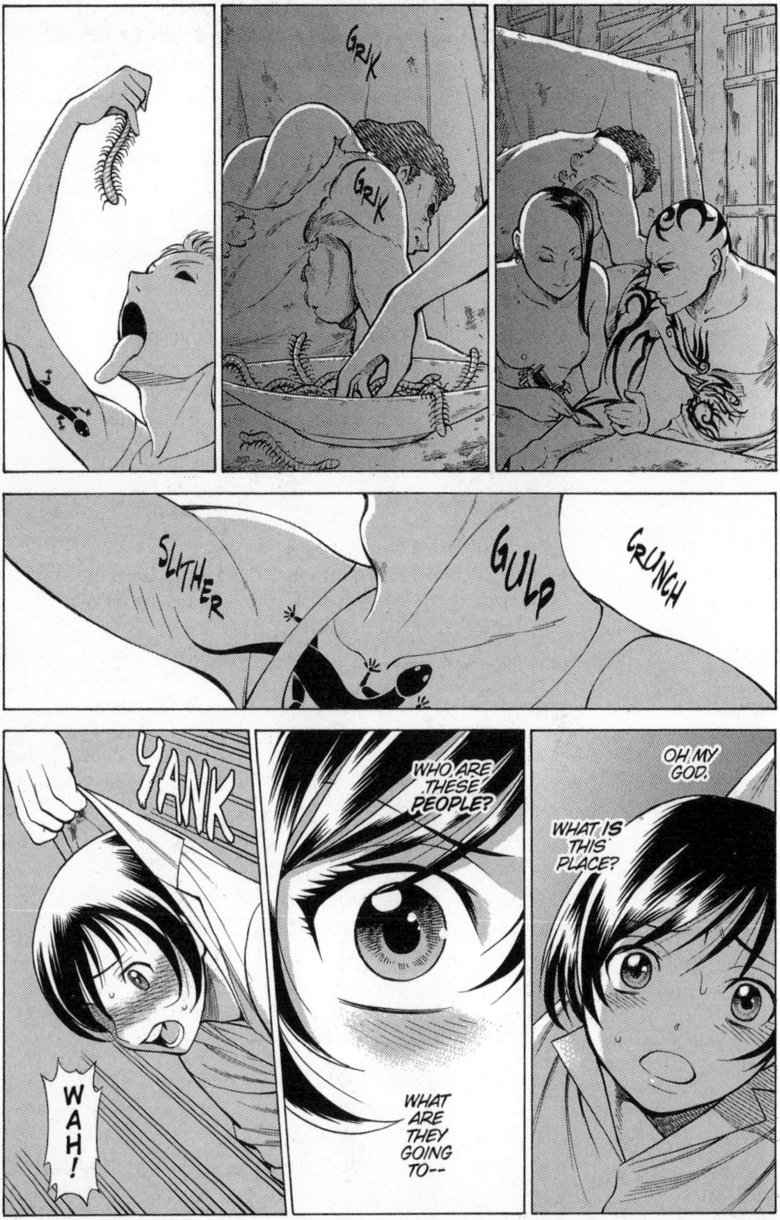
GRIK
GRIK
CRUNCH
GULP
SLITHER
OH MY GOD.
WHAT IS THIS PLACE?
WHO ARE THESE PEOPLE?
WHAT ARE THEY GOING TO--
YANK
WAH!

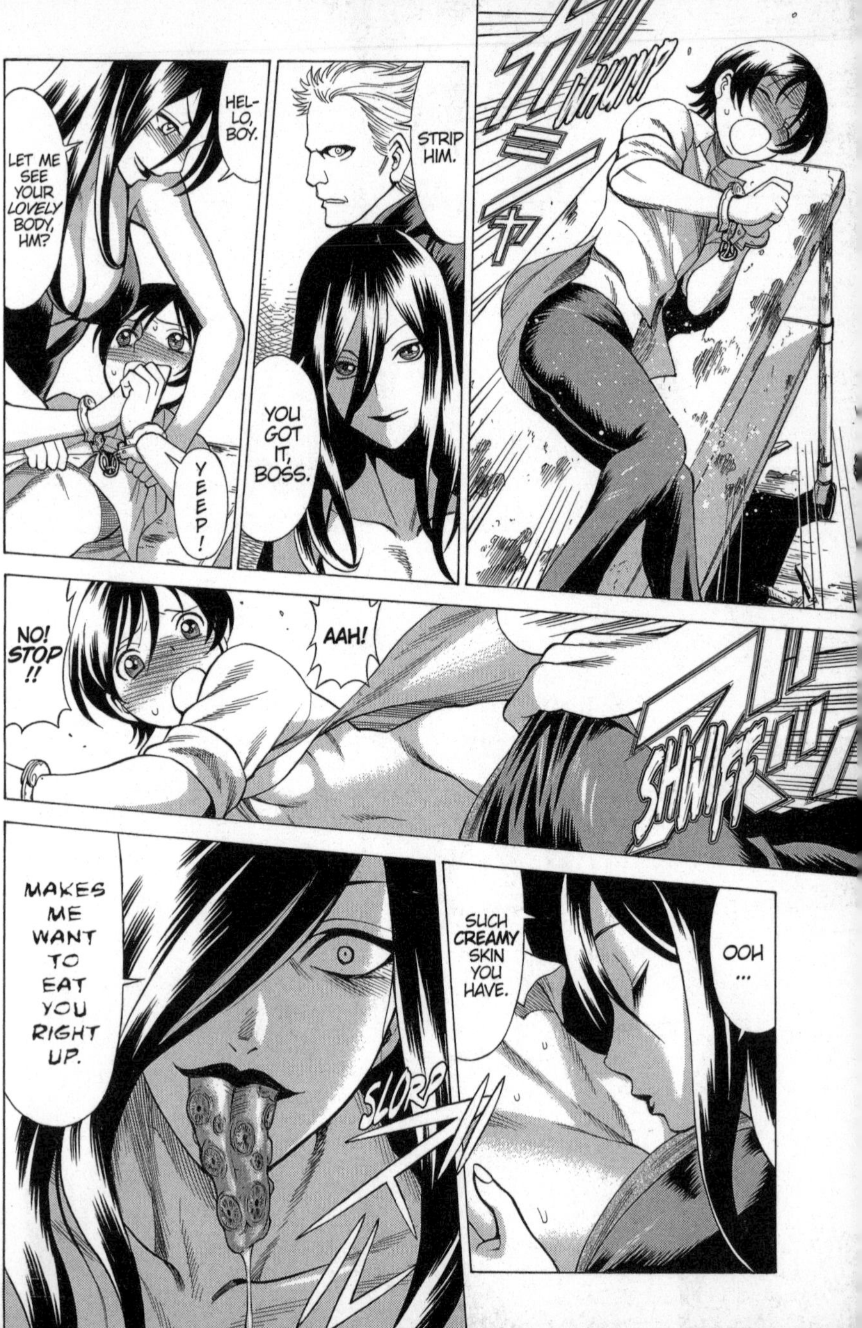
STRIP HIM.
YOU GOT IT, BOSS.
HEL-LO, BOY.
LET ME SEE YOUR LOVELY BODY, HM?
YEEP!
SHWIFF
AAH!
NO! STOP!!
OOH...
SUCH CREAMY SKIN YOU HAVE.
MAKES ME WANT TO EAT YOU RIGHT UP.
SLORP

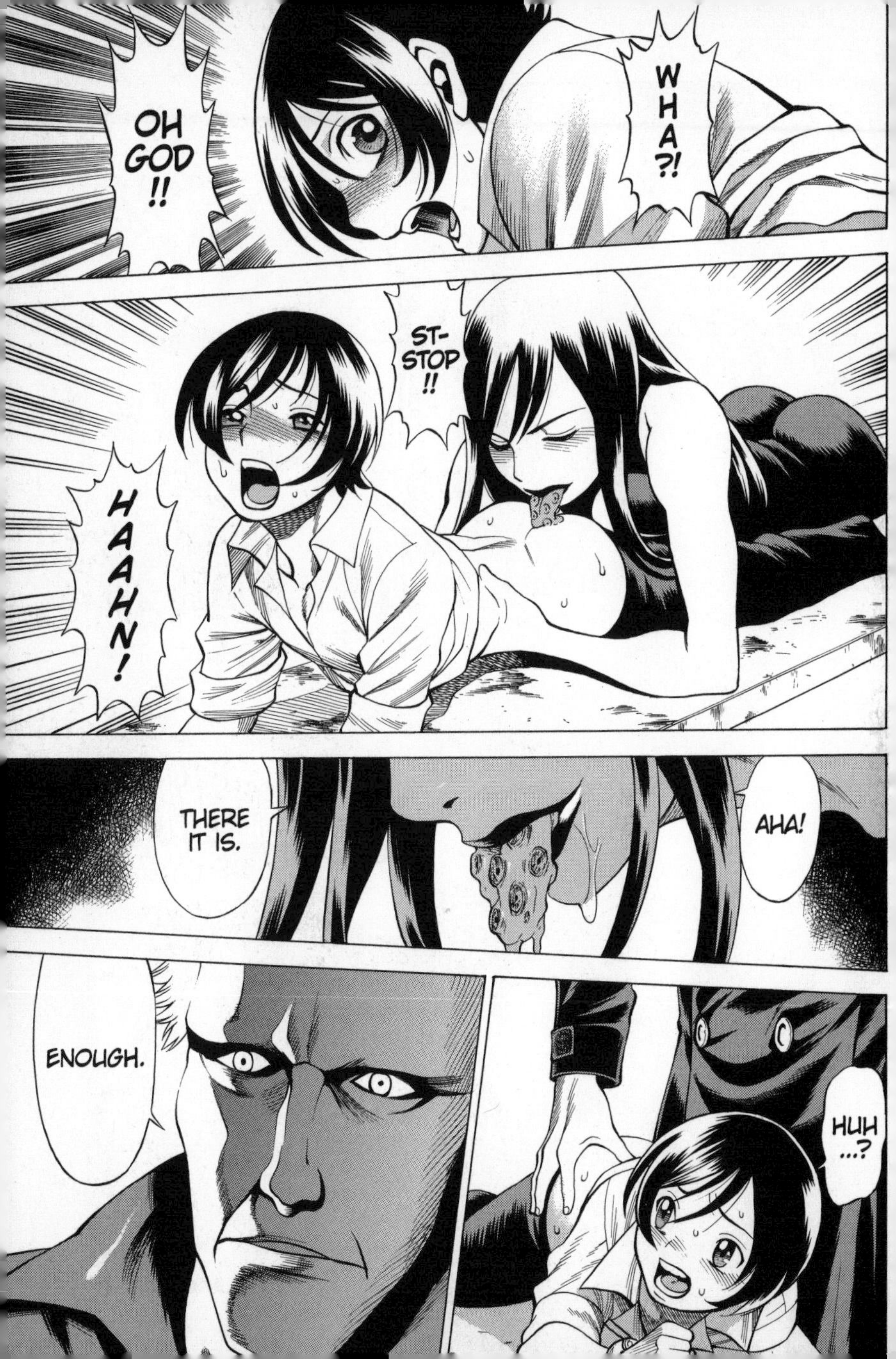
WHA?!
OH GOD!!
ST-STOP!!
HAAAHN!
AHA!
THERE IT IS.
HUH...?
ENOUGH.

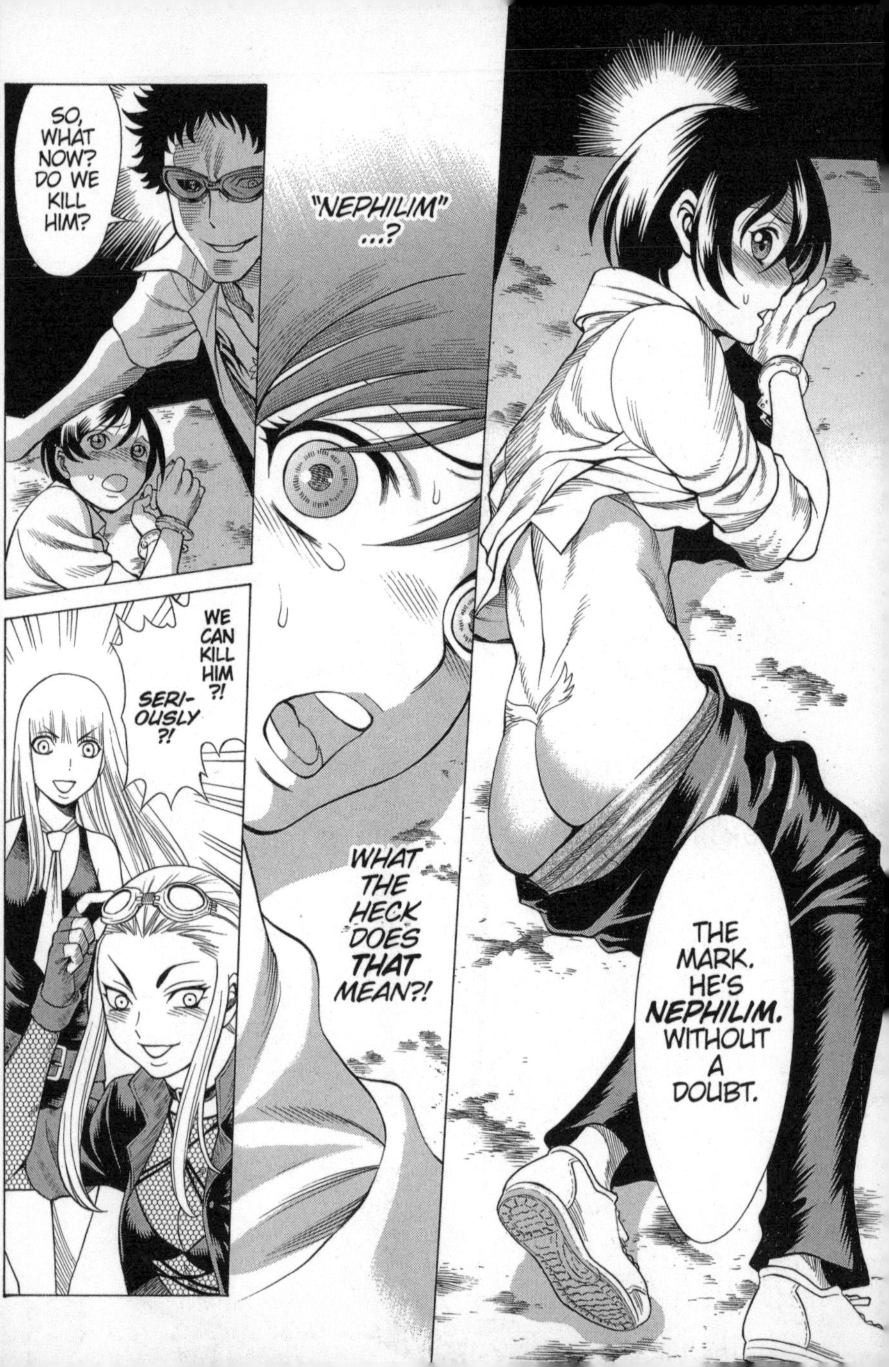
THE MARK. HE'S NEPHILIM. WITHOUT A DOUBT.
"NEPHILIM" ...?
WHAT THE HECK DOES THAT MEAN?!
SO, WHAT NOW? DO WE KILL HIM?
WE CAN KILL HIM?!
SERI-OUSLY?!

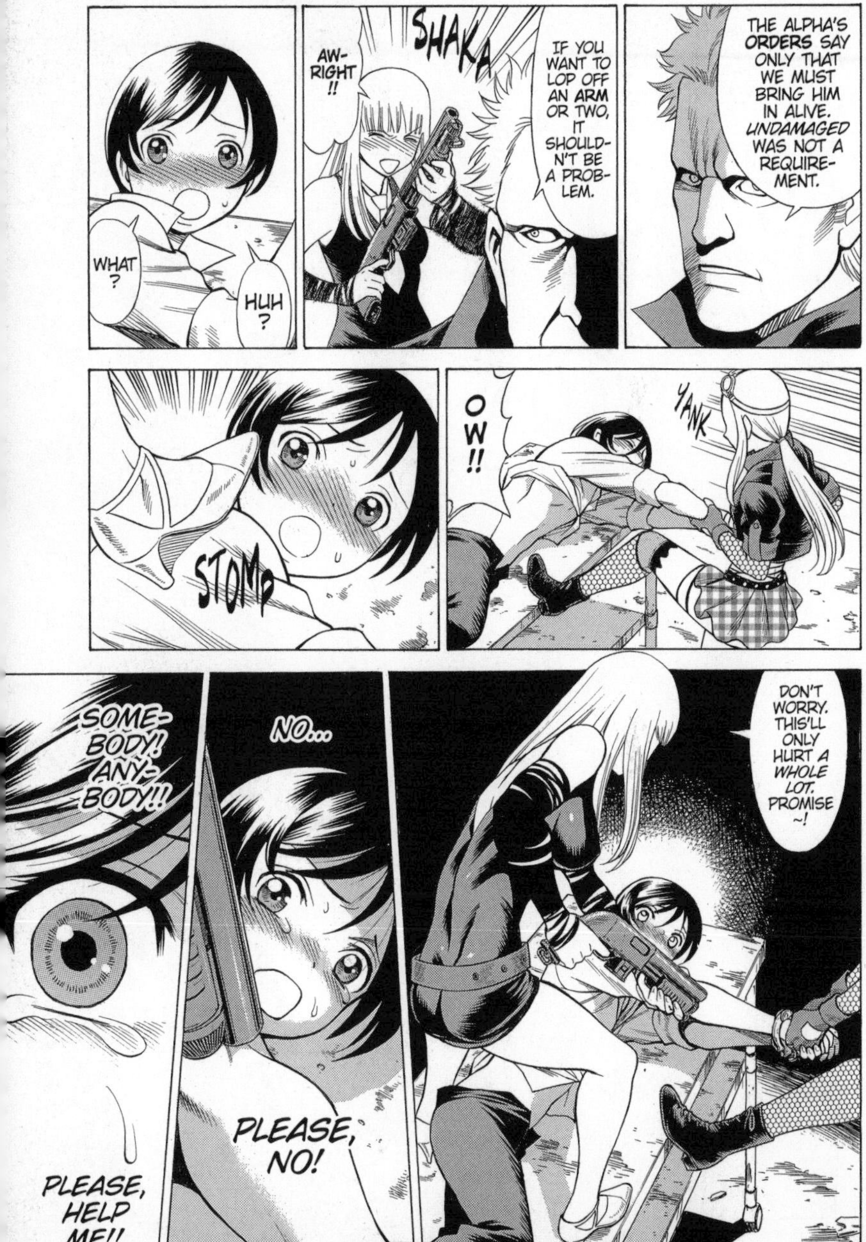
THE ALPHA'S ORDERS SAY ONLY THAT WE MUST BRING HIM IN ALIVE. UNDAMAGED WAS NOT A REQUIREMENT.
IF YOU WANT TO LOP OFF AN ARM OR TWO, IT SHOULDN'T BE A PROBLEM.
SHAKA
AW-RIGHT!!
HUH?
WHAT?
YANK
OW!!
STOMP
DON'T WORRY. THIS'LL ONLY HURT A WHOLE LOT. PROMISE~!
NO...
PLEASE, NO!
SOME-BODY! ANY-BODY!!
PLEASE, HELP ME!!

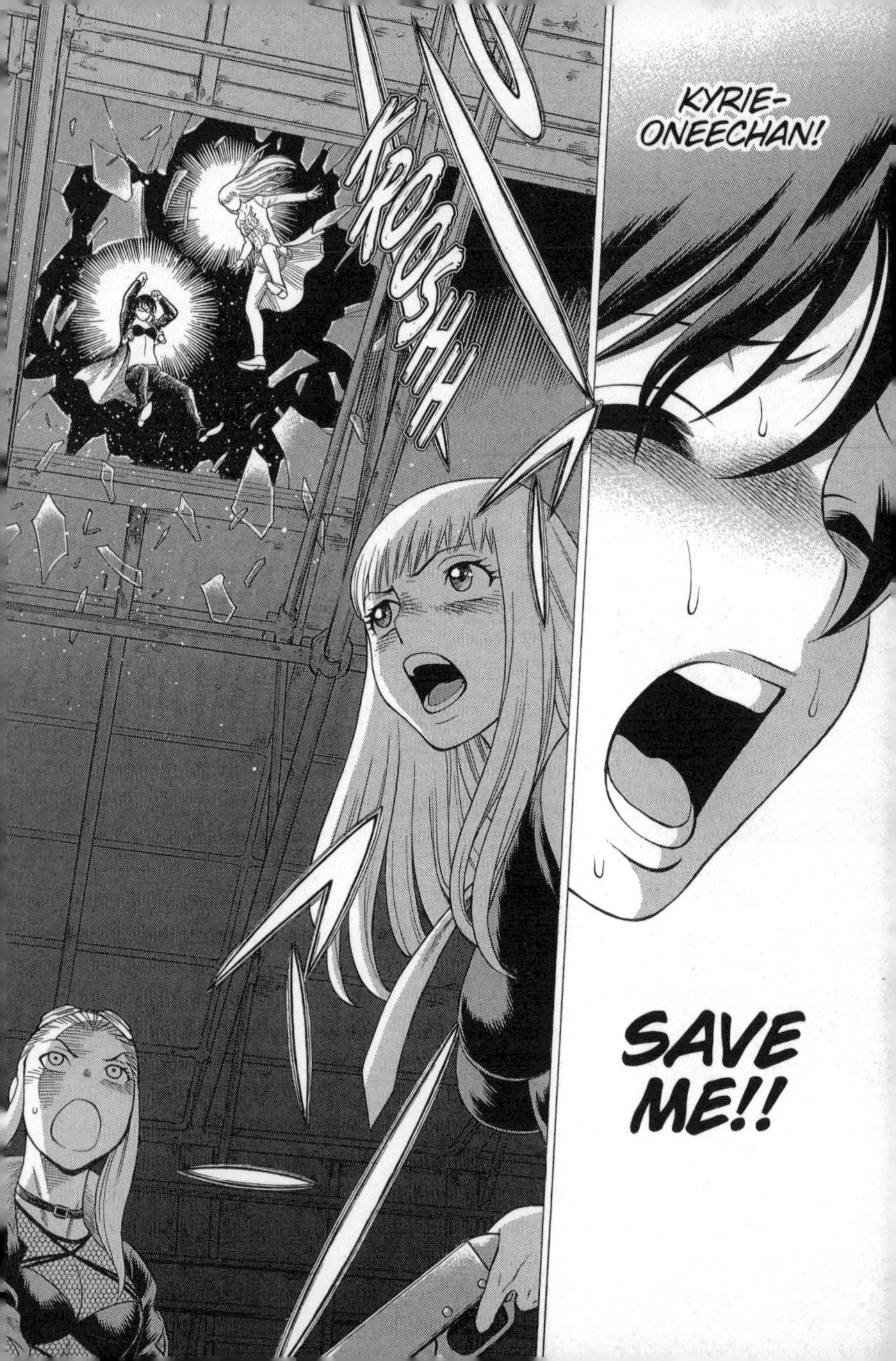
KYRIE-
ONEECHAN!
SAVE
ME!!
KROOSHH

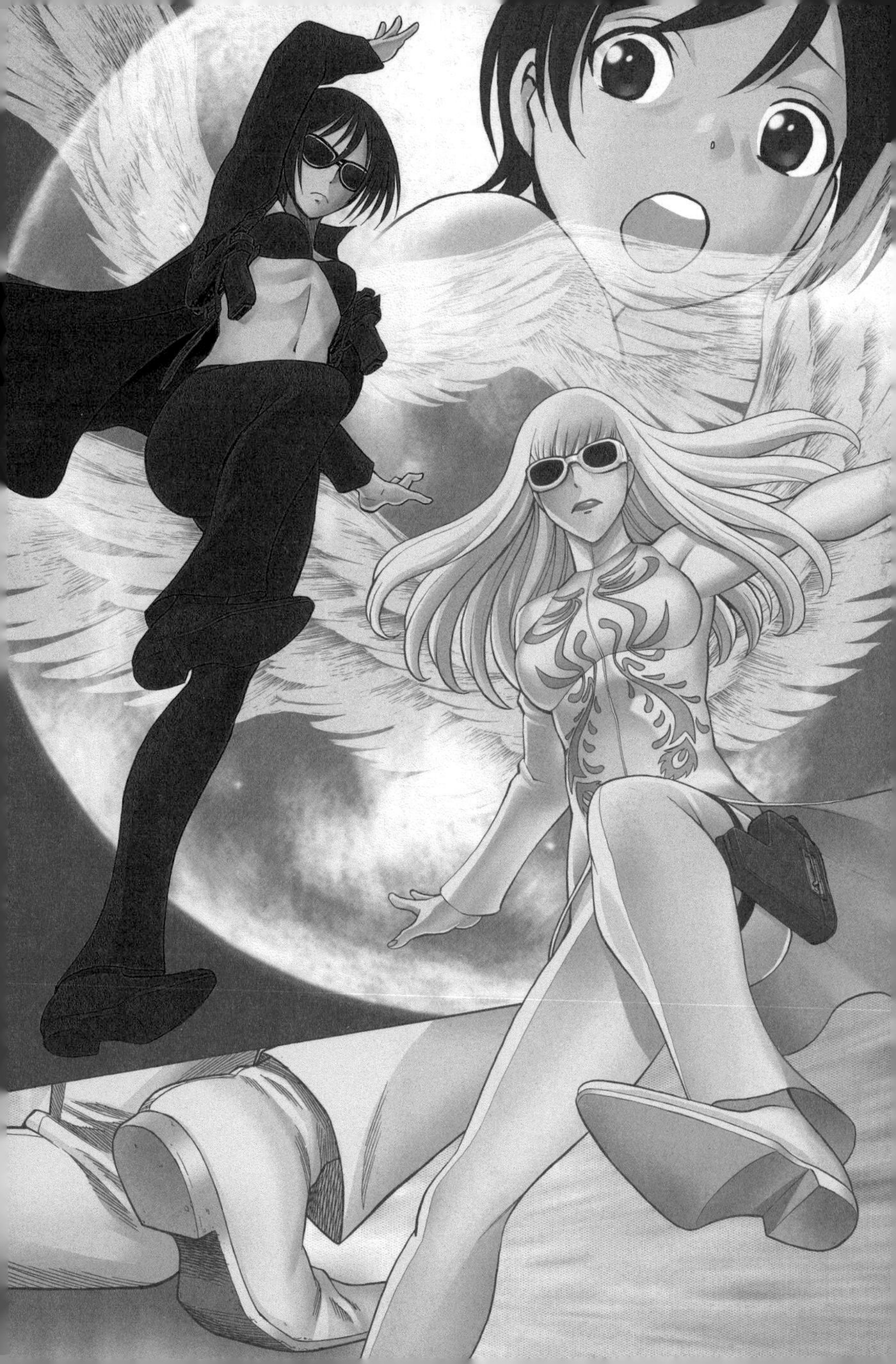

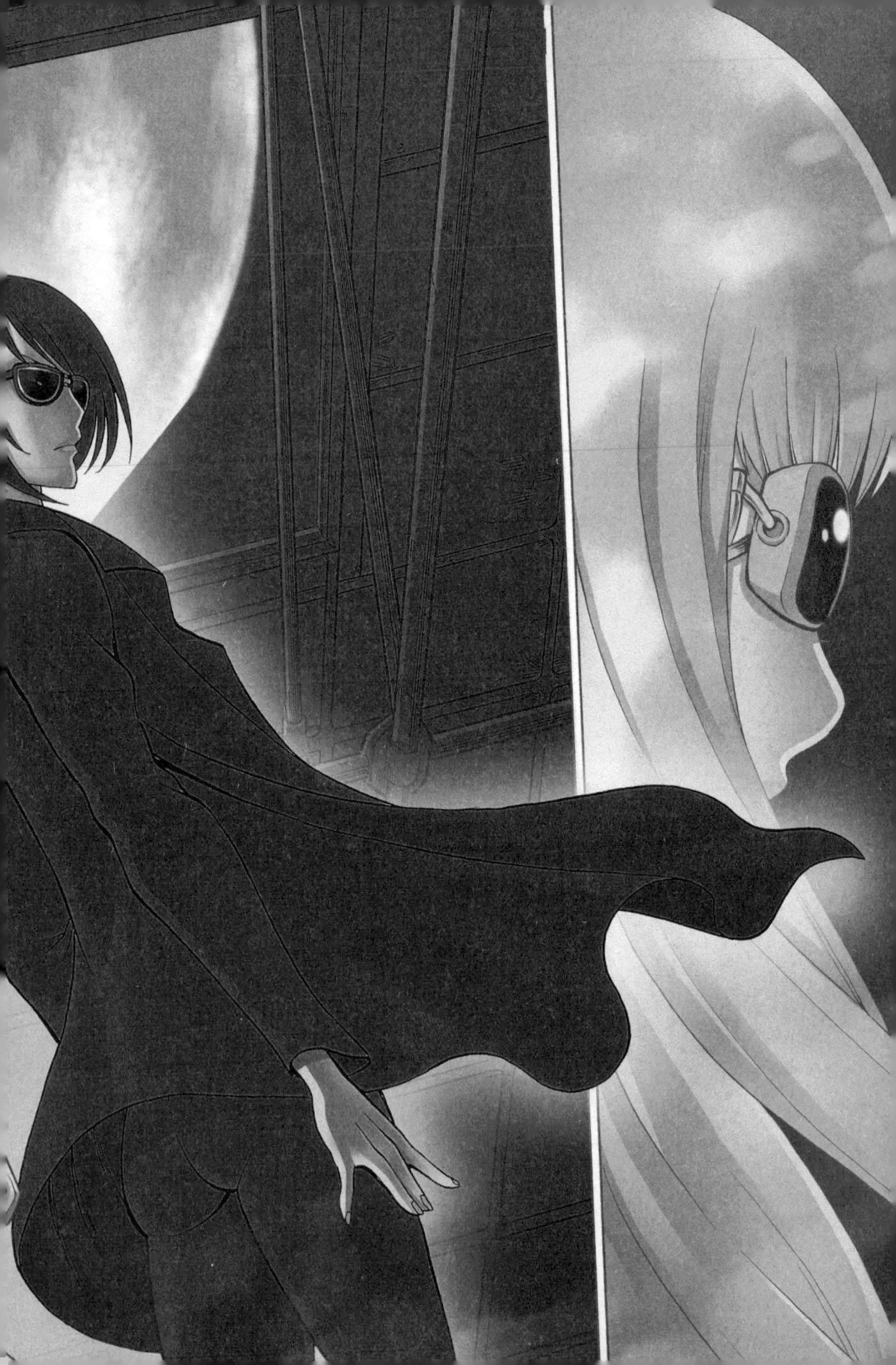

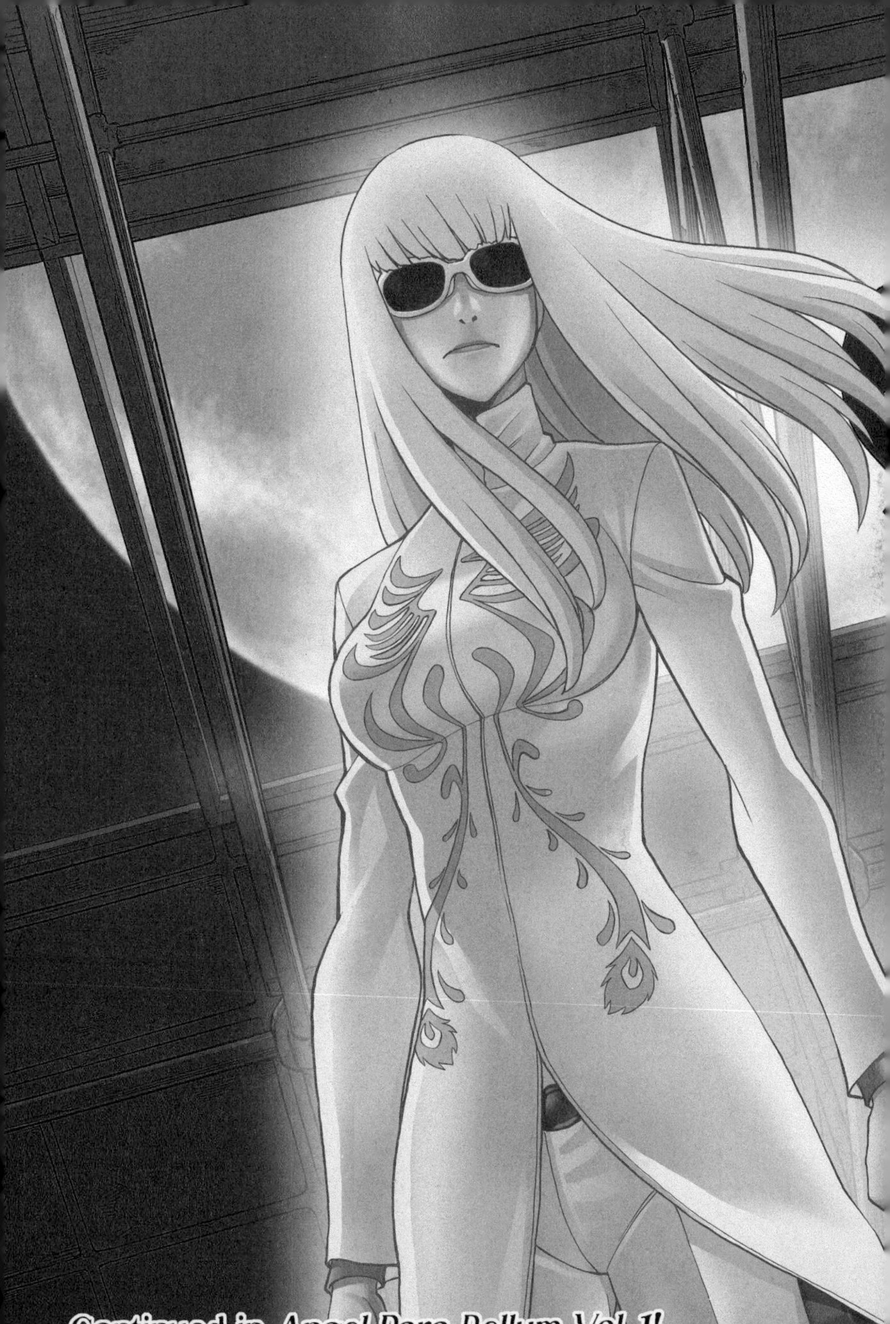

Continued in *Angel Para Bellum* Vol. 1!

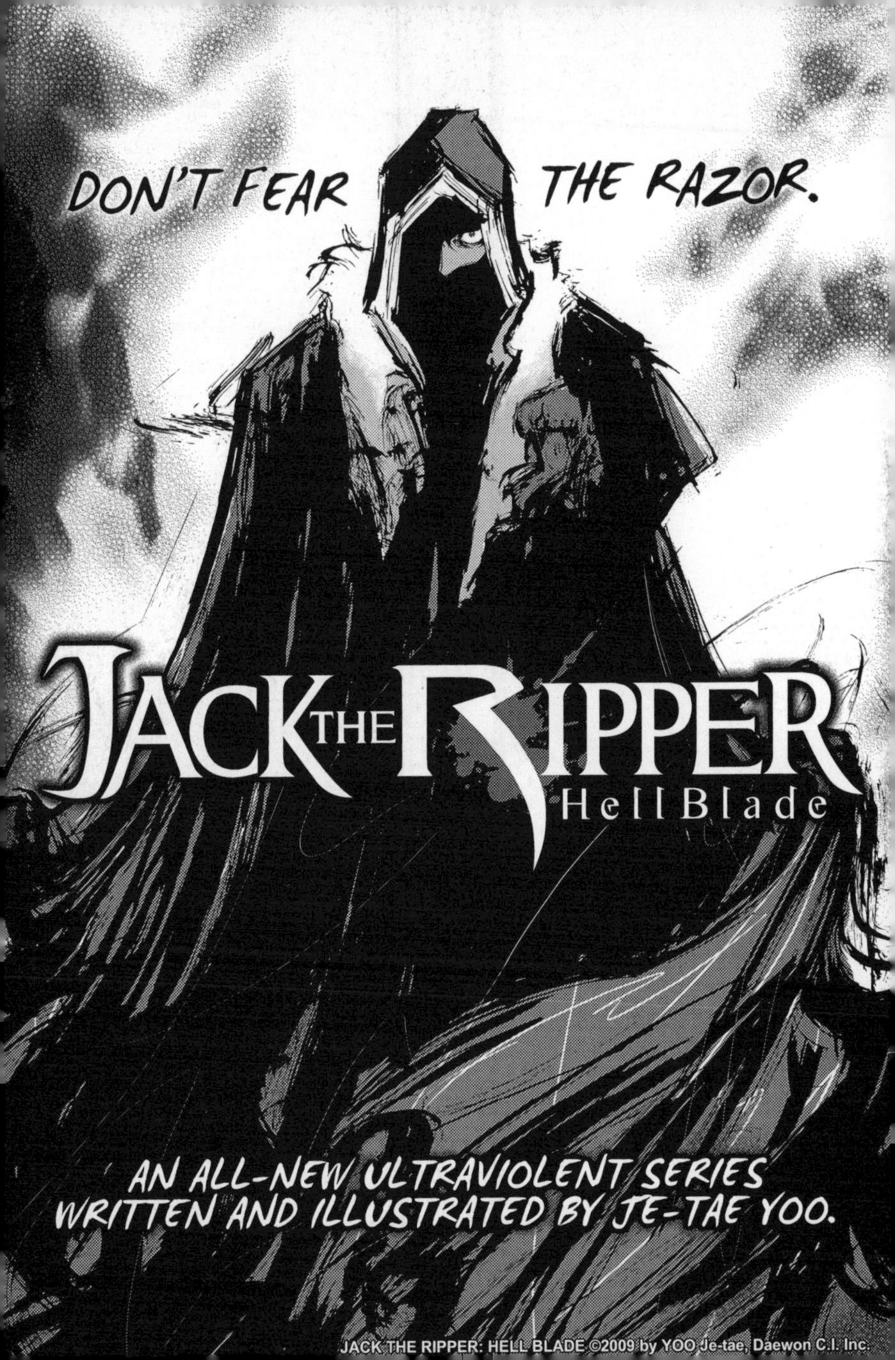
DON'T FEAR THE RAZOR.
JACK THE RIPPER
HellBlade
AN ALL-NEW ULTRAVIOLENT SERIES
WRITTEN AND ILLUSTRATED BY JE-TAE YOO.
JACK THE RIPPER: HELL BLADE ©2009 by YOO Je-tae, Daewon C.I. Inc.

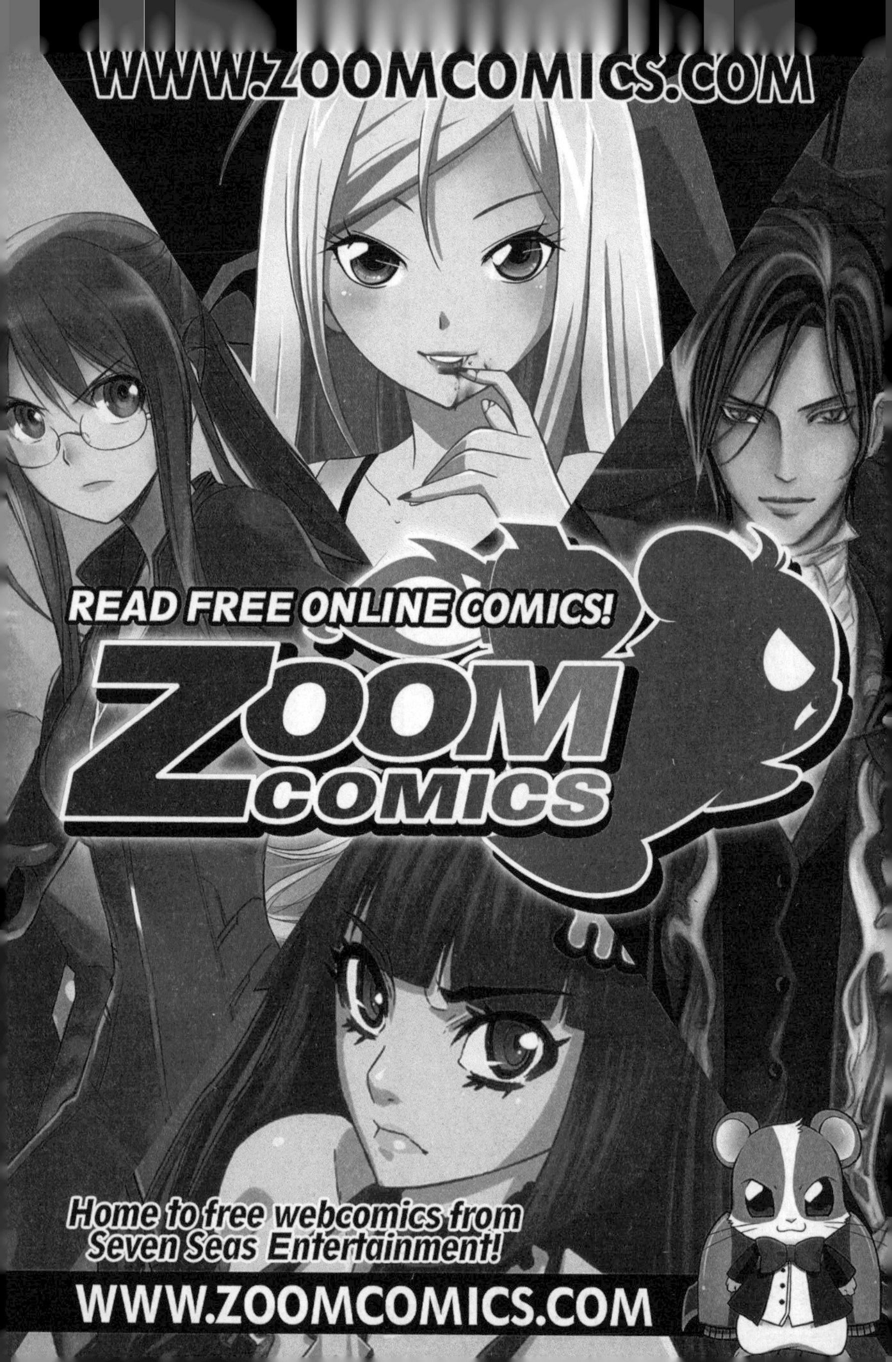
WWW.ZOOMCOMICS.COM
READ FREE ONLINE COMICS!
ZOOM COMICS
Home to free webcomics from
Seven Seas Entertainment!
WWW.ZOOMCOMICS.COM

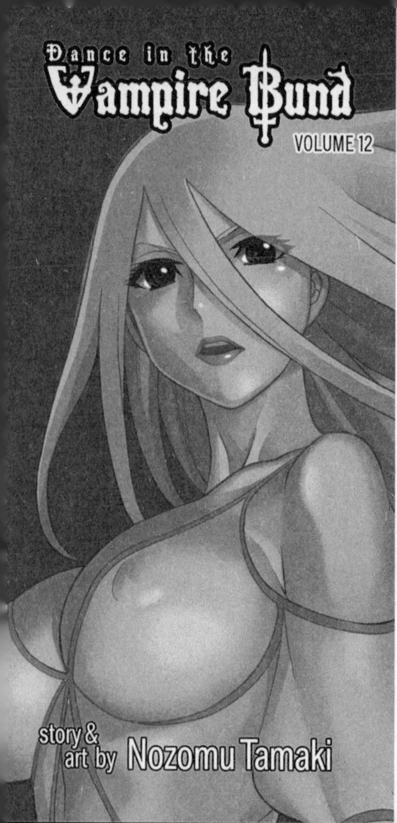
Dance in the
Vampire Bund
VOLUME 12
story & art by Nozomu Tamaki

STAFF CREDITS

translation Adrienne Beck
adaptation Janet Houck
lettering Roland Amago
layout Bambi Eloriaga-Amago
cover design Nicky Lim
copy editor Shanti Whitesides
editor Adam Arnold

publisher Jason DeAngelis
Seven Seas Entertainment

DANCE IN THE VAMPIRE BUND VOL. 12

ISBN: 978-1-935934-72-1

Printed in the USA

First Printing: June 2012

10 9 8 7 6 5 4 3 2

Seven Seas

READING DIRECTIONS

This book reads from *right to left*, Japanese style. If this is your first time reading manga, you start reading from the top right panel on each page and take it from there. If you get lost, just follow the numbered diagram here. It may seem backwards at first, but you'll get the hang of it! Have fun!!

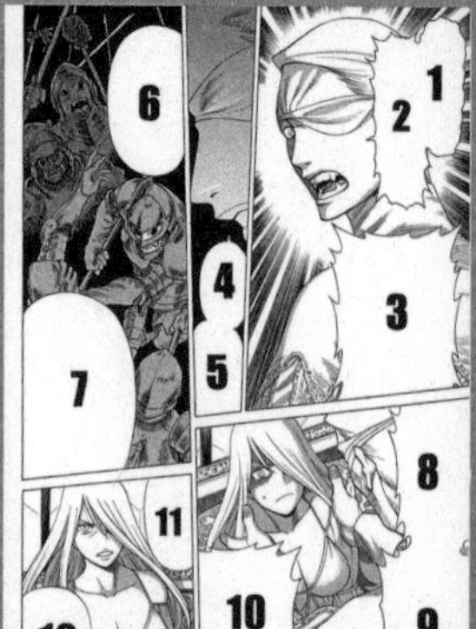
1
2
3
4
5
6
7
8
9
10
11
12

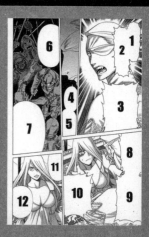